RESPONSIBILITY AT WORK

JB JOSSEY-BASS

RESPONSIBILITY AT WORK

*How Leading Professionals Act
(or Don't Act) Responsibly*

Howard Gardner, Editor

John Wiley & Sons, Inc.

Published by Jossey-Bass
A Wiley Imprint
989 Market Street, San Francisco, CA 94103-1741—www.josseybass.com

Wiley Bicentennial logo: Richard J. Pacifico

Jossey-Bass books and products are available through most bookstores. To contact Jossey-Bass directly call our Customer Care Department within the U.S. at 800-956-7739, outside the U.S. at 317-572-3986, or fax 317-572-4002.

Jossey-Bass also publishes its books in a variety of electronic formats. Some content that appears in print may not be available in electronic books.

Library of Congress Cataloging-in-Publication Data

Responsibility at work: how leading professionals act (or don't act) responsibly / Howard Gardner, editor.—1st ed.
  p. cm.
Includes bibliographical references and index.
ISBN: 978-0-7879-9475-4 (cloth)
1. Leadership—Moral and ethical aspects. 2. Social responsibility of business. 3. Business ethics. I. Gardner, Howard.
  HD57.7.R467 2007
  174'.4—dc22   2007011634

Printed in the United States of America
FIRST EDITION
HB Printing   10 9 8 7 6 5 4 3 2 1

CONTENTS

ACKNOWLEDGMENTS

THE GOODWORK PROJECT, WHICH FORMS THE BASIS FOR THIS BOOK, has involved over fifty researchers at seven universities since 1995. I want to thank these devoted individuals—some senior researchers, others researchers-in-training—for their valued contributions to this complex endeavor. Without their efforts neither the data collection nor the data analyses reported here would be possible.

The project has been generously and flexibly funded by several individuals and several foundations. Profound thanks are due to the following:

Atlantic Philanthropies

Bauman Foundation

Carnegie Corporation of New York

COUQ Foundation

Nathan Cummings Foundation

J. Epstein Foundation

Fetzer Institute

Ford Foundation

William and Flora Hewlett Foundation

John & Elisabeth Hobbs

Christian A. Johnson Endeavor Foundation

Robert Wood Johnson Foundation

John F. Kennedy School of Government, Harvard University

Thomas H. Lee

John D. and Catherine T. MacArthur Foundation

Jesse Phillips Foundation Fund

Rockefeller Brothers Fund

Louise and Claude Rosenberg Jr. Family Foundation

Ross Family Charitable Foundation

Spencer Foundation

John Templeton Foundation

Finally, it has been a pleasure to work with Lesley Iura at Jossey Bass. I appreciate both her initial enthusiasm for the project and her excellent editorial suggestions throughout the process of preparing this book for publication. Thanks are also due to Dimi Berkner, Justin Frahm, Kate Gagnon, and Susan Geraghty.

Cambridge, Massachusetts   HOWARD GARDNER
June 2007

ABOUT THE CONTRIBUTORS

LYNN BARENDSEN is a project manager at the GoodWork Project. She has published articles on African American and regionalist literatures and taught courses in literature and film, English and American literature, and expository writing. Lynn has been working on the GoodWork Project since 1997 and has published work on young social and business entrepreneurs and the elements of leadership.

○

KENDALL COTTON BRONK is assistant professor of educational psychology at Ball State University. She received her doctoral degree in child and adolescent development at Stanford University and has published several papers on young people's sense of purpose in life.

○

MIHALY CSIKSZENTMIHALYI is professor of positive developmental psychology at the Claremont Graduate University in California. He taught for thirty years at the University of Chicago and is the author of *Flow* and eighteen other books.

○

WILLIAM DAMON is professor of education at Stanford University, director of the Stanford Center on Adolescence, and senior fellow at the Hoover Institution on War, Revolution, and Peace. For the past thirty years, Damon has studied moral commitment at all ages of life.

○

WENDY FISCHMAN is a project manager at the GoodWork Project. She has published a book and several articles on the development of young professionals and is currently working on an application of the research to be used in schools and other educational settings.

○

HOWARD GARDNER is the Hobbs Professor of Cognition and Education at the Harvard Graduate School of Education. He is a leading thinker about education and human development and he has studied and written extensively about intelligence, creativity, leadership, and professional ethics.

o

LAURA HORN was a researcher at the GoodWork Project for four years. She has a B.A. in psychology from Amherst College and a massage therapy license. She currently works in the Harvard Medical School Division of Medical Ethics and plans to pursue graduate work in psychology.

o

CARRIE JAMES is a project manager at the GoodWork Project. She has been studying higher education, medicine, philanthropy, and, more recently, young people's conceptions of trust and their engagement with the new digital media at the Harvard Graduate School of Education. Her research interests include the relationship between gender and approaches to ethical dilemmas at work and at play. Carrie has an M.A. and Ph.D. in sociology from New York University.

o

HANS HENRIK KNOOP has led the Nordic branch of the GoodWork Project since 1998, investigating the domains of education, journalism, and business. He is associate professor at the Danish University of Education and director of the Universe Research Lab, investigating learning, creativity, and the teaching of science. He has authored or co-authored five books and numerous articles on a broad range of topics related to learning, creativity, complexity, and social responsibility.

o

JEANNE NAKAMURA is assistant professor in the School of Behavioral and Organizational Sciences, Claremont Graduate University. Her current research interests include engagement, mentoring, and positive aging.

o

ANDREAS SCHRÖER is director of research at the Center for Social Investment at Heidelberg University. He has published on change management in nonprofit organizations and is currently studying philanthropic and nonprofit leadership.

o

JEFFREY SOLOMON spent several years as a researcher on the GoodWork Project, at Harvard University. His published work has focused on how professionals create and maintain a sense of meaning for themselves. He also has published on how professionals carry out work that embodies qualities of wisdom. Currently he is a researcher at the Center for Health Quality, Outcomes and Economics Research at the Bedford, Massachusetts, VA Medical Center.

––––––––––– o –––––––––––

SUSAN VERDUCCI is assistant professor of Humanities at San Jose State University and former researcher at the GoodWork Project. Her primary interests include moral philosophy, moral education, and the ethics of professional work. She recently edited *Taking Philanthropy Seriously: Beyond Noble Intentions to Responsible Giving* with William Damon (Indiana University Press, 2006).

––––––––––– o –––––––––––

SETH WAX was a researcher at the GoodWork project. He is currently pursuing graduate studies in Buddhist philosophy, meditation theory, and the contemporary adaptation of meditative practices.

RESPONSIBILITY AT WORK

INTRODUCTION

WHO IS RESPONSIBLE FOR GOOD WORK?

Howard Gardner

I recommend that the Statue of Liberty be supplemented by a Statue of Responsibility on the West Coast.
—Viktor Frankl

The price of greatness is responsibility.
—Winston Churchill

THE GREAT PSYCHIATRIST VIKTOR FRANKL, who escaped the death camps of World War II and became a leading thinker of the twentieth century, believed that responsibility must go hand in hand with liberty. He had a vision that one day a large statue would greet visitors, including immigrants, to the western shores of America. That statue would remind us of the responsibilities that all human beings should assume by virtue of their being human (www.sorfoundation.org). Efforts to construct such a statue are under way, and perhaps by the time you read these words, the Statue of Responsibility will already be in place. Meanwhile, such a monument—envisaged to be a 330-foot structure, with the hand of liberty clasping the hand of responsibility—serves as a virtual icon for the topic of this book.

As individuals living at a time of affluence, most of us are accustomed to thinking in terms of rights—our individual rights of life, liberty, and the pursuit of happiness, and the right of every human being to a good and

comfortable life. If we have attained global consciousness, we broaden
our perspective to include the provision of medical care, education, and
political and economic freedom to those who live in less privileged corners of the globe. Of course we all recognize in principle that we have certain responsibilities, and at least some of us take these responsibilities
seriously. Yet a monument that forefronts the concept of human responsibilities rather than human rights can still jar.

Once we begin to think in terms of responsibilities, the ledger fills up
quickly. Productive adults are expected to assume responsibility in a
number of realms: for our own health and welfare; for those who
depend on us—spouses, offspring, and as they age, grandparents
and parents; for those at our workplace; for those in the various
communities—such as professional, neighborhood, and regional—in
which we live; and to the extent that we have the opportunity and the
means, for our global society. No wonder many of us find it more comfortable to perseverate on the abstract concept of human rights: the
numerous and disparate areas for which we could assume responsibility
threaten to overwhelm us.

Most human beings spend a third of our lives, and at least one half of
our waking hours, at work. We give a great deal of ourselves at work,
and over the years we have gained some measure of control over the conditions in the workplace. For many of us, especially the less fortunate,
work entails burdens; for a smaller, more fortunate number, work is
a privilege garlanded with rewards. The latter is especially true for
professionals—individuals who are accorded status, prestige, and a comfortable livelihood in return for which they are expected to offer high-
level services and clear-minded judgment.

Always timely, issues of responsibility have taken on new urgency in
recent years. Across the professions, examples abound of work that is
clearly irresponsible. The energy-trading giant—Enron—and the accounting titan—Arthur Andersen—have become the poster children for work
that flouts every ethical convention. Companies such as World.com,
Global Crossing, and Adelphi are almost as notorious. Within government, personal corruption and policy misrepresentations are reported
with numbing regularity. Questions of responsibility arise when physicians enter into special arrangements with high-paying patients and when
lawyers seem indistinguishable from corporate executives. And the news
media, on whom the public depends to learn about flagrant instances of
irresponsibility, have themselves been subject to searing (and often
deserved) critiques. Serious inquiry into this troubling state of affairs is
overdue. We need to understand better both implications of this book's

title: how responsibility at work is apportioned and how it can and should operate.

In the pages that follow, a number of researchers focus on the set of responsibilities that arise in the workplace. We do so chiefly from the perspective of a large-scale research project called the GoodWork® Project.[1] That Project has revealed the most impressive forms of responsibility, the various factors that cause or catalyze a sense of responsibility, the threats and obstacles that lead to compromised or irresponsible work, and various educational interventions that can foster a greater sense of responsibility. Before detailing the Project, along with the essays that have emanated from it, I offer a few comments on the key concepts with which we will be concerned.

Work

Ever since Adam and Eve were expelled from the Garden of Eden, human beings have had to work "by the sweat of our brows." For most of human prehistory and much of recorded history, work has not been an activity on which we have had much perspective. We have worked so that we could eat, have shelter, survive, be secure, and protect our families, particularly those too young or too frail to fend for themselves. Some individuals have been officially designated as slaves. Most farmers and laborers have had to work for long hours, and only a few have been able to enjoy leisure and exert dominion over others.

The rise of great civilizations, in both classical and modern times, saw an increasing division of labor and hierarchization of work. Men's and women's work became increasingly specialized, and a greater proportion of the population worked in organizations with mutually acknowledged structures of authority. Those in positions of power had latitude in how they approached their work and how they allocated their time; depending on their personal inclinations and on the messages that pervaded the wider society, these leaders could render working conditions relatively benign or relatively stressful. Those who possessed specialized knowledge took advantage of their expertise: in the middle ages they formed guilds; in the modern era, they constituted the prototypical professions such as law and medicine, as well as less prestigious professions such as teaching and nursing. (For an excellent review of the history of work in the West, see Applebaum, 1992.)

---

[1]The GoodWork® Project is a registered trademark. For ease of reading, we do not repeat the trademark sign in this volume.

Responsibility

Paradoxically, for those of us who live in the privileged, rights-dominated twenty-first century, the history of responsibilities dates back many centuries. The great religions have devoted the bulk of their attention to enumeration of what individuals should and should not do, and to outlining the consequences of inappropriate, venal, or *irresponsible* activities. The Code of Hammurabi, the laws detailed in Leviticus, the Ten Commandments, the Analects of Confucius, and the books of Plato's *Republic* all devote many more words to duties and consequences than to privileges and rewards. References to human rights and privileges, as articulated in classical Athens or pre-Imperial Rome, in the Magna Carta, or in the Glorious Revolution, the American Revolution, and the French Revolution, represented scattered cries for various liberties, against the much noisier and far more prevalent regimes marked by authoritarian or totalitarian rule. Indeed, the solitary Chinese man standing and confronting the tanks in Tiananmen Square in June 1989 symbolizes the assertion of human rights against one more heavy hand imposed by yet another punitive state.

But responsibility can also be construed in a more constructive vein. If we are to have a society that is open and fair, individuals must willingly, even energetically, be prepared to carry out crucial actions—ones required for the achievement and maintenance of such a society. This is the heart of the Kantian sense of duty: we must act toward others in the way in which we would want all others to behave, and we should avoid those actions—however tempting—that could not be universalized in this way. The classical view of politics entails a commitment to act as a responsible citizen. The classical view of a profession entails a commitment to act as a responsible worker. In this view, a responsibility is seen not as a burden but rather as a privilege of living in a civilized world.

Work and Responsibility

A key notion that marks the intersection of the realms of work and responsibility is that of *vocation* or *calling*. Both of these words—and their equivalents in non-Latin, non–Anglo Saxon societies—capture the intuition that one does not simply carry out work. Rather, the work one carries out is work that one has been "called" to execute—in Protestantism, a direct call from God. Moreover, work ought not simply be carried out in a slipshod or thoughtless manner. Rather, one is expected to carry out work carefully and responsibly—for one is thereby realizing God's agenda. Moreover, in the traditional Calvinist version—still dominant in many places in the United States and northern Europe—one's own cumulative achievements at work constitute a "sign" that one is a member of the elect (compare Weber, 1950).

It need not be so. When work is considered "just a job," the realm of responsibility is necessarily circumscribed. We are responsible for carrying out the letter of our job description—nothing more. We get paid for what we do, as long as we do it. And when a better opportunity arises, or when our organization decides that our services are no longer needed, we move on.

It is not necessary to be religious, let alone a Calvinist, to deem work sacred. Indeed, many of those who treat work with the greatest seriousness are not religious in the conventional sense and might not even be aware of the Protestant (or Jewish or Confucian) ethic. Increasingly, in the modern era life centers around work we want to do, like to do, and feel—for internal or external reasons—needs to be done well. And for at least some of us, there is the additional desideratum that work needs to be "good."

The Concept of Good Work

Nearly all of us would prefer to live in a society that features good work—work that exhibits three connotations of the word *good*. We crave work that is of *excellent technical quality*, work that is *ethically pursued and socially responsible*, and work that is *engaging, enjoyable, and feels good*. Of course such work is more easily described than achieved. Not all work is executed at a level of excellence, not all work is carried out in an ethical manner, and alas, not all work engages the passions of the worker. Still, to the extent that our work is under our control, we like to do what we can to become good workers ourselves and to encourage good work on the part of those with whom we come into contact and those over whom we exercise some control.

Once we move beyond exhortation, however, a nagging question arises: Which individuals, institutions, or regulating entities carry the burden for—or share the privilege of—bringing about good work? Framed differently, how are we, as individuals or as a society, going to discourage or prevent work that does not meet these three criteria of good work? To introduce the theme that animates this volume, *Who is responsible for good work?*

The chapters collected here tackle this question head on. Our focus falls particularly on the second facet of good work: how to achieve work that is socially responsible, ethical, and moral. Building on a project that has studied good work for more than a decade, we present a model of the factors that underlie good work, chronicle the lessons learned from informants representing several professions, and put forth recommendations on how best to increase the incidence of good work. Much of what we present comes directly from our informants; in that sense, it is descriptive, a view of responsibility as construed by workers themselves. We do not, however, skirt issues of value. Shifting explicitly to prescription, we also put forth our own views on responsibility: how it can be achieved, who is responsible for its achievement or nonachievement, and what steps might be taken to enhance responsible work.

The GoodWork Project: Background, Model, Findings

Following a year of informal consultation (September 1994–June 1995), psychologists Mihaly Csikszentmihalyi, William Damon, and I embarked on a formal collaboration that lasted until 2006. (In 2006, we reverted to our earlier, informal personal and professional ties.) Eventually called the GoodWork Project, our study consisted primarily of in-depth interviews of more than twelve hundred Americans working in nine professional domains: journalism, genetics, theater, higher education, philanthropy, law, medicine, business, and precollegiate education. Most of the subjects were well-known veteran practitioners, but we also spoke to workers-in-training as well as to selected individuals who had already retired. We conferred the honorific title *trustee* on the most exemplary senior members of the cohort. (For an introduction to the project, see Gardner, Csikszentmihalyi, and Damon, 2001; for updates, see http://goodworkproject.org.)

During the interviews, which typically lasted an hour and a half or more, subjects were asked about the mission of their work, their most cherished values, the obstacles to the achievement of their goals, the strategies adopted to deal with those obstacles, the changes that had taken place in their field over the years, the training they had received, the individuals who had had the most profound impact on their work (positively or negatively), and (where appropriate) the mentoring they had provided to younger workers. The basic questions asked of all subjects were the same, but of course there were variations based on the nature of the professional field and on the age and experience of the subject. In most cases, standardized interventions, such as a Q-sort of values and a set of posed dilemmas, were also included. Our methods spanned the gamut from in-depth case studies to qualitative analyses of major themes to quantitative comparisons and statistical tests of selected hypotheses. (For further details on our methods, see Gardner and others, 1997.)

One question asked of nearly all subjects proved particularly revealing: *To whom or what do you feel responsible in your work?* Most subjects had not considered this question in any depth before, so we were far less likely to get pat, rehearsed, or socially desirable answers. A few subjects seemed

Figure I.I. A Graphic Rendition of the Principal Elements of GoodWork.

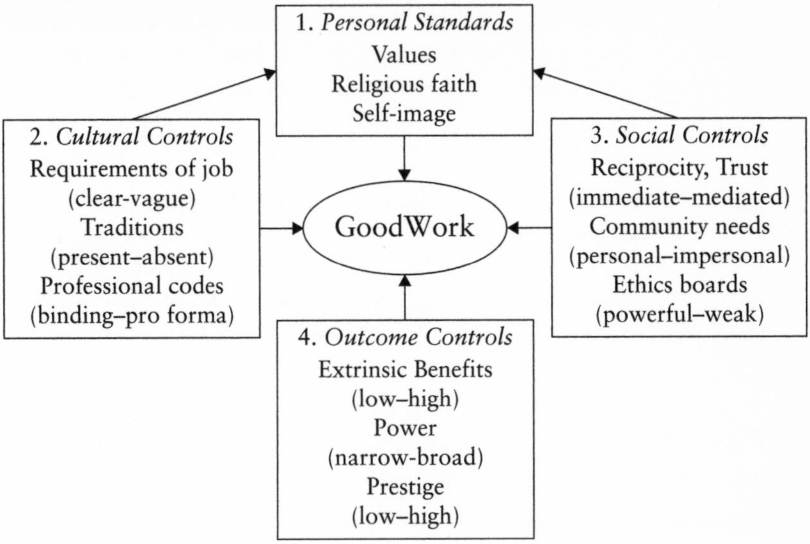

```
                    ┌──────────────────────┐
                    │ 1. Personal Standards │
                    │       Values          │
                    │   Religious faith     │
                    │     Self-image        │
                    └──────────────────────┘
┌─────────────────────┐                        ┌──────────────────────────┐
│ 2. Cultural Controls│                        │  3. Social Controls      │
│ Requirements of job │                        │  Reciprocity, Trust      │
│   (clear–vague)     │      ⬭ GoodWork ⬭      │  (immediate–mediated)    │
│    Traditions       │                        │  Community needs         │
│  (present–absent)   │                        │  (personal–impersonal)   │
│ Professional codes  │                        │  Ethics boards           │
│ (binding–pro forma) │                        │  (powerful–weak)         │
└─────────────────────┘                        └──────────────────────────┘
                    ┌──────────────────────┐
                    │ 4. Outcome Controls  │
                    │  Extrinsic Benefits  │
                    │     (low–high)       │
                    │       Power          │
                    │   (narrow-broad)     │
                    │      Prestige        │
                    │     (low–high)       │
                    └──────────────────────┘
```

genuinely perplexed by the question, while others gave brief, almost perfunctory responses. But in a large majority of cases, the subjects pondered the question and gave thoughtful and revealing answers. These answers, and the reasoning behind them, proved to be an invaluable lens on professional life in the United States today—and perhaps elsewhere as well. These probed responses constitute the heart of the present volume.

As befits a large project involving many investigators over a lengthy period, the GoodWork Project has already yielded a number of products, and others are in the pipeline. The project has also forged a model for conceptualizing good work. This diamond-shaped model, show in Figure I.1, underlies many of the analyses carried out.

Constituents of Good Work

As we see it, the attainment, or nonattainment, of good work entails consideration of four discrete elements:

1. The individual *worker.* Relevant here are the worker's belief systems, motivation for carrying out good work, and personality, temperament, and character, which codetermine whether the individual will hold to high standards or, alternatively, cut corners, "go along," or engage in compromised or irresponsible work.

2. The *domain* of work. Every profession and nearly every other line of work harbors a set of core values and beliefs. These conceptualizations have developed gradually over the years; they are known to workers and carry a certain degree of force. The prototypical example is medicine; for more than two thousand years physicians have taken and sought to adhere to the core commitments of the Hippocratic Oath.

3. The forces of the *field* that operate on the domain. Mediating the core values of the domain are various social entities: the gatekeepers who determine entry into the domain, the individuals who provide or deny opportunities or prizes, and the evaluators who determine the merit of the work in the short run or over the long haul. The domain can be thought of in epistemological terms, as the structure of knowledge and core values; the field can be thought of in sociological terms, as the individuals and institutions that hold power and make consequential decisions. Formulated differently, the sum of the domains (all professions, arts, crafts, and disciplines) at any moment constitutes the culture; the sum of the field entities (all the organizations, gatekeepers, and evaluators) constitutes the society.

4. The larger *reward system* of the ambient society. Individuals, domains, and fields are embedded in the larger society, be it medieval Europe, the China of the Ming dynasty, or the market economy of the United States today. This broader society embraces various rewards and sanctions, and these in turn exert influence over and above the signals that may permeate a particular domain or profession.

These four elements are always present and operative, though they may well be invisible to individual participants or observers in the society. Our studies suggest that good work is most likely to emerge when these four elements are well aligned, that is, when the individual beliefs, the values of the domain, the forces of the field, and the reward system of the society all point in the same direction. Such alignment does not, of course, guarantee good work, but it clarifies and simplifies the job of the individual worker. To the extent that her beliefs and values coincide with those of the domain, the field, and the broader society, the worker is free to proceed with her practice in ways that make sense to her. Conversely, to the extent that the four entities pull in diverse directions, it becomes more difficult to achieve good work; indeed, it may even be difficult to determine what is, and is not, good work.

Consider a concrete finding from the first phase of our work. In the late 1990s, research in genetics was very well aligned in American society.

The individual researchers, the core values of science, the goals and orientations of the gatekeepers, and the overall signals from Americans all pointed in the same direction—the achievement of longer and healthier lives. Geneticists felt empowered to pursue their work in ways that made sense to them; most of them could not wait to get to work each day; they felt cheered on by the rest of society. The ethical issues that have arisen in more recent years—issues surrounding cloning, stem cell research, and genetically modified foods, for example—had not yet become salient in the American context. Issues of responsibility did not explicitly arise, and good work seemed to be there for the taking.

In sharp contrast, the domain of journalism proved to be poorly aligned in the late 1990s, and it remains so today. Journalists who honored the core values of their domain—the careful and thorough investigation of important issues, and the resulting reports that are fair to all concerned—felt pulled in various directions: the often sensationalist tastes of their readers; the search for ever-larger profits on the part of shareholders in the companies that owned the journalistic outlets; and the messages from editors and publishers to avoid controversy, support principal advertisers, and placate powerful interest groups. These factors combined to make many journalists unhappy and to render the achievement of good work more elusive. Many spoke of the loss of a "golden age" with its honored, highly responsible trustees (star foreign correspondent Edward R. Murrow, trusted broadcast anchorman Walter Cronkite, respected publisher Katharine Graham); and quite a few stated their intention of leaving the field (a phenomenon not encountered among the geneticists).

Despite these vastly different landscapes, alignment alone is not enough to determine whether good work is carried out. Our study of journalism documented many individual journalists who carry out good work despite the numerous pressures to compromise. These individuals drew on strong senses of personal responsibility (newscaster Carol Marin resigned her position rather than go along with the hiring of a coanchor who was principally an entertainer), shifted their employment to institutions that honored good work (reporter Ray Suarez left lucrative commercial television to work with public radio and, ultimately, public television), started their own organizations that embody the core values of the domain (Frances Moore Lappé launched the American News Service, dedicated to civic journalism).

Conversely, in the area of genetics, we encountered subjects or learned about colleagues who ignored the line between research carried out with government support and that carried out for profit-making enterprises who misrepresented the nature of their findings in order to achieve priority, or who abused their positions of power in the laboratory. Compromised, irresponsible, or bad work can arise even when the conditions of work are benign.

Domains, Professions, Realms

The careful reader will have noted that, in the description of the Good-Work Project, I have so far abstained from using the word *profession,* instead favoring the more neutral (if more obscure) term *domain.* This choice is intentional. *Profession* has a clear connotation in our society. It refers to those spheres of work that feature a prescribed educational path and a license; only those people designated professionals in a particular field can call themselves such, and at least in theory, a person can be disbarred for malpractice. More generically, professions are groups of individuals who are afforded a certain degree of autonomy and status for tackling important individual or societal problems involving complex judgments under uncertainty, and for doing so in a thoughtful and disinterested manner. In our study, law, medicine, genetics, and higher education clearly qualify as professions. (compare Abbot, 1988; Freidson, 2001).

Other spheres of work definitely fall outside the realm of the professional. Neither the businessman nor the artist fulfills the requirements outlined here. Anyone can call herself a businessperson or an artist, anyone can rise to the top of these elective spheres, and the only obligation attendant to this label is to obey the law.

Certain spheres are borderline. There are no official requirements for being a journalist or a philanthropoid (the term of art for someone who gives away money accrued by someone else). Yet these spheres have core values and a cohort of persons who believe they are adhering to these values; they would distinguish themselves from pseudojournalists and from amateur philanthropoids. Precollegiate teaching has the official imprimatur of a profession, but its principal defining features are constantly under attack—recently by those who endorse quick alternative certification. Following terminology favored by sociologist Nathan Glazer, we might label school teaching, social work, and nursing "minor professions."

For our study it is important to underscore that, in the final analysis, each individual must decide for himself or herself whether to behave in a professional manner. Many individuals who belong to authorized professions behave in ways that are distinctly nonprofessional; they aggrandize themselves as much as possible, cut every corner they can, and benefit parasitically from colleagues who behave in a more professional manner. Conversely, many individuals in the humblest of trades behave in ways that are highly professional—a case in point being the punctilious butler immortalized in Kazuo Ishiguro's novel *Remains of the Day*. These individuals confer respect on spheres or domains that would not ordinarily be assimilated into the realm of the professions. The crucial difference across these spheres inheres in the delineation of responsibility. In the standard professions, responsibilities have emerged explicitly over the long run; professionals are expected to know these responsibilities and to act in accordance with them. In other, less professionalized spheres of work, responsibilities have emerged informally; far more of the burden of delineating these responsibilities falls on the individual practitioner.

Other consequential distinctions have emerged from our work. We distinguish between those professions that highlight caring for specific individuals (such as medicine, nursing, and teaching) and those in which such personal caring is not a high value (such as journalism and law). Philanthropy occupies an intermediate position here: not direct caring, but providing resources for those in the caring professions. We distinguish between those professions that highlight knowledge (journalism, higher education, and science) and those that focus more on service (philanthropy) or performance (theater). These distinctions turn out to have consequences for the delineation and execution of responsibilities.

Responsibility Across the Age Span

Our preliminary analysis as well as findings from developmental psychology suggest that the realm of responsibility might be seen as a set of ever-widening concentric circles. That is, the young person—say, under the age of fifteen—sees responsibility as chiefly involving himself and perhaps the few family members and friends to whom he feels closest. Until then, it is others who have assumed responsibility for him.

Depending on the society in which he lives and the age or stage at which work officially commences, a series of additional responsibilities gradually comes into play. He assumes responsibility *to* a larger number of persons, including those supervisors and peers he encounters only, or chiefly, in the workplace. To the extent that he receives rigorous training in a profession, he also acquires a sense of responsibility *to* the core values of a domain—for example, he is not just an employee of the *Boston Globe;* he is also a journalist, and therefore must adhere to certain beliefs, values, and practices.

In most cases, the sphere of responsibility never broadens beyond the ambient field and the core values of the domain. To be sure, responsibilities accrue within these realms. Increasingly, we become responsible at work *for* certain persons, such as interns or new hires, and for certain tasks, such as governance of our home institution. More responsibilities arise in the personal sphere: our children, our aging parents, perhaps our role in the community. These accumulating and conflicting responsibilities are more than enough to keep most of us busy, if not overwhelmed.

But of special interest are those workers whose sphere of responsibility eventually extends to the health of the profession more generally. From this vantage point it does not suffice if we are good workers in science, journalism, law, or business. What happens when we look around and observe dubious practices among our peers, both those we know personally and those about whom we hear or read?

Enter the role of the trustee. Especially toward the end of their career, certain individuals stand out because they take on the status and stature of their chosen profession. This role may entail leadership within a professional organization—not in the sense of management but rather in service of the preservation or promulgation of cherished values. It can also take the form of more disinterested criticism and guidance—the sort exercised by John Bogle of Vanguard when he criticizes the securities industry, in which he made a fortune; or Anthony Kronman (1995), one time dean of the Yale Law School, when he laments the decline of the lawyer-statesman.

Values, Ethics, Morality

In putting forth the above score sheet and in identifying trustees, we enter the realm of values. For many associated with the GoodWork Project, journalists Carol Marin, Ray Suarez, and Frances Moore Lappé are heroes; these prototypical good workers honor the core values of their profession rather than succumbing to the pressures of their supervisors or the seductive lures of the marketplace. By the same token, we withhold the epithet "good worker" from those who use their positions to enhance their pocketbook, achieve credit unfairly, or abuse those over whom they have authority.

The aforementioned judgments would not be particularly controversial. Yet we are well aware that not all ethical issues and judgments of quality are as clear-cut. Some ethical dilemmas involve right versus right: Should the journalist try to help a group that has been underserved, thereby bringing the scales of justice into better balance? Or should the journalist remain steadfastly neutral between the powerful and the powerless? Other ethical issues involve shades of gray: Is it better for the physician to serve a larger population less thoroughly than he could a smaller one, or to initiate a concierge practice, in which enrolled patients are well served but only those with the means to pay for it are beneficiaries? Other ethical decisions draw on valid but sharply contrasting value systems: Should the lawyer give her all for a client, no matter how nefarious that client, thereby carrying out one facet of her role? Or should she, as an officer of the court, draw on a broader sense of justice?

Recognizing the complexity of ethics is not the same, however, as embracing relativism. That the answer is not always clear-cut or that judgments may be controversial is scarcely a license for "anything goes." My colleagues and I believe that in most cases one path is superior to another, that consensus as to the proper course should be found within a society, and that in many cases consensus might be obtained across societies. Bribery may be part of doing business in many parts of the world, but few would defend a system of bribery as superior to one that bans or punishes bribery.

Indeed, we contend that work that is ethical exhibits the following characteristics: The worker has a set of values that she can state openly. These values draw chiefly on the longstanding values of the domain, though they may be nuanced in various ways. The worker attempts to operate according to those values, even when they clash with immediate self-interest. The worker recognizes issues of moral complexity, wrestles with them, seeks advice and guidance, reflects on what went right, and seeks to right the course in the future when similar circumstances arise. Put generically, she takes the challenges of responsibility seriously and seeks to behave in as responsible a way as possible.

Organization of This Volume

Our purpose here is to go beyond these general considerations to investigate responsibility in a rigorous conceptual and empirical manner. Our work proceeds in a series of ordered steps.

The opening section of the book features models of work that is responsible in the fullest sense of that term. In Chapter One, William Damon and Kendall Bronk describe three exemplary figures: corporate executive Max De Pree represents the employer who is impressively responsible to those who work at his company, Herman Miller; publisher Katharine Graham demonstrates how one can exercise responsibility to an entire profession—in this case, journalism; and most dauntingly, John W. Gardner is described as a public citizen who over the years has addressed several of the most pressing problems in American society—to use the aforementioned term, an exemplary trustee. These figures, and the spheres they represent, stand as embodiments of high responsibility.

Susan Verducci, in Chapter Two, chooses to focus on the quality of caring—the assumption of personal responsibility for the lives and fortunes of others. She delineates the chief properties of an ethic of caring: receptive attention to others, the willingness to honor the motivations of other persons, and an abiding and enduring concern with relationships. Six of her subjects demonstrate these virtues to an impressive degree. The seventh, journalist Daniel Schorr, makes an instructive contrast. Abjuring the forms of personal caring exhibited by the other subjects, he instead displays a sense of caring for the profession of journalism as a whole.

The form of caring embraced by Schorr exemplifies the state of affairs discussed by Mihaly Csikszentmihalyi and Jeanne Nakamura in Chapter Three. These authors describe how highly creative individuals exhibit a powerful sense of responsibility for the fate of the domain to which they are devoting their creative energies. They honor the past of the domain by their mastery of it; at the same time, sensitive to the pressures and conditions of their own times, they mobilize their skills to lead the domain in positive, new directions. Their form of responsibility assumes a more abstract, less person-centered form than that embraced by the caring individuals portrayed in Verducci's chapter.

During its earliest manifestations, the GoodWork Project was called the Humane Creativity Project. Its stated goal was to understand how individuals who were highly creative—in the sense described by Csikszentmihalyi and Nakamura—could at the same time behave in a humane way. In her contribution, Wendy Fischman, in Chapter Four, revisits the concept of humane creativity. Focusing on the vocations of precollegiate education, social entrepreneurship, and philanthropy, Fischman shows how workers in these fields focus sharply on a widely perceived need in society. In addition to creating a tangible product, they have internalized the responsibility to meet this felt need and are prepared to commit themselves wholly and passionately to the task. Like other creators, they "think big," are flexible in the means they use, and influence others by their personal example as well as by their achievements.

The authors in the second part of the book focus on specific factors that contribute to a sense of responsibility or that make responsibility problematic in various ways. One of the features that characterizes professional life today is pressures on the use of time. Although present across the professional landscape, these pressures may be especially acute for those whose work involves caring for individuals. Jeffrey Solomon explores in Chapter Five the ways in which time pressures affect two vital professions: medicine and teaching. He discerns an intriguing and important distinction. Physicians respond to temporal constraints by spending more than the allotted time with individual patients, and teachers draw a line between their personal and their professional personae.

Surprising is Seth Wax's finding, presented in Chapter Six, that religious factors per se do not play much of a role in the senses of responsibility exhibited by the professionals in our study. However, once we move beyond religion in a strict sense, spiritual elements emerge in a number of instructive ways. Waxman delineates four distinctive forms of spiritual involvement: an orientation to a spiritual vision, a sense of calling to responsibility, the enactment of specific spiritual practices, and the direct experiencing of a divine reality. Each of the varieties of spirituality tends to be associated with specific professions—for example, an orientation toward spiritual visions is most frequent among those in the helping professions; a direct experience of the divine, among actors, musicians, and scientists.

In Chapter Seven, Andreas Schröer investigates the sense of responsibility as it is apprehended by individuals at different stages in the life cycle. Focusing on leaders, he discerns contrasting patterns. Senior leaders have achieved a sense of integrity; they have assumed responsibilities in ways that make sense to themselves and to the constituencies with whom they work. In contrast, young leaders struggle with a number of competing responsibilities that they have yet to resolve. Sometimes the struggle occurs at the workplace—Which constituency should be favored?—sometimes it is one of personal identity—What role should be assumed?—and most frequently, it is a struggle between responsibilities at work and those at home. Only time will tell whether the younger leaders will eventually achieve the equilibrium that characterizes the older leaders or whether different patterns will come to determine the course of the younger cohort.

Revisiting themes raised initially by Verducci, Lynn Barendsen probes in Chapter Eight the differences between professions that have an explicit caring dimension (such as teaching, nursing, and social entrepreneurship) and those that are better described as compartmentalized (such as journalism, law, and business). Specifically, Barendsen delineates three features that are particularly characteristic of the caring professions: imbalance between work and family life, overlap between professional and personal values, and strong identification with the constituency they serve. In certain respects, these factors complexify the lives of those in the caring professions, yet they also confer a coherence that may be lacking in the more compartmentalized professions.

In Chapter Nine, Carrie James presents another surprising finding: the senses of responsibility displayed by women and men in our study turn out to be surprisingly similar to another. One has to squint to discern significant trends. James's inquiry into gender differences yields a distinction that may be important, particularly in the professional realm. Professionals—and professions—can be instructively distinguished from one another depending on whether the responsibilities to self and to others are conflicting (as often happens in law), coexisting (found with some frequency in journalism), or in the happiest case, congruent (possible anywhere but somewhat more noticeable among actors).

Nearly all of the empirical work of the GoodWork Project has taken place within the borders of the United States, in the period from 1995 to 2005. During most of that time we are fortunate to have had the collaboration of an intrepid colleague from Denmark: social scientist and educator Hans Henrik Knoop. On the basis of his studies of business executives, journalists, and educators in Denmark, Knoop presents in Chapter Ten a portrait of good work in the Nordic context. In this way, he directs our attention to a final variable: the role of culture in delineating the scope and form of responsibility. In general, Knoop confirms the impression of informed observers that Scandinavia remains an area of the world characterized by good work and good workers. However, he also discerns a number of troubling trends that are most acute in journalism but that can be discerned in other professions as well. Unless extreme market forces can be countered by an Olympian spirit—in which victory is less crucial than a sense that the rules have been fairly employed—good work may be vulnerable in that corner of the globe.

The third part of the book focuses on threats to responsible work. When the conditions enabling good work are enfeebled, the possibility arises for work that fails to exemplify the properties of excellence, ethics, and engagement. In Chapter Eleven, Laura Horn and I investigate the limits of responsibility as they are delineated by practitioners. In one form of limitation, common among geneticists, professionals limit their responsibility by adhering to the rules of the domain. In a second form, common among physicians, individuals weigh the competing demands before limiting responsibility in one or another form of medical practice. In a third approach, which may be more common today in less secure professions like journalism, individuals limit their responsibilities by straying from the core purposes of the profession.

Picking up on the theme of the previous chapter, I turn my attention in Chapter Twelve to work that is best deemed irresponsible. Using journalism as my principal example, I describe work by individuals (such as *New York Times* reporters Judith Miller and Jayson Blair) that does not pass the test of responsibility. Then focusing on irresponsibility at the institutional (management and board) level, I review recent events at the *New York Times*. Finally, probing irresponsibility across a profession, I examine the broad trends in American journalism—ones that magnify those already mentioned by Knoop. While institutional and societal regulations can be helpful, I conclude that, in the end, responsibility resides in reflective and courageous individuals who strive to behave ethically whatever the obstacles.

In the fourth and final section of the book, we turn our attention to the practices that can enhance good work. Jeanne Nakamura's inquiry in Chapter Thirteen is directed at institutional responsibility. She examines the practices and culture at three tertiary institutions—Swarthmore College, Morehouse College, and St. Mary's College—each of which was nominated as an example of good work in higher education. Nakamura highlights the importance of a central mission that is widely recognized and embraced, as well as specific practices that serve to embody the core mission of the institution. The methods of investigation she describes are being used at colleges and universities that have been engaged in self-inquiry; these measures of alignment can also be adapted in other kinds of institutional settings.

In Chapter Fourteen, Lynn Barendsen and Wendy Fischman describe the GoodWork Toolkit, a set of materials that are being used primarily with secondary and collegiate students. The Toolkit familiarizes students with the kinds of ethical issues that arise in the workplace and helps them to anticipate and deal successfully with these dilemmas; this instrument also addresses issues that arise in students' current work—getting into college, in the case of secondary students, and making wise choices among the opportunities and temptations that arise in the relatively unstructured environment of the liberal arts college. The Toolkit has been used successfully in a range of settings and can be adapted for other venues in the future.

In a brief concluding essay, I survey the chief results of the lines of inquiry pursued in complementary ways by the volume's authors. I then chronicle investigations that are already under way and suggest further lines of work that might be undertaken in the future.

REFERENCES

Abbot, A. (1988). *The system of professions: An essay on the division of expert labor*. Chicago: University of Chicago Press.

Applebaum, H. (1992). *The concept of work: Ancient, medieval, and modern*. Albany: State University of New York Press.

Freidson, E. (2001). *Professionalism: The third logic.* Chicago: University of Chicago Press.

Gardner, H., Csikszentmihalyi, M., and Damon, W. (2001). *Good work: When excellence and ethics meet.* New York: Basic Books.

Gardner, H., Gregory, A., Csikszentmihalyi, M., Damon, W., and Michaelson, M. (1997). *The empirical basis of GoodWork: Methodological considerations.* Available at http://goodworkproject.org.

Kronman, A. (1995). *The lost lawyer.* Cambridge: Harvard University Press.

Weber, M. (1950). *The protestant ethic and the spirit of capitalism.* New York: Scribner's. (original publication: 19040)

PART ONE

POWERFUL
MODELS OF
RESPONSIBILITY

TAKING ULTIMATE RESPONSIBILITY

William Damon
Kendall Cotton Bronk

It's not enough that we do our best;
sometimes we have to do what's required

—Sir Winston Churchill

The buck stops here.

—Sign on President Harry Truman's desk

SOME PEOPLE, WHEN THE CHIPS ARE DOWN, can be counted on to step forward and do whatever they can to salvage a difficult situation. They "take responsibility" for finding a solution, no matter how burdensome, risk-laden, or even hopeless the situation may seem. Others, fearing the personal costs of becoming entangled in a hard problem, find excuses for absenting themselves or looking the other way. They disclaim the problem, perhaps because they believe it was not of their making, or because they have not been given sufficient resources to solve it, or because they have other business that they consider more pressing. Whether explicitly or not, they proclaim "it's not my problem," assuming that someone else will step in to fix things.

Stories of people who have assumed difficult responsibilities to a heroic degree are well-known, as are those of people who have famously (or infamously) shirked them. Mother Teresa, for example, felt an intense personal responsibility to care for the ill and impoverished. She once said, "When a poor person dies of hunger, it has not happened because God did not take care of him or her. It has happened because neither you nor I wanted to give that person what he or she needed. Make us worthy, Lord, to serve those people throughout the world who live and die in poverty and hunger. Give them through our hands, this day, their daily bread, and by our understanding and love, give them peace and joy" (Global Catholic Network, n.d.).

Mother Teresa did not leave this consuming job to others, nor did she merely pay lip service to it. Instead she labored for years to help some of the world's neediest citizens. Even though she knew she could never eradicate hunger or end human suffering entirely, she did as much as she could. "I heard the call to give up all and follow Christ into the slums to serve Him among the poorest of the poor. It was an order" (Global Catholic Network, n.d.). Unlike many of us who are concerned about the world's poor but fail to do much about it, Mother Teresa took ultimate responsibility for helping them.

On the other end of the responsibility spectrum was Emperor Nero of Rome. In about 64 A.D., a devastating fire swept through Rome, destroying everything in its path. According to the Roman historian Suetonius, the self-indulgent emperor "sang and played the lyre while Rome burned" (Bible History Online, n.d.). No psychologist was present at the time to analyze Nero's behavior, but we might speculate that he threw himself into a state of denial because he felt inadequate to cope with this formidable challenge. Or perhaps it was all a self-serving ploy: at the time it was rumored that Nero had started the fire himself in order to make space for a new, more beautiful palace. But whatever the reason, it is clear that rather than taking responsibility for the people he ruled, Emperor Nero shirked his duty in dramatic fashion, thereby becoming an emblem for irresponsibility.

While Mother Teresa and Emperor Nero provide extreme historical examples of responsibilities assumed and shirked, more ordinary instances abound in contemporary society. Our focus in this chapter falls on the workplace. In most work settings, some team players can be counted on to stay until the job is completed while some leave as soon as their part is done, regardless of the state of the project. Some are committed to seeing a project succeed while others are content seeing themselves succeed. Why are some people willing to put themselves on the line in order to resolve a tough problem while others around them think it more prudent to withdraw? (Compare Horn and Gardner, Chapter Eleven, this volume.) How, that is, do some people acquire a sense of *ultimate responsibility* for the way things turn out?

The Psychology of Ultimate Responsibility

In recent years, psychologists have taken an interest in life goals. Such goals have been referred to, variously, as "current concerns" (Klinger, 1977), "life tasks" (Cantor, 1990), "personal projects" (Little, 1989), "personal goals" (Brunstein, 1993), and "personal strivings" (Emmons, 1999). In the Emmons formulation, which is closest to our own framework, personal strivings are aimed at enduring objectives that motivate the person's behavior over the long haul (Emmons, 1999). Many people strive for enduring objectives in their lives, but there is enormous variation in the intensity of their strivings, in how well articulated the strivings are, and in how much influence they exert on the person's life choices. Personal strivings that are especially profound, long-lasting, and central to the person's identity (who I am, what I'm here for, what I'm trying to accomplish with my life, what kind of person I want to be) are considered *ultimate concerns* that transcend and guide the person's lower-level goals. (Emmons, 1999).

Ultimate concerns differ from other types of personal goals in important ways. A personal goal, such as acing a math test or finding a date to the spring prom, is typically short-term; in contrast, an ultimate concern, such as finding a cure for cancer, reflects a long-term purpose that subsumes a string of short-term goals. Short-term goals can act as means towards the fulfillment of ultimate concerns (or they may come and go on their own, without larger significance). Ultimate concerns, however, are ends in themselves. An ultimate concern may serve as an organizing feature for one's personal goals. Returning to the cancer example, someone may have the short-term goal of getting a high mark on a test in order to be admitted into a competitive college so that he or she can go on to medical school and begin researching cancer cures. In this way, personal goals may move the individual closer to achieving an ultimate concern.

People with ultimate concerns usually act in service of those interests, and such activity can provide profound and enduring sense of purpose for their lives. A purpose may reflect a commitment to faith, a social cause, a talent, or a domain. A purpose may be noble or ignoble. Hitler clearly had a purpose in his life, though it was surely not a moral one. Although distinguishing between noble and ignoble purposes can be difficult, it is possible; however, that challenge is beyond the scope of this chapter.[1]

---

[1]For a discussion of ways to distinguish noble from ignoble purposes, we suggest the following source: Bronk, K. C., Menon, J., and Damon, W. (2004). *Youth purpose: Conclusions from a working conference of leading scholars.* Available online at http://www.stanford.edu/group/adolescent.ctr.

In a study of adolescents, we interviewed a seventeen-year-old girl whose ultimate concern was caring for the environment. She felt it was her duty as a human being to preserve and protect her natural surroundings.

> What I believe is that God created [the environment], and God created [it] for us to take care of it. . . . All those little trees out there, and every bird that flies and every unique sunset and sunrise, was created by God for me to be able to see and enjoy, but if I don't take care of it, it's not going to be there for me to enjoy. So I guess that's one of the big parts of why I'm so passionate about what I do. Because this is given to me, for me to take care of, so I need to do my part for it to be there later for somebody else. [Bronk, 2005, p. 214]

This young woman did not just talk about her passion; she eagerly tackled a local environmental problem. Farmers with no place to dispose of significant amounts of motor oil were pouring it into their fields and the oil was beginning to contaminate the local water supply and damage the vegetation. This enterprising young woman started an innovative oil recycling program that became so successful that it was eventually implemented statewide. Creating and expanding the oil recycling program gave her life a purpose because she was able to work toward her ultimate concern of conservation. She then enrolled in a college environmental engineering program as a further means to advance her longstanding purpose and is eager to pursue a career toward that end as well (Bronk, 2005).

An ultimate concern may take a variety of forms. For some people, the call of a particular responsibility can become an ultimate concern—for example, responsibility to a person (such as a spouse or child), a community (such as one's country or company), a cause (such as civil rights or liberty), a value (such as truth or compassion), or an ideal (such as personal integrity or excellent work). In such cases, responsibility may be fueled by a deeper purpose, often a moral one. Mother Teresa's stated ultimate concern was serving God. That concern inspired a deep sense of responsibility for God's children, particularly the neediest of them. Caring for God's children provided a moral purpose for her life. In this way, Mother Teresa's sense of responsibility, driven by a powerful moral purpose, became an essential and inextricable part of her ultimate concern.

When is responsibility guided by a deeper purpose? How does that happen? In this chapter we argue that responsibility is likely to become an ultimate concern when (1) it stems from a highly articulated sense of moral identity, (2) it reflects the moral purpose at the center of that moral identity, and (3) it is supported by an organized group of respected peers and mentors (such as a faith community, a profession, an army or business team, a nongovernmental organization, and so on). Such personal and social conditions maximize the likelihood that people will strive to take ultimate responsibility, although in the end this stance remains to some extent a personal choice subject to the vagaries of will. In other words, while such conditions make it likely that people will take ultimate responsibility, they do not guarantee it.

Moral Identity and Moral Purpose

People differ in the centrality of their moral concerns to their senses of who they are and who they want to be. For some, moral convictions largely define who they are—these are people with strong senses of moral identity. For others, material concerns (how much money they have, how powerful they happen to be, and so on) are far more central. It is the former who are most likely to act in accord with their moral beliefs. We have found that moral identity is the best predictor of a person's commitment to moral action, because it determines not merely what the person considers to be the right course of action but also why the person would decide that "I myself must take this course." For example, most persons will express the belief that allowing others to starve is morally wrong, but only some of these people will conclude that they *themselves* must do something to prevent this occurrence in a particular circumstance, such as a famine in Africa. Moral identity engenders a sense of *personal responsibility* for taking action: it provides a powerful incentive for conduct because it triggers a motive to act in accord with one's conception of one's ideal self. Moral judgment alone cannot provide this motive: it is only when people conceive of themselves and their life goals in moral terms that they acquire a strong propensity to act according to their moral judgments.

Colby and Damon (1992) found that the moral exemplars they studied were convinced that the work they were doing fulfilled both their personal *and* moral goals. People who define themselves in terms of their moral goals see moral problems in everyday events, and they see themselves as necessarily implicated in dealing with those problems. From this sense it is a direct step to taking responsibility for seeking a solution.

In the workplace, moral identity means defining the self in a way that includes not only work-related skills and interests, but also the purpose for one's work, one's sense of ethical restrictions, and one's responsibility to one's community. In this way, personal responsibility in the workplace is fostered by a strong moral identity.

Over the course of human development, when a person makes a moral choice regularly, the choice becomes habitual: a child who has learned to tell the truth does not usually need to decide whether to lie, cheat, or steal every time the chance arises. The honest behavior comes naturally—or to use a familiar idiom that in this case has psychological validity, it becomes "*second nature.*" Through a system of acquired action, the behavior becomes habitual. Well-established moral habits are commonly known as virtues, which in turn form the behavioral basis of moral character.

People who function at the highest levels, maximizing all their potentials, strive for a unity in the self as a kind of ultimate concern in itself (the concern of personal integrity). Although absolute unity is rarely achieved (other than by extraordinary moral exemplars with high degrees of moral commitment), every person can approach this ideal over time. Cultivating a strong moral identity—the sense that moral concerns play a primary role in determining who I am and who I want to be—is the psychological means to this end.

Often at the center of one's moral identity a powerful moral purpose resides. The moral purpose may serve as an organizing feature for one's moral identity, compelling an individual to define himself or herself not only in moral terms but also in terms of his or her moral purpose.

A moral purpose is a stable and generalized intention to accomplish something that is at once meaningful to the self and of consequence to the broader world (Damon, Menon, and Bronk, 2003). There are two important features of this definition. First, a purpose is a goal of sorts, but it represents a long-term aim rather than a short-term goal such as to learn a new computer program or to finish the laundry. Second, purpose is a part of one's personal search for meaning, but it also has an external component: the desire to make a difference in the world, to contribute to matters larger than the self. Purpose is always directed at an accomplishment toward which one can make progress. This accomplishment may be material or nonmaterial, external or internal, reachable or unreachable. Its necessary characteristic is not its concreteness but the sense of direction it provides in creating an objective for purpose. Returning to the example of Mother Teresa is helpful here. Her purpose was to serve God, and this long-term, overarching aim clearly had an external focus. It served as a compass, providing direction throughout her life.

People who possess a moral purpose that is central to their lives feel obliged to act in service of that purpose. They feel responsible for its outcome. In this way, purpose may fuel a sense of personal responsibility.

In the empirical study mentioned earlier, we found a dozen adolescents who exhibited intense dedication to their individual purposes. Their commitments tended to be driven by a strong sense of moral identity (Bronk, 2005). In other words, their sense of who they were revolved around their purposes. So the environmentally minded young woman called herself "a tree hugger" and a religious adolescent described herself first and foremost as a Christian. The young people identified themselves by their purposes, and when this happened they felt personally responsible for working in service of their ultimate concerns. When a twelve-year-old boy learned that people in Africa were dying from a lack of clean drinking water, he felt personally responsible for raising the money to build wells in the neediest parts of the continent. His belief that he was ultimately responsible for providing clean drinking water likely resulted from a strong sense of moral identity, and in taking responsibility for the cause, he found a purpose for his life. Similarly, workers who find purpose in their jobs are more likely to take ultimate responsibility for resolving difficult issues at work.

Finally, a sense of ultimate responsibility is more likely to develop when social support for that effort exists. In the empirical study of adolescents, social support took the form of mentors, clubs, organized or informal groups of like-minded peers, faith communities, and supportive families (Bronk, 2005). In the workplace it may take the form of advisors, mentors, and professional associations.

In sum, regardless of the form it takes, social support in conjunction with a personal sense of moral identity and moral purpose maximizes the likelihood that people will develop a sense of ultimate responsibility for the work they do.

Ultimate Responsibility in the Workplace

In the GoodWork study, we sought out people with a deep sense of personal responsibility for their work. We conducted in-depth interviews with them to examine their personal beliefs, histories, and strategies for accomplishing good work. The interviews were semistructured and extensively probed, in the tradition of "clinical interviews" that we and others have used in previous studies to examine moral commitment and judgment (Colby and Damon, 1992).

In the GoodWork study, we found three types of ultimate responsibility in the workplace: (1) responsibility for the ethical conduct of an organization and its workers, (2) responsibility for fulfillment of the organization's professional or business purposes, and (3) responsibility for the broader social good. For this chapter we have selected three cases to illustrate these three types of ultimate responsibility.

While each of our examples exhibits all of these types of responsibility to some degree, each provides an especially powerful example of one type in particular. For example, Max De Pree, who worked in the business domain, illustrates the first type of ultimate responsibility; he took ultimate responsibility for the ethical conduct of his organization and its workers. Katharine Graham, who worked in the journalism domain, exemplified a strong sense of responsibility for the fulfillment of journalism's professional or business purpose. And John W. Gardner, who worked in the philanthropy and nonprofit domain, took ultimate responsibility for our society as a whole.

Max De Pree

While Max De Pree illustrates aspects of all three faces of ultimate responsibility, he provides the clearest example of someone who exhibits a sense of responsibility for the ethical conduct of an organization and its workers.

De Pree is chairman emeritus of Herman Miller, Inc., an innovative company in the furniture business. Under De Pree's leadership, Herman Miller was regularly included in Fortune's list of the twenty-five most admired companies in the United States. In addition to writing several books on leadership, De Pree was elected by *Fortune* magazine to the National Business Hall of Fame and won the Business Enterprise Trust's Lifetime Achievement Award.

De Pree owes his success in business to his innovative leadership style. In his book *Leadership Is an Art* (2004) De Pree shares his decidedly humble approach to being a leader. He begins his book with a short story that contains a simple moral: "no one is perfect" (p. 5). His approach to leadership naturally flows from this premise. Admitting that individuals are neither perfect nor all knowing "enables us to begin to think about being abandoned to the strengths of others" (p. 9). Accordingly, De Pree encourages leaders to identify others' talents and to remove obstacles in order to allow them to use their talents to the greatest extent possible. De Pree endorses Greenleaf's (1977) concept of servant leadership; rather than workers serving leaders, leaders should serve workers.

De Pree's confidence in others stems from a strong sense of moral identity. Central is his belief that "each of us is needed. Each of us has a gift to bring. Each of us is a social being and our institutions are social units. Each of us has a desire to contribute" (p. 66).

De Pree's moral identity reflects a moral purpose at its core. In his capacity as a leader, his purpose was to run a business that served its customers' needs fairly and ethically. This goal entailed helping his employees use their strengths to make their own contributions to a larger cause. In an interview with us he said, "For me, one of the very important things that happened in the course of a business career was the slow discovery that business and business people have to be a positive part of a society." De Pree defined himself by the work he did, and he encouraged his employees to do the same. He believed that the way people see themselves as workers should not differ from the way they see themselves as individuals in other contexts. People should strive to live at work according to the same value system by which they strive to live in other areas of their lives. "For many of us who work there exists an exasperating discontinuity between how we see ourselves as persons and how we see ourselves as workers. We need to eliminate that sense of discontinuity and to restore a sense of coherence to our lives" (2004, p. 32). Because De Pree believed that people should act at work as they would in their personal lives, he tried to create a corporate culture that encouraged ethical practices and a strong sense of responsibility to one's community.

Through his powerful sense of moral identity De Pree took personal responsibility for his company and his employees. One way he took responsibility for his employees was through a program he instituted called silver parachutes. The company was functioning in a time when hostile takeovers were common, and De Pree felt it was unfair for only the top executives to receive significant financial compensation, or golden parachutes, in the case of such a takeover. So he instituted a program by which all employees were entitled to compensation should the company be acquired. In our interview with him he told us how this program served two aims: "If [another company] really wanted to take you over, they had to pay the extra cost, which helped to inhibit the idea that you could take us over. But, you see, it wasn't primarily designed to prevent a takeover. It was primarily designed to bring equity." Such a program points not only to De Pree's business acumen, but also to his deep concern for the welfare of his employees. This program evidences De Pree's sense of responsibility for the Herman Miller workforce.

A critical component of De Pree's philosophy on leadership was accountability. Leaders, he believed, should have enough faith in their workers to allow those workers to be personally accountable for the work they do. De Pree put this idea into practice at Herman Miller through the Scanlon Plan, a program that offered financial rewards to workers who saved the company money and that gave employees partial ownership of the business. By making his employees owners, he gave them a personal stake in the company's performance. In *Leadership Is an Art* (2004) he wrote, "Another implication is that everybody must live up to some important expectations. In the position of owners, we become more accountable for our personal performance. Owners cannot walk away from concerns" (p. 99). Of course, another word for accountability is *responsibility*. This is yet another way that De Pree encouraged his workers to take ultimate responsibility for their work, and in which he took responsibility for his employees.

Not only did De Pree take responsibility for his employees but he also took responsibility for the company's practices. He assumed that the ethical integrity of his company was *his* job to promote and enforce. Unlike so many of the corporate chieftains who have made news in recent times with their claims that they were blithely ignorant of their employees' or associates' criminal shenanigans, De Pree made it his business to communicate high ethical standards all through the ranks of the company and to ensure that his employees were acting accordingly. Evidence of this was the strict policy that De Pree set against accepting bribes—in those days a common practice for doing business overseas. In our interview with him he shared an anecdote regarding this practice:

> One of our senior salespeople was dealing with an important decision-maker at [unnamed company]. We were talking about it, and my recollection is that it was about a $12 million order. And the guy said, "Well, I can arrange for you to have this order, but we have to talk about what my share is going to be." And our man said, "Well, there isn't going to be any share for you. Our company doesn't do this." "Sure," the guy said, "everybody does it." "No," [our man] said, "we don't." And [their man] said, "Well, I'm going to have to call your boss, and you'll probably lose your job." And [our man] said, "Oh no, we just lose the order." Because he knew that's what I'd say.

De Pree believed strongly in ethical business practices and he took ultimate responsibility for seeing that his company functioned accordingly.

De Pree had a series of mentors who helped him see his work in a broader context. In our interview he talked about the important role that ethical businesses play in the support of the societies they serve. "I think that my business career was a kind of pilgrimage away from, you know, how can you build up the revenues . . . towards a goal of figuring out what are the preserving principles of the free market system in a democracy." Mentors helped De Pree connect his work life to his religious life. They helped him see how his work life could serve society and, in doing so, serve his religious aims as well. As a result of the powerful role that mentors played in his life, De Pree later served as a dedicated mentor to others. In addition to having the support of mentors, De Pree had the support of his family. Before him his father and his brother had run the company, and both of these men supported De Pree in his "social approach" to business.

In sum, not only did De Pree help his workers feel personally invested in their work but he also took ultimate responsibility for the ethical conduct of Herman Miller and for the welfare of its employees.

Katharine Graham

The second example of responsibility in the workplace is Katharine Graham. She provides a powerful example of someone who exhibited responsibility for the fulfillment of the organization's professional or business purpose.

Graham grew up in New York and Washington, D.C., the fourth of five children in a wealthy, politically active family. Her mother was a socialite with a deep appreciation for books, art, and politics, and her father was a wildly successful businessman with a keen sense of civic responsibility. As a child, Katharine admired both of her parents, but as she grew older she became particularly close to her father, Eugene Meyer. As a young man, Eugene had plotted a "map of life" in which the first twenty years of his life were to be spent learning. Accordingly, much of this phase was spent in school. The next twenty years he planned to dedicate to earning a living to support his family, which he did through a variety of highly successful business ventures. Finally, the last twenty years of his life were to be devoted to public service. During this time he moved his family from New York to Washington, D.C., to assume a series of political positions. He also bought the struggling *Washington Post*. While Eugene ran the paper, he and Katharine routinely engaged in discussions about journalistic ethics and political issues.

Once leaving home, Katharine majored in journalism in college and worked briefly as a reporter for the *San Francisco News* and the *Washington Post*. She married Philip Graham, a lawyer who clerked for Supreme Court Justice Felix Frankfurter. Phil and Eugene became close friends, and when Eugene was ready to retire from the *Post*, he installed Phil as its new publisher. Phil grew the paper's readership and acquired other media companies. In his forties Phil began to suffer intense bouts of depression and committed suicide. Katharine, fearful that her family could lose the paper, took over as publisher. For a wealthy woman in

1963 this was a surprising move; women of means at that time did not typically work. Initially Graham planned to assume the role only in title and until her son was old enough to take over. However, she soon realized that being publisher required a good deal of time and attention, and she found the demanding job surprisingly engaging. During her tenure as publisher, Katharine made enormously difficult publication decisions, including whether to publish stories about Watergate and the Pentagon Papers; these decisions evoked the fury of the administration and the justice department at that time.

Graham's sense of moral identity included at least three distinct facets, and each played out in the context of the journalism domain. First, Graham saw herself as someone who owed something to the community in which she lived. In her autobiography she wrote, "We grew up with the belief that no matter what you did professionally, you automatically had to think about public issues and give back, either in interest in your community or in public service—you had to care" (Graham, 1997, p. 46). She saw her role as publisher as an opportunity to serve the public good. Like her father, she believed that "a newspaper was a public trust, meant to serve the public in a democracy" (p. 63).

Second, her moral identity included a deep concern for people of lesser means. In her autobiography she recounts the following story: "Once in 1952, after a visit to a Utah copper mine that had yielded my father great financial gains, [my mother] wrote in her diary, '[The mine] was an interesting sight but the village that led up to it appalled me. . . . This is where [the money] comes from and I spend it on Chinese art but it was a shock to think that we live on money that is produced under such conditions'" (1997, p. 52).

Upon hearing this story Graham could have moved to Utah and taken personal responsibility for the miners' welfare. With her wealth she could have significantly improved their working conditions. Instead she took her concern for the miners and embedded it in the mission of the paper. Rather than becoming a class paper that catered only to the wealthiest readers, she saw to it that the *Post* remained a paper for the masses, serving readers from all socioeconomic levels, including, as she told us in her interview, "Maryland housewives . . . [and] the government people and the guy behind the State Department desk." In doing so, she did not completely ignore the miners' plight. Instead she took responsibility in the area of her moral identity, using the paper to serve the public good. Her personal mission, or purpose, interacted with the mission of the domain to produce good work, as her concern for the masses played out in the context of trustworthy journalism.

Finally, humility was another important part of her moral identity, and it too played out in her job. As a publisher she insisted that her editors listen to readers. "You have to make them listen," she said in our interview. She also listened to readers and made an effort to hear not only their praise but their critiques as well.

Graham's highly articulated sense of moral identity was revealed by her decision to publish the Pentagon Papers. This was a very controversial choice that essentially defined her tenure as publisher. In our interview with Graham she told us that she had about thirty seconds to make the call. Her ability to make this snap decision reflects a powerful sense of moral identity. She did not need long to consider the decision; the right course of action was "second nature" for her. In Colby and Damon's 1992 study, moral exemplars exhibit this same strong sense of moral identity. Rather than waffling over difficult decisions, these individuals clearly determine the proper course of action. The ability to make decisions like this quickly points to Graham's powerful sense of moral identity.

Running the *Washington Post* was more than a job to Graham; it gave her life a purpose. She cared deeply for the paper, and throughout her autobiography and in her interview with us she often spoke about the *Post* almost as though it were another member of her large family. She described her "passionate devotion" to the paper and said she always "cared a lot and invested a lot" in it, just as a parent would in a child. Graham felt a deep sense of responsibility for the paper, and just as parents routinely fight for custody of their children, she worked hard to keep the paper in her family.

Graham's moral identity reflected her purpose of running a high-quality newspaper. As a publisher she believed that being a profitable paper was important, but it was not her primary aim; it was simply one necessary step toward achieving her ultimate concern. In her interview she said, "I used to make pious speeches to Wall Street about profitability and excellence going hand in hand. I really started on that theme. . . . I had to convince them that I really wanted to be profitable, which in fact I did, because you have to be profitable to survive. You have to be profitable if you want to invest in editorial—you know, reporters and quality people." Graham's purpose, to run a superior newspaper, subsumed her aim of profitability and gave her life a deep sense of meaning. Because this was her purpose, Graham took ultimate responsibility for seeing that the paper served its readers.

Graham's ability to take ultimate responsibility for the paper was scaffolded by the social support she received. Both her husband and her father felt the same way about the paper. In her autobiography Graham said of her husband, "[Phil] insisted that newspapers should not 'brush off our defects by blithely saying that people can cancel their subscriptions if they disagree'" (1997, p. 184). Like Katharine, Phil felt that the paper served an important civic function. When Katharine took over as publisher she continued many of the practices her husband and father had put in place. For example, her father started a policy of not endorsing presidential candidates because he did not want the paper to appear biased, and Graham kept this policy in place.

Like De Pree, Graham took ultimate responsibility for her work. She felt responsible to the paper and to the civic function it played in supporting a democracy. This strong sense of responsibility was fostered by the social supports and resulted from a well-articulated sense of moral identity.

Unlike De Pree, however, Graham was working in an area—journalism—that had a long and noble tradition as a professional domain serving the public interest. As our GoodWork model indicates (see Introduction), the mission and standards of domains can play a strong role in helping individuals find and accomplish their moral purposes in the workplace. GoodWork, as we have written, arises from interactions between people and the fields and domains in which they are working. In Graham's case, she had the benefit of the grand tradition of journalistic ethics as well as the company of people, such as Ben Bradlee, her distinguished editor, who were pillars of the field of first-rate news reporting. The evolution of Graham's own moral identity owed a significant debt to these associations. Graham's own moral choices as an individual were critically important for the good work she accomplished; but the historic domain of journalism also played a part in shaping the nature and directions of her decisions.

John W. Gardner

John W. Gardner, former president of the Carnegie Corporation; former secretary of Health, Education, and Welfare; and founder of Common Cause and Independent Sector, is our third illustrative case. In his distinguished and widely celebrated life as the foremost leader of the American nonprofit sector, Gardner exemplified ultimate responsibility for the broader social good.

Gardner was born in Los Angeles in 1912. He received his doctorate in psychology in 1938 and taught briefly at the University of California, Connecticut College for Women, and Mount Holyoke College. In 1943 he joined the U.S. Marine Corps and served as an intelligence officer.

When he was released from active duty he joined the Carnegie Corporation of New York, a large and influential philanthropic foundation. He served as vice president in 1949 and as president in 1955. Also in 1955 he became president of the Carnegie Foundation for the Advancement of Teaching. In 1964, President Lyndon B. Johnson awarded Gardner the Presidential Medal of Freedom, the nation's highest civilian honor, and in 1965 named him U.S. Secretary of Health, Education, and Welfare. Gardner held this position until 1968, when he resigned to become head of the National Urban Coalition. In 1970 Gardner founded Common Cause, a nonpartisan citizens' lobby. He served as its chairman from 1970 to 1977. He also chaired the organizing committee that led to the founding of Independent Sector, a national forum for organizations in the voluntary sector, and served as chair until 1983, when he became professor of public service at Stanford University. Engaged throughout his adult life in a variety of civic pursuits, Gardner is impossible to pigeonhole. Independent Sector's Web site refers to him as "the ultimate builder of ideas and unifier of people and causes" (n.d.). His varied resume is held together by the common commitment to community building.

Gardner was driven by a strong sense of ultimate responsibility not for himself and his own organization, as De Pree was, nor for a domain, as Graham was, but for all of his society. His adult life was spent in pursuit of jobs that would allow him to strengthen the social fabric.

In our interview with Gardner he spoke at length about the values that constituted his moral identity and served as a source of ultimate concern for him. These values guided his life. "You run a lot of risks when you try to articulate neatly your value system. . . . It starts with the first week in life, and by the time you are ten you have downloaded so much in terms of values and ways of looking at the world that it is impossible to sort it all out." While Gardner found it difficult to talk about his complete value system, he had no problem identifying a particularly salient personal value. "I want to stress one [value] that you have heard me talk about before, and that is responsibility. . . . It clearly traces back to childhood and early development of a sense of responsibility for the other." "Responsibility for the other" was the basis of Gardner's moral identity. It defined who he was and what he spent his life trying to do. This striving was central to Gardner and to his ultimate concern with improving society.

Gardner believed that a sense of responsibility among citizens was essential to solving social problems. A community could not function effectively, he argued, without a populace that felt personally responsible for its vitality. "Responsibility is the absolute key to community." So

Gardner took ultimate responsibility for encouraging people to feel personally accountable for the health of their communities.

Working to improve society gave Gardner's life a purpose. Throughout his life he moved from job to job as opportunities to work on social problems presented themselves. While he talked about how it was "extraordinary luck that Carnegie Corporation" offered him a position, in his interview with us he acknowledged, "I was determined to find work that exposed me to a broader range of social issues, social problems, the way the world functioned." He intentionally sought out opportunities to work on improving the society in which he lived. In his book *Self-Renewal: The Individual and the Innovative Society* (1963) Gardner wrote, "The storybook conception [of happiness] tells of desires fulfilled; the truer version involves striving toward meaningful goals" (p. 97). According to Gardner, true happiness required a purpose, and taking responsibility for the betterment of society served as a deeply meaningful source of purpose for him.

Responsibility for the other served as the basis of Gardner's moral identity, but humility was another important aspect of it. Though he did not directly talk about humility in our interview with him, his actions repeatedly point to the central role it played in the way he viewed his role as a philanthropist. For example, when discussing the role of philanthropy in a democracy, he pointed out that foundations need to grant the groups they fund a high level of autonomy.

> We let people do the thing they want to do within a moral framework, but still letting them be creative in their way. . . . I think one of the very worrisome things today is the tendency of foundations to gravitate toward a view that "we around this staff table or board table really know what the truths are. Let's find people, let's go out and find people to pursue those truths. We'll support them to do what we want them to do." You'd be surprised what a live impulse that is. You have a pot of money and you feel that entitles you to make decisions.

Humility played an important role both in the way he viewed the social role of philanthropy and in the way he pursued his ultimate concern.

In addition to possessing a well-articulated moral identity and a powerful sense of purpose, Gardner sought out mentors who supported his aims and assisted his efforts. "I had marvelous mentors . . . [and I've been] spared untold missteps and disasters by my mentors." In our interview he spoke about a number of mentors who helped him use each new position he acquired to tackle social problems effectively. With the support and assistance of these people he was able to effect serious social change.

Conclusions

De Pree, Graham, and Gardner shared some important characteristics. For example, they all functioned, either intentionally or unintentionally, as servant leaders. DePree talked about his high regard for Greenleaf's servant approach to leading and spoke at length about his intentional efforts to be a servant leader. As such he sought to remove obstacles so that his employees could do their best work.

While Graham did not use the term *servant leader* to describe her leadership style, her actions suggest that she also embraced the philosophy. For example, in our interview with her she talked about the delicate way in which she worked with her editor. Rather than simply telling him which stories to publish and which ones to omit, she served as a sounding board for him and typically allowed him to make the final decision.

Gardner too acted as a servant leader. For instance, a creative effort he led to build a low-income housing development aptly demonstrated this leadership style. Rather than simply building the community for the residents, he and his team empowered the would-be residents to build their own community using Gardner and his team as a source of support and guidance.

> You go in and you say, "If you want some affordable housing, we'll show you how to get it." The neighborhood people . . . don't know how to design a housing plan. It takes people very familiar with construction, financing, et cetera. You give them the pattern. You go with them to the insurance company, to the banks, even to the city council. . . . You say, "It's your project, not ours. . . . [But] you can always call on us for technical assistance."

This approach to building their domiciles fostered a sense of ownership in the future residents that led to a greater sense of neighborhood. In this way, being a servant leader helped Gardner achieve his aim of community building.

The servant leader concept was so central to Gardner that it shaped his sense of philanthropy's primary mission. "There isn't anything you can congratulate yourself on except spotting good people. I financed David Riesman's first book. I am proud of that. I financed John Kenneth Galbraith's first book. I am proud of that." Gardner saw his philanthropic role as one in which he provided the means for others to do great acts. In this way he functioned as a servant leader.

Consonant with the servant leadership approach, humility was another hallmark of this group. Despite their positions of power, the exemplars exhibited a sense of openness to new ideas and new approaches. They made a habit of listening to others, even if the people speaking had less expertise than they did. They recognized the strengths of their colleagues and used those strengths to advance their efforts. According to Tangney (2000, 2002), these practices characterize an authentic form of humility. In describing his approach to leadership, De Pree called for giving employees a good deal of responsibility and then stepping back and letting them do their work. He believed that leaders should tell employees what needs to be done but not how to do it, because workers are better equipped than leaders to determine the best way to do their jobs.

Graham's humility was particularly evident in her practice of listening intently to her readers. "I used to go out and have lunch with communities in various places and take the editors and circulation people and just talk to them and let them criticize us." Listening and learning allowed her to assume successfully the position of publisher with minimal prior journalistic experience, and to be effective in taking responsibility for the domain of journalism.

Gardner also demonstrated a surprising degree of humility. In our interview with him he repeatedly described himself as a "learner" and spoke of the importance of listening to others. "I thought of myself as an observer, a student, trying to understand." Had he not possessed this humility, he likely would not have been able to involve himself in as many different projects as he did with as much success as he achieved.

An authentic sense of humility allowed the exemplars to be effective in their efforts. Had they not listened to others or been open to new ideas and novel approaches, it is unlikely they would have achieved the success they did in taking responsibility for their respective concerns.

Finally, each of these individuals was also willing to take risks. In De Pree's book *Leadership Is an Art* (2004), he talked about how he never wanted Herman Miller to be the largest furniture company because then it could not risk losing its leading position. Instead, he sought to keep Herman Miller relatively small and to make it an innovative company that was not afraid to try new things.

Graham too was a risk taker. Her career was defined by two significant risks. First, she chose to take over as publisher of the *Post* with very little professional experience. She had minimal experience in journalism and no experience managing people, yet her risk-taking personality allowed her to assume the position anyway. Her second major risk was publishing the Pentagon Papers. In making this decision she risked her professional reputation.

Finally, Gardner's professional life was also defined by risk-taking behavior. In our interview with him he said,

I have always been a risk taker. I thought I was going to be a writer of fiction until I was about twenty-one and had a big investment in that and dropped it to become a psychologist because I felt I had to earn a living. . . . When I left psychology, many of my colleagues just thought I was crazy. Assistant professor, great chance of moving ahead, just leaving the field. . . . I have very little sensitivity to risk.

Gardner was self-aware enough to recognize his own propensity for risk. He not only accepted it but also seemed to thrive on it. While most people feel that attaining a high level of proficiency at their job is a desirable goal, Gardner consistently left positions when he reached this point. "For a good year before I was offered the job, I had a real feeling that my situation was too comfortable. I knew all the answers to being a foundation president in New York City. I was able to open practically any door and deal with my problems, and that's not a good sign."

In this way, Gardner shared with our other two exemplars a willingness to put himself on the line for the sake of his ultimate concern, even in conditions that others would find unacceptably risky in a personal sense. As with the moral exemplars in Colby and Damon's (1992) study, none of the three discussed here worried much about such risks: they shared an almost instinctive sense that they had no choice in the matter, that their ultimate concerns could broach nothing less than their full commitments, that their sense of ultimate responsibility demanded nothing less than doing whatever it would take to get the job done. None of these exemplars could have taken ultimate responsibility had they been deterred by the risks that confronted them; and they dealt with these risks preemptively, by not allowing them to enter into their considerations in the first place. In short, they did what they had to do, and knowing that this was the course to which they were committed liberated them from worrying about the personal consequences.

Although these individuals shared some characteristics, they also differed in many ways. They each had a very different moral identity. De Pree saw himself as an ethical business leader, while Graham saw herself as a protector of journalism and Gardner saw himself as an agent of social change.

All three prized certain values, but those values varied greatly in content. De Pree sought to abide by the virtues of equity and fairness, as evidenced by the company stock option plan he introduced. Graham valued truthfulness and transparency. Her decision to publish the Pentagon Papers points to her desire to be open and honest with the public. Finally, Gardner's entire professional life revolved around the value he placed on responsibility to others.

Neither these commonalities nor these contrasts were accidental. Instead, all three individuals were prepared for their positions by their moral identities and the experiences that shaped them.

As these examples illustrate, people can assume ultimate responsibility in the workplace at different levels of societal concern. For this chapter we chose our three exemplars of ultimate responsibility to illustrate three different levels of concern. The three cases reflect purposes that are all highly moral but that deal with different sorts of social issues arising from work.

De Pree took personal responsibility for his employees and for his company. Through the Scanlon Plan and the silver parachutes program, he took care of his employees. Through policies such as not allowing his employees to accept bribes, De Pree took ultimate responsibility for his company's ethical practices. But his reach ended, figuratively, at the outer walls of his company.

Graham's sense of responsibility was broader. She took responsibility for the integrity of a domain—journalism—that plays a crucial role in any democratic society. Graham saw to it that her paper served the public good by implementing the mission and standards of good journalism, because she firmly believed that a free press exists to support democracy. Accordingly, she made sure that the *Post* remained a paper for the masses and made choices like publishing the Pentagon Papers in order to keep her readers informed. She believed in the potential of the journalism domain and took responsibility for seeing that it was used to benefit the general public.

Gardner's sense of responsibility extended ever more broadly than Graham's. It did not stop at the edge of a particular domain; instead he accepted responsibility for all of society and worked to ensure society's well-being in whatever domain he felt he could be most effective. In the course of his legendary career, Gardner moved across domains, from philanthropy to politics to social entrepreneurship, always in pursuit of his broader mission of progressive social change. The working life he forged for himself created a model of leadership and a standard of social commitment that is widely emulated in the present and will likely remain influential for years to come.

Those who assume ultimate responsibility for the choices of any group, whether a company, a professional domain, or an entire society, place themselves in a pivotal position. They subject themselves to the requirement of constantly evaluating the choices and, when necessary, resisting or altering the choices in order to bring them in line with their own moral commitments. Such a role is always difficult and often risky. Sustaining it is possible only when it is consistent with the purposes that emanate from a firmly established moral identity.

It has been said that people create their own destinies through the choices they make over the course of their lives. Society's destiny too reflects choices made by people, sometimes collectively and sometimes as individuals. Most make conventional choices that contribute to society's prevailing trends; but some people leave their mark on history by resisting or altering the trends. Although there is no way to do this without facing opposition and accepting the attendant risks, it is the only course that those who exert moral leadership in transformative times can take.

REFERENCES

Bible History Online. (n.d.). *Emperor Nero.* Retrieved March 6, 2006, from http://www.bible-history.com/nero

Bronk, K. C. (2005). Portraits of purpose: A study examining the ways a sense of purpose contributes to positive youth development (Doctoral dissertation, Stanford University, 2006). *UMI ProQuest Digital Dissertations,* AAT 3187267.

Brunstein, J. (1993). Personal goals and subjective well-being: A longitudinal study. *Journal of Personality and Social Psychology, 65,* 1061–1070.

Cantor, N. (1990). From thought to behavior: "Having" and "doing" in the study of personality and cognition. *American Psychologist, 45,* 735–750.

Colby, A., & Damon, W. (1992). *Some do care: Contemporary lives of moral commitment.* New York: Free Press.

Damon, W., Menon, J., & Bronk, K.C. (2003). The development of purpose among adolescents. *Journal of Applied Developmental Science, 7*(3), 119–128.

De Pree, M. (2004). *Leadership is an art.* New York: Doubleday.

Emmons, R. A. (1999). *The psychology of ultimate concerns: Motivation and spirituality in personality.* New York: Guilford Press.

Gardner, J. W. (1963). *Self-renewal: The individual and the innovative society.* New York: Norton.

Global Catholic Network. (n.d.). *Mother Teresa: Her words.* Retrieved March 8, 2006, from http://www.ewtn.com/motherteresa/words.htm

Graham, K. (1997). *Personal history.* New York: Vintage Books.

Greenleaf, R. K. (1977). *Servant leadership: A journey into the nature of legitimate power and greatness.* Mahwah, NJ: Paulis Press.

Klinger, E. (1977). *Meaning and void: Inner experience and the incentives in people's lives.* Minneapolis: University of Minnesota Press.

Independent Sector (n.d.) *The life of John W. Gardner.* Retrieved March 6, 2006, from http://www.independentsector.org/about/gardner.html

Little, B. R. (1989). Personal projects analysis: Trivial pursuits, magnificent obsessions, and the search for coherence. In D. M. Buss & N. Cantor (Eds.), *Personality psychology: Recent trends and emerging directions* (pp. 15–31). New York: Springer-Verlag.

Tangney, J. P. (2000). Humility: Theoretical perspectives, empirical findings, and directions for future research. *Journal of Social and Clinical Psychology, 19*, 70–82.

Tangney, J. P. (2002). Humility. In C. R. Snyder & S. J. Lopez (Eds.), *Handbook of positive psychology* (pp. 411–419). New York: Oxford University Press.

2

THE ABILITY TO RESPOND

Susan Verducci

*I always think that's one of the great myths—that
you separate [yourself] in business.*

—Anita Roddick, Founder and Owner of The Body Shop

EXPLORING THE CONCEPT OF RESPONSIBILITY is like dancing with an
octopus. Just when you begin to groove, an unattended arm of the concept taps you on the shoulder, disorienting you. When you finally corral
that wayward arm and reestablish your rhythm, yet another arm taps and
the cycle begins anew. Conceptually, responsibility challenges even the
best dancers.[1]

In this chapter, I leave that dance behind by bracketing the inherent complexities of the way we commonly understand responsibility. I focus on a
single and literal arm of the concept—*response-ability,* that is, one's ability
to respond to needs. Of course everyone possesses the ability to respond to
needs. We respond to being cold by putting on a sweater, we respond
to hunger by trying to find food. If we did not respond in simple ways, we
could not survive. What separates and distinguishes us is *how* we respond
to certain stimuli. In this chapter I examine how good workers respond to
their perception of the needs of others in their professional lives. More specifically, how does recognition of the needs of others influence how they

---

[1]Thanks to musician Red Norvo for his vivid image of dancing with an octopus.

conceive of and go about their work? By narrowing my subject to this particular question, I intentionally tie down all but one of the octopus's arms. I know they are there, straining to be let loose, but for the moment I am free of them.

But another octopus appears: What do I mean by "perception of the needs of others"? To frame answers to this question (and others that are sure to arise), I move to the moral domain. The workers examined in this chapter were selected by their peers and by experts in their field for doing "good work"—that is, work that is both excellent in quality and socially responsible. The latter component, social responsibility, places the good work squarely in the moral domain.[2] There are, however, many ways in which morality is understood and explained. In this chapter, the moral lens I use to understand responsibility is borrowed from the *ethics of care,* particularly from philosopher Nel Noddings's work.[3]

Whereas concern for right action characterizes most traditional approaches to morality, forging and maintaining moral relations serves as the primary concern in the ethics of care. The moral nature of acts of caring was first identified by Carol Gilligan in her groundbreaking book *In a Different Voice* (1982). Gilligan suggested that females may possess a moral orientation different from the traditional justice perspective delineated by, for example, philosophers Jeremy Bentham, Immanuel Kant, and John Rawls, and in particular, developmental psychologist Lawrence Kohlberg. This "female" orientation holds *caring* as its moral center. Work on caring since then has delimited its connection to women and its oppositional position in relation to the justice perspective. On the whole, caring is now considered a moral orientation of both men and women that is at times compatible with the ends of justice.

Gilligan's psychological findings were made philosophically coherent and vivid by Nel Noddings (1984), whose approach to understanding

---

[2]I use *ethics* and *morality* interchangeably in this chapter. I recognize that in academic discourse *ethics* usually refers to the interpretation of morality by social institutions (think *code of ethics*) and not to morality itself. I ignore this distinction for a number of reasons. First, most people use the two terms interchangeably and conceive of morality and ethics as the same. Second, this chapter focuses on individuals, not social institutions. Third, many individuals I examined articulated what might be considered their own *personal* ethical codes by which they abided in their work and lives; in other words, they developed conceptual frameworks and structural systems to guide them to be socially responsible.

[3]The ethics of care is not a singular entity. Many theorists are working in this vein, each with her own particular focus.

morality can be helpful in understanding how good workers exhibit responsibility in their work. The ability to identify and respond appropriately to the needs of others—response-ability—grounds and centers her approach to thinking about the moral world. Caring, as a philosophical approach, rejects the detached, universal, impartial, and abstract requirements of traditional moral theory. The notion of moral agents seeking to maximize utility or perform obligations for their own sake is antithetical to the notion of caring. Instead, relationships and responsibilities replace (or are prior to) rights and rules. Moral caring is characterized by receptive attention to others, motivational displacement, and concern for restoring, maintaining, and building relationships with others.

With this theory in mind, the questions explored herein can be reframed. Do good workers respond to the needs of others in ways described by the ethics of care? Which workers do? Which do not? In other words, *Who cares?*

Methods

I examined the interview transcripts of two sets of workers: seven "exemplary" workers and ten "good" workers. I sought to find indications (or the lack thereof) of guidance by an ethics of care and of differences in terms of frequency of articulated guidance between the two sets of workers. The seven exemplars were selected by the GoodWork Project's researchers; they were considered to be the best and most inspirational of the good workers we interviewed and studied for the project. They were nominated without the researchers' having prior knowledge of the working hypothesis of this chapter. Workers nominated multiple times were considered, and the attempt to represent multiple professions and both genders influenced who ultimately was selected. The three men and four women came from five professions: two from journalism, two from business, one faculty member from higher education, one executive of a philanthropic foundation, and one surgical doctor in the field of obstetrics and gynecology (OB-GYN).

From each of these five professions two good workers were randomly selected to compare with the exemplary workers. They were selected from the same professional niche. For example, although we interviewed *donors* in philanthropy, given that the exemplar was an *executive* of a foundation, the comparison workers were also executives. Likewise, the comparison subjects in higher education were faculty members, and all the doctors specialized in OB-GYN.

What does it mean for these seventeen workers to "care" in the sense that Noddings intended? In the transcripts of the interviews with these people, I looked for three features derived from the primary characteristics of Noddings' ethics of care. The first feature, defined by Noddings as *receptive attention,* attempts "to grasp or to receive a reality rather than to impose it" (1984, p. 22). Noddings wrote, "When my caring is directed to living things, I must consider their natures, ways of life, needs, and desires" (p. 14). In terms of receptive attention, I sought evidence of listening and gathering information from others, meeting others where they are (rather than imposing one's own agenda on others), and bias against hierarchy (rejection of the power differential between oneself and others). The second feature I looked for was examples of what Noddings called *motivational displacement* (pp. 16, 18), instances when good workers consciously pushed aside their own motives in order to take on those of others. Finally, I looked for evidence of the fundamental characteristic of caring: concern for relationships. The evidence I noted was concern for creating connections with others and caring for community (restoring community, conserving community, or building community).

Who Cares? or What They Say

Did the workers I studied articulate the three characteristics of the ethics of care? The simple answer to this first question is yes. The transcripts provide an overwhelming amount of evidence that these workers were guided in their professional lives by an ethics of care. Were the exemplars guided by this ethics more (or differently) than the good workers? The answer to the second question is not quite so simple. When the aspects of caring I looked for were grouped together, the exemplary workers articulated the features of caring more often than the good workers (see Figure 2.1).[4]

What cannot be captured by an analysis of the frequency of these connections is the *depth* of the exemplars' discussion of the features in their work lives. Most good workers did not speak about caring in the rich way the exemplars did. For many of the exemplars, the perception of the needs of others formed the central chord in their reflections on the processes, purposes, and motives in their work. Although they might mention the aspects of receptive attention only twice, they might discuss each instance for five minutes. For the others, receptive attention was simply

---

[4]This difference was computed by a one-way analysis of variance and was statistically significant at the .05 level (p = .028).

Figure 2.1. Comparison of Exemplars and Good Workers
on Features of Caring.

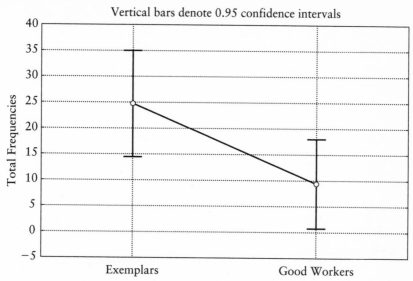

one of many chords in their work. Although the notes of caring were heard in all the interviews, they were heard more often and in more detail among the exemplars.

In what follows I use the words of these exemplars to trace the nuances of how they talk about caring, and I emphasize the many ways they respond to the perception of the needs of others.[5] On the heels of this presentation, a near-perfect exemplar anomaly is introduced. The chapter concludes with a brief discussion of the implications of caring in workers who do high-quality and socially responsible work.

Receptive Attention

The exemplary workers we interviewed consistently signaled that they approach others with the characteristics of receptive attention: they listen and gather information from them, they talk of meeting them where they are, and they reject hierarchical relationships.

Three of the seven exemplary workers mentioned listening to and gathering information from others. The following is only one of eleven times

---

[5]Certain subjects requested that their interviews remain anonymous. Although their words appear in what follows, their names do not.

that Anita Roddick, founder of The Body Shop, brought the topic up in the course of a two-hour interview:

> I think my success comes through the ability to gather around women and get their stories out of them and the stories of the body and the stories of the rituals of the body—I think I've done that. So when I opened the shop I had all these amazing stories. . . . I was in Sri Lanka and the women would eat the pineapples and not throw the skins away and rub it on their body. And years later you realize it's because this particular protein that gets rid of god knows what is in there, acid. And the industry knows all about that, but these tribal women or fishing women knew all about that too. So all those type of stories. . . . In a world [of cosmetics] that then was very "the magic ingredient X," we were telling the stories. We were going the route of indigenous peoples' wisdom.

The late John W. Gardner was also eloquent on this subject when we spoke to him just a of couple years before his death in 2002. During his life he had founded a number of important social institutions and held many high-powered positions. As U.S. secretary of health, education, and welfare; chairman and CEO of the Urban Coalition; founder of Common Cause; chairman of the Commission on White House Fellowships; founder of Independent Sector; and Haas Professor in Public Service at Stanford University, he was a powerful advocate and dedicated public servant. We spoke to Gardner about the work he did in philanthropy as a program officer and as president of the Carnegie Corporation.

Following is one of six examples that Gardner provided of how he integrated listening into his work in philanthropy:

> The Nigerian government had asked me . . . to come over there when they first became independent because they wanted to think about the future of their educational system. . . . And I thought, they need the land grant pattern. They need the land grant pattern. That will really enable them to do the things that were needed at the ground level. Well, Ken [Dike, president of the University of Nigeria, Ibadan] came in, and I would guess that five minutes into the conversation I introduced the land grant pattern as a thought. And he said, "Well, I'm thinking about something else." He said, "We dig up—our local people dig up these historical objects, obviously with some religious significance, totems or idols or whatever. We don't know what they are. We don't know our own history. It's a mystery to us. Here we keep running across this evidence that we have a history as a people,

and we don't know it." And he said, "It's shameful and it's humiliating." Well, he just washed that land grant idea out of my mind, and we supported what I'm pretty sure was the first black studies program, and it was because I listened and I didn't go with my kind of fixed idea, but I listened to the person who walked in the door. I can give you lots of examples, but that's the basic thing. And I think you can go far with that. And I think you can go far in assuming that talent is out there, judgment is out there, and that you can gather it around you and learn from it.

In addition to discussing how listening and gathering stories was important to their work, four out of the seven exemplars also talked about meeting others where they are. The most extreme example of the importance of being able to meet others and adjust to them came from an OB-GYN surgeon. When asked if she ever felt conflict between what was meaningful to her and what was best for a patient, she responded:

Not much anymore because I really value the individual. . . . I actually had a woman die when I was an intern. A woman who was about twenty-three weeks pregnant, with sickle cell disease. And I was the person who sat with her every day. . . . My team challenged me with "You go in and make sure she accepts a blood transfusion. She needs blood." I said, "But she's a Jehovah's Witness; they don't want that blood." "Yeah, but you need to convince her she needs blood. . . ." By the end of the week . . . she looked really horrible and I said, "You know, you're going to die and you need to have a transfusion." And she looked at me and said, "You can save my physical being but spiritually I'm dead and would not be welcomed into the Kingdom of Jehovah." And she was a young woman but I heard her. And then I was at peace when she died. And from that day forward it has impressed me that no matter what my belief system is, I need to know what is important to you, and once I appreciate that and you appreciate the fact that I appreciate it, again that's another level we can act on in a positive way and I'm OK with that. And people look at me all the time, how can you take care of these patients? Because I can and I respect them.

Aligning a focus on listening and gathering information with meeting others "where they are," five out of the seven exemplars discussed eschewing the hierarchies and power differentials that are typical of their professions. An activist who was embarking on a project in the field of journalism told us, "Everything that I see, that I'm doing, contributes to that shift from a hierarchy and domination mode to one more truly democratic and inclusive." In her own typically passionate way Roddick also remarked, "I loathe hierarchy. I loathe it. You've got a job giving you $250,000 a year. I don't give a toss that I have to talk to you first. . . . I'm a grassroots, ground, down-and-dirty person. I'm a troops person. I'm less at home in high managerial status. 'I'm here by deign of my title'—I'm so anti that."

Listening and gathering information from others and meeting them where they are (which in the case of these professionals included breaking down hierarchical relationships) are defining features of what Noddings (1984) calls receptive attention to others. These features are clearly present in the exemplars' descriptions of their work. Five of the seven exemplars consistently and frequently mentioned placing their attention on the needs, desires, and reality of others. They explicitly connected this sort of attention to their deep and due respect for others. And they used this information to determine their responsibilities.

Motivational Displacement

Receptive attention, according to Noddings (1984, p. 16), allows for the possibility of taking on another person's reality "as possibility" for the self. This in turn results in the feeling that one has to act "as though in my own behalf, but in the behalf of the other" (p. 16). Noddings refers to this second feature of caring as *motivational displacement*.

Among the exemplars, motivational displacement did not exist in the way that Noddings describes. First, it was not mentioned nearly as often as the other features of caring—only five times in 186 pages of single-spaced transcripts. Second, instead of responding to others' needs as if they were their own, these exemplars recalled their initial motivational forces as being highly personal. Their personal experiences motivated them to act on the behalf of the needs of others. This state might be better described as *motivational integration*.

Two subjects recounted pivotal moments when the death of their fathers catalyzed their movement toward the advocacy work they both do in their professions. The OB-GYN surgeon told us,

> I've always been interested in people and I've always been a caregiver. I always wanted to help. . . . Then my dad died in my arms when I was thirteen years. . . . You know, fifty-three-year-old Afro American man dying from a heart attack. I lived in an area of Brooklyn that wasn't well served. . . . I was there by myself and called EMS and they

arrived in maybe, in a half an hour. . . . And just the response I got from them. You know, black man in the ghetto. You know, just that interaction and maybe really feeling that I could deliver better health care and it really struck me when I was thirteen. . . . [T]hat was me as a kid, that was my perspective: that nobody really cared. So yeah, that was a main driving force.

Roddick spoke of being similarly catalyzed to attend to the needs of others:

[After the death of my father] I was just like a fly, hitting my head against a wall and not knowing how to deal with this. I picked up a book on the Holocaust—first printed edition of a paperback with photographs. And I think that sort of emotional kick started me into that sense of "*umph!*" And from that day on my mum said I was always organizing. I was organizing marches. I was up challenging the MPs, or whatever it was, I was out there. . . . And from that [point] on there was this rabble-rousing champion for the underdog, or the anonymous, whatever. It was always there. My whole life it's been there. I don't challenge it anymore. It's like somebody fashions your identity, your psychopathologies, and you just walk down that road; and you don't bloody challenge it anymore.

In a different vein, a journalist spoke of how her feelings of personal betrayal after reading a book on governmental deception during the Vietnam War catalyzed her to work for the good of others.

There was one book, I'll never forget, called *Vietnam White Papers,* which was the early documentation of deception—our government's deception about the Gulf of Tonkin and all of that. So I started reading on my own, and that was like the first turning point for me. It was when I realized that my government was, in effect, lying to me. It was then, it was the first break to see that what's wrong is much deeper than just cleaning up things around the edges. And it's very, very, very traumatic.

A minute later she went on to say,

Once I realized that the problems were not just sort of around the edges, that . . . there is something fundamentally amiss in our society as a whole, in the root, in the grounding assumptions, I thought, well, the thing to do is to go and to work very directly with the people who are suffering the most from whatever it is that is the root of the problem.

In these examples, self-concern shifts to care for the welfare of others. Although their own suffering may have been the initial motivating experience, it translated into active concern for and response to the needs of others. Their own pain connected them to the pain of others.[6]

Deeply ingrained religious beliefs served as another source of motivational integration. Two of the exemplars explained their response-ability to act for the good of others in these terms. One business owner recounted, "I think of it more in my religious Jewish upbringing, that doing good and being of service to other people is the greatest good deed, mitzvah, one can do. And that's embedded really deeply in me, from the cradle on. It's in there deep."

These exemplars complicated Noddings' notion of motivational displacement. They did not settle for a simple conception of the motives of the goals they pursued. They did not claim to work selflessly. Nor did they claim to work only for their own selfish purposes. These exemplars embraced their personal motives and integrated them with the motives of others. Instead of dichotomizing serving themselves and serving others, they integrated the two. With strict motivational displacement, "caring is always characterized by a moving away from self" (Noddings, 1984, p. 16). With these people, caring for others seems to be not only a movement toward others but also a concurrent movement toward self—toward defining and understanding self—and toward self-fulfillment. Thus their motivations to care for others in their work can also be seen as means of fulfilling their responsibilities to themselves.

Connection to Others: Focus On Restoring, Conserving, or Building Community

Caring, at its core, is a means of protecting, maintaining, and nurturing connective relationships. All but one exemplar spoke directly and frequently about working to foster connections with and among others. They articulated their professional goals as including restoring, conserving, and building community.

John W. Gardner identified community as the locus and generator of responsibility. He told us, "responsibility is the absolute key to community"

---

[6]In 2001, Wendy Fischman and colleagues examined the formative influences of Schweitzer fellows and of health care and social services graduate students dedicated to community service. This research also found that "difficult childhood experiences prompted these individuals to develop and recast their life perspectives to include a commitment to helping others suffering similar plights" (p. 3).

and that at the center of community lie shared beliefs and "mutual obligations." He dedicated much of his life's work to countering what he saw as the slow disintegration of both community and responsibility.

There is a point at which everything crumbles if a community does not have this web of shared beliefs. Mutual obligations, shared values, responsibility, trust, and caring hold a culture together, whether it is Muslim or Central African or Peorian.

Gardner reiterated the necessary relationship between responsibility and community:

> People say to me that [through technology] we've got a way of linking people into new kinds of communities. The only problem is that those communities are not communities in my sense of the word or any traditional sense of the word. Mutual obligations! Just because you're in touch with somebody in South Africa or Indonesia doesn't mean that you have the sense of reciprocity of obligation, of trust.

Tammy Metcalf-Filzen, a faculty member and women's basketball coach at Carleton College, talked most often about community. When we spoke to her, her team had just won the division championship of the National Collegiate Athletic Association (NCAA), an unlikely feat at a small liberal arts college ranked fifth in its institutional category by *U.S. News & World Report*. Metcalf-Filzen discussed a number of ways she cultivates connections with people. First, she aims to cultivate community within her team:

> I mean the basketball team is kind of a small community with lots of different people. We have such varied perspectives and beliefs. . . . But to take a group of people like that and bring them together to work towards a common goal I think helps them while they're here and also afterwards, whether it's in business or family things or whatever.

Second, she consciously acts to cultivate community across her campus. She started a guest coaching program, first with the dean's food service people, then with the academic faculty.

> If we're playing a Saturday game, they'll come to practice on Friday. They'll sit down and watch practice. We'll give them programs so they can start to figure out who everybody is, and then they sit behind the bench during the games. We have a little pre-game where we talk to them. My assistant usually talks to them about what our game plan is and that kind of thing, and they sit behind the bench. And they really like that. And a lot of times they had no idea what was going on

down here. It was something that I wanted to do to begin to connect the faculty with our students and really give them an appreciation for what our students are doing down here.

The coach not only wants people across the campus to connect with and respect her students' work on the court; she also respects the work that students do with others off the court and works to enhance those connections. She notes that in four years her team has missed class only once, to go to the NCAA tournament. "We go to great lengths so that our kids don't miss a class."

Being respectful not only of the students' time but also of the faculty's time with students has had positive consequences across campus:

> We were playing in front of standing-room-only crowds in the gym, so we were drawing twelve to thirteen hundred people.[7] And to hear professors say, "I've been here thirty-seven years and I've never seen this community come together like this." Things like that really meant a lot to our team.

Third, Metcalf-Filzen pushes her students to understand their responsibilities to those beyond the local community. While in San Antonio, Texas, for a game, before practice the team spent the morning working in a soup kitchen. She also took the team to Thailand and used "basketball as a bridge" in order to learn about women's issues. While there they traveled to remote villages to offer basketball workshops and to learn from those they met. At the time of her interview she was in the planning stages of bringing together all the varsity athletes to work with kids at a Native American reservation over spring break. Her focus on building community among those on her team, among those on the larger campus, and between the campus and other communities speaks to her commitment to care not only about her own work but also about developing response-able students.

Similarly, an exemplar journalist provided an example of commitment to building community. She shifted the focus of the media from the celebration of celebrity and breaking news to portraying the community:

> The reason that we want to redefine what the media considers to be news is because we believe that the kind of democratic social change necessary for a fully functioning democracy, which really likes serving society, can't exist unless many, many more people are themselves

---

[7]Carleton is located in a small, relatively isolated Minnesota town of fewer than twenty thousand people. Its current enrollment is 1,750.

involved in public life. . . . [In the current media, the] whole universe of what real human beings are doing in their communities to solve public problems is largely ignored. So therefore people don't see people like themselves rewardingly engaged and therefore they withdraw into private concerns and reject any public life involvement as just what famous people or quirks do. So, the motive of founding the news service [was] to enlarge the definition of news ties very tightly back into the original goal . . . of drawing people into public life.

This goal reinforces what she believes human beings need in order to thrive. She emphasized that "we are defined by our relationships, our animalness, in terms of our need for social connection and all of that. . . . All of that has a major, major influence on me."

A businessman discussed his commitment to the community in which his family had built its business. "So, since the first World War, the guys who have been successful have moved out of this area. They consider textiles labor intensive, and they go to an area where they can get cheaper labor, cheaper hands. So they moved out of here, and we stuck, because we thought it was the right thing to do." At one point, a fire decimated this man's factory. Instead of cashing in on his insurance and retiring, he kept his employees on the payroll while he rebuilt his factory. His reasons for rebuilding his business in the same expensive area honor the importance of community. "The community is here. And if I am in business here and trying to make my profit here, my community is here in the Lawrence area. . . . Had the decision been made differently, to retire and just take the insurance money, the community of Lawrence-Methuen would have been very badly damaged."

John W. Gardner summed up sentiments that can be found in the words of all but one exemplar: "Fortunately, the human species is a community-building species. That's one of our gifts . . . we have that capacity." In their interviews, these exemplary subjects showed that they prized and cultivated this caring gift in themselves and others. They recognized community connections as the locus of responsibility and considered it their own responsibility to restore, conserve, and cultivate these connections.

The answer to the question *Who cares?* is *all the workers I studied.* The exemplary workers, however, articulated a *focus* on the ethics of care in their work. They discussed the values of repairing, cultivating, and maintaining relationships, particularly those within the community. They consistently considered the nature, needs, and desires of others, and they integrated their own motives with those of others. They conceived of and went about doing their work with the care of others in the foreground of their minds.

A Perfect Anomaly

One of the exemplars seemed to be an anomaly in all three categories of caring (receptive attention, motivational displacement, and concern for relationships). In his interview, journalist Daniel Schorr exhibited a single-minded care for something that none of the others did: his profession. Whereas the other subjects integrated (or balanced) their caring relations with their professions, Schorr's passionate care for his profession was rarely balanced by the concerns of caring that have been formulated here. Why might this be?

This difference might stem from the profession itself: journalists are not responsible to individuals or to particular groups of people; they respond directly to the news. Their commitment is to act as middlemen, bringing the news directly and impartially to the general public. This professional stance can require something antithetical to caring—detachment and depersonalization.[8] The desire to respond to the needs of individuals and groups of others is not valued; in fact it may even harm a journalist's ability to do his job. Schorr prides himself on his lack of this type of response-ability.

> Well, there is an anecdote that I like to tell and I'm not sure anymore whether it happened literally as I remember it, but it is really emblematic and telling about me and the journalistic profession. But the way I remember it—it's either partly true or maybe even all true—as a kid of about twelve growing up in the Bronx, we lived in a ground-floor apartment and with no air conditioning—hardly existed—and on a hot summer day the windows were open. And I heard an enormous plop right outside the window. I went and looked and there was a man who had jumped or fallen from the roof.
>
> I went out and looked. I waited until the police arrived. I asked the police what they knew, whether they knew his name or anything more about him. And putting together what I thought I knew, I learned about him. I called the local newspaper, the *Bronx Home News,* which was offering five dollars for news tips. I called and dictated a story to them, earning my first five dollars, journalist five dollars, at the age of twelve.
>
> And what I remember of it was that my mother and others remarked about how cool I was, how unaffected I was myself, emotionally, by the

---

[8]Not all journalists agree with this point. Schorr does.

fact that a person had died almost in front of my eyes. And instead, had gone about this professional thing of what more can we learn, what do we know about, all of that. That anecdote, whether literally true or not, has colored my entire professional life, the ability to detach myself.

Schorr tells a similar story about the importance of detachment when reporting in Poland. It captures how the professional requirements of journalism are in opposition to the value of caring. In 1959, Schorr was doing a documentary for Edward R. Murrow's *See It Now* program.

It was pretty strong stuff at Auschwitz, as I look back through my script, it was very strong stuff. There was a time, for example, when I was saying in my script, and this is where they came out of the gas chamber and then they pushed them into the ovens over here. And the ovens were running at a rate of sixty thousand a day, but they couldn't get all the people they were killing, so some of them were just burned from the ovens and thrown into empty trenches over here, which are now these places full of water. And if you run your hand along the bottom, you will come up with splinters of bone, and so on and so forth.

I did that very journalistically. I didn't faint, I didn't feel overcome by it all, I didn't relive the Holocaust. I just did my job. It may well be—there were members of my family two generations ago who were lost in the Holocaust. They had lived in what is now Belarus. Some of them may well have died at Auschwitz, but I was doing a job there and I did the job.

The "job" of being a journalist required that he disconnect himself from his feelings, from his ability to respond. It further required detachment from others and connection with the principles and ethical standards of his profession.

Is journalism, then, antithetical to caring? And if so, why did the other journalist exemplar provide numerous examples of the features of caring? First, the other journalist was not originally a journalist. She began as an activist and writer, and her activism led her into journalism. Second, she was not a reporter; the "living democracy" project she started focused on different responsibilities and ethical codes. These two facts may explain the difference. They may not though.

Daniel Schorr's example raises deeper questions for this study of the response-ability of good and exemplary workers. It seems that the professional codes of journalism may truncate a reporter's willingness to respond to the needs of others. In journalism, the public need for "truth" can trump the responsibility of the journalist to "care" about the needs of the individuals and groups concerned. A good worker in journalism may not be able to express or act on caring in the same way as workers in other professions can. Journalists do *not* integrate their motives with those of others; they do *not* aim to forge, maintain, and cultivate relationships with others (unless it is appropriate to their work in reporting the news). Journalists are *not* response-able in the ethics-of-care sense. They are responsible to the standards of their profession.

Noddings (1984, pp. 116–118) had something to say about this. She asserted that institutions and organizations cannot, in and of themselves, be ethical. She argued that institutions can in fact require behavior that at times "diminishes" the vision one has of one's best ethical self (p. 117). In these circumstances, people act according to their understanding of the institutional requirements, not their understanding of what they would need to do to live up to their own ethical ideals. She cited as examples institutions such as the military, unions, political parties, fraternities, and religious organizations. She might as well have added professions to her list. It is easy to imagine ethical diminishment happening in the field of medicine, particularly when the business demands of the profession require doctors to act against their sense of what is best for the patient. It also seems possible that the ethical codes of journalism can conflict with what an individual journalist might think is the moral thing to do. Schorr himself endured a remarkable ethical dilemma of just this nature—one in which he acted on his own ethical sights and not on those of the profession.

> I was faced—during that same period, working in Poland—I was faced with a big professional ethical problem. We were roaming around the country; we were somewhere in the eastern corner of Poland, near the Soviet border . . . and as we walked through a village and looked around, we ran into an amazing sight—a group of people with all their furniture, furnishings piled up on horse-drawn carts, like a scene from *Fiddler on the Roof*. And we went up and asked what this was. . . . [T]hey spoke Yiddish and I can still speak some Yiddish. They explained to me that they were on their way to Israel. . . . And this was quite remarkable, because this was in 1959, in a period where the Soviets and Soviet satellites were not allowing any emigration to Israel in order not to offend the Arabs. So how could they be going to Israel? I interviewed them. . . .
>
> [I] went back to Warsaw, went to see the Israeli Minister in Warsaw— was something of a friend of mine, we used to play chess together—and I told him what I saw. And I said, "What is the story with these people

going to Israel?" And he said, "You saw them? And what, you filmed them and [conducted] interviews?" "Yeah." "All right sir, since you know this much, I'll tell you the rest of that story and then you decide what you're going to do with it. These people came to that part of the Soviet Union (which used to be Poland, until a couple of years ago), and they're very unhappy to be in the Soviet Union. And the Soviet Union government doesn't want them very much either. So we made them an arrangement; we worked out a secret agreement between the Soviet government and the Polish government and the Israeli government that these people would be, quote, repatriated, unquote, to Poland, but they would not stay in Poland, because they didn't want to. They would go right on, as fast as possible, to Israel. The Soviets said they would go along with this arrangement unless it became public. If it became public, it would stop."

"And so," he said, "Mr. Schorr, you have your story. And now decide what you want to do. If you broadcast this, several, fifteen thousand Jews will be lost in the Soviet Union."

If I have any ethic, any journalistic ethic at all, the major part of that ethic is that you don't stand between—you don't censor the news. You're not God. What you legitimately find out that's interesting has to be passed on. And here I was facing this question. I would love to have talked to Murrow about it and asked what he thought, but if you talk on an open phone from Poland, that wouldn't work.

The cameraman, at the end of every day, would pack up the film that we shot that day and ship it off by plane to New York. This reel of film, I said, "let me hold this for a day or so." And I held it for one day, and two days, and three days, and four days. And I never shipped it.

Clearly the professional code of ethics for journalism conflicted with Schorr's notion of the "right" thing to do. Luckily for those fifteen thousand Jews, Schorr allowed himself at that moment of personal ethical expression. What is notable is his tagline to the story. After stating "And I never shipped it" he said, "And I could not today articulate what my justification was for not shipping it, because I would be embarrassed." Now, most of us could easily justify his actions and would have a difficult (and embarrassing) time justifying sending the film to the newsroom. But Schorr so internalized the codes of his profession that such humane and caring actions, even on such a grand scale, embarrassed him because they betrayed his notion of what it is to be a good journalist.

Perhaps then there are different sorts of caring in one's role as a professional. First, there might be a type of caring exemplified by Daniel Schorr. This caring focuses on doing the job in the best way one can. Schorr cares about being a great reporter. This is not a dispassionate or disinterested sort of care; it is full of feeling and requires enormous personal interest. It is not easy to live up to the standards of a profession. This type of caring can even be ethical, because one's professional ideal might contain certain features of ethics. This type of caring, however, is not the sort explored in this chapter. The second type of caring, and the focus here, is caring about and for others. It includes the human dimension of how one treats others and how one considers others in the course of one's work. Other types of caring might occur in professional life, but this distinction between caring about the job and caring for others can be helpful in explaining how Daniel Schorr remains an exemplary worker but one who usually does not prioritize caring for others (as formulated in this chapter) over caring for his idea of what it means to be a good journalist.

It is also important to note that there is a significant difference between the first two situations in which Schorr found himself (reporting the suicide and reporting from Auschwitz) and the last situation (not reporting the Polish-Soviet immigration to Israel). In the first two cases there was nothing left to be done. Schorr could not have an impact on the outcome of the Holocaust, nor could he affect his neighbor's suicide. All he could do was share the stories of these events. The immigrants' situation was different. Schorr could directly contribute to the fate of these people. This distinction is akin to what is commonly referred to in ethics as the *trolley problem*. First posed by philosopher Phillipa Foot (1978), this thought experiment goes something like this: A trolley is out of control. There are five people working on the track who cannot see the trolley coming. Fortunately you can flip a switch and the train will change tracks. Unfortunately, there is a single worker on that second track. The question is, should you flip the switch? Whatever action or inaction one chooses (to flip the switch or to keep the footage), ethical tensions remain.

Implications

In the course of working with these data, the concept of *integration* was frequently brought up and seemed relevant, though not in the sense of motivational integration, developed earlier. I went back to the transcripts to see if another sort of integration was salient. Five of the seven exemplars indicated they were concerned that their work be integrated with their personal lives, beliefs, and values. The business owner who rebuilt his factory after a fire spoke consistently and eloquently on this other sort of integration:

> I'm trying to make a blend of two strategies that are not blended here in the United States, one being maximizing the profit for the shareholders, and the other being trying to do something good and worthwhile on this earth, not only for the shareholder, but for employees, community, the environment. And in the United States, these two concepts are split completely and they're isolated. And one has nothing to do with the other. You work real hard in business and there's a ruthless kind of principle in business, that—it's absolutely impersonal. It's a battle for money and it's a battle for profits and it's a battle to accomplish, and it has nothing to do with trying to do the good or what's right on this earth. That's being relegated to another position. When you go home after your work in which you behaved in an inhuman way, . . . if you are so inclined, you could be charitable to others. . . . [I aim for] a unification of the economic process with the ethical.

Likewise, Anita Roddick organized her company in terms of the activism she holds so dear in her personal life: "Why do we as a company spend so much time in community trade or campaigning for human rights? That's the DNA of our company." After talking about the seamless connection between her activism, love, and work, and an inability to compartmentalize the three, she continued:

> I always think that's one of the great myths—that you separate [yourself] in business. You know, you go in, wear a suit, and become a new identity. . . . I just thought life was love and work, end of story. I think the thing was like one creative stew. And so I was an activist—was, is. And my little office—who I was employing—were all people marching with me, or in Greenpeace marches, or whatever. So it seemed to be just an extension of my own kitchen.

The journalist in the midst of organizing the newswire service echoed Roddick and the businessman:

> I feel what happened in the sixties of my generation is people sort of not learning how to integrate [public] engagement with satisfying personal lives and family lives, and so I think the biggest single message would be that the good life is the engaged life. . . . It's about figuring

out a whole lifetime of how can your profession and your relationship with your children, your spouse, or whatever it is, how can it all weave together?

Not only did these exemplars conceive of the needs of others as integrated with their own needs, but they conceived of the relationship between their personal and professional lives as integrated as well. As Anita Roddick so aptly said, echoing a well-known aphorism of Sigmund Freud's, "I just thought life was love and work, end of story."

One might hypothesize that the sustenance and continual renewal of the exemplars' response-ability depends on this integration of work and life. When motivation is internally generated as well as externally reinforced, the vibrancy and longevity of caring may be improved. Further, when one's conception of one's self (identity) is connected to others (as when one cares) *and* to the profession itself, then caring in work is a natural focus. In starkly egocentric terms, if I am caring for you in my work, I am by extension caring for myself.

A form of this integration of personal and professional life as a function of personal identity can even be found in Daniel Schorr, our anomaly. He told us that his identity was completely and inextricably tied to his work. "My mother wanted me to be a lawyer. I didn't want to be a lawyer. It's almost inconceivable to me that I could be anything other than a journalist. If there were no journalism, there would be no me."

Conclusion

In the course of studying these workers it became clear that although they all discussed caring, six of the seven exemplars explicitly focused on the dimensions of this topic. In detail missing from the accounts of the good workers, they described how they worked to consider the natures, needs, and desires of others. They spoke of working to repair, cultivate, and maintain relationships. They spoke of integrating their own motives with the motives of others. This integration even extended to blur the line between their professional and personal lives.

Perhaps the lesson to be drawn from this study is that response-ability in the best workers stems from their seeing themselves as profoundly and inextricably connected to others and to their professions. For most of the exemplars, this vision motivated them to be socially responsible in their work. They saw their professional lives integrated with their personal lives, and this, we might conclude, is what motivated them to care.

REFERENCES

Fischman, W., Schutte, D., Solomon, B., & Lam, G. (2001, September). The development of an enduring commitment to service work. In M. Michaelson & J. Nakamura (Eds.), *Supportive frameworks for youth engagement.* New Directions for Child and Adolescent Development, no. 93. San Francisco: Jossey-Bass.

Foot, P. (1978). *Virtues and vices and other essays in moral philosophy.* Oxford, UK: Oxford University Press.

Gilligan, C. (1982). *In a different voice.* Cambridge: Harvard University Press.

Noddings, N. (1984). *Caring: A feminine approach to ethics and moral education.* Berkeley: University of California Press.

3

CREATIVITY AND RESPONSIBILITY

Mihaly Csikszentmihalyi
Jeanne Nakamura

Fatti non foste a viver come bruti ma
per seguir virtute e conoscenza.[1]

—Dante, *The Divine Comedy, Inferno*, Canto 26, 118–120

IN THE POPULAR IMAGINATION, creative individuals are often seen as oblivious to the ties of responsibility that hobble lesser mortals. They tend to be depicted as arrogant and insensitive, disdaining social values and obligations. In part this image has been the unintended result of Europe's emancipation from the weight of tradition that followed the humanistic turn of the Renaissance. The still largely conformist masses, on the one hand, were gradually estranged from the few individuals who, on the other hand, were ready to break away from tradition. Those who rejected the constricting ethos of the

---

This chapter focuses on the cultivation of responsibility for others. It does not explore—despite their prominence as aims of undergraduate education—the cultivation of responsibility for self or the nurturing of responsibility for a particular domain or discipline.

[1]You were not born to live like brutes do, but to pursue virtue and knowledge. (Ulysses, trying to convince his shipmates to be the first to sail out into the open Atlantic Ocean)

Middle Ages and developed new maps of the heavens or dissected cadavers to see how the body was put together were often suspected of breaking the boundaries not only of knowledge but of morality as well.

Even artists who explored subjects beyond traditional religious themes and adopted new styles were suspect. When Vasari wrote the first biographies of Western artists in 1550, he complained bitterly about their lack of polish and morality: they "had received from nature a certain element of savagery and madness, which, besides making them strange and eccentric . . . revealed in them rather the obscure darkness of vice than the brightness and splendor of those virtues that make men immortal" (Vasari, 1959, p. 232).

Centuries later, the ideology of Romanticism emphasized the chasm between the creative individual and the conforming masses. In Goethe's masterpiece, Faust rejects traditional morality in order to gain knowledge and experience novelty—even at the price of selling his soul to the devil. The perception that to be creative one must reject social mores led to a vicious circle: Young people who sought recognition found it easier to attract attention by acting extravagantly rather than by actually producing valuable novelty, thus reinforcing the stereotype (Kasof, 1995).

It is therefore not surprising that when Cesare Lombroso, in 1889, wrote the first modern treatise on creativity and mental health, *The Man of Genius,* he argued that artistic creativity was a form of inherited insanity. Creative scientists had an equally dubious reputation. Frankenstein's monster and *Dr. Strangelove* of Stanley Kubrick's film are prototypes of what happens when a person's *hubris* lets him trespass the limits that keep most mortals in line.

But is it actually true, as popular wisdom suggests, that men and women at the cutting edge of culture operate without a moral compass? Our claim in this chapter is that, to the contrary, the culture has much to learn from the distinctive ethical sense that directs most creative individuals. An extremely intransigent sense of responsibility is a distinctive trait of creative persons. They feel an almost religious respect for human accomplishments of the *past,* at least within the domain of their interest and activity. Musicians revere the classics of the past, and scientists revere the laws of nature and those who uncovered them. So a sense of responsibility for staying true to the best practices of one's domain is a constant aspect of creativity. Conversely, creative individuals also respect the possibilities of the *future.* They are open to novelty and curious about how to make things better. Whenever they can, they try to combine the achievements of the past with the possibilities of the future and express them in the *present.* Thus, responsibility for good work in the present that combines the best of what was and the best of what is to be is the hallmark of creativity.

What binds the behavior of creative persons is a response to a call that is neither less urgent nor less essential to the well-being of humankind than the dictates of conventional morality. The responsibility felt by creative persons involves integrity, honesty, and excellence in the performance of their tasks—qualities that are not always foremost among conventionally moral people. Thus, understanding the creative ethos might help expand our notions of what constitutes responsible behavior and provide a broader basis for moral education.

In what follows, we examine interviews conducted with approximately one hundred creative individuals in an attempt to extract what these persons consider the most important guiding principles in their lives and work. The participants in the study included artists, scientists, inventors, businesspersons, and politicians who had in some ways transformed their domain and the broader culture. Eleven of them had been recognized with the Nobel Prize (Csikszentmihalyi, 1996).

In an analysis of a subset of forty-seven interviews from the study, Choe and Nakamura (1996) found that these creative individuals mentioned at least three values that reflected concern for responsibility: *responsibility* (the tenth most often mentioned value), *doing good work* (the seventh most frequently mentioned value), and *social concerns* (the fourth most often mentioned value out of eighty-one cited altogether). These three coded values overlapped substantially, and hereafter we shall refer to them collectively as *responsibility*.

What did *responsibility* mean to these creative individuals? Most of our interviewees employed a language that stressed notions of calling, duty, loyalty, obligation, and responsiveness. In the most circumscribed instances, these notions applied to the conscientious performance of professional roles. Doing careful, sound, original work was a value essential to their self-image. One scientist defined it as "dealing with information rigorously," another as "getting things right and formulating things perfectly"; an astronomer aimed to "collect very good data" and a poet said "one wants really to write very good poems."

But in at least one third of the cases, the sense of responsibility extended much further. Some felt they owed a duty to mentors, colleagues, and students, to be available, supportive, critical, or responsive, as needed. Others felt they had to enhance the visibility and status of the discipline in which they worked. On a more idiosyncratic note, a novelist expressed "concern that what I write is not destructive [to readers]," and a leading journalist embraced his mission of being "the eyes and ears for the little guy."

Finally, several of these eminent scientists and artists extended the scope of their concern far beyond the boundaries of their discipline.

For instance, nuclear physicist Victor Weisskopf became a vocal opponent of the Cold War arms race "to see that the negative influences of science are mitigated"; so did Benjamin Spock, the pioneering pediatrician. Linus Pauling, who earned a Nobel Prize in chemistry in 1954 and eight years later the Nobel Peace Prize for his courageous stand against the irresponsible use of nuclear energy, was detained by the police for his efforts. In fact, at least a dozen of the ninety-one creative individuals studied were jailed or attacked for their beliefs—for supporting union strikers in the United States, for standing up to Stalin or Hitler in Europe, or for expressing candid views about cultural and religious changes in Egypt, as happened to Nobel Prize novelist Naguib Mahfouz, who just months after our interview was critically wounded by a Muslim fundamentalist assassin.

Responsibility as a Call to Excellence

Of all the forms of responsibility that these creative persons mentioned and demonstrated in their lives, perhaps the most important is their duty to do excellent work as defined by the traditions and current standards of the particular activity in which they are engaged. To know how a person learns to heed this call is enormously important for society, because the excellence of the whole depends disproportionately on the energy and commitment of those few who, in all walks of life, want to change society for the better. Yet the link between creativity and responsibility is little understood.

It is easy to assume that by *responsibility* we mean only a contractual obligation that develops between a person and a community that imposes certain moral expectations. According to this limited view, each of us internalizes, consciously or not, a set of rules and demands that we then feel obliged to follow.

But responsibility is often also manifested in a broader form. The term itself derives from the noun *response* and connotes a feeling that one must answer a call, a summons, that comes from somewhere outside the person. Thus the notion of responsibility overlaps with what in Christian religious thought, and later in the sociology of Max Weber, has been referred to as a calling or vocation—the sense a person has that he or she must answer a call and take on a task that a higher power expects him or her to fulfill. When a person is immersed in a religious worldview, the call is interpreted as coming from God. This is how billionaire investor Sir John Templeton, for instance, recalls his response to the call: "When I was very small, maybe as young as eight years old, I wondered why humans were created . . . and coming from a religious town, I thought God must have made people for some purpose. . . . I wanted to find out what God wanted me to do." After reflecting on his strengths and weaknesses, when he reached college Templeton decided that investing in technologically less advanced countries would help him "accelerate God's creativity," and this is the call he has followed ever since (Csikszentmihalyi, 2003, p. 159). Creative individuals—and most people to a greater or lesser extent—seem to hear intimations of such a vocation, even though the personal call from a divinity is often missing. But if not from God, from whence does the call to excellence come?

The Call of the Past

The interviews suggest that in most cases creative individuals recognize a specific talent or strength they possess, and if they take this advantage seriously, they react to it in a way that is not unlike the acceptance of vocation or calling that people with a religious background describe. In other words, they feel they have a responsibility to do their best to use the special tools that genes, family, or sheer luck has given them. The bottom line is, they feel responsible to do work of such high quality that it would stand up to the best of what one's predecessors were able to accomplish.

To do so means internalizing the highest standards of the past. When asked what he felt responsible to at the time of the interview, Canadian novelist Robertson Davies, who was eighty years old then and spending much time giving public talks about his latest book, answered, "I feel that I must be very careful about what I say and not just talk off the cuff, you know, because that is so shallow and stupid, and it's not fair to the people who've asked you to speak."

Care in avoiding shallowness and stupidity was a constant theme in all of the interviews. Whatever one's craft is—art or science, medicine or engineering—one can aim either to do well or to just get by. It is difficult to achieve eminence in any field if one is not committed to the first of these two choices.

It is clear that the network of loyalties to which Davies felt responsible was wide and complex. Above all else, he felt responsible to his own experiences; even though he knew they were subjective and probably unique to him, he defended their reality and importance. It is out of these personal memories that Davies constructed his dense narratives. He had no doubt that all novels are essentially autobiographical—their value depends on the author's faithfulness to what he or she actually feels

("You remember that story about Gustave Flaubert when someone said to him, 'Where did you achieve this extraordinary knowledge of feminine psychology that appears in Madame Bovary?' and he said, 'Madame Bovary, *c'est moi.*' And he was right, where else would he get it from? Not out of a book, certainly").

Extending beyond his own experience, Davies felt a sense of responsibility for his ancestry and ethnic roots—his Welsh paternal lineage ("because of my father, I always had one eye turned toward the past, almost looking back toward the days of King Arthur. . . . The Welsh have very long memories"), and the British loyalists on his maternal side who were exiled from New England to Canada after the United States gained its independence ("and so I had both the old land and the new land constantly before me in my childhood and in the things that influenced me, and I was always turning from one to the other, and feeling the pull of one against the other").

Davies illustrates two common sources of responsibility reaching out from the past. Although accessible to everyone, these sources are rarely noticed by most people. One is the call of excellence in one's task, the second is responsibility to one's experience and to one's roots. These are among the most insistent voices to which creative individuals respond.

Although this pattern is most evident among artists and humanists, it is also present in a less obvious form among scientists. For them, responsibility to the demands of the craft is so taken for granted that it seldom even comes up. Thorough knowledge of the best work in one's field is a given. Excellence that demands hard work is well illustrated by Freeman Dyson, the mathematical physicist who has laid down the formal theory of quantum electrodynamics:

> I have always to force myself to write. . . . You have to put blood, tears, and sweat into it first. It's awfully hard to get started. . . . You have to force yourself and push and push and push with the hope that something good will come out. You have got to go through that process before it really starts to flow easily, and without that preliminary forcing and pushing, probably nothing would ever happen.

Like all other creative scientists, Dyson believes that one cannot do anything new without first becoming thoroughly immersed in the past. Respect for the insights of previous scientists is essential; they know, as did Isaac Newton, that if they are able to see farther than others, it is because they are standing on the shoulders of giants. Similarly, scientists are committed—almost by definition—to take seriously their responsibility to evidence, to their own experience.

Less clear in the case of scientists is the link to their personal past or ethnic origin. Yet in most cases those interviewed remembered a parent or teacher they admired and whose strengths they wished to emulate. For instance, Dyson spoke with respect of his father, an orchestra conductor who sat down at his desk at home every day to compose music: "I remember very well when we were children, he would compose quite systematically for three hours every morning. . . . He had a very strong self-discipline. His hero was Haydn. He also, like Haydn, put on his best suit when he was composing . . . and I think that is very largely true of me as well." Respect for past excellence is not restricted to one's own craft, but can emanate from any form of outstanding accomplishment.

But how does a person learn to respect and emulate the accomplishments of others? While there are almost as many ways to do so as there are creative persons, some qualitative similarities emerged in the interviews. Creative persons tend to become interested, intrigued, almost obsessed with an aspect of life for which they have a special knack—a small advantage over their peers. When the interest becomes established, the budding creator tries to find out as much about it as she or he can, approaching with wonder the skills and knowledge that previous generations achieved in that domain. E. O. Wilson, the great naturalist, described how this process occurred in his childhood, when in grade school he and a friend became deeply interested in fire ants:

> We would go over to the zoo in Washington and to the National Museum . . . I was enthralled by the grandeur, by federal grandeur, the idea that the citizenry of this great country could make magnificent institutions, full of animals and insects and scientists who studied them and so on. This was grand stuff, and I just wanted to be part of it. And Ellis and I soon got a copy of an advanced textbook in entomology, which I now realize is one of the most . . . densely technical books ever written. Quite unnecessarily so. But we were awestruck by this. You know, there was the mystique that goes with terminology and complex drawings and so on. Well, we started studying it together. And this gave us new impetus, something to shoot for, that we would be competent enough to do that kind of work some day. Oh, I was, I was committed from then on.

One note of caution about perhaps overestimating the importance of respect for the past is the fact that all creative individuals studied, whether by us or by others, tend to be adults at the time they are interviewed. So it could be that a sense of responsibility to the best work of the past is more the result of maturity than of creativity. Perhaps when they were young the Dysons and Davies had no interest in or respect for their predecessors; perhaps all their energies were focused on leaving their mark on the domain by rejecting traditions. This is certainly a popular view in the social sciences; for instance, Bourdieu (1993) attributes the historical change in science and art to the struggle between older cohorts intent on preserving the past and younger cohorts bent on dethroning them.

Certainly many older creative persons recalled that by their teens they felt a sense of awe for the best work of their predecessors. As Wilson's recollection suggests, wanting to continue in their forerunners' footsteps was something they felt early; it does not seem to be a later reconstruction from an adult perspective. It is difficult to resolve this issue without following cohorts of young people in a longitudinal study and determining whether respect for tradition differentiates creative individuals early in life as well as late. In any case, our present uncertainty suggests an interesting topic for future research: The hypothesis is that, other things being equal, young people who feel a sense of responsibility for the past are more likely than those who do not to become creative as adults—provided, of course, that they also feel responsible for improving on what their predecessors accomplished. While *deference* to the past can be paralyzing, *responsibility* for it can be liberating and constructive.

The Call of the Future

Respect for the past is not sufficient to provide an ethos conducive to creativity. In fact, by itself an excessive concern for past accomplishments might breed excellent performance, but it is unlikely to lead to novelty, let alone striking originality. As one might expect, creative individuals are also extremely interested in future possibilities. For them the old adage *rerum novarum cupidus*—lusting for new things—is an apt description.

Robertson Davies, the writer who described himself as being constantly pulled back and forth between the "old land" of his ancestors and the "new land" where he grew up, expressed this dynamic in his works. In his last book, he traced the trajectory of how his city, Toronto, emerged from provincialism into a dynamic metropolis: "One of the principal themes in it is the growth of a city, and the city is this city, Toronto. I have seen it in my lifetime emerge from a place which was still gripped in the form of a British colony into an independent place. . . . What the book is about is [this growth] as seen by a single character who observes it . . . without, by any means, taking the line that progress has always been positive."

At age sixty-nine, Freeman Dyson was also still "lusting for new things." Having ridden the crest of quantum physics fifty or so years earlier, he now found physics too specialized, too congested: "When I first came into physics, I would go to meetings of the American Physical Society, and essentially all the physicists of the United States would be there in one room, you know? I mean it was still a small community. . . . Now, of course, the Physical Society has twenty-five thousand members, and meetings are completely different . . . specialized." As a result, Dyson has become more interested in astrophysics and is searching out colleagues in that still manageable field, learning from them and contributing to their thinking. "There are about twelve young astronomers in this building who are doing fantastic things. I mean, astronomy is now in a golden age, much as physics was forty years ago. . . . In astronomy there are new things being discovered every week. . . . Those people are really enjoying themselves." In fact, one could say of any of the individuals interviewed what has been said of Paul Cezanne: "He was obsessed with tradition and obsessed with overturning it" (Trachtman, 2006, p. 82).

Of course an excessive focus on what is to come presents its own dangers. It can breed impatience with what is at hand. Lusting for new things may lead to risky shortcuts, to a disregard for process in favor of the desired outcome. Without roots in the best practices of the past, a commitment to the future can easily become out of touch with lived experience and result in chaos instead of creativity. The emphasis on novelty for the sake of novelty that has become so prevalent in the contemporary visual arts is just one of many examples.

Past and Future Folded into the Present

How past and future excellence can be combined in a fulfilling quest for creativity in the here and now is shown by the life of ceramicist Eva Zeisel. She was born to a prominent intellectual family in Budapest in the early part of the twentieth century. Two of her relations eventually obtained Nobel Prizes in science. She was a very independent young girl, in part because she believed she lacked her mother's social graces and her brother's intellectual ambition and training. In her late seventies she still remembered that as a teenager she overheard some people sitting a couple of rows back in a theater talking about her: "Her grandmother is such a clever, bright, intellectual person. Her mother is such a beauty. And now, look at her."

Zeisel turned out to have one talent that was missing from the rest of the family: drawing. She meant to become a painter, but in the meantime she also dabbled in making ceramicware—vases, plates, pitchers, and bowls. Eventually she took it upon herself to become a "professional" ceramicist, which involved the unheard-of step, for a girl from a good family (or any girl for that matter), of apprenticing to a master potter so she could get an official guild certificate at the end of the training.

In this decision she was inspired, in large part, by her belief that well-designed objects of folk art were being replaced by cheap, mass-produced tableware and that poor people were being deprived of one of the last opportunities to be surrounded by things of beauty. At the same time she understood how quixotic it would be to try to provide handmade plates and glasses to those living close to poverty. So she decided next to study the mass production of china; toward this end, she went to work for a large factory in Germany.

When she felt ready to combine her appreciation of beautiful ceramics inspired by tradition with the new manufacturing opportunities, Zeisel asked herself, Where could I apply this knowledge? In the early 1930s, one obvious answer presented itself: in the Soviet Union, the paradise of the proletariat. So Zeisel went to Russia and offered to set up a factory to manufacture beautiful chinaware cheaply. The Soviet regime appreciated the public relations opportunity—daughter of wealthy Western family comes to work for Russia—and accepted her offer, putting her in charge of an existing factory.

To make a long story short, Zeisel soon came into conflict with the Soviet authorities, who wanted her to make things cheap but did not care about how they looked. The conflict ended with her being imprisoned, in solitary confinement, waiting any moment to be executed. The Soviets finally relented because of international pressures and allowed her to leave for Turkey. From there Zeisel moved to New York, where her inexpensive but elegant lines of chinaware became best sellers all over the world and are now exhibited at the Museum of Modern Art and other museums.

Although in no way a moralistic person by conventional standards, Zeisel responded to the calls for excellence that issued from many directions. She felt responsible for continuing what was best in traditional folk art, and she felt responsible for sharing beauty with those who could not otherwise afford it. These senses of responsibility led her to learn modern ceramic technology so she could satisfy these two calls. At every step she was directed by the enjoyment she derived from making the most beautiful objects she could at the least expense.

Although she was always playful in her work, the responsibilities Zeisel shouldered were no trifling matter. While in solitary confinement in Moscow she was tempted to commit suicide several times. In her loyalty to beauty, she showed the steely determination that one usually associates with religious martyrs determined to follow their vocation to the bitter end.

Another example of how respect for the past and a vision of the future come together in a creative present is provided by Ravi Shankar, Indian composer and musician. Shankar trained since childhood as a *sitar* player and composer, and reached great fame in doing so. He felt enormous commitment to the traditional roots of this music and to its preservation. But by the middle of the twentieth century he realized that these traditions were endangered by a variety of economic and cultural changes: "[In] the olden days, when the maharajas and all these aristocrats were sponsoring famous musicians, it was no problem keeping fifteen or twenty students, you know. . . . And for all these years they would really concentrate [on] learning and practicing—that's all they did." Now, however, with the maharajas gone, young people had to earn money to support themselves and could no longer focus on learning the traditional skills.

Shankar saw the possibility of combining the traditional music of India with the avant-garde music of the West. In the 1960s he became the guru of George Harrison and performed with Harrison and the other members of the Beatles—thus revitalizing both the content of the music and the economy that supported it. Respect for the past and respect for the unfolding reality of the future together allowed Shankar to keep doing good work in the present.

The notion of responsibility shown by these people is not the usual kind based on ethical values and conformity to community pressures. It is based instead on a desire to do good work for its own sake—to achieve excellence in a domain at any cost. While the desire for excellence may actually lead to questionable outcomes—as with Robert Oppenheimer's fascination with the "sweet problem" of how to build a nuclear bomb—it is also a necessary component of the evolution of culture. Without reverence for the achievements of the past and a clear-eyed respect for the unfolding reality of the future, one can expect only chaos or rigidity.

The Sources of Calling

Table 3.1 summarizes the responsibilities that attract the allegiance of creative individuals. The eighteen cells of the figure are not intended to be exhaustive; they are provided only to suggest how a full classification might

Table 3.1. Major Sources of the Call for Responsibility Mentioned by Creative Individuals.

		Past	Present	Future
Domain (culture)	Chosen discipline	Learn	Act	Expand
	Relation to the discipline	Learn	Integrate	Expand
Field (society)	Coworkers	Be trained	Collaborate	Train
	Broader social milieu	Respect traditions	Support community	Innovate
Person (self)	Personal growth	Find meaning	Act with integrity	Reshape goals
	Relation to others	Filial	Partnering	Generative

be developed. Basically, the taxonomy refers to the direction from which the call for action is perceived to be coming, and thus the direction toward which the person is likely to commit his or her energy. It contains three time dimensions of concern for excellence: the past, the present, and the future; and three major areas of investment: the culture, society, and the self. Each of the nine cells and the intersection of these dimensions can in turn be subdivided into at least two subsets.

For example, the first row refers to the responsibility a creative person is likely to feel toward the content of his or her discipline—for a doctor, the knowledge of medicine; for a mechanic, the craft of making a car run. Practitioners of any domain would be remiss if they did not master the knowledge of the past, did not apply it in their own work, and did not try to expand the existing knowledge so that their domain would contain more of it in the future.

The second row in Table 3.1 refers to the fact that many creative achievements take place at the boundaries of domains. When the quantum theory that had been developed at the subatomic level was applied to chemistry, the latter domain was able to expand exponentially. Sometimes ideas from music, art, and literature influence neighboring forms of art, and even science. Thus creative individuals are often patrolling the borders of their domain to see if they can learn something from outside them that can be integrated into their own work and thereby expand the domain.

The third row of Table 3.1 indicates that creative individuals feel a sense of responsibility toward the people who trained them—such as the master craftsman, the guru, or the lab head who shaped their approach to the craft. They also learn continually from peers and often collaborate with them, or are involved in the organization of the field of practitioners as reviewers, editors, department chairpersons. They are also involved in training the next generation of practitioners and may take responsibility for how the discipline will be practiced in the future.

The fourth row suggests that eventually many creative persons feel the call of the larger human context in which they live and get involved in causes beyond the borders of their discipline, first by becoming involved in the community as it is, and then by working to change it in line with their values—as did Benjamin Spock, Eva Zeisel, and Linus Pauling, among others.

The fifth and sixth rows of the table deal with the personal development that creative individuals tend to pursue throughout their lives, not only in their professional role but also in their full humanity. Starting from a firm foundation of curiosity, interest, and meaning, they try to act in the present in conformity with the self-image they have created. But this image does not become static: even in the late decades of their lives they often find new knowledge to learn, new activities to engage in, and new goals to pursue. The relationships that define them also reflect this threefold attachment—to their origins, ancestors, and family; to their partners and colleagues; and to the generations that will follow.

The Implications of Creativity for an Expanded View of Responsibility

The most important message that creative individuals have to convey on this matter is a simple but vital one: there is no responsibility without care. Persons who do not care enough for *something* are unlikely to extend themselves except for reasons of self-interest. But if they care enough for something, then they feel responsible for the well-being of the object of their care. If they do not care, they do not even hear the call; or if they hear it, they do not bother to respond.

The most obvious and universal objects of care are other people we love: our parents, siblings, friends, spouses, and children; the members of our sport team or army platoon; our coworkers, fellow parishioners, and compatriots. When they call, we hear and heed the summons. Then we feel responsible to the institutions that order our lives—the laws, the church, or the workplace. We also feel responsible to legal, professional, religious, and civic virtues that we have learned make a good person and a good citizen.

All of these reasons for caring are necessary for civilized human existence. But creative individuals show us yet another way of caring.

Their concern is for all aspects of life—for galaxies and molecules, for towering buildings and subtle human feelings. They care for the excellence of human artifacts such as music or mathematics, life sciences or poetry. They care not only for the best examples of the past, but also for how best to perform in their chosen medium right now—and how to improve and enrich the tradition.

The call to excellence is a joyful calling: Creative people may at times be lonely, depressed, and even suicidal; but when they respond to a call, they feel connected to the dynamic trajectory of human evolution. It is an ecstatic experience that benefits everyone—the creator who is lifted out of limited individual existence, and the community that is enriched by the quest for excellence.

Is this kind of care something only geniuses feel, or can the rest of us benefit from their expanded view of responsibility through education? It seems quite obvious that we not only can, but we also desperately need to apply the lessons of creativity to the rearing of children in all walks of life. Alas, formal education is not overly concerned with teaching passion, which is the prerequisite for caring, and hence for beginning to feel responsible for something beyond self and the closest circle of one's social network. Some teachers understand the importance of getting students to care about some aspect of life, whether the fire ants that so fascinated naturalist E. O. Wilson or the pottery that Eva Zeisel so loved. But it is very difficult for teachers to do so under the current conditions of schooling, where numbing tests take top priority and even sullen obedience is difficult to achieve, let alone burning passion.

In fact, one of the most distressing changes in the context of child rearing is a widespread reduction of opportunities for children to care and to feel responsible. In the prevailing environment of a century ago, on the farms and in the small towns of America, children learned that cows had to be milked each morning, chickens needed to be fed, the garden plot needed to be watered, the firewood had to be split, and so on and so forth—and if the tasks were not completed competently and on time, the consequences were felt by all, and the responsibilities could be clearly assigned. This kind of experience is now very rare. Many children grow into adulthood with hazy notions of how cause and effect work in the real world—notions made even more confusing by the steady diet of virtual reality absorbed from the media.

Visionaries and some educational pioneers have pointed at possible solutions that might serve as stimuli for planning what we should do next. In his novel *Island*, Aldous Huxley described a utopian community where the first formal training of children was to learn rock climbing.

This way, the author argued, they would learn to take responsibility for their own lives as well as those of their partners on the rope. Moreover, they would learn to trust their peers by placing the responsibility for their own life in the hands of their partners. Huxley's educational program has never been implemented, to our knowledge, but less extreme versions have entered child-rearing practices quite successfully. For instance, one of the major goals of Montessori teachers is to get children to learn to care for their clothes, their food, and the well-being of their peers; as well as to care for the orderliness of the classrooms and the learning tools they contain. Children who learn to care for such simple things will be able to care for increasingly more complex objects, ideas, and forms of order.

Creative lives bear witness to the fact that one can learn to care and be responsible for practically any aspect of the world and of human activity. How to implement their experience into a viable pedagogy, however, is a challenge that still needs to be confronted. Some initial suggestions include the following:

Help the child find his or her interest. The passion of creative persons often arises serendipitously, by chance. It is aroused by an exceptional event or experience. But just as often it seems to be prepared for by the intervention of parents and teachers. We know only a little at this point about how to ignite a child's passion.

One obvious way is to expose the young person to as many forms of experience as possible, without pressure or coercion. Role models who love what they are doing help, and so do exemplars of excellence. Taking traditional accomplishments seriously is also useful. So is considering future possibilities in the child's life, in connection with possible careers in various fields.

Basically, the issue is to communicate to the child a love for life in its myriad forms, in the hope that the child will find a connection between his or her interests and some aspect of the world. Once the connection is established, the child is likely to begin caring for that aspect in its past, present, and future forms.

Trust the child while helping to develop the child's interest. If the child learns to care for an object or activity, a dialectic spiral of autonomous learning tends to develop. Care implies a desire for excellence, which leads to more skilled activity—a desire to play the piano better or to solve more advanced calculus problems, for example. In turn, this cycle leads to deeper caring for the medium, and hence a greater sense of responsibility. When this commitment coalesces, the adult needs only to stand on the sidelines, ready to lend a hand when needed or to point to the next level of challenge.

The love for learning that develops in a child needs to be sustained into maturity if it is to lead to responsible adult behavior. A physician or businessperson who sees his or her work exclusively as a means to wealth or prestige is likely to take the easy way out when hard choices are called for. A plumber who does not care for excellence is going to be more prone to take shortcuts in his work than one who does care for excellence. A civil society depends on institutions that support in people a feeling of responsibility to their callings. As John W. Gardner so aptly wrote, "An excellent plumber is infinitely more admirable than an incompetent philosopher. The society which scorns excellence in plumbing because plumbing is a humble activity and tolerates shoddiness in philosophy because it is an exalted activity will have neither good plumbing nor good philosophy. Neither its pipes nor its theories will hold water" (Gardner, 1961, p. 86).

Unfortunately, training in the occupations, and even in the professions, is ignoring the fact that good work depends on whether workers come to love and respect what they are meant to do. The notion that one's work is a calling, a vocation, is not a fashionable one to hold these days. The close mentoring, the teaching by example, that used to be a safeguard that young workers would recognize the beauty and value of a job well done, is getting harder to find. Yet if a young person fails to learn this and sees instead that success and promotion in the workplace depend on cleverness and compromise rather than on responsibility to the craft, the temptation to be irresponsible becomes more attractive. Of course the responsibility that a budding poet learns for his craft or that a young biologist learns for hers might not transfer to other aspects of life outside their respective domains of interest. The extremely punctilious businessperson and the uncompromising plumber could be lax and remiss as citizens. But considering the alternative—cohorts of children growing up without any interest in or concern for the past or the future, without any motivation to do their best—it is hard to argue that life in the next generation would not improve if children learned to care for at least one aspect of the world, and thus be led to appreciate excellence in it and to feel responsible for preserving and improving it.

REFERENCES

Bourdieu, P. (1993). *The field of cultural production.* New York: Columbia University Press.

Choe, I., & Nakamura, J. (1996). *Values of creative individuals.* Unpublished manuscript.

Csikszentmihalyi, M. (1996). *Creativity: Flow and the psychology of discovery and invention.* New York: HarperCollins.

Csikszentmihalyi, M. (2003). *Good business: Leadership, flow, and the making of meaning.* New York: Viking.

Gardner, J. W. (1961). *Excellence: Can we be equal and excellent too?* New York: Harper & Row.

Kasof, J. (1995). Explaining creativity: The attributional perspective. *Creativity Research Journal, 8,* 311–366.

Lombroso, C. (1889/1891). *The man of genius.* London: Walter Scott.

Trachtman, P. (2006). Cézanne, the man who changed the landscape of art. *Smithsonian, 36*(10), 80–89.

Vasari, G. (1959). *Lives of the most eminent painters, sculptors, and architects.* New York: Modern Library. (Original work published 1550).

4

A CALL TO SERVE

AN EXPLORATION OF HUMANE CREATORS

Wendy Fischman

*I think I differ in that I'm constantly looking for a connection
between how you give back to society and do your work
at the same time . . . and more people I know and who I work
with say, "I'm going to do my work first and then I can give
back to society. I don't have the time right now"—[whereas
I believe that] you can do both at the same time.*

—Business entrepreneur

PEOPLE CHOOSE DIFFERENT KINDS OF WORK FOR MANY REASONS—a salary, location, years invested in training, obligations to family, or some combination thereof. Some people know at a young age what they want to do for work, while others sample many jobs before they settle on the "right" kind of work. Other workers—probably a relatively small number—are driven to particular work because it meets a need they feel responsible to fulfill. Some doctors, service workers, lawyers, journalists, and educators, for example, initially choose to go into their respective fields to help others, indeed sometimes a particular group or community. Their passion to serve others inspires them to choose particular careers. These individuals want to do "good work"; they are committed not only to a mastery of technical skills and knowledge, but also to pursuing

81

work that goes beyond self-fulfillment (Damon, Colby, Bronk, & Ehrlich, 2005).

Some individuals believe that the needs they discern are not being met through traditional professional roles. Troubled by these voids and passionate about carrying out work that can be helpful to others, they create new techniques—and in rare cases, new professional domains—to facilitate change. The deeply felt responsibility to create "good" for society drives them to extend or redefine the conventional jobs and career paths from which most people select. In other words, these individuals not only *choose* a kind of work to help others, they *create* it. For these "humane creators," the nexus of creativity and responsibility forms the basis of work. They devise new opportunities, approaches, and products to respond to unmet needs and challenging external conditions, with the larger goal of serving society.

Several factors contribute to creativity, including attributes of the individual (such as inborn or acquired talents, training, and age), the context in which the individual lives (such as period of history and type of community), and judgments by informed others (such as acceptance or denial of new ideas, rewards, and notoriety). Combining these elements, Csikszentmihalyi has described creativity as the "synergy of many sources": (1) a culture that contains symbolic rules, (2) a person who brings novelty into this symbolic system, and (3) experts who recognize and validate the innovation (Csikszentmihalyi, 1996). According to Csikszentmihalyi, "a genuinely creative accomplishment is almost never the result of a sudden insight, a light bulb flashing in the dark, but comes after years of hard work" (Csikszentmihalyi, 1996, pp. 1, 6).

Creative work does not always imply "good work." Certainly many individuals are recognized for the "good" uses of creativity in their work (for example, scientist Niels Bohr, theater artist Anna Deavere Smith, musician Yo-Yo Ma,), but the ability to think in new and different ways does not necessarily lead to admirable work. Artistry and inventiveness can also produce intentional or unintentional negative consequences. Consider, for instance, Jayson Blair, the talented young journalist who fabricated stories for the *New York Times* (see Gardner, Chapter Twelve), or Kenneth Lay, the CEO of the purportedly innovative company Enron who misled employees, shareholders, and the general public about business operations and profits. It is unlikely that Lay's and Blair's activities would be defended by anyone knowledgeable about the facts of the case and the norms of journalism or business.

Terrorist Osama Bin Laden's attacks on several international groups represent an extreme example of creativity deployed for irresponsible ends. Certainly by the standards of civilized nations we do not accept the methods and strategies Bin Laden created; we must concede, however, that among those who embrace his ends, Bin Laden's inventions may very well be deemed creative and even socially acceptable.

The "humane" value of creative work lies in its purpose—the extent to which an individual wants her work to have a positive influence on other individuals or on the natural environment (for example, improved health, cleaned air, preservation of species). *Humane creativity*, a concept coined by the GoodWork Project, refers to an individual's intent to use creativity in a humane way—to create responsibly and to be mindful of the consequences of work for others. In the mid-1990s, when the just-launched project was named the Humane Creativity Project, the principal investigators posed a key question: *As demands, expectations, and standards change at the workplace or within a domain, who are the individuals who responsibly respond by considering the potential outcomes of their work on others?* The original study was designed to examine the individuals and institutions that *successfully* combined cutting-edge creativity with a sense of social responsibility. Specifically, researchers sought to understand the beliefs, values, personal experiences, and external conditions that lead certain people to meld humane and creative concerns. They asked, *With rapid advances in technology and the warp speed at which work is expected to be carried out, would innovation fan or dampen social progress?*

In this chapter I revisit the original research question regarding humane creativity with the data collected about "good work"—work that is excellent, ethical, and engaging. As discussed in Chapter One of this volume, well-known paragons like Katharine Graham and John W. Gardner are powerful exemplars of people who are driven by passion and ultimate responsibility—who spend their professional lives working to improve the lives of others through their work. However, there are also individuals who serve as important role models for those who invent new socially oriented domains and new sets of practices within already existing domains in order to satisfy the unmet needs of the more traditional roles and responsibilities of their respective domains. In this respect, the discussion about humane creators serves as a transition in this volume to consideration of individuals who strive to be responsible but are less illustrious than the aforementioned paragons.

In particular I examine individuals who travel the extra mile and exemplify humane creativity in three domains: education, business, and philanthropy. Within these domains, I focus on precollegiate urban educators, social entrepreneurs, and venture philanthropists.

In many ways, individuals in these latter two roles view their missions similarly. They use the labels *social entrepreneur* and *venture philanthropist* to describe themselves, regardless of their respective domain affiliations.

What does humane creativity look like for these workers? To explore this question, I consider the beliefs and values, personal experiences, and external conditions that have led particular individuals to combine humane and creative concerns in their work; I examine as well how the responsibility that drives them to carry out "good work" differentiates them from others with whom they work. Specifically, I use coded interviews conducted by the GoodWork Project to compare the ways in which individuals in these three domains described the purpose of their work, their awareness of needs, and the strategies they devised to satisfy particular needs.

Precollegiate Urban Educators: Creative Responses to Constraining Environments

At first blush, precollegiate education in public schools appears loaded with constraints. The bureaucracy can be cumbersome, with school principals, district superintendents, state commissioners, and government officials all trying to manage the work that takes place. However, though teachers in public schools must follow certain mandates (such as state testing), they ultimately control the focus and priorities in their own classrooms, often describing them as their own "labs" or "planets," in order to experiment with different teaching and learning techniques (Fischman, DiBara, & Gardner, 2006). Some teachers focus on "teaching to the test," while others concentrate on ways to make content engaging for students. In urban schools, teachers spend a lot of energy developing meaningful relationships with students. In the end, numerous decisions, such as how to grade work, handle disciplinary issues, and manage parent participation, are made by individual teachers themselves.

With relatively little agreement across American society about the goals and purposes of their work, teachers can be easily frustrated and overwhelmed. What is most important: student retention rates? standardized test scores? developing students into lifelong learners? These questions and complexities not only leave teachers confused but often stimulate pressures to meet all of these demands. For many teachers, managing the struggle becomes exhausting; others use the challenge as motivation to find new ways to fulfill students' needs.

Andrea Grimes: The GIVE Project

Andrea Grimes is a young social studies teacher at Leominster High School, an urban school outside of Boston, Massachusetts.[1] In her sixth year of teaching, she explains that when she tutored in high school, she knew that teaching would "fit" her personality. She believes that, aside from disciplinary knowledge, the most important traits and skills for being a "good" teacher are a deep care for students and an ability to connect with them on a personal level. In her words, "it's so important to recognize where kids are at, recognize where they're coming from, and work with the whole kid, all their baggage, everything, not just assume that they can leave their baggage at the door." Many of the students in Andrea's school come from broken homes—some live in foster care—and must work to provide a first or second income.

A self-proclaimed parent to many of her students, Andrea feels the need to help them with their personal problems: "If some kid is having a problem with their girlfriend or their boyfriend, they are not going to care what is going on in social studies, English, math, science. Until they sort through some of that, then they'll be able to deal with what's going on in the classroom." Furthermore, Andrea worries that if she does not address the "emotional baggage," many of her students will not have a reason to come to school. She explains, "I've had so many [students] withdraw this year for personal reasons, and it's not necessarily a school failure, it's just that they emotionally didn't have what they needed to be able to follow through."

Andrea realized that as an individual, her efforts could have only a limited impact. To reach more students, she developed a community service club called GIVE (Getting Involved in Volunteer Experiences). She thought that the experience of "giving to others" would increase students' self-esteem and, at the same time, help them to "stop thinking about [their] own problems . . . and start thinking about the problems of someone else." Enrolled students participate in one service project per month, as well as help organize a schoolwide fundraiser. In what is described as the biggest club at her school, participating students complete more than one thousand hours of community service throughout the year. Nearly three-quarters of the students from Andrea's school who

---

[1]In the profiles that follow, some names have been changed to ensure confidentiality. In cases where permission was granted, identities have not been further disguised.

applied to the National Honor Society had been involved with the club. She comments on why it has been so successful:

> [It] is a perfect example of kids who want to do good; I mean these kids, they constantly amaze me. They want to do nice things for other people. They want to be appreciated for the right reasons. It's just amazing, so I'm hoping that people will start to recognize that more kids do good works . . . and participate in good things that benefit other people.

Not only is Andrea pleased with the interest the club has generated among students, but she also recognizes the positive influence it has had on the adults in the building. Sometimes, she experiences tension with other faculty because they are worried that she spends too much time with her students. The friction with her peers intensified when teachers learned that Andrea actually accompanies students as they do the community service work rather than simply coordinating the list and sending students off-site. Some teachers are resentful of her "extra" efforts because they think she is raising unrealistic expectations for others. Recently, though, as the club has become a stronger presence in the school, she has received more support from other teachers: "I've had these teachers randomly appearing at my room, and some of them are teachers I don't even know . . . but I think that people see that there's some value in it, and it's doing wonderful things for the kids."

Andrea readily admits that sometimes "I don't know when to say when," and that she has to be "careful" not to overempathize with students' problems. She says, "I feel like I almost absorb their failures as my own if they can't make something work. . . . That's hard . . . almost to the point that it's painful." At the same, however, she explains, "I love what I do. I wouldn't do it if I didn't love doing [the work]." Andrea has always felt that community service is a spiritual experience that "feeds my soul."

For Andrea, teaching is not just an occupation; it is a "way of life"— an opportunity to be a positive role model for students both inside and outside the school building. Though she is sometimes overwhelmed, Andrea does not let others, including resentful peers, dictate the boundaries of her job. She describes the responsibilities she feels as a teacher: "[Focus] is always on the kids. It doesn't matter what's going on in the building, what is going on amongst the faculty . . . the kids are who we're here for . . . the priority is always making sure the kids have what they need." Andrea sees her "ultimate destiny" as giving beyond her school. She wants to create an opportunity for students throughout the country to participate in work that gives perspective on their own lives even as they help others in society.

Mary Skipper: Tech Boston Academy

In 2002, Mary Skipper created Tech Boston Academy (TBA), a pilot school in Boston, Massachusetts. A former teacher and administrator committed to the public school system, Mary recognized the need for urban students to acquire discrete skills and knowledge in technology as preparation for future work. She also believed that technology can "transform" the ways in which students learn and engage in other disciplines. Her goal in creating TBA was to fashion for students an experience that provides high expectations and standards, quality instruction, and deep personal connections with faculty.

TBA enrolls approximately 350 students, accepting roughly 100 for the freshman class each year from a lottery of interested families. Students commit to a longer school day than any other school in their district, beginning at 8 A.M. and ending at 4 P.M. All students receive laptops, which they bring to every class and leave at school overnight. On their personal computers, students are trained to take notes, complete assignments, and even read whole books. Mary believes that technology helps students visualize key concepts, keeps them focused, and fosters ownership of their own learning process.

As a school leader, Mary describes herself as an innovator and creator, "a balloon [without] the string," who could not refuse the opportunity to start something new "from a fresh slate, with nothing on it." She credits TBA's existence to her own entrepreneurial skills in raising funds: "You should be able to count on a certain amount of funding [from the district]. And that's it. From that point on, you need to figure out how to raise your funds, and you need to figure out how to align your resources."

In addition to raising the necessary funds to support the school, she also describes her role as a visionary, "a bridge builder of the vision." Mary believes that a good school leader must have a clear mission as well as skills to communicate and sustain the mission over time. A clear vision, Mary believes, keeps teachers satisfied and not overwhelmed:

> There are so many different gods that teachers are trying to worship. Is it content? Is it methodology? Is it relationship? Is it collegiality? What's the most important thing that they should be doing with one another, with their kids? Again, I think the clearer the vision of the

school leader as to what's important and the support the school leader gives, the healthier the environment for the teachers.

Mary points to other skills that have been important for the growth of TBA, including careful hiring, setting the management structure, evaluating teachers, and communicating with faculty, students, and parents. She works to instill a culture that encourages "citizenship" among the student body:

> There's a great deal of Ignatius in my school. Even though it's a public school . . . there's an ethical and moral framework that exists . . . to make TBA students really good people and help them to be the best people they can be. And that ranges across citizenship, community service, respect, love . . . those are words we use on a daily basis at TBA, which aren't typically used in public schools. . . . And I'm not embarrassed about them. I help my kids.

These achievements have helped her to "beat the odds" of working within a difficult urban environment with underachieving students, poor building condition, and limited resources; 94 percent of the graduating class in 2006 enrolled in higher education programs.

Creating and leading a school is not easy, but as Mary says, "for me personally, I thrive on challenge." Being strategic and reflective, and having a good sense of humor and an ability to "roll with the punches," enables Mary to stay positive when "things get crazy." She also describes herself as a spiritual person who "prays for wisdom" when confronting difficult situations. Though sensitive and respectful, she is also a risk taker. As she says, "You know, I probably break fifty thousand laws. That's the only way I know how to educate. . . . It's probably a good thing I'm a pilot school because if TBA wasn't, I probably would have been fired like three years ago."

Though Mary's primary focus is to sustain the culture she has created and support the teachers, she ultimately feels responsible to the students with whom, even as the school leader, she connects on a daily basis. Mary stands in the middle of two main hallways in between classes, says hello to everyone by name, and knows where they are supposed to be going. She congratulates those who have shown academic improvement, gives a hug to someone who has been out sick, and sets up meetings with students who have concerns. Recognizing the need to engage students in school itself, Mary has created an environment that provides them with meaningful experiences to which they might never have been exposed without TBA's presence.

o

THOUGH ANDREA AND MARY OCCUPY DIFFERENT POSITIONS within their schools and have varying years of experience in education, they agree that finding ways to connect with students keeps them committed to school. With little agreement in their field, Mary's and Andrea's responsibilities to students guide their work, regardless of the "extra" time involved or how they may be perceived by their peers.

In our study of teachers who work in urban settings, we found that many individuals share a similar sense of responsibility for their work.[2] Almost all of the participants identified students as their primary responsibility. Though some teachers also mentioned a responsibility to students' parents, school administrators, and colleagues, the students almost always took precedence in their teachers' minds (Fischman, DiBara, & Gardner, 2006). Teachers believe that, with the deterioration of family bonds and the rapid pace of society, students experience more need than in the past. For the most part, the teachers we interviewed responded to this perceived increase by broadening their responsibilities; they strove to meet the academic needs of students as well as their social, developmental, and emotional needs.

Though teachers often broaden their sense of responsibility, they also recognize the risk of becoming overinvolved in students' problems and sometimes taking them on as their own. As much as teachers want to develop close relationships with students, they worry about blurring personal and professional boundaries, and about preserving their own time for family, friends, and hobbies. They are also concerned that eventually they will not be able to find enough ways to meet the needs of students and remain vitally engaged in their work—the third facet of good work. Many teachers assert that once they fail to meet students' needs, they will have to give up teaching altogether.

Entrepreneurs in Business: What Is the Bottom Line?

In contrast to urban education, business has a clear and simple purpose: to make money for owners and investors. Within business, however, various kinds of enterprises and roles exist. Here I focus on entrepreneurs,

---

[2]We interviewed forty teachers in four urban high schools who had been identified by a group of educational experts for "good work" in precollegiate education. At each school, half of the teachers were nominated by school leaders and the other half were randomly selected. All of the teachers had at least a few years of experience in their positions.

particularly those who have a social orientation. The goal for any entrepreneur is to devise something that does not already exist in order to create or to capture an untapped audience. With innumerable possibilities and few, if any, standards for how to set up these ventures, this variety of business tends to attract individuals who have a propensity for risk and creativity. Research has shown that in general entrepreneurs are individuals who are energetic and dominant, socially adroit and autonomous, but who also display lower conformity and a lesser sense of responsibility than many of their peers (as cited in Bird, 1989). Furthermore, entrepreneurs seek ownership and control. In fact, according to Kent, Sexton, and Vesper (1982, p. 55), "typically, it is only after deciding to start a business that they determine a product or service." This "internal locus-of-control" plays an important role early on in determining the kind of business or company that will result—in terms not only of product but also of the type of workplace created. For most businesspersons, making a profit is the end goal, whereas for those who are particularly interested in social change, profit is the means toward executing good work.

Lauren Creamer: Firefly Toys

Lauren Creamer, a young entrepreneur in her second year of business school at Babson College in Wellesley, Massachusetts, recently launched Firefly Toys, Inc., a therapeutic toy company. The toys and accompanying guidebook help facilitate conversation between children and their parents (and caregivers) about difficult life transitions such as divorce, illness, and death, as well as about less epochal challenges, including nightmares and bullying. The goal of these products is to "help communication and provide [individuals with an opportunity] to really work together to get over whatever the situation is, as opposed to alienating each other, which tends to happen for kids at any age." The mission of Lauren's business is to provide a product and a service that is "needed in society," and to provide opportunities to individuals working with children who want to "do something good."

Interestingly, Lauren had never thought about business as a career option: she had considered medicine, and specifically becoming a pediatric oncologist. As a young child she frequently expressed desire to work with children in her future career. One of the aspects of working with children that Lauren has found most rewarding is using creativity to navigate the inherent challenges. She always sought the "hard kids" who "don't want you there," because she liked to solve problems and "think out of the box" about new approaches and strategies to engage these children. Lauren now sees creativity as a key ingredient for business: "The thing that makes you successful or not in business is your creativity and your drive. If you are really motivated and passionate about being successful and doing it, you'll become successful."

After she finished college, Lauren went to Ecuador for a year and worked with girls living in an orphanage. To raise their self esteem and sense of empowerment, Lauren came up with an idea: she would help girls build their own business, to create and sell products. Though she enjoyed seeing the positive difference this work made in the lives of the children with whom she worked, Lauren also realized that she enjoyed business herself.

Lauren became aware that business offers the potential to continue to do "the good work that I was doing with the kids" without having to scrounge for money all the time: "I was looking for a way to merge those two desires of doing something really good for society . . . while at the same time being able to be self-sustaining." Lauren was also looking for ways to take on work about which she felt passionate. She pondered why people always worry about balancing passion and work in their lives: "Shouldn't there be a way to do your work and [do something] that you love, so that it becomes a part of who you are?"

In her graduate studies, Lauren often finds herself at odds with peers and some professors in business about their approaches to work and the mission of work. She often feels like the "black sheep," because she does not see business decisions as "black and white," and takes more of a "holistic" perspective, thinking about how decisions affect "everybody and everything." She also claims that many individuals affiliated with her academic program do not fundamentally agree with "what it means to help another human being and that the choices that you make on a higher level can actually influence individual people." Lauren believes that most of her peers are more interested in money, influence, and the power they can attain than in their potential impact on society.

Certainly Lauren hopes that her company will turn a profit, but she sees money as a way to validate the importance of her work, not necessarily as a way to increase her own wealth. She explains, "I want to make money. I've never had an issue with that . . . because I think in making money you show to other people that doing this kind of work is valuable on all levels. It's not that I'm sacrificing one for the other [money for helping people], it's that you can put the two together."

Lauren is best thought of as a *social entrepreneur*—an individual who creates new approaches to a social issue in order to bring about change (Barendsen, 2004). Her mission for Firefly Toys is not directed toward one particular social cause (such as fighting homelessness or divorce), but rather is fashioned to provide a product that can help children and adults experiencing a range of social problems. Lauren is a "special" kind of business entrepreneur—someone who carefully combines passion and responsibility to fulfill needs in society.

Steven: Home Products

Working unhappily as a marketing manager, Steven looked for ways to make his free time on weekends and evenings meaningful. His favorite hobbies consisted of making things, so he began to create home products such as laundry detergents and hand lotions for peers at work as a way to pass the time and do something he truly enjoyed. Steven stated, "As long as I can . . . be making things and [be] inventing or be creative, I think I will always be happy." Many of his colleagues inquired about buying his products as gifts for others, and as these requests mounted, he thought about starting his own business.

Eventually Steven started a company to provide people of varying income and marital status with the opportunity to create a comfortable, pleasant home environment. He explained, "Everyone can build a home, even if you are a single mom or if you are a single parent with five kids or whatever and you make $5,000 a year. It's not the money, it is what you do within your home. . . . Everyone has the capability of having a nice home. . . . I try to provide that through products."

Ironically, Steven received a lot of resistance from members of his family when he decided to start his own company, because they were concerned that he was leaving a "decent-paying" job with insurance and other benefits. He explained, "In no uncertain terms [they] told me that . . . I didn't know what I was doing [or] what I was going up against." However, despite this pressure, Steven stuck with his decision. Though he was not particularly tied to business as a career, he felt strongly about the mission of his company. He became convinced that this pivotal decision was the right thing for him to do and that ultimately it gave him strength and confidence to handle other difficult situations.

Even though it has been years since the inception of his business, Steven's determination clearly influences the way he leads the company. He described a steadfast commitment not to compromise the quality or message of the products he produces, even when the stakes are high. Steven says that if a product is not "up to par," the company recalls it, even if the client might never have noticed. He explained, "I don't follow my nose to where the money is. . . . You don't just move to the front of the line because you have more money."

Like Lauren, Steven views money as a secondary goal of his work. His primary interest is to make a difference in people's lives through the products he creates. He believes that having a mission that helps others is important; he wants to ensure that his venture does not become "just another company that is making money." Likewise, Steven views business as "an outlet for people to survive and sustain themselves with something that they love" rather than as an opportunity primarily to generate personal wealth. Similarly to Lauren, he struggles to work with people in business who do not share his goals. He finds that most people are just trying to "make a buck."

Interestingly, when specifically asked to whom or what he feels responsible, Steven describes his primary responsibility as being to himself. However, unlike other business entrepreneurs who describe this responsibility as generating income for themselves, Steven is most concerned with how to stay true to his mission.

○

BOTH YOUNG AND IDEALISTIC, Lauren and Steven are attracted to business primarily because it provides an opportunity to carry out work they enjoy and that will benefit others. Neither of them started with a particular interest in business. Instead, they each recognized the opportunity—indeed, the responsibility—to meet a particular need in society. Lauren explained, "I'm not tied to an industry as much as I am to what [I] want to do." Though they view themselves as business entrepreneurs, the kind of responsibility at the core of their work sets them apart from other business entrepreneurs in the GoodWork Project.[3]

On the surface, business entrepreneurs exhibit traits similar to those of Lauren and Steven: driven, determined, confident, and open to risks. Many business entrepreneurs report that their personality fits the skills they see as necessary for success in business. They look for work that enables them to use creativity and problem-solving skills. One business entrepreneur stated, "I like to go after something that has never been done before with great

---

[3]We interviewed eighteen business entrepreneurs between the ages of twenty-one and thirty-five who were just beginning their careers. Half of the entrepreneurs had already started their own companies, the other half were in graduate school with a focus on business. Some of the entrepreneurs had already made career shifts and job changes.

passion and without worrying about what all the naysayers are saying." On the whole, the group explained that "being a good person" is important in business—that you have to be careful how you treat others with whom you work, both inside and outside of the workplace, especially when you are just starting your own company. Many of these entrepreneurs were well aware that their reputation was at stake: to raise funds, network, and gain respect from others in the field, you have to be well-liked.

In fact, in describing their primary responsibilities, some of the business entrepreneurs alluded to preservation of their reputation as a "good person." One entrepreneur stated, "I'd rather fail knowing that I'm doing the right thing, rather than succeed doing the wrong thing. . . . it's important for me to stand for something." However, unlike Lauren and Steven, most of the business entrepreneurs identified responsibilities to their shareholders, employees, and the company's overall financial success. Some of them also mentioned a responsibility to their families.

Few of the business entrepreneurs talked about a responsibility to the wider society, and even in these cases the responsibility was not integrated into their work but rather carried out in their spare time. For example, one entrepreneur stated that it is important to "give back" to society, but he would do this at "some point in my life. . . . I'd like to see myself doing some kind of public service . . . and give back to the system which I've clearly profited from." Another entrepreneur agreed that he would like to have a positive impact on the world, but this is different than being *responsible* for the impact: "I feel a responsibility to do the most with what I've been given. And I would say that's to me."

Venture Philanthropy: Reconstituting the Notion of Giving

Philanthropy in the contemporary United States depends heavily on businesspeople—both those active today and those who accumulated fortunes in the past. Traditional foundations, family foundations, corporate foundations, and individual donors give away money to nonprofit organizations, such as schools, homeless shelters, and research institutions, as well as to charismatic catalysts for social change who need money to do work that is not profitable. Though there are limitations on how these foundations are initially set up, there is relatively little accountability for how money is distributed.

In an effort to instill accountability between the grantor and the grantee, venture philanthropy was launched. Many venture philanthropists come from a business background themselves; some started their own companies and have experience building the infrastructure and seeding the culture to allow for growth and development. These philanthropists help nonprofit organizations create plans that set direction, build systems for monitoring the spending, and devise ways of measuring and reporting progress.

Paul Brainerd: Giving Back to the Environment

After selling a lucrative technology company he founded in 1984, Paul Brainerd established both a family foundation and a venture philanthropy organization. His attraction to philanthropy was catalyzed by his upbringing in a small town, where his family lived modestly. Paul reported that the concept of giving back to one's community was established for him at an early age and modeled through the actions of his mother.

Paul had accumulated considerable capital in the assets he earned from selling his company. Rather than giving to an existing philanthropy, he wanted to start a new organization that would meet needs in his community. He cited an ability to "build new things" and "think strategically about what is needed and how [to] meet [these needs]." After meeting with more than one hundred individuals, including scientists, journalists, and local politicians, Paul established a family foundation dedicated to environmental and conservation needs. He asked environmental experts, "If you had three checks to write, to whom would you write them?" As soon as he formulated the program areas, Paul tried a new approach to reach potential grantees. He facilitated a series of open community meetings. At these meetings, he and his newly hired executive director gave presentations about the mission of their foundation and sought feedback. As far as Paul knows, this approach had never been implemented before.

Not only was Paul interested in preserving the environment, but he also wanted to improve the ways in which philanthropic foundations operated. Cognizant of the abuse of power associated with many philanthropic organizations, Paul set out to create a respectful, accountable, and responsive organization. He also developed an internal structure to encourage staff to be mindful of the potential "harms" and to respond immediately upon noticing inappropriate acts. He explained, "We've put in place . . . a peer process that ensures . . . that if anybody does begin to get beyond the boundaries or go up against the line of not listening or being disrespectful in any way, shape, or form, that we know about it right away."

Two years after launching his family foundation, Paul established a new venture philanthropy organization. His goal was to involve his peers in philanthropy in meaningful ways. He wanted to provide an alternative to the model in which interested individuals volunteer and then get "asked to lick envelopes and put stamps on and send out a mailing." Paul and his assistant spent a year researching giving models and came up with a plan.

Social Venture Partners (SVP) is a giving circle in which donors become partners. SVP started with two goals: to work closely with nonprofits, and to educate the partners. This model has been replicated in more than twenty cities. Now serving as an informal advisor to SVP, Paul reflected on the outcomes of his work: "I knew there were people out there that really cared about giving back to their communities, but just didn't have a structure to work within. And this model, for a lot of people, is one they could relate to."

Paul commented on the difference between this work and that of a business: "In a business you're expected to set direction and get to move in that direction quickly, and in philanthropy the people engaged have a different set of values . . . not that I don't still value getting things done and moving forward, but I just acknowledge the fact that it may take three months versus a week or two." Because of Paul's goal of creating meaningful ways to contribute to society himself and, at the same time, help others "give back," he was willing to take risks in a field that was new to him. He concluded, "I've made plenty of wrong decisions. I just accept the fact that there's risk associated with it and that's part of life and you can learn from those mistakes and move forward and hopefully not make the same mistake again, or at least too many times."

Sara: Helping the Economically Disadvantaged

After becoming financially successful through business, Sara created a new philanthropic foundation in the mid-1980s. Unlike Paul, however, Sara was inspired by a single event—the stock market crash of 1987. Living in San Francisco, young, full of energy, and equipped with the financial resources to contribute, she decided to get involved in philanthropy. Once she made this decision, she started to pay attention to how others who had money contributed to society. Sara noticed that a lot of the "socialites" readily gave to music and arts institutions, but "you couldn't raise a penny" to help disadvantaged communities. She said, "Nobody really cared about what was happening to the rest of the world that was being left behind."

Days after the crash, Sara called all her friends and acquaintances who might be sympathetic to her cause and said, "We've got to do something to help the people that are going to be destitute." This initial group started monthly meetings in her home with the mission of providing aid to "any organization that was helping people in economically disadvantaged communities."

Sara started her own foundation because she felt strongly that "if you want to do something right, you've got to do it yourself." In other words, like Paul Brainerd, she did not want to develop a philanthropic arm of an existing institution; she wanted to begin with a "clean playbook" and be "guided by our hearts" rather than by existing organizational dynamics. Sara wanted to create a foundation in which donors had an understanding about how their money would be spent. She wanted donors to feel good about their contributions—to know that the money was helping others in society rather than being devoted to operational costs.

Sara used her business skills—conducting due diligence, devising strategy, and developing a management structure—to create something new. Through her experience volunteering with other philanthropic organizations, she knew how to develop an organizational mission that had explicit goals and clear benchmarks for achievement. Sara believes that "just because you spend a lot of money and give a lot of time, it doesn't mean that there is going to be improvement." She wants donors to see that their investments have "real returns," just as people expect in business. Sara was determined to stay focused on results-based philanthropy.

Sara's foundation has raised more than $100 million from more than three thousand donors. In reflecting on the success of her foundation, Sara underscored the importance of her board, particularly the way it was formed and its current mode of operation. In contrast to most other institutions, the board currently underwrites all of the fundraising and administrative expenses incurred by the organization. Sara explained that the board has an "entrepreneurial spirit": it is dynamic, active, aggressive, and expansionary. It is necessary to convene a group of individuals who are not afraid to put together what others might reject because of the risks involved. Sara claimed that "at the end of the day, there's no greater satisfaction in the world than helping somebody elevate themselves. It's the single greatest joy you could possibly ever derive, I think, on earth, just about, except for maybe watching your own kids grown up."

○

FINANCIALLY SUCCESSFUL AS A RESULT OF COMMERCIAL VENTURES, Paul and Sara used many of their already mastered strategic skills to structure new foundations and new opportunities for informed giving. Without necessarily trying to start a new trend, now known as *venture philanthropy*, both Paul and Sara looked for meaningful ways for people to "give back." Though raising money is always the main priority in philanthropy, Paul and Sara wanted individual donors to be "engaged"—to put their skills and expertise to use for others and to understand how their efforts (financial or otherwise) were being implemented. They each felt a responsibility to encourage people to do more than just write checks: they believed that getting involved with the actual work might increase the likelihood that donors would constitute sufficient resources to meet a particular need in society.

Most of the venture philanthropists with whom we spoke reported similar traits and approaches.[4] They underscored the importance of discipline for their work, as well as the ability to get along with others. Some of the venture philanthropists spoke about having their "heart in the work." Most participants also expressed a desire to give back and to integrate their passion for business with their interest in serving a larger community. A young woman, for example, who worked for a well-known venture philanthropy organization specifically sought a business degree in order to help the poor and the homeless. She felt that her passion could go only so far and that she needed skills to manage the "business" of helping the homeless.

However, when asked specifically about their responsibilities, a number of venture philanthropists expressed loyalty to the smooth running of their respective organizations and to the individuals who support them. Though venture philanthropists ultimately want to make positive changes in society, many are focused on the immediacy of improving their organization's capacity to help a cause. Many of these venture philanthropists operate on the principle expressed by one participant: "Through stronger organizations come stronger communities."

The Ripple Effect: Results of Humane Creativity

For the humane creators described in this chapter, the potential to make a difference and have an impact on society is the driving force for their work. These individuals are not only inspired to create something tangible—a

---

[4]After a careful selection process, we interviewed thirteen venture philanthropists. Most of the individuals had come to venture philanthropy from other fields (for example, business, education). Some of the individuals did not necessarily refer to themselves as "venture philanthropists," as this term has become controversial.

philanthropic foundation, a school, a program, a consumer product—but they also feel responsible to create work that will influence others. What makes these individuals different from other highly creative individuals is the humane component of their work—the ability to recognize and articulate a need in society, as well as the commitment and passion to devise solutions regardless of the challenges. One participant described this phenomenon:

> I came up with this analogy because you see so many people doing great work. And when their work stopped, the system just sucked them up and it was like they did not ever exist. . . . It's like [any individual], they're just tiny drops in a bucket of water. And they're swimming like mad trying to get someplace, and then their time's up, and they're pulled out of the bucket, and the water goes perfectly still like they were never there. When you get pulled out of the bucket, what you really want to do is hope that some ripples still exist after you're gone.

In the areas surveyed here, humane creators differentiated themselves from others in their respective domains by three features: passion for work, ability to transfer and adapt technical skills, and a propensity to think about large-scale, systemic change for society.

Passion

Many individuals who participated in the GoodWork Project spoke of the enjoyment and excitement that have sustained them for the long term. These humane creators stressed enjoying what they do, but mostly they emphasized the passion to meet a particular need in society. The responsibility to fulfill this passion—and thus contribute to society—is what has led them to challenge the conventional paths of their respective domains. The business entrepreneurs, Lauren and Steven, were not originally drawn to business because of their interest in the industry per se, but rather because of the opportunity to create products that could help a specific sector of society. Similarly, the venture philanthropists, Paul and Sara, did not set out to work in philanthropy; rather, because they were frustrated with the more traditional ways of giving, they decided to develop a new approach. The two educators, Andrea and Mary, were already rooted in their domain, but each developed new ventures based on their thinking about how to engage students in the learning process. Rather than leave the field of education, they extended the boundaries of their roles to meet the needs they recognized.

These six humane creators underscored confidence as a vital element, because it enabled them to overcome skepticism from other individuals. Humane creators may hear the doubts and criticisms, but they keep focused on the ways they can most effectively carry out their responsibility to bring about change and improve the lives of others. Interestingly, although some of them identified mentors, training opportunities, religious upbringing, and other formative influences as helpful resources, their own passion and inner confidence seemed to be the most important ongoing supports for their work.

Ability to Transfer and Adapt Skills

Humane creators are able to transcend the traditional boundaries of their work because of an ability to adapt their skills for different purposes and new situations. Csikszentmihalyi (1996, p. 51) claimed that "creative individuals are remarkable for their ability to adapt to almost any situation and to make do with whatever is at hand to reach their goals." Paul and Sara noted that their abilities to devise strategy, develop management structures, and build boards in their profitable business endeavors did not fully prepare them for their work in venture philanthropy. They mentioned the sensitivity required to develop trust in nonprofit organizations, the slower pace around decision making, and the challenge of attracting personnel with specific areas of expertise. To be successful in this new context, Paul and Sara drew on business skills but significantly altered their particular techniques.

Without formally changing their domains of work, educators and business entrepreneurs who exemplify humane creativity must also adapt conventional skills. For example, Lauren and Steven needed money in order to validate the quality and usefulness of their work, but unlike in business, money was not their "bottom line." Therefore, they used their skills in marketing, advertising, recruiting, staff supervision, and setting culture in a way that deviated from their earlier experiences. Andrea and Mary used their interpersonal skills in combination with the techniques they honed in education—strong classroom management, disciplinary knowledge, and appropriate assessment techniques—to engage their students in learning.

Thinking Big

The passion to produce work that can satisfy a need, coupled with the ability to transfer domain-specific skills, leads humane creators to "think big" about systemic change. A venture philanthropist who participated in the GoodWork study articulated what it means to think about addressing large-scale problems:

> If there's one philosophical point I would make: people cannot deal with the total cost of full life-cycle solutions. They want to deal with the immediate things, and the reality is the problem with big things is they always require a system solution. System solutions are very expensive and you've got to look at the whole picture. That's why today we are building more prisons than good school solutions, because we treat the symptoms and fail to provide a systemic solution approach, and I don't believe you can change things unless you change systems.

Bill Gates, creator of one of the most profitable corporations in the world and head of a multibillion-dollar foundation that works to promote global health and prevent deadly diseases, has said that he wants his tombstone to read, "Ended Malaria" (Greene & Symonds, 2006). Though not as wealthy or well-known, the six humane creators examined in this chapter shared Gates's broad goals for making a difference in the world. Paul wanted to change the way individuals are engaged in "giving back to society," Mary looked to influence the way in which school leaders structure learning environments for the "average student." Lauren sought ways to build self-esteem and open lines of communication for youngsters experiencing difficult personal problems. Similarly, Andrea articulated her mission to "spread" her community service organization so that inner-city students would not only feel better about themselves but also be viewed differently by the rest of society.

All six of these humane creators hope not only to influence those within their particular school, foundation, or company, but also to affect peers in their domain and individuals in the larger society. In other words, in addition to contributing a specific product or service, these humane creators want their work to serve as points of departure for others—to lay the groundwork on which others can build. Both Paul and Sara, for example, developed a rotating position for board chair of their foundation to ensure that new individuals would be brought in to participate and that the foundation would not rely on any one particular person, such as one of the founders. They both described their roles at this point as "informal advisors." Similarly, after witnessing the first senior class graduate from her school, Mary confided that she was thinking about her next step in work: possibly training other school leaders. She viewed her likely departure as a positive turning point for the school—as affirmation that her ideas had not become coextensive with her presence. The six humane creators described their efforts as "replicable models": they hoped that their contributions would be not just a single drop in the bucket but rather a ripple felt by others.

Conclusion

As our research team hypothesized more than a decade ago, individual workers face an ethical dilemma: how to stay true to the central mission of service when the expectations of peers, authority figures, and the wider society clash with the original calling of the domain. Humane creators differentiate themselves from other individuals facing these dilemmas by responding to challenging situations in creative ways and by producing new forms of work that directly addresses the needs they strive to meet.

Although the contexts of work vary across the diverse professional landscape, humane creators are marked by commonalities. They exhibit a broad perspective about the impact of their work, have passion and drive to fulfill a need in society, and can alter their skills as dictated by circumstances. They feel responsible, and indeed compelled, to make a difference for individuals and, by doing so, to create long-lasting change for the larger society. Their adaptability helps them to overcome domain-specific challenges—powerful bureaucracies in education, limited opportunities for training in philanthropy, and lack of mentorship and role models in business. Because of their felt responsibility to meet the needs of others, they find creative ways at work to navigate challenges.

Although the humane creators portrayed here seem well on their way to achieving their lofty goals, their work is not easy. Aside from the challenge inherent in creating something new, these individuals have also described risks: the potential of overempathizing with the people they are trying to help; resentment from peers, family, and society for choosing a messy line of work in the first place; public scrutiny about their approaches; and the possibility that their endeavor will fail and possibly have a negative impact on those they are trying to serve. These humane creators recognize these potential harms and talked about their concerns. Specifically, Andrea and Mary worried that students would rely too much on the teachers who care for them and have a false sense of security when they move on to college or the world of work; Lauren and Steven were concerned about how to hire people who embrace the organization's mission while not being afraid to turn a profit; and Paul and Sara talked at length about how nonprofit organizations drift away from their original missions.

Despite these difficulties, these humane creators exhibit perseverance in pursuing the work they feel is important to carry out. They are energized to do work that is engaging and meaningful and that will positively affect others. These humane creators have a special ability to, as one participant described it, "latch on to something like a bull terrier and hang on to it." This ability or trait begs an important question: How can humane creators be nurtured or recruited, and what would this mean for their colleagues and the nature of work itself?

As discussed in several chapters in this volume, responsibility (just like morality) is learned and developed over time. To be sure, positive influences at early ages, including attentive parents, teachers, religious beliefs, and supportive role models and mentors at work, are certainly strong predictors that an individual will feel responsibility for others in society. However, many people *feel* a responsibility but fail to *act* on it, for many reasons, including fear of consequences, lack of support, or sometimes laziness or no sense of urgency. Humane creators are individuals who not only feel a responsibility for their work but also need to act. They stretch their thinking and go "above and beyond" to change the ways in which they work (either through creating a new domain or devising new strategies) because they want to satisfy the needs they believe cannot be met through traditional methods and approaches. Humane creators act with both a deep-rooted responsibility *and* a broad perspective about the purpose of work. They describe their work not as a *job* but rather as a *mission*.

Therefore, in addition to helping students and novice professionals develop a wider responsibility for work—recognizing the consequences of their work for others—we also need to give young individuals in school and at the workplace regular opportunities to consider the mission or calling of particular areas of work and to reflect on how their particular roles and assigned tasks help to fulfill this mission (Fischman, Solomon, Greenspan, & Gardner, 2004). These kinds of opportunities may also help veteran professionals, whose experience over time will provide important insights for younger and newer individuals. Veteran professionals should model the important and delicate balance of fulfilling daily responsibilities while keeping an eye on the broader mission of the workplace and domain.

REFERENCES

Barendsen, L. (2004, April). The business of caring: A study of young social entrepreneurs, GoodWork paper 28. Retrieved October 5, 2006, from http://pzweb.harvard.edu/eBookstore/detail.cfm?pub_id=156

Bird, B. (1989). *Entrepreneurial behavior*. Glenview, IL: Scott, Foresman.

Csikszentmihalyi, M. (1996). *Creativity: Flow and the psychology of discovery and invention*. New York: HarperCollins.

Damon, W., Colby, A., Bronk, K., & Ehrlich, T. (2005). Passion and mastery in balance: Toward good work in the professions. *Daedalus, 134*(3), 27–35.

Fischman, W., DiBara, J., & Gardner, H. (2006). Good education against the odds. *Cambridge Journal of Education, 36*(3), 383–398.

Fischman, W., Solomon, B., Greenspan, D., & Gardner, H. (2004). *Making good: How young people cope with moral dilemmas at work*. Cambridge, MA: Harvard University Press.

Greene, J., and Symonds, W. (2006, June 26). Bill Gates gets schooled. *Business Week*, pp. 64–70.

Kent, C., Sexton, D., & Vesper, K. (1982). The entrepreneur. In *Encyclopedia of entrepreneurship* (pp. 55–56). Englewood Cliffs, NJ: Prentice-Hall.

PART TWO

FACTORS THAT MODULATE RESPONSIBILITY

5

A BALANCING ACT

HOW PHYSICIANS AND TEACHERS MANAGE TIME PRESSURES AND RESPONSIBILITY

Jeffrey Solomon

Had we but world enough and time
—Andrew Marvell

MOST PROFESSIONALS, whether they be engineers, artists, or bank executives, share a common frustration with time constraints and demands on their work. By and large, workers wish there were more time to generate ideas, put together projects, and carry them through to completion. But the reality of most forms of professional work is that time is limited. Perhaps there is a contractual agreement with a client that work should be completed by a certain date. Perhaps one's supervisor has established a deadline that must be met for the sake of a project as a whole (and in fairness to one's coworkers). Or perhaps the self-imposed limiting of time spent on a project—say, writing a novel—is in one's best interest; after all, spending ten years producing a single work of literature crowds out the possibility of writing other books.

In certain professions, time constraints and demands are particularly acute and have important implications for whether and how people carry out their work. Such is the case for physicians and K–12 teachers. Although there are important differences in how time plays out for these two groups of workers—differences based on the conditions impinging on their respective professions—both physicians and teachers face demands on their time that pose serious risks to their capacity to serve the needs of patients and students, respectively. Indeed, in interviews for the Good-Work Project, physicians and teachers expressed a sense of primary responsibility to patients and students, but also suggested that various types of time constraints and demands can make it especially challenging to tend to the needs of their respective clients.

Yet, at the same time these professionals—who were interviewed precisely because they were reputed to be good workers—have developed revealing strategies for managing time constraints. These strategies, which I detail throughout this chapter, consist of subverting the very time constraints that physicians and teachers perceive to be at play in their work. More specifically, physicians counter restrictions on the amount of time they are allowed to spend with patients either by making the individual choice to spend the time anyway—and accepting the consequent penalties—or by structuring their medical practices in a manner that makes it possible to take the necessary time to consult with patients. Teachers respond to ongoing demands to put in long hours at the expense of personal or family time by establishing strict boundaries between work and home.

The Interview Sample

The interviews conducted with physicians and teachers were based on the general protocol used for the other branches of the GoodWork Project, albeit with some modifications to account for profession-specific circumstances. Therefore, physicians and teachers were not asked how time figures into their work, yet time constraints were mentioned spontaneously and at a numerically impressive frequency. A qualitative thematic analysis of verbatim interview transcripts was conducted to identify the topic of time restrictions.

Thirty-eight physicians from the specialties of internal medicine, obstetrics and gynecology (OB-GYN), and cardiothoracic surgery were interviewed in the Boston area. Ninety percent of the internists and OB-GYNs mentioned, with no direct prompting, the deleterious effects of time restrictions on their work. (The surgeons were an anomaly. Because of the nature of their work, time constraints were not prominently mentioned).

Nearly all of the physicians were affiliated with Harvard Medical School in one way or another. Some were on the faculty, some had practices in a Harvard-affiliated teaching hospital, and some had both roles; others had admitting privileges at a Harvard hospital but practiced in a suburban setting quite apart from the daily workings of the school. Clearly the physicians' affiliations with Harvard—and its myriad privileges as well as professional expectations and obligations—limits the degree to which my findings can be generalized to the physician population of the United States as a whole. Nonetheless, I believe that important lessons can be gleaned from my research sample.

Thirty-seven teachers from four high schools in Massachusetts and one in southern California were interviewed. Of these, 76 percent spontaneously commented on the difficulties presented by time limitations on their work. The teachers were drawn from urban school districts, which, as is well-documented, present a range of challenges ordinarily not seen in other types of districts. Although the difficulties encountered in urban settings are more extreme than elsewhere, the strategies used by the teachers in my sample are instructive for teachers in a wide range of settings.

Of course there are important differences between medicine and teaching that render my analysis a less-than-pure comparison. In American society, physicians are well compensated, relatively autonomous and powerful, and highly regarded by society. In contrast, teachers are not well paid; are constrained by numerous school, district, and state policies; and are relatively undervalued by society. Such differences inevitably influence how physicians and teachers respond to time constraints and pressures. Yet between the two groups there are enough similarities—being accountable to the specific population served as well as to institutions or organizations—to render comparisons between physicians and teachers appropriate.

The Nature of Physician and Teacher Responsibility

As one might expect, both the physicians and the teachers cited a type of responsibility that is informed by the traditional aims of their respective professions. The physicians discussed responsibility for putting patients above all else as part of their mission to solve health problems and alleviate suffering. The teachers talked about responsibility for imparting to students the knowledge and associated skills pertaining to various subject areas, such as math, English, and the sciences.

But the physicians and teachers also mentioned a second type of responsibility that was somewhat less expected. This form of responsibility has to do with enabling patients and students to realize their full potential and flourish, psychologically speaking. Acting on this sense of responsibility requires taking into account a patient's or student's goals, background, and values. The physicians and teachers emphasized that it is inappropriate to impose predetermined notions of optimal development on those they serve. Only through careful listening and observation can one discern what truly matters to a person. This focus on patients' and students' perspectives is in line with philosopher Anthony Appiah's (2005) concept of *ethical individualism* (adapted from the writings of John Stuart Mill), whereby people are granted the autonomy to pursue life projects that are meaningful and fulfilling, as long as the well-being of the larger community is not compromised.

The Nature of Time Constraints

The primary time constraint cited by physicians emanates from policies imposed by managed care insurers, hospitals, and medical practices. These policies stipulate that more patients must be seen per hour by decreasing the amount of time spent with each patient. The standard amount of time allotted for a patient visit is now fifteen minutes. The overriding rationale for restricting physician-patient contact is often couched in the euphemistic term *efficiency,* which actually means pursuing ever-higher levels of revenue. The problem is well-documented in the research literature (see, for example, Davidoff, 1997; Dugdale, Epstein, & Pantilat, 1999; Fuchs and Emanuel, 2005; Grembowski et al., 2002; Landon, Reschovsky, & Blumenthal, 2003; Linzer et al., 2000; Ludmerer, 1999; Reed, Vratil, Stoddard, & Hargraves, 2001; Safran, 2003; Woo, 2006) and even in the popular media:, limiting the duration of office visits often does not allow sufficient time to address a patient's full medical and psychosocial needs. After all, human disease and symptomatology do not obey the arbitrary timetables established by insurance companies or hospital administrators. Although in some cases fifteen minutes is more than enough time—to diagnose an ear infection, for example—in many other instances it is wholly inadequate. There is widespread evidence that both physicians and patients are unsatisfied with this arrangement. The question becomes, then, How can physicians meet their full responsibilities to patients when the very structure of their work is in many respects antithetical to providing optimal care?

It is particularly striking that even though physicians have the financial means to pay for child care and to take care of other domestic matters, they are still greatly frustrated by the lack of time they are afforded to carry out their professional work. This frustration speaks to the great extent to which managed care has shaped the very nature of physicians' work.

But teachers, as we will see, have fewer resources for outsourcing domestic matters to third parties, a situation that accounts in part for their expressed need to draw clear boundaries between work and home. In other words, teachers need to get home to take care of the very types of responsibilities that physicians often can afford to pay someone else to address.

The teachers spoke repeatedly about the overwhelming time demands of their work and about the threats these demands pose to their personal and family time. In the popular imagination, teaching is often depicted as an undemanding and luxurious job—relatively short official school hours, summer vacations, and the like. But the reality for most teachers is quite different. Preparing for thoughtful and thorough lessons, attending to the learning and developmental needs of often troubled individual students (and the concerns of their families), participating in compulsory school meetings and various professional development programs, grading and assessing student work, and being involved in student extracurricular activities, among other things, together make an all-consuming experience, in terms of both time and emotions. In addition, teachers are accountable to multiple constituencies beyond their students, including fellow teachers, school administrators, parents, the community at large, the district administration, and the state. In other words, this array of pressures makes it very challenging for teachers to achieve a sense of alignment between their own goals and those of the various stakeholders in the education arena.

Summers offer little relief because many teachers use the time away from the classroom to plan for the upcoming year, to attend required continuing education courses, or in some cases, to take on temporary work in an unrelated field to make up for relatively low teachers' pay. In districts with fewer financial and infrastructure resources, the demands and strains placed on teachers are intensified. The conditions of teachers' work in combination with threats posed to their personal and family time can lead to the phenomenon of teacher burnout, which in turn increases the likelihood that teachers will leave the profession (Black, 2003; Moore Johnson and Birkeland, 2003; Peske, Lui, Moore Johnson, Kauffman, & Kardos, 2001; Woods and Weasmer, 2002). Furthermore, when teachers are burned out, their capacity to meet their responsibilities to students is obviously diminished.

To set the stage for understanding how physicians and teachers manage time demands and constraints, I turn first to a more detailed examination of the pressures bearing down on these two groups of professionals.

Physician Time Constraints

The one time constraint that applies to nearly all of the internists and OB-GYNs, regardless of type of medical practice, is insurance-mandated limitations on how much time is to be spent consulting with patients during office visits. One OB-GYN commented that such restrictions have changed the very nature of clinical encounters from focusing on long-term prevention and well-being to responding only to problems presented by the patient. She explained:

> The reimbursement schedule is such that you have to see a lot of patients. You can't just spend time talking to patients, as you used to be able to do. That [insurance policies] cuts a lot into the doctor-patient relationship. I started practice back when you could spend more time with a patient, do more of a complete evaluation of the patient, not just a problem-oriented [one]. Now it's very problem oriented.

The inability to spend time talking with patients is an enormous source of frustration for physicians, for two reasons. First, internists and OB-GYNs hold the conviction that much of what ails their patients can be discerned from a well-crafted clinical interview in which patient attitudes and behavioral patterns provide clues to the nature of the presenting symptoms. This more subjective realm of patients is referred to as the *psychosocial dimension* of illness and well-being; there is ample evidence that the onset and course of many symptoms is influenced by how patients lead and think about their lives, as well as by the environments in which they spend their time.

The second reason that physicians lament restrictions on interactions with patients is because they have found such relationships to be deeply meaningful. Nearly all of the physicians explained that they became clinicians to begin with because of the tremendous satisfaction derived from having ongoing relationships with patients, being part of their lives, addressing their concerns over time, watching their children grow, and so on. To take away time spent cultivating the doctor-patient relationship is to be left with medical facts alone, a prospect that is unappealing to physicians.

In addition to the time constraints imposed by insurers, some physicians face group-practice policies that dictate how much time is to be spent with patients. An internist who works in a large hospital-based practice commented that

> medicine has changed so dramatically over the past ten years, twenty years, in terms of, not just in terms of managed care and sort of pushing in. We obviously don't control our days the way [we did] twenty years ago. Even in this practice you would have had forty minutes to see patients, at least, or more if you needed it. I don't get that. I can force a forty-minute time slot, but then I lose revenue. So, in other

words, it is split into RVUs, relative value units. And I get report cards essentially every three months telling me where I am in terms of where I should be.

It's a very interesting way of looking at your life, in relative value units. And the things I do that are important to me, like spending a little bit more time with the ninety-five-year-old patient who's struggling with X, there are no relative value units that our society or our sort of business, hospital infrastructure, assigns to that. I don't get points for that. I get points with me for that, and I get points with the patient and the family, but I get points taken away for spending that time, and that's very frustrating in this day and age.

This is the first year where the practice has decided there are a certain number of RVUs that you need to meet; if you go below it, you lose salary. . . . So you're competing, you're almost working against yourself sometimes. So I have twelve patients scheduled in a four-hour session. If two people don't come, on the one hand it gives me a little bit more time with some of the other people, but I'm losing salary.

This physician has highlighted a commonly cited frustration: the erosion of professional autonomy. Indeed, as Schindler and colleagues (2006) have documented, physicians in academic medicine—such as the one just quoted—are increasingly facing pressures from institutions to bring in more revenue by seeing more patients per hour. But if physicians are not supported to take the time to make decisions about what patients need without having to endure reductions in income, then who will serve the best interests of patients? Of all the professions, medicine has the longest-lasting and most involved training, all geared toward the goal of developing the specialized knowledge and highly refined skills to treat illness, relieve suffering, and promote health. Group-practice administrators or other agents do not possess such training and therefore are not in a position to evaluate what is best for patients.

Related to the time restrictions imposed by group practices, some physicians interviewed discussed the additional burden of institutional policies that either discourage or penalize time spent with patients. An internist in a large teaching hospital provided the following example:

I was in the emergency room admitting this patient and I wanted to admit her under my name to cardiology because I know her well. However, the way she could be seen the fastest is not to admit her under my name but instead to admit her to the cardiology service because there are some barriers to how quickly people will be seen, which seems sort of silly. By the way, if I do that, then I can't charge for the time I just spent [consulting] with her. . . . I would not be compensated for that time. . . . A lot of the things that I think are very important aren't compensated.

If she comes into the hospital and goes to cardiac catheterization and needs a surgical procedure, to get all that done, it's a win-win-win. If she comes in and it turns out that she doesn't need the cardiac cath, and it's actually her knees and her shoulders, then that's a financial loss for the institution because she took up a bed of somebody else that could be there. And then the right thing to do is to get her home as quickly as possible, which is what she wants, but then it's going to make it more difficult for me to do what I think her knees need. However, if I can get her onto the surgical service to get her knees operated on, then it's a win for the institution.

So, in other words, at the moment, the way the payment systems work, procedures or surgeries are highly compensated. Thought and discussion and reassurance are not compensated. That's the whole medical system at the moment, and on a daily basis I do battle with that and try to ignore that and work with it.

In this example, then, institutional policies explicitly dissuade physicians from attending to the "softer" realms of care—time spent consulting with patients—and reward them instead for routing patients toward more lucrative medical procedures.

Indeed, another physician based in the same hospital noted that she has been under a great deal of pressure from top-level administrators to create a "concierge" practice whereby services are provided only to "members" who pay high fees in exchange for complete physician attention. But this shift would mean that those from the physician's current case load who are unable to pay such fees—and most of them would not be able to do so—would no longer have access to the physician. And although this physician has thus far resisted the hospital's pressure on ethical grounds, administrators have let their values be known: increase revenue at the expense of the needs of the majority of patients.

Teacher Time Demands

When it comes to the teachers in the study, many used vivid metaphors to convey the tremendous time demands they face. As one teacher noted, "Time restrictions: your day, you're all over the place. And there are a lot of demands. Everybody's taking a chunk out of you. And sooner or later there aren't any chunks left."

Another teacher cited planning student fieldtrips as just one example of the time consumed by the tasks involved in teaching:

> To get through field trip permission slips and finding a bus and finding money to have all this happen is a mountain of paperwork and a mountain of time when I know that field trips are the best thing for the students to do. And it really starts to push and pull me around a little bit because time is just not elastic. I don't have time to do all of the up-front work that the district wants for a field trip to be insured and okay, and yet I know that it's the most important thing for the students.

Yet another teacher, who also has sports coaching responsibilities, talked about his sense of always being on the go, with no reprieve:

> My life is so busy; I just go boom, boom, boom. I get here at 6:15 in the morning and I'll get home at 9:30 at night because of [coaching] sports, and then grade papers and then go to bed. And then boom, I'm up the next day. I'm just constantly on the go. You just get used to being run down and spread so thin, and it's been like this for twenty years, I guess. I'm just like, "I'm ready to retire."

Finally, one teacher commented that despite having a period set aside during the day for planning, her work life is all-consuming:

> We're given free time, prep time, which is why I was so adamant about my prep time. I can't lose a free period because I can't afford to. I spend every second. I don't even like to stand and talk to people in the hallways and be sociable anymore because I'm thinking, "Oh, my God, I've got all those reports to do. I've got papers to correct. I've got to create, I've got to do a lesson or make a test up".

I discerned at least two reasons why teachers seek to maintain strict boundaries between work and home life. First, they spoke of the pleasure derived from pursuing personal interests or spending time with family. They mentioned the enjoyment of hobbies such as reading, writing, and playing music, or simply being with spouses and children. One teacher even noted that he resents his work when he feels he's giving more to his students than to his own children.

A second reason for preserving personal or family time is because spending quality time beyond work is rejuvenating, thereby enabling teachers to approach their jobs with reduced levels of psychological stress as well as a broader perspective on work. In the face of the time demands of teaching, then, involvement in other activities serves as an important counterbalance.

Strategies for Managing Time Constraints and Demands

For both teachers and physicians, the ability to manage time constraints and demands effectively represents more than simply coping with perceived burdens. Developing creative strategies regarding time is a means of acting on the responsibilities that teachers and physicians believe they have for the well-being of students and patients, respectively. By establishing sharp boundaries between work and home, teachers not only make time for the things that matter to them in their personal lives, but they also preserve the downtime they need to ward off burnout and therefore approach teaching from a perspective of renewal (J. W. Gardner, 1981). Physicians resist the limits imposed on patient visits precisely because of their conviction that such restrictions are not in the best interests of patients. The inability to spend the necessary amount of time addressing patient concerns is an affront to physicians' very notions of what it means to be a doctor, as well as to their views of the responsibilities that the profession of medicine has for those it serves.

So how do these professionals manage time constraints and demands in order to serve the needs of patients and students?

Physician Strategies

The most common time-management strategy for physicians is simply to take the time they deem necessary to help patients, despite the known financial consequences of exceeding permissible limits. Most of these physicians expressed a willingness to earn less money as a result of seeing fewer patients per hour. For example, an internist who works in a large hospital-based practice makes it a habit to visit her patients in the hospital. Such visits are not billable to insurance companies and therefore are not compensated. But this physician follows up on her patients in the hospital because she believes her responsibility for them does not end once they have left her office. Here's how she conceives her role:

> When my patients get admitted, which they do three or four times a week, I follow them into the hospital, which is not the routine at all anymore for an internist. . . . I ultimately think [that] when somebody is in the hospital, it makes a big difference to have their doctor there.

You know, it's playing a role and it is sort of leading the team. And I actually think that the care is better so it is something that I have chosen to do and continue to do.

This internist went on to explain that her practice of seeing patients in the hospital can have unexpected rewards. She cites the example of one hospitalized patient whom she wouldn't have expected to express appreciation for being visited in the hospital:

> She's very professorial. She's gotten mad at me in the past. We've had a very good relationship in many ways. We've sort of gotten through stuff. I'm proud of that relationship. But when I went to her bedside for all of five minutes, she was genuinely, overwhelmingly appreciative that I was there, and I didn't do anything but come and visit and talk to her for a little bit and sort of tell her what was going to [happen]. So for me, that brings value because I feel like I really made a difference. And that's nice, feeling like you made a difference.

For many professionals who are accustomed to conceptualizing their work as an exchange of time for money this example might prove somewhat perplexing. One might argue that because the hospital is already staffed by many capable doctors who will check on the status of the patient, it is a better use of the internist's time to remain in her office, where she can see more patients (and therefore meet their needs) while earning more money.

But when we look more closely, it becomes clear that there is more than money to be considered in the internist's decision to visit patients in the hospital. First, she believes that patient care is better when she is able to check up on her patients in the hospital. Other physicians interviewed for our study made the same observation. As capable as hospital physicians might be, there is no substitute for the knowledge that a primary care doctor has about a patient's medical history and about the particular qualities of the patient that might affect the course of treatment.

Second, the internist in this example speaks of the great personal rewards accrued from knowing that she has gone out of her way to help patients. The satisfaction of "making a difference," as she calls it, is the very reason that she, like many of the other physicians in our study, chose to enter the profession of medicine. This more intangible and yet important quality regarding the meaningfulness of the internist's work outweighs the extra income that would have been generated from seeing more patients in her office.

To point to another example, an OB-GYN doctor noted that she takes the time necessary to serve patients despite pressures from the hospital that employs her to generate increasing revenue. She commented that the mission of her practice is to

> [go] overboard with compassionate care, which is really important to me. To me that means giving patients the time that's necessary. We don't run a factory here. We don't run patients in and out of here every ten to fifteen minutes. The day that I need to do that I will leave medicine. I just will not do that. I'd rather take a hit financially, if I need to, than become that kind of a patient mill. Being able to sit down and talk to my patients is really, really important for my job satisfaction, and also to provide good care, as far as I'm concerned.

Lest one have the mistaken notion that talking to patients is merely a "feel-good" exercise with little bearing on patient well-being, this OB-GYN went on to explain how time taken to listen to patients' life stories reveals key clues for addressing serious problems:

> I think the kinds of questions that you ask people about their life and about their family and how their marriage is, how their job is, that you may not get from other physicians, is a really important part. . . . And often those kinds of questions will really lead down the path of marital difficulties that they're having, or an abuse situation that they're involved with, or problems with their kids. I'm not a social worker, and I'm not here to solve those problems. I feel that I'm here to sort of screen for those kinds of problems and get them the help that they need. And that's what I do, try to get them the help that they need.

As with the example of the internist cited earlier, this OB-GYN spoke to the relationship between taking time with patients and the satisfaction she derives from doing so, as well as its positive effects on the course of patient care. But *patient care* here means something much broader than is customarily conceptualized in medicine. Although there have been some important developments in medical education in recent years, illness is still by and large thought of among physicians as emanating from discrete physiological processes. This OB-GYN, however, like so many of the other physicians in our study, thinks more broadly about patient well-being. In this view, a patient's psychological well-being is just as important to consider as his or her physical state. Physical abuse, for example, might have a negative impact on a woman's ability to maintain proper gynecological health. And in worst-case scenarios, abuse might itself be the cause of gynecological problems.

Restructuring Medical Practices in Response to Time Demands

What stands out about the pattern we have seen thus far is that physicians make time for patients *despite* prevailing disincentives to do so. Some physicians, however, spoke of another, more dramatic strategy for managing time constraints. These physicians, although relatively few in number, have altered the structure and overall functioning of their practices to make it easier to spend time with patients. More specifically, physicians in this group have created concierge practices and devised regimens based on the notion of the continuity of care.

It is worthwhile to examine these cases of practice restructuring. First, as increasing numbers of physicians have become frustrated with the constraints of practicing medicine, those who are establishing alternative practice formats can be seen as pioneers who are potential bellwethers for the future direction of the profession. Indeed, the consensus among physicians at large, as well as among health care policymakers, is that the current managed care system is becoming untenable. Calls to change how medicine is structured, practiced, and reimbursed are on the rise. But the unresolved and staggeringly complex question at this point is, what new system should be put in its place? The examples offered by those in our study suggest some possible options to consider.

At the same time, one needs to consider potential negative implications of these restructuring efforts for both doctors and patients. For physicians, as for anyone who attempts to launch a new way of conducting business, there is no guarantee that the intended results—serving patients well, continuing to feel satisfied with their work, and earning a sufficient livelihood—will materialize. For example, the physicians interviewed spoke about the legislative threats looming over their concierge practices as well as about the outcry they have had to endure from fellow physicians who are opposed on ethical grounds to such practices.

There are risks to patients too. Most obviously, patients who do not have the financial means to pay the typically steep membership fees for concierge practices are shut out from the opportunity to obtain the thorough medical care afforded to more affluent patients. But patient risks are not limited to concierge practices. One internist who runs a community health center that provides continuity of care for its patients described the challenges of remaining financially solvent due to the reluctance of insurers to pay for this model of care. If the practice cannot sustain this model of care, its patients will be on the losing end. When taken together, then, the risks posed to patients and physicians by alternative practice structures points to the challenges of breaking free from the dominant paradigm.

So how do alternative practice structures enable physicians to spend the time they deem necessary with patients? Two of the internists we interviewed had taken the dramatic step of creating concierge practices. As already noted, this model—which has come into existence only within the past few years—limits most of its patient slots to those who pay a high annual membership fee (although for both of the concierge practices included in our study 10 percent of the slots are reserved for reduced or waived fees). In exchange for the fee, patients can expect that visits will not be rushed (and therefore will be thorough), that doctors will be accessible by phone at any time for questions and consultations, and that there will be no limit to the number of visits per year.

As a testament to the privilege of belonging to such a practice, the decor of both of the concierge practices we visited was relatively upscale. In one practice in particular, the waiting room resembled a spa more than a medical office, with soothing lighting and colors, quality artwork on the walls, expensive coffee-table books on display, and complimentary healthy snacks available. In other words, the message communicated by these practices is that patients' needs and feelings come first, medical functionality comes second.

Both of the concierge physicians (internists) worked in traditional medical practices before striking out on their own. They both cited long-term frustrations with the burdens of excessive patient caseloads and constraints on providing care as the bases for starting concierge practices. But what does concierge practice offer that a traditional practice cannot? Both physicians spoke about, more than anything else, the freedom to offer patients generous amounts of time and attention, which is precisely what they believe good doctoring is in the first place. Here is how one of the physicians described her availability to patients:

> There are a lot of novel solutions that I think are possible in this kind of practice. I've made house calls. I am a runner. I love running. . . . There have been a couple times where people called me and I was running. I was like, "I really do want to [see] you but I'm in my running clothes, is that OK?" So I've met them here at the office in my running clothes, which I wouldn't have ever done before [in previous type of practice]. I had someone [for whom] I made a house call and I actually made it in my running clothes because I was, like, "Well, I'm out here now." And he really needed to see me. I wanted to see that ulcer that he has on his butt. And so I said, "I'm going to stop by, but I'm probably sort of smelly because I was out running, but this is the only time I can really do it right now."

This physician, like the other concierge practitioner in our study, does not experience such interruptions in her personal routine as burdens because her caseload is very small (roughly three hundred patients). She derives great pleasure from attending to patients' needs in a manner that accords with her vision of a good doctor. As she went on to say, she would not have gone to such lengths to see patients in her previous, more traditional practice, precisely because the costs, both financial and other, would have been unacceptably high.

As mentioned earlier, one of the physicians in our study—an internist—created a practice that emphasizes continuity of care. In contrast to the typical internal medicine practice, which passes patients off to specialists or other facilities with little follow-up, this physician offers continuing care to patients beyond the walls of her office. Here is how she explained the concept of care continuity:

> What we've done is developed a house calls program where nurse practitioners and physicians work in pairs and go out and see patients at home. One of the common themes throughout the practice, my practice and the entire group practice, is this idea that [although] you see people in the office, people you see over time at a certain point may become too frail. And so if they get to a point where it's too difficult for them to come into the practice or, for instance, you can't optimally care for them because you don't really see the whole picture, I mean you see them in the office, you don't really know how they're taking their medications, or you really don't know how physically they're managing, there comes a time when it makes more sense to deliver their care at home.
>
> For us viscerally we always feel as if when somebody who has been in our practice we know really well gets sick and is in the hospital, what a terrible time to hand their care over to somebody else, that's when they really need somebody who knows what their house looks like, knows what their baseline function is, knows what the bigger picture is of what is and isn't a safe discharge because of who may or may not be present to support in the household. So we see them at home. And then if, for example, they need to go to a nursing home for rehab or long-term, we then also have the ability to follow our patients there. So for us that feels very much like the right way to take care of people, because too often what happens when people are sick is they just get bounced from one setting to another and their medical history becomes a series of black boxes and no one ever really knows them. And it's a very scary thing, especially for people with a lot of problems. So that's

> why we like doing it the way we do it. . . . And it's unfortunately a
> model of care that is a nightmare to sustain financially. All of it loses
> money, but it's also addictive.

As described by this physician, time takes on a whole new meaning. Patients can expect that care will not be limited to clinical encounters in the office but will extend instead to home or other facilities when necessary. Access to physicians in this practice, then, is broader and deeper than in most internal medicine practices.

Teacher Strategies

The teachers in our research sample spoke of two strategies for managing the time demands of their work. First, teachers draw strict boundaries between their school life and their home and personal lives to enable them to spend time with family or by themselves, without the intrusion of work demands. (As Barendsen emphasizes in Chapter Eight of this volume, creating school-home boundaries is not always easy to do.) Second, some teachers use their time away from school to engage in hobbies or other activities that they describe as rejuvenating. Teachers reported that a feeling of rejuvenation is necessary for enabling them to maintain a reservoir of motivation for doing their work. It is important to emphasize, however, that the stress that teachers place on life outside of teaching does not mean they leave the school building the moment the afternoon dismissal bell rings. Quite to the contrary, many teachers noted that they stay long after students depart in order to get work done so there is less need to bring work home. For example, one teacher said:

> I've learned to get as much done here as I can—lesson plans, getting
> work ready for tomorrow, next week, grading, getting the grades done,
> putting them onto the computer here—getting everything done as much
> as I can while I'm here in the building so that I'm not doing it at home,
> so that when I get home I have time to play with my son. . . . If I need
> to look at my things at night, not until he's in bed. I don't bring it out
> at all just because that's our time, and the time with my husband too,
> but he doesn't get home as early. That's just a major contributing factor,
> and especially on the weekends. I like to be able to call it a weekend for
> me too, not just the students. And on breaks, if I don't give them home-
> work, I certainly don't want homework. So I really try and get it done
> here like a normal person who has a nine-to-five job.

Another teacher echoed the sentiment of wishing to preserve weekends for personal and family pursuits. In addition, she noted that she had adjusted her expectations of how much work to produce within given amounts of time:

> So I think just using, trying to find a way to use the time that I'm in this school in the best way is the only thing that will help. But I have, like on Saturdays, now I refuse to do work, because before I used to take it with me. And I guess also just realizing I can only do so much, so if we take a test today, they want it back the next period. And before, I was just like, "Oh, I have to get this done for tomorrow," but now I realize, "You'll get it in a couple of days," or "You'll get it when you get it."

In some cases teachers commented that preserving a strict boundary between work and home is necessary for meeting pressing family concerns. As one teacher explained,

> And at home, I have a twenty-five-year-old who still lives at home, but he works in Boston. I take him to the train station at 5:40, and then I have a thirteen-year-old who I have to make sure is ready to get on the bus as soon as I leave. And my husband, he leaves about the same time I do. I also have my ninety-year-old mother living with us who's got Alzheimer's, so I have to make sure that she has everything set, ready to go, and she's got some instructions written down, her lunch is made, and notes saying, "You have to find it in the refrigerator," because otherwise she'll forget to eat or she'll just raid the cookie jar. I have to hide the cookies and candy on her sometimes.

> I come home late at night too because I like to get most of my work done at the building, so I stay very late. Very often I don't leave here until 4:30 or 5:00 because if I get home and it's "Help me [with] the homework," or my mother is stuck with something because of her Alzheimer's, and then my husband comes home late because he's also a teacher but he is a music teacher, so he does after-school instrumental lessons, so he comes home very late.

Teachers spoke of an array of hobbies and activities that serve as a source of rejuvenation for their work, including knitting, traveling, performing music, and exercising.[1] Without such opportunities for what John W. Gardner (1981) called "self-renewal," teachers stated that they would

---

[1]These findings accord with other research carried out as part of the GoodWork Project. Journalists, biologists, and jazz musicians spoke at great length about the importance of rejuvenating activities that had a positive impact on their work. For more on this idea, see Morway, Solomon, Michaelson, & Gardner, 1998.

be at greater risk for succumbing to burnout. As an example, one teacher described the routine he has instituted for clearing his mind and relaxing:

> Recently I learned about the importance of balance in all things. . . . Yes, I have a little book, and I set personal and professional goals each week, and at the end of the week I assess the extent to which those goals were reflected. I also have a little pie chart that says what I'm going to focus on this week professionally and personally.
>
> For example, music is a part of my life, and it centers me, and it was getting pushed aside because of [his sixteen-month-old] baby and because of stuff. And I said, "I need thirty minutes a day, and I'm going to play. I'm going to go downstairs and I'm going to practice my guitar, and I'm not taking grading home or on vacations anymore." It was those sorts of things, trying to really differentiate between the personal and professional.
>
> There are also mental things that you do. You learn and you train yourself. I said earlier, "not to sweat the small stuff," but that takes constant repetition, or to remind yourself. Some people call it *The Serenity Prayer*: Let me change the things I can change and let go of the things I can't change. There's a lot of stuff at school that I can't change, and I've got to let go of it. One of the things I decided three years ago was I am not chasing kids in the hall down anymore for behavioral issues; I'm just not, because it's making me bitter and unhappy. . . . And I'm just going to let it go. . . . And I try really hard not to bring the classroom home. It's like: How do I cope?

Another teacher cited combining many activities as a strategy for gaining perspective on her work and provided needed rejuvenation:

> I exercise regularly. I go to the gym. . . . You may have thought I was being corny when I said it, but I would try to stop at the Hallmark store before I'd pick up my own children, to just read cards, to try to help me to calm down a little bit, so that I didn't take things out on my own children. I try to laugh. I try to find humor. . . . And I try to travel a lot. I try to let me clear my head. Lying on a cliff on the edge of the ocean in Ireland last year just gave me a chance to just be free of lots of things, and school being a big part of that.
>
> But trying to just, I mean, daily I go to the gym, daily. I've started knitting again, to just give me a spot of time to just be me, I guess, and to think, and to relax a little bit. But then the travel and bigger things at the end of the year, to try to, or during the year. Just try to

get away and gather my thoughts and try to move back and take on another day. And some days are harder than others. Some days you need more Hallmark cards to read than other days, or more time at the gym. But just trying to soothe yourself a little bit.

As a final example, yet another teacher spoke of the importance of exercise, but with a somewhat different emphasis. As she noted, finding pockets of silence is especially valuable:

> I exercise a lot. Yes, I really do, that's the thing for me. I work out a ton and I just need it to decompress. I ran a marathon last year to just let go. I needed three hours of running, no music, no students, silence. I need silence after being in such a loud, constant talking, and I'm incredibly social and incredibly talky, and normally I would go out with my friends and shoot the shit and talk a lot. But because this is such an intensive, constantly, when you're talking, you're thinking and you're not reflecting as much, but you're just going, you're just producing, you're responding, you're listening. I need some quiet, quiet time to read a book, to make dinner, I need quiet.

Discussion

How can the differences between teachers' and physicians' uses of time be explained? In other words, why do physicians respond to the time constraints they face by spending more time with patients, while teachers deal with their time demands by drawing a line between the personal and the professional? Answers to these questions emerge when three levels of analysis are taken into account for both professions: the domain (the profession), the field (bodies of practitioners who establish professional policies and procedures), and individual workers (Csikszentmihalyi, 1998; Gardner, 1994).

Physicians

THE DOMAIN. The domain of medicine has been characterized, since its establishment as a profession, by an ideal of patient care that is informed by scientific excellence and attention to the whole patient. Indeed, one of the reasons managed care has caused such a stir among physicians and the public at large is the perception that economic dictates and time restrictions threaten to undermine the enduring ideals of the profession. Although it would be foolish to overromanticize medicine in the pre-managed-career (there were plenty of MDs whose bedside manner was less than exemplary), the consensus among older physicians and scholars of the profession is that there has been a significant qualitative shift in how medicine is practiced and how patients are cared for.

The physicians interviewed for our research revealed an unwavering commitment to the ideals of their profession. In fact, in their own words, many decided to become an MD because of the opportunity it would afford to blend science and caring for the "whole patient." When these physicians are confronted with the choice of either adhering to new time and economic policies or not complying and enduring the resulting consequences, the ideals of the domain figure prominently in their minds as they decide to buck the system. In other words, the domain's ideals serve as a moral compass of sorts for guiding physician behavior.

THE FIELD. The choices that physicians make to spend time with patients beyond what is allotted in managed care or institutional policies can also be traced to certain features of the field of medicine. Specifically, how medical students are acculturated into their profession, especially during internship and residency, leaves its mark on them regarding the role of time in patient care. As is well known, internship and residency are defined by an extremely long work week. Until a mandated eighty-hour work week was imposed a couple of years ago (which by most people's standards is still a long week!), it was not uncommon for interns and residents to log more than one hundred hours a week. Although many of the physicians interviewed for our research acknowledged the hardships that they and their peers endured while in training, they also spoke of the value of such intensive immersion in the direct care of patients. The experience of giving so much time to the profession in one's early years apparently has instilled in physicians a conception of time that is open-ended and for the primary purpose of serving patients. Ironically, even in this era of managed care, internship and residency continue to be defined by long hours spent primarily in a hospital setting.[2] In other words, medical students typically are not introduced to the time restrictions they will face upon completing their training.

---

[2]Some physicians we interviewed complained that this model of training is out of step with the realities of practicing medicine. First, spending so much time in a hospital does not give students enough exposure to the outpatient settings where the majority of patients currently seek care. Second, hospital patients often suffer from problems that are unusual and therefore not broadly represented in the larger patient population.

A second feature of the field of medicine must be taken into account. Notably, many of the physicians we interviewed hold academic positions. This means that part of their official job responsibilities is to teach students by giving lectures or providing direct clinical instruction and to carry out various administrative functions. An academic position is salaried and, as a result, a reliable stream of income puts less pressure on physicians to generate revenue exclusively through patient consultations. Furthermore, because there is less pressure to see more patients, physicians can take more time with individual patients than do their colleagues who devote 100 percent of their time to clinical work.

THE INDIVIDUAL. The influence of domain ideals regarding patient care, as well as the manner in which physicians are acculturated into their profession, provides the backdrop against which individual practitioners come to understand what it means to be a physician. Following from this, physicians develop and refine a repertoire of dispositions and behaviors that they view as being in accordance with the meaning and purpose they impute to their professional role. Put another way, physicians have clearly articulated notions of a professional identity.

More than an abstraction, identity is a phenomenon that emerges and is reinforced in ongoing, lived contexts. Psychologist Jerome Bruner has noted that such contexts "are always *contexts of practice*: it is always necessary to ask what people are *doing* or *trying* to do in that context" (1990, p. 118) in order to grasp what a person's identity might be. The "contexts of practice" for the physicians are spending time with patients and attending to the psychosocial dimensions of well-being and illness. Indeed, not having a well-formulated identity would leave physicians without a blueprint for action.

Clearly, given the state of affairs in medicine these days, there is an ever-increasing risk that physicians' identities will be eclipsed altogether by restrictions on how they practice. In fact, several of the physicians noted that they see little or no room for further compromise, precisely because they are not willing to eschew the professional identities that give meaning and purpose to their work. The ultimate risk, many noted, is having to leave the profession.

Teachers

The factors that influence teachers' responses to the demands of time—namely, making sharp distinctions between work and home—differ significantly from the factors that shape physicians' responses to time constraints. First, in the profession of education there is little consensus about a domain ideal. Although some educational philosophies and practices are well-known and have attracted a following, there is not the same degree of consensus on how best to teach arithmetic, for example, as there is in medicine on diagnosing and treating strep throat. If anything, individual teachers and principals have the reputation of selecting their own guiding theories of education on the basis of little more than the idea that it feels right on an intuitive level. To the extent that teachers can be said to share a domain ideal, it is the notion that they understand their purpose to be helping children learn.

When it comes to the field, there is nearly as much variation in the substance and rigor across schools of education as there are theories. Some schools of education grant master's degrees in one year while others require two years of coursework. Furthermore, some schools of education are known for a rather lightweight curriculum while others insist on greater rigor. And once one has graduated, it is remarkably easy in some states to obtain certification while in others the process is more involved. There are also plenty of cases when a bachelor's degree alone is sufficient to enter the classroom.

Having said all this, however, there is a notable feature of the field of education that does influence the patterns of teacher behavior I have been describing. Most public school teachers, unlike physicians, are unionized workers. This means that teachers have contractual agreements concerning the number of hours they are to work, how long they are required to be in the school building, and so on. Although I am not asserting that belonging to unions is the principal factor shaping teachers' responses to time demands, it is a contributing factor. Because teachers are relatively low-paid professionals, and because of the seemingly endless demands placed on teachers, unions exist to protect them from being exploited. Inevitably, viewing one's work through the lens of a contract that is designed to protect a teacher's time is bound to shape one's sense of how to demarcate boundaries between work and home.

Physicians, as we saw, have well-articulated senses of professional identity that are drawn in large measure from domain ideals and that inform their "contexts of practice." But what about teachers, whose domain lacks an agreed-upon and enduring set of ideals? My view is that teachers too have strong professional identities to anchor their work, but of a somewhat different type than doctors have. On the one hand, teachers' identities are shaped by education theories and practices that they find particularly appealing. However, on the other hand, because of the fragmented nature of the domain, teachers bolster their identities by drawing on aspects of their personal and family life. This situation explains in part why teachers impose clearer boundaries between work and home than physicians do. For teachers, meaning and purpose are derived more evenly from the spheres of work and home. Therefore, it makes sense that teachers strive to preserve personal and family time; this realm of experience accounts to a significant extent for how they understand who they are. Physicians reference the importance of home much less because their identities are tied more directly to a clear domain ideal.

Conclusion

Despite the differences between teachers and physicians when it comes to how time pressures and demands are managed, a key similarity is important to emphasize. Notably, both physicians and teachers in my sample responded to time challenges by resisting them rather than unhappily complying. My view is that this resistance is not a mere matter of preference; rather, physicians and teachers are exercising their professional autonomy to the extent possible to act on their senses of responsibility to patients and students, respectively. Physicians resist the amount of time allotted per patient visit in order to best serve their patients. Teachers resist having work encroach on valuable personal or family time so that they can replenish themselves, tend to their sense of who they are, and ultimately meet their perceived responsibilities to students.

Given that both medicine and teaching are facing intensifying pressures, however, it is unclear how long the strategies for managing time that I have discussed will be sufficient for helping physicians and teachers put into practice their senses of responsibility to those they serve. After all, there is only so much that individual professionals can do. Ultimately the problems plaguing medicine and education are complex and structural. In the end, righting these professions for the benefit of patients and students will require large-scale and well-thought-out systemic reforms.

In American society, talk of systemic reform is often assumed to be equated with *regulation,* a concept that has taken on increasingly negative connotations over the past generation. Although there are many reasons that Americans—especially those of a conservative political ilk—are uneasy with systemic reform, perhaps the most salient of these reasons is the fear that cherished individual liberties will be quashed under the homogenizing policies of governmental agencies or other powerful organizations. But this need not be the case.

Systemic reform can be accomplished in part by the members of the professional organizations that directly serve medicine and public school teaching. Organizations such as the American Medical Association (AMA) and the National Education Association (NEA) are important vehicles for addressing the needs and concerns of physicians and teachers, respectively. Several years ago the AMA recognized the deleterious effects of residents' working excessive hours. The AMA responded by introducing a new policy that prohibits residents from working more than eighty hours per week.[3]

Although both the AMA and the NEA have been the target of much criticism from their respective constituents as well as from observers, individual physicians and teachers can, by virtue of their membership in these organizations, take the initiative to work toward bringing about changes. Of course doing so is not easy or straightforward. Indeed, for those whose efforts are not rewarded, the option remains—in line with the spirit of American entrepreneurship—to found alternative professional organizations. The very plethora of physician and teacher organizations speaks to such possibilities.

But systemic reform, in my view, cannot be accomplished without some form of governmental involvement. Lest this notion set off alarm bells in the minds of some readers, it is useful to step outside the typically held assumption that governmental policy is diametrically opposed to the interests of individuals. Consider that medicine and teaching are unique among the professions because of the degree to which they touch our entire citizenry. Indeed, a person does not have a chance to activate individual initiative without the proper education or requisite state of health. Seen from this view, governmental policies regarding how physicians are compensated (doing away with the restrictions of managed care), on the one hand, and the amount of compensation earned by teachers (paying teachers much more), on the other, could go a long way toward serving these professionals and, by extension, the individuals—all of us—served by medicine and education.

---

[3]This has not been uncontroversial. Some of the physicians interviewed for the GoodWork Project argued that capping resident hours threatens patient care by removing the physician most familiar with particular cases.

REFERENCES

Appiah, A. (2005). *The ethics of identity.* Princeton, NJ: Princeton University Press.

Black, S. (2003). Stressed out in the classroom. *American School Board Journal, 190*(10), 36–38.

Bruner, J. (1990). *Acts of meaning.* Cambridge, MA: Harvard University Press.

Csikszentmihalyi, M. (1998). Implications of a systems perspective for the study of creativity. In R. Sternberg (Ed.), *Handbook of creativity* (pp. 313–338). New York: Cambridge University Press.

Davidoff, F. (1997). Time. *Annals of Internal Medicine, 127*(6), 483–485.

Dugdale, D. C., Epstein, R., & Pantilat, S. Z. (1999). Time and the patient-physician relationship. *Journal of General Internal Medicine, 14,* S34–S40.

Fuchs, V., & Emanuel, E. (2005). Health care reform: Why, what, when? *Health Affairs, 24*(6), 1399–1414.

Gardner, H. (1994). *Creating minds.* New York: Basic Books.

Gardner, J. W. (1981). *Self-renewal: The individual and the innovative society* (2nd ed.). New York: Norton.

Grembowski, D., Ulrich, C. M., Paschane, D., Diehr, P., Katon, W., Martin, D., et al. (2002). Managed care and primary physician satisfaction. *Journal of the American Board of Family Practice, 16,* 383–393.

Landon, B., Reschovsky, J., & Blumenthal, D. (2003). Changes in career satisfaction among primary care and specialist physicians, 1997–2001. *Journal of the American Medical Association, 289*(4), 442–449.

Linzer, M., Konrad, T. R., Douglas, J., McMurray, J. E., Pathman, D. E., Williams, E. S., et al. (2000). Managed care, time pressure, and physician job satisfaction: Results from the physician worklife study. *Journal of General Internal Medicine, 15,* 441–450.

Ludmerer, K. (1999). *Time to heal: American medical education from the turn of the century to the era of managed care.* New York: Oxford University Press.

Moore Johnson, S., & Birkeland, S. (2003). The schools that teachers choose. *Educational Leadership, 60*(8), 20–24.

Morway, L., Solomon, J., Michaelson, M., & Gardner, H. (1998, August). Contemplation and implications for good work in teaching. Good Work Project Report no. 6. Available at http://www.goodworkproject.org

Peske, H., Lui, E., Moore Johnson, S., Kauffman, D., & Kardos, S. (2001). The next generation of teachers: Changing conceptions of a career in teaching. *Phi Delta Kappan, 83*(4), 304–311.

Reed, M. C., Vratil, A. K., Stoddard, J., & Hargraves, J. L. (2001). Managed care, professional autonomy, and income. *Journal of General Internal Medicine, 16,* 675–684.

Safran, D. (2003). Defining the future of primary care: What can we learn from patients? *Annals of Internal Medicine, 138*(3), 248–255.

Schindler, B. A., Novack, D. H., Cohen, D. G., Yager, J., Wang, D., Shaheen, N. J., et al. (2006). The impact of the changing health care environment on the health and well-being of faculty at four medical schools. *Academic Medicine, 81*(1), 27–34.

Woo, B. (2006). Primary care: The best job in medicine? *New England Journal of Medicine, 355*(9), 864–866.

Woods, A., & Weasmer, J. (2002). Maintaining job satisfaction: Engaging professionals as active participants. *Clearing House, 75*(4), 186–189.

6

PLACING GOD BEFORE ME

SPIRITUALITY AND RESPONSIBILITY AT WORK

Seth Wax

*You can't help but be a little spiritual as a scientist
because everyday you're living on the edge of
what is known and what is unknown.*

—Genetics graduate student

RELIGIONS HAVE TRADITIONALLY SERVED as powerful forces the world
over, inculcating social mores and regulating behaviors. Providing frameworks that dictate how people should act, they have also established priorities and responsibilities: to family, to elders, to community, and above all
in monotheistic religions, to God. But after attacks on public religion following the Reformation and the Enlightenment (Casanova, 1994), along
with the more recent explosion of lifestyle choices and the disruption of
stable social networks and communities in the United States, formal religions and ecclesiastical institutions have weakened considerably. While
some religious entities have strived to reassert their public role in recent
years, they have largely ceased to exert the influence they did in the past.

Many thanks to Courtney Bender, Harvey Cox, Howard Gardner, Ron Hogen
Green, Carrie James, Alison Jones, and Jeffrey Solomon for their advice and
assistance on the current and previous versions of this chapter

Yet the fact remains that 94 percent of Americans claim to believe in God or a higher power (Lyons, 2005) and that alternative forms of spirituality—including yoga, Buddhist meditation, charismatic Christianity, and mysticism—are increasing in popularity. These trends confirm that private, individual religion or spirituality—often idiosyncratic personal beliefs and practices—has not diminished and may in fact have supplanted involvement with traditional religious institutions.[1] And although these beliefs and practices are characterized by a high degree of autonomy and are often criticized for promoting moral relativism and social disengagement, they affect the ways in which contemporary Americans conceive of and carry out their responsibilities, especially at work. Despite what critics may claim, those who take spirituality seriously often place on themselves the responsibility to do good work.

In this chapter I examine how workers bring metaphysical beliefs and spiritual practices to bear on their work. The study is based on a survey of 671 transcripts gathered from professionals in eight domains, and on an in-depth analysis of 105 interviews of subjects who explicitly connect their spirituality and work.[2] Four major orientations emerged from among these subjects (see Table 6.1):

1. *Spiritual goal.* For one third of subjects connecting spirituality and work in this study ($n = 35$), metaphysical beliefs act as a frame, often directing their activities to fulfill spiritual goals. As a result, work becomes a vehicle to achieve these goals. For medical professionals, this orientation could be construed as taking part in Christ's healing mission;

---

[1]This is not to say that religious institutions exert no influence at all today. Religion naturally impacts the ways in which people speak of their beliefs, and many for whom spirituality is highly salient are involved with religious groups.

[2]The domains examined include journalism, the sciences, the performing arts, law, business, medicine, and K-12 and collegiate education. The survey revealed that an additional nineteen subjects maintain some spiritual beliefs or practices, but because they do not connect them to their work, they were not included in this analysis. Moreover, the divergence between the 94 percent of the general population that claims to believe in God or a higher power and the paltry 20 percent of our subjects who profess spiritual beliefs may be attributed to the fact that most subjects interviewed for the project were white professionals living near urban areas outside of traditionally religious regions. Yet consistent with findings about contemporary spiritual belief, our data show that "traditional" views of God are increasingly uncommon, and only sixteen subjects (1.5 percent) in this sample reported feeling responsible to God, a higher power, or their religion.

Table 6.1. Four Orientations to Spirituality at Work.

Spiritual Goal	Call to Responsibility	Spiritual Practice	Divine Pursuit
One engages work within a spiritual framework, in many cases to advance a spiritual goal.	One feels an imperative to do specific work.	One takes up a spiritual practice (such as meditation) and engages in it at work.	Deep engagement in work yields a bonus: awareness of the spiritual reality.
Imperative from self	Imperative from God/higher power	Imperative from self	Imperative from self
Explicit Responsibilities			
clients, people at work, God, family	clients, people at work, family, God/higher power/religion	not asked	beneficiaries (public, audience, and so on)
Implicit Responsibilities			
mission, doing good work	God/higher power, quality of work	personal spiritual growth, quality of work	quality of work, oneself

for Buddhists, choosing work that will help to end the suffering of others; and for others, maintaining a commitment to social justice through hands-on service work. Having developed their beliefs through religious training or reflection, they view their work as venues to actualize their beliefs.

For example, Aaron Lieberman, a Jewish social entrepreneur, noted that the concept of *tikkun olam*, or "repairing the world," is a particularly salient frame for his work. Originally a mystical concept concerning Jews' responsibility to unite fractured pieces of God through ritual practices, tikkun olam is interpreted today as an imperative to respond to injustice and suffering throughout the world. For Lieberman, tikkun olam provides a metaphysical framework in which he orients his actions. Prompted by a deep commitment to this concept, he created an organization for improving educational outcomes for preschoolers. Although the impact of his organization may so far be localized, he conceives of it globally, in keeping with his broader mission to repair the world: "You have a limited amount of time, and you try to fundamentally change as many lives as you can through the work that you're doing." Lieberman takes upon himself the responsibility to do good work, motivated by his spiritual commitment to social justice.

2. *Call to responsibility.* In the aftermath of the Reformation, Luther's and Calvin's writings on being "called" to work brought this concept to the forefront of Western discussions of work, spirituality, and one's relation to the divine. One-quarter of subjects who connected spirituality and work ($n = 27$)—committed Christians as well as those who believe in a "higher power" that permeates reality—asserted that they have a purpose and are meant to be engaged in a specific line of work; they are responsible to exert themselves diligently in it. Nearly half of subjects in this group demonstrated characteristics of born-again Christians; they feel a personal connection to a God who cares about them as individuals, who has ordained a specific task for them, and who has given them the skills and gifts to accomplish it.

A women's basketball coach at a small liberal arts college maintained that she is on earth for a purpose and that God wants her "to use the gifts that I have to reach other people." Aside from employing a spiritual cosmology to explain her role in God's plan, she also demonstrated other characteristics of "the call": the certainty that God has commanded her to do something specific, and that what she does matters on a cosmic scale. God wants her to teach and coach, which she views as "a form of ministry or a form of mission work," and God gave her the skills to do it well. As a result, she is responsible for working hard and doing her work to the best of her abilities.

3. *Spiritual practice.* Spiritual practices are the ways in which people engage practically in religion or spirituality. A variety of techniques exist for enhancing awareness of the metaphysical, including prayer, chanting, visualizing the divine, offering food or incense, and meditating to develop concentration and awareness. One-fifth of interviewed subjects who connected spirituality and work ($n = 24$) engage in meditative practices from Buddhist, Hindu, and Jewish sources and explicitly bring them into their work in ways that shape their behavior, commitments, and responsibilities. At work they practice vipassanāa (also known as insight) and Zen meditations, which entail cultivating moment-to-moment awareness and attention during formal sitting periods and in daily activities. Individuals attempt to maintain focused attention through routine tasks as well as complex interactions with coworkers and clients.

A human resources executive who practices vipassanāa meditation brings the techniques into her work as she continuously strives to cultivate moment-to-moment awareness and attention in her interactions with personnel. She works to stay present with individuals and teams who come to her with problems, and strives to respond appropriately rather than react to her own meandering thoughts and emotions. In this way, work becomes part of a broadly construed spiritual practice. Such practices are not limited to ritual settings but are extended to all work. By taking them up, individuals explicitly claim responsibility for their spiritual growth, and implicitly accept responsibility for the results of their efforts at work.

4. *Divine pursuit.* Connecting with the spiritual often requires conscious effort, yet for some artists and research scientists ($n = 19$), such intuitions emerge through active engagement with work. In the process of creating a theater production or pushing the boundaries of biological knowledge, these individuals have transcendent experiences and claim to connect to a spiritual reality, thus making the divine present.

A prominent Boston-area jazz pianist spoke of peak performing experiences as spiritual. At times he is so engaged while playing that he loses conscious control as a "God energy" flows through him, the music, and the audience. When he surrenders himself to it and "gets [out of] the way of it," the creative process opens up and he is able to deliver music with increased passion and skill. While such an epiphany does not impel individuals to act in certain ways or to do good work per se, these experiences may encourage a certain sense of responsibility. If performers or scientists wish to experience a transcendent dimension at work, it can come about only when they are fully committed to the work at hand.

Orientations and Their Accompanying Features

Although an individual could theoretically demonstrate characteristics of more than one of the orientations, the data suggest that subjects generally fall into only one category. In the analysis that follows, I examine how each orientation is associated with work-related features (such as the type of work, the dominant discourses in a given domain, autonomy, and so on) and aspects of spirituality (such as types of spiritual beliefs, salience of spirituality, frequency of ritual observance, and so forth).

Spiritual Goal

Spiritual beliefs often furnish a believer with a cosmology in which he can place himself, helping him to establish a sense of identity and location in the world. Metaphysical beliefs, whether in an omnipotent creator, a higher power transcending the universe, or a divinity that emerges when people come together, help people orient themselves toward an expansive reality.

Cosmologies provide lenses through which individuals view themselves and their environments, both at and beyond the workplace. When individuals take their beliefs seriously and allow them to serve as a guiding framework, such beliefs can deeply affect how work is conceived and the purposes for which it is carried out. Not only will work be spoken of through religious or spiritual metaphors, but the work itself will be understood as fulfilling spiritual goals.

Spiritual traditions often shift practitioners' conceptions of reality to help them see things in a new light, and many people today attempt to see the divine in everyday life. Father Philip Linden, a professor at Xavier College in New Orleans, attributed his perspective to his school's founder, Saint Katherine Drexel, who taught that religious members of the college community "ought to be involved in the adoration of the Eucharistic Christ around the clock." In practical terms, they should not only "start the day in the presence of the [ritual] Eucharist in the chapel," but also keep the image of Christ in their consciousness throughout the day. By keeping this image in mind, Linden argued, "when you teach the Native or the American Negro, you are standing in the presence of the Eucharist." As a result, the work of teaching the underprivileged is conducted "in the presence of the Eucharistic Lord because [it] is manifested through this kind of service." Spiritual beliefs serve as a framework through which the world is filtered and interpreted. These beliefs fundamentally change the larger purpose of one's work, transforming it into a task of ultimate importance and impelling one to engage in behavior that will promote the welfare of others.

For others oriented to work in this manner, spiritual beliefs provide a deep-seated motivation for work—it is done for the sake of achieving a spiritual goal. In most cases, the mission entails a responsibility to serve others in need. Earl Phalen, a social entrepreneur and director of an organization working to improve the educational and social outcomes of black and Latino children in poor urban areas, was raised in the Catholic tradition but was also influenced by Baptist teachings. He firmly believes that all human beings have been created in God's image and, accordingly, deserve humane treatment. Moreover, because he has been given talents to help these children, he has been charged with the task of lifting them up from their condition. Phalen sees underprivileged children not merely as victims of an unjust economic and political system, but rather as manifestations of the divine, for whom he must work tire-lessly. Given the gifts and benefits that he has received, he feels not only a spiritual responsibility to help them, in a manner similar to the approach of Aaron Lieberman, discussed earlier, but also a broader mis-sion. His responsibility to the child becomes an expression of that broader spiritual mission of providing assistance to inherently divine human beings.

A life coach who is also a Zen Buddhist articulates how spiritual beliefs construct a vision of reality that motivates action at work. She is commit-ted to working toward the goal of her own enlightenment, or "waking up" to her true nature. In Zen Buddhism, one vows to become a bodhi-sattva, a being who commits to helping all sentient beings end their suffering and reach enlightenment. For her, the assumptions of Buddhism and her commitment to the bodhisattva vow form the basis of her work. On a surface level, she identifies her work as a life coach as "implicitly Buddhist" because it is concerned with helping clients cease habits and behaviors that produce suffering. However, the goal of her work is ulti-mately spiritual. It is to help all people "wake up" to their enlightened nature, and this aim ultimately trumps the provisional professional goals. She noted, "In some ways, I don't really care about coaching. But what I care about is helping people wake up. So if coaching can provide a vehi-cle for me to do that—great. . . . Now, it's more like the work is just a vehicle to express the practice."

EFFECTS OF WORK-RELATED FEATURES. Among the thirty-five subjects who frame their work and align their goals with spiritual cosmologies, three-quarters ($n = 26$) are involved in a helping profession, be it teaching, medicine, social entrepreneurship, or the nonprofit sector. Embodying principles consistent with spiritual beliefs about providing assistance to the needy, these domains may attract those who embrace spiritually inspired ideas of service. Most of these subjects also tend to work in domains that afford them a high level of autonomy.

EFFECTS OF SPIRITUALITY FEATURES. The most consistent belief among respondents who demonstrated this orientation is a belief in social justice, which was reflected by nearly half of the subjects ($n = 17$) and ranged from a commitment to repair the world (the Jewish concept of *tikkun olam*) to the importance of Catholic social gospel teachings. Specific conceptions of God also seem related to how subjects approach their work, with fifty-seven percent ($n = 20$) referring to the divine as "God" or a variation of "Christ," using language consistent with mainstream religious denominations.

The social justice beliefs and conceptions of God found among these subjects suggest the broad impact of religious denominations, namely mainline Protestantism, Catholicism, and Judaism, in which such themes are central. Accordingly, two-thirds of subjects ($n = 24$) demonstrating this orientation report having grown up with or being exposed as an adult to some form of religious training. Perhaps then it is of little surprise that spiritual belief or practice is salient to a similar number of subjects.

Framing one's work in this way also carries important implications for how workers understand their responsibilities for doing good work. By perceiving themselves and their behavior within a cosmic context, they enhance the value of what they do. In attempting to improve the world, serve God, or simply help other beings, they take upon themselves the responsibility to ensure that their work is effective. For those who take it seriously, there is no opportunity to hand off responsibility to another; they become ultimately responsible. "You can never be too tired or too busy to [do] what you have to do," noted a former prominent public defender in citing the impact that his spiritual beliefs have had on his drive to help clients. Despite the fact that only six of these subjects noted that they ultimately feel responsible to God, nearly all reported feeling responsible to the beneficiaries of their work and their colleagues. Spirituality may help them commit themselves to the goals they perceive need to be met.

Call to Responsibility

Ever since Luther reinforced the connection between God's will and a believer's occupational activities, the notion of "the call" and the view of reality that it promotes have had a strong impact on Western discussions of work. Weber (1930) indicated that Luther's and Calvin's interpretations of the call were among their most influential ideas about religious commitment, because they made both mundane and elite labor "a duty instead of a curse" (Muirhead, 2004, p. 106). For many religious people in the United States today—especially Protestant Christians—a calling is the means by which the believer can serve God; these individuals view their "secular work as a divinely appointed duty" (Wuthnow, 1996, p. 300).

In recent years, social scientists have drawn attention to how work conditions and institutional aspects of religion can lead people to think about their work as a calling rather than a career or job (Davidson and Caddell, 1994; Wrzesniewski et al., 1997). Yet because 20 percent of the subjects in this study spoke of their work as a calling without clearly affiliating with a religious identity or group, it is clear that personal spiritual belief plays an important role. This orientation implies a deep sense of purpose and a responsibility to the higher power that has ordered one's task. In other words, these individuals feel a deep sense of responsibility to meet the call of good work.

Half of the subjects who demonstrate the calling orientation embrace a vision of the divine that is consistent with that of born-again Christians. These individuals generally accept a traditional Christian theology as outlined in the New Testament; they believe in a personal God with whom they have an intimate relationship and who is interested in enhancing their lives; and they are committed to practices that reinforce this relationship with God (Roof, 1999, p. 183).[3] Exemplifying a traditional view, some perceive God as omnipotent—"in control of many, many things"—and omniscient—knowing innumerable details about each person. In imagining a deeply personal relationship with God and by recognizing God's closeness, these believers consciously allow God into all aspects of their personal lives, intensifying their behavioral and ethical expectations.

A Lutheran high school teacher illuminated the sense of commitment that emerges through belief in a personal God. God not only thinks of him often, he argued, but God has a specific mission for him, a responsibility for him to meet: "I feel like I have a sense of vocation or calling. And I think there's a standard that I feel held to in terms of my conduct, my commitment to my students, and to my profession that is about what I think God would want me to do." God's expectations for him relate specifically to ways in which he conducts himself at work and the extent to which he accomplishes his goals. If he does not live up to these expectations, he lets down not only his students but also God. Accordingly, his ultimate responsibility to God is fulfilled via his responsibility to others at his work.

---

[3]Roof chooses the phrase *born-again* to describe a wide range of Christian affiliation—from evangelical Christians, such as some Baptist and Methodist denominations, to Charismatics, such as Pentecostal or Holiness—in order to draw out some of the most prominent features and similarities while glossing over the differences in doctrine and practice among the various groups. Only a scant number of subjects explicitly identified with a denomination that could be characterized as born-again; the remainder have been grouped in this category due to the ways in which they conceptualize and speak about their religious beliefs and commitments.

Nearly a third of subjects who spoke of their vocation as a calling did not describe a deity per se as directly commanding them to engage in specific work. Rather, they perceive a higher power or a broader order of the universe. These individuals see themselves within an expansive metaphysical reality that is beyond normal sensory perceptions; they acknowledge invisible forces that have a broad and subtle impact on them. One social entrepreneur who considers himself spiritual but not formally religious commented, "I believe that I was meant to do what I do right now. . . . I believe that this was the path that I was supposed to take and I have a role to play now. And I will play it to the best of my ability." While he did not speak of a deity, he believes that there is an order to the universe, and within that order he needs to engage in a specific line of work.

This individual illustrates another aspect of the calling doctrine that was demonstrated by many subjects: that the transcendent force dictates the specific type of work to be taken up. A teacher who identified herself as Baptist and demonstrated characteristic features of born-again Christianity, noted, "We all have something we need to accomplish in this life, and whatever we do, we should do the best we can." Having been assigned a task to carry out in this life, she has an explicit responsibility to engage it. Such attitudes could simply be reflections of the high level of satisfaction that these subjects derive from their jobs; yet what clearly underlies their work is a deep belief in something beyond themselves. The importance for many subjects lies not necessarily in fulfilling a goal but in doing what they are meant to be doing.

Viewing work as service to others is often central to a sense of calling, regardless of specific metaphysical beliefs. The Lutheran high school teacher discussed previously looked to lessons he learned from his father that exemplify service in one's calling, specifically that "the importance of a career is not simply putting food on the table for your family but also something that can be seen as an act of service," that responds to a need that God wants fulfilled. Similarly, a physician who identified as "spiritual as opposed to religious" spoke at length of the formative influence of her Christian upbringing and the weight of the "Presbyterian burden." Despite her rejection of Protestantism, she continues to believe that one is "put here for a purpose, and you need to do something to make things just a little bit better in your lifetime to justify your existence." In viewing their work as a calling and an act of service, such individuals demonstrated a complex nexus of responsibilities: to the work at hand, to the beneficiaries, and perhaps above all, to the divine. They placed themselves at the center of this web, binding themselves to doing their work effectively and to helping others in the process.

EFFECTS OF WORK-RELATED FEATURES. A number of work-related features correlate with a sense of calling, yet they do not seem to depend on a specific profession.[4] Fifty percent of subjects work in a helping profession such as teaching, medicine, or social entrepreneurship, which may correlate with seeing one's work as an act of service. Most respondents (74 percent, $n = 20$) who reported being called to their work also seemed to sustain a high level of volatility or stress in their work and to receive low-to-medium compensation (70 percent, $n = 19$). These conditions may contribute to a desire to see a cosmic order encompassing both their stressful lived experiences and the transcendent. It also seems plausible that their sense of calling may lead them to tolerate stress and lower compensation for the greater reward of serving God and the associated benefits.

EFFECTS OF SPIRITUALITY FEATURES. A number of aspects of spirituality seem relevant in leading individuals to believe they are called to a specific occupation. Despite the fact that we did not explicitly gather data on religious affiliation, it appears that beliefs consistent with born-again Christianity figure prominently. Perhaps the most significant aspect of these beliefs, as alluded to earlier, is the sense that God guides these subjects through life, providing them with a task to perform. One-quarter of subjects who demonstrated this orientation also indicated that they pray frequently, and it seems likely that many more do as well. Because spiritual beliefs are also affected by broader discourses, this finding also points to the impact of religious denominations, such as evangelical, Pentecostal, and other born-again groups, that promote these beliefs, as well as the likelihood that workers have had some type of formative religious experience in which they have come to accept God and become serious Christians.

Among the less formally religious, the dominant belief tends to be in a vague "higher power." Spiritual affiliation and practice are naturally less important among these individuals, as is the frequency of religious training. It seems likely, given the relative uniformity in how these individuals spoke of the divine, that they are influenced by contemporary spiritual narratives in popular culture.

Regardless of whether one believes that a supreme deity has ordained that one must engage in a certain task on earth, by virtue of adopting this belief one implicitly takes on responsibility for it. For those who believe

---

[4]This idea follows the argument of Wrzesniewski et al. (1997), who claim that the idea of calling (and even viewing one's vocation as a job, career, or calling) is "not necessarily dependent upon occupation" (p. 22).

in a personal God, this avowal could manifest in a desire to please God and gain rewards at the end of life or avoid possible punishment. Admittedly, the drive to take responsibility for good work may be weaker among subjects who do not hold such concepts of God. Indeed, it seems plausible that one's sense of calling in work may not drive one to pursue good work and may arise only when one is feeling good about it.

Interestingly, when asked explicitly, *To whom or what do you feel most responsible?* only five subjects who demonstrated the calling orientation claimed to feel a responsibility to God or their religion. The remainder, if asked, cited supervisors, colleagues, clients, and their families and communities. Of those who specified responsibility to God, three embraced, to various degrees, belief in a personal divinity, while two spoke either of God more generally or of a higher power.

Spiritual Practice

Whereas spirituality can provide a framework in which believers may contextualize and give meaning to their lives, it also enables them to transform the ways in which their work is carried out. Zoketsu Norman Fischer,[5] a former abbot of the San Francisco Zen Center, described a Zen Buddhist attitude toward time and work, drawing on a central aspect of this school's practice of cultivating continuous moment-to-moment attention. Speaking about the daily activities in which humans engage, he noted that, at its root,

> everything is work—being alive and in a body is already work. Every day there is eating and shitting and cleaning up. There is brushing and bathing and flossing. Every day there is thinking and caring and creating. So there's no escape from work—it's everywhere. For Zen students there's no work time and leisure time; there's just lifetime, daytime and nighttime. Work is something deep and dignified—it's what we are born to do and what we feel most fulfilled in doing. [Fischer, 1996, p. 13]

Fischer further distinguishes two types of work as part of spiritual practice: repetitive, manual work (such as shoveling or cleaning) that is approached as a meditation and in which one pays close attention to the physical sensations of the experience; and work as an offering to others, done not for financial or status rewards but to benefit others. Any task, if

---

[5]Not interviewed as part of the GoodWork Project.

taken up with the proper intention and frame of mind, can be part of Zen spiritual practice.

Such a description of work aligns with the Zen Buddhist approach to life, but it is also recognized more broadly among those involved in a spiritual tradition that provides specific non-devotional contemplative practices. These individuals view reality through a spiritual lens, as described earlier, but they also align with traditions that prescribe specific techniques in which to engage. Moreover, the techniques and implied attitudes reinforce the idea that the methods must be engaged at all times. In this way, there are no distinctions between spiritual practice and life in general.

For many who engage in meditative practices, spirituality consists of active engagement with the techniques. They take responsibility for continually approaching experiences in accordance with the teachings and practices of their tradition. This accountability is then transferred to work, and occupational activity becomes a part of spiritual practice. Practitioners must take responsibility for doing work that is in accord with the principles of their practice, thereby implementing their spiritual beliefs in a practical manner in the workplace.

For some who practice meditation, its application in their work lives translates into their becoming calm, flexible, and aware at work; they try not to be thrown off course by its vicissitudes. For others, the impact is greater still and reflects the high degree of agency accepted by those who take up spiritual practices. This assumption of responsibility and the use of specific techniques directly impact the manner in which work is approached. Eric, an HIV-AIDS counselor and vipassanāa practitioner, brings into his interactions with clients a meditative practice that is aimed at cultivating awareness and cutting attachments to ideas that distort reality. Rather than trying to pigeonhole a client by recommending a specific treatment, reacting to a complaint in a self-protective manner, or obsessing over positive results in order to validate himself, Eric strives to observe his own thoughts and actions as he interacts with clients. By increasing his awareness of how he thinks and feels and by attempting to stymie hasty reactions, he can perform his work more skillfully. In addition, by engaging in a practice aimed at developing equanimity, he is able to let go of his desire for specific results while remaining committed to broad positive outcomes. Through practicing meditation and cultivating positive qualities, he can connect with his altruistic intentions and reinforce his professional responsibility to those with whom he works.

Spiritual techniques can also help guide work toward accomplishing spiritual goals, as in the case of Cheryl Conners, a former prosecutor and legal educator. Conners began practicing Tibetan Buddhism by first engaging in some mind-training techniques and then undertaking a thorough examination of her personal beliefs and those of the culture in which she worked and lived. These experiences helped her to understand the conditioned and oftentimes incorrect ways in which she had reacted to and interpreted the world around her. As part of this self-examination, she also reflected on her occupational experiences and her legal training: "I also began to inquire about how the mental habits which I had developed through law training and practice influenced my own well-being, the well-being of clients, courts, and those with whom I had contact. I began to re-examine many elements of legal doctrine, analysis, argument, the adversary system, and professional roles in light of my new understandings" (Conners, n.d.).

The competitive nature of the legal system, its negative psychological effects on others, and its failure to acknowledge the humanity of the individuals involved troubled Conner. Accordingly, at work she began applying Tibetan Buddhist spiritual practices that are aimed at shifting one's consciousness, cultivating compassion and awareness, and changing the ways in which one interacts with others. Instead of adopting the traditional perspective of viewing opposing counsel as a party to defeat in battle, she began to see them as "co-creators of problem-solving." In an attempt to avoid the use of negative language and thoughts that would leave destructive karmic imprints on herself and others, she practiced using language devoid of aggression; when judges would treat her and her fellow prosecutors harshly, she tried to see them more holistically, as individuals who were uncomfortable with themselves and who had learned that being abusive was an appropriate way to deal with people. She has endeavored to bring this approach to the legal profession through teaching meditation techniques at law schools, by forming a consulting group, and by promoting restorative justice projects that encourage victims, perpetrators, defense attorneys, and prosecutors to move beyond their strictly defined roles and to approach crime resolution as a healing process.

Conner's spiritual practice has thus become integrated into her work, transforming the motivations behind and methods for it. In the process she has also reconsidered her relationship to her occupation and to the world, recognizing that beings are "all inter-connected." This insight profoundly shifted the way she considers her own and others' responsibility for behavior and actions; as she argued, "We are all responsible for each plaintiff, each defendant, each newly created nonprofit corporation, profit-making Limited Liability Partnership, agency, conflict, war and prison. We must go from being poised for action into the most deeply informed powerful action that we can muster."

EFFECTS OF WORK-RELATED FEATURES. The type of work one does or the domain in which one works appears to have little bearing on this orientation to spirituality and work. Yet there may be a relationship between professional autonomy and the propensity to do spiritual practice at work. Three-quarters of subjects ($n = 18$) work in sectors with medium to high pay, and they demonstrate a high level of autonomy and stability. Such characteristics may provide the latitude for individuals to incorporate spiritual practices into their work; they may also reflect the fact that many of those who engage in meditation come from the upper socioeconomic levels of our society.

EFFECTS OF SPIRITUALITY FEATURES. The emphasis on everyday practices is clearly tied to specific types of spirituality, in particular the practice of meditation. Spirituality is not simply an abstract concept to be pondered on occasion; it is a highly salient aspect of life that demands continuous engagement and involvement. Use of religious terminology was rather uniform among these subjects: four who identify as Jewish articulated a mystical view of God, as imminent in existence, while those who practice Buddhist or Hindu meditations spoke of interconnection, "buddha-nature," and cosmic consciousness. Interestingly, half of those demonstrating this orientation ($n = 12$) reported having been raised in a Western religious tradition—Judaism, Protestantism, or Catholicism—thus confirming reports regarding movement away from traditional religious denominations and toward involvement with Asian religions and practices, especially among the middle class.

The majority of subjects practicing meditation were not explicitly asked to identify their responsibilities, yet their narratives point to intriguing possibilities. Their accounts suggest the importance of personal spiritual growth and the need to do quality work. The traditions from which these meditation practices derive, especially Buddhism, promote ethical conduct and steady increase in spiritual knowledge through observance of the practices. Oftentimes it is believed that practice leads to greater understanding of and adherence to ethical precepts. In turn, this stance may inculcate responsibility for affairs beyond the domain of spirituality to work and to practitioners' interactions with others in daily life. Moreover, it seems possible that by considering the workplace as a venue in which to make spiritual progress, these subjects experienced a heightened sense of the importance of their work and its effect on others. In the absence of belief in a deity actively intervening in human affairs, the onus or responsibility for positive outcomes falls squarely upon the individual.

Divine Pursuit

People often tell stories about becoming aware of the divine while standing atop a mountain, watching a beautiful sunset, or witnessing a birth. Such experiences need not be limited to nature or miraculous events. Among those in professional fields that entail the creation of new knowledge, ideas, or art, recognition of the divine mystery is more common, taking place through work activities. These intuitions require individuals to interpret their experiences through spiritual metaphors; subjects who demonstrated this approach spoke of the experience of coming close to God or a divine power through deep engagement in their work.[6]

Although stark differences exist between the attitude in the arts and the attitude in the sciences toward religion and spirituality, this orientation was found principally among actors, musicians, and scientists. Theater and other performing arts professionals frequently discussed their work's connection to ancient Greek theater and its historical religious and public significance. They pointed to features of religious ritual in theater, considering the stage to be modeled after an altar, scripts to be adaptations of hymnals and prayer books, and the audience to be a congregation that sits in pews, quietly paying attention during a performance. With their dedication to objectivity, empiricism, and independent verification of results, scientists have traditionally maintained a hostile attitude toward religion, and some have dismissed it outright as simpleminded mythology.[7] Yet in both domains, some practitioners (performing arts, $n = 12$; science, $n = 7$) admitted to sensing the presence of a spiritual entity or feeling through their work. Here we encounter a fascinating yet rarely discussed aspect of professional work. For actors and musicians, the sensing emerges as energy or higher power. For scientists who associate the search for truth through the scientific method with spiritual discovery, it is an appreciation of the seemingly limitless, potentially explicable, and yet still mysterious bounds of nature.

---

[6]See also Csikszentmihalyi and Nakamura, Chapter Three, this volume.

[7]A surprising 1996 study of one thousand scientists nevertheless found that nearly 40 percent believed in a personal God, a level unchanged from when the survey was first administered in 1916 (Larson & Witham, 1997).

Spiritual belief plays an important role in constructing these performers' and scientists' senses of responsibility; yet they do not conceive of a commanding divinity, nor do they take up ritual or practice obligations. Rather, their spiritual intuitions come when they are thoroughly engaged in their work and when it seems to be of the highest quality. Therefore, they must first be dedicated to doing good work in order the experience the transcendent.

Location and space are critical aspects of this approach to integrating spirituality and work. Among performing arts professionals, the divine is encountered onstage, and among scientists it occurs wherever work is taking place. For some actors, the stage may replicate an actual altar or at least become a location where, in the words of Shakespeare & Co. director Tina Packer, "God is seen or heard." Ron Savage, a prominent jazz drummer, explained that he is in touch with his spiritual side and God during performances, and one young Hindu actor located the cosmic vibration OM onstage. Among scientific researchers, awareness of the divine often emerges in a specific location. For some ecologists, it may be outdoors, where there is direct contact with nature, while for bench researchers insights arrive as they collect and analyze results in the lab. While they seem to differ in their conceptions of a higher power, both performers and scientists perceive the work location as a locus where that power can be contacted.

A key feature of this approach is that the higher power is not immediately accessible; it is latent and therefore requires the expenditure of energy, intention, and in some cases certain rituals by the worker if it is to be actualized. The Hindu actor commented that the primordial sound OM that "pervades all existence . . . can happen onstage," but only if he and other actors take it upon themselves to "treat the stage as a holy place . . . giving the true respect to the audience, ourselves, and to the art form." Likewise, prior to taking the stage at a performance Ron Savage actively engages in a personalized prayer in order to "clear my mind and focus and channel my energy. So when I pray, that puts me more in touch with God and my spiritual side. That's where I'm trying to play from . . . this purely spiritual side. . . . Whatever I'm studying is so everything I do musically is purely spiritual. And everything else, [so that] there's nothing to hinder that flow."

In order to encounter or glimpse the divine, scientists must deeply engage in their work and demonstrate openness and willingness to letting the divine emerge. One postdoctoral geneticist explained that nature is mysterious, but through deep engagement with research he can "understand how the world works, how the universe is organized," which will bring him "as close to God as you can get." Especially among scientists, spiritual encounters involve recognition of the immensity and incomprehensibility of the natural world, leading to a sense of wonder. A veteran geneticist spoke of the "awe and respect both for the science itself and the people you do it with," while a graduate student noted, "You can't help but be a little spiritual as a scientist because every day you're living on the edge of what is known and what is unknown. . . . But everything works like clockwork every single day. Nature works like clockwork. So you can't help but be a little spiritual and say, Well, maybe if not an intelligent being, at least some force is coordinating and organizing all of this." While pursuing these experiences does not guarantee good work, appreciating the mystery of nature may lead scientists to respect it and feel responsible for engaging in work that is ecologically or socially responsible.

EFFECTS OF WORK-RELATED FEATURES. When one considers work-related features associated with this pattern, prevailing discourses about good work in performing arts and sciences seem important. Both domains stress that practitioners continually discover and express that which is new. Actors and performers explore ideas through their performances, and scientists generate new knowledge. The most highly rewarded workers in both domains are those who can produce the most innovative performances, theories, or results. The discourses that promote such breakthroughs are conveyed through professional training, and subjects who demonstrate sensitivity to intuiting the divine seek its manifestations in their respective domains. Given the emphasis on personal interpretation in the arts, one might expect artistic training to be amenable to spiritual beliefs while that of science discourages such views. And given that fewer scientists than artists demonstrate these inclinations, it would seem that science generally succeeds at suppressing spirituality or that it attracts those not inclined toward it. Yet the evidence presented by these subjects suggests that commitment to science and spiritual belief are not necessarily mutually exclusive. When individuals work in domains that promote creativity, it remains possible to pursue the divine.

EFFECTS OF SPIRITUALITY FEATURES. Certain characteristics of spirituality are common among those who believe that the divine emerges from their work. The conceptions of the divine are remarkably consistent: it is often characterized as a vague, impersonal sense of spirit; as God-energy, a cosmic vibration, a spiritual force inside physical matter, "chaos and stillness," or an awe-inspiring force. Such conceptions, as well as the low incidence of reported practice or religious upbringing, imply low or medium salience of spirituality in these individuals' lives. These approaches to spirituality are generally weak and are not difficult to maintain. They are simply articulations of a spiritual awareness that can be achieved through everyday work activity.

Although this type of spirituality may demand little of individuals, it may still contribute to how they think about their responsibilities. As noted earlier, one of the most consistent aspects of this orientation is the responsibility it places on individual practitioners to engage in their work wholeheartedly according to the accepted methods and expectations of their domains. Moreover, Wuthnow observes that as artists emphasize their "personal experience with the sacred," they also "take responsibility for their own spirituality" and for playing "an active role in shaping events," both spiritual and secular (2001, pp. 166–167). If they do not take responsibility for their actions and do good work, they will not have spiritual intuitions. As a result, contact with the realm of the spirit may function as a reward for high quality work and as encouragement to continue it. Ron Savage plays his best only when he is in touch with his spiritual side; OM emerges only when actors treat the stage, the craft, the audience, and one another with respect and honor; glimpses of the spiritual on the research bench occur only when the boundaries of human knowledge are pushed to their very limits. Accordingly, emergent spirituality can encourage responsibility for good work in the domains of the arts and the sciences.

Conclusion

Given the highly autonomous and personalized nature of contemporary spirituality, it would appear at first glance to have little impact on how individuals behave in the workplace. Yet the examples outlined here show that when spirituality is taken up as a serious endeavor, it can inspire individuals to reflect on the meaning of their work, those it will affect, and the need to do it well. Those who visualize a cosmology and attempt to fulfill spiritual goals in their work take on responsibility to help others by actively choosing occupations that will enable them to respond to problems in the world. Those who believe they have been called to their work experience a visceral sense that their work is necessary and that they must ensure it is done well. When primary motivations are more oriented toward the self, as they are among dedicated meditators, artists, and scientists, the devotion to doing good work emerges from a commitment to full engagement with the task. Meditators feel responsible for their spiritual growth and generally approach their practice with a commitment and energy that carries over to their work. And for their part, artists and scientists, with the locus of their spiritual experiences at the workplace, strive to do their best to merit a transcendent encounter. These individuals can interface with the spiritual when they assume responsibility for doing good work.

For the subjects treated in this study and for many others, spirituality reflects an abiding concern with existential matters: the nature of the self and the transcendent; how to respond to suffering, crisis, and wonder; and how to live in a world where one's actions take on cosmic significance. Spiritual questions can lead to deep reflections on one's place in the world and can dramatically affect how one thinks about and interacts with it. As one chaplain at a liberal arts college commented during an interview with our project, "Spirituality has more to do with working on yourself. . . . It is being concerned about the individual and being concerned about society. Spirituality is concerned about an awakened world."

Yet spiritual engagement does not guarantee that a person will do good work. Moreover, many who do not hold spiritual beliefs frequently take on the responsibility to respond to societal and global problems in their work, and the specific ways in which a spiritually oriented person does his or her work does not appear to differ in any specifiable manner from the ways of someone who is not spiritual. At the same time, evidence from this study suggests that spirituality not only helps to connect one's personal beliefs with one's work, but it is also capable of awakening a person to the desperate need for good work in our world. Rather than a self-centered diversion, spirituality can help people take responsibility for their actions and their work. Indeed, it seems quite clear that spirituality, in its various guises and formulations, can lead individuals to carry out work that is both excellent in quality and vitally important for the broader world.

REFERENCES

Casanova, J. (1994). *Public religions in the modern world.* Chicago: University of Chicago Press.

Conners, C. (n.d.) Cheryl L. Conners, Bio. San Francisco: Project for Integrating Spirituality, Law and Politics. Retrieved May 19, 2006, from http://www.spiritlawpolitics.org/people/cheryl_conner.html

Davidson, J. & Caddell, D. (1994). Religion and the meaning of work. *Journal for the Scientific Study of Religion, 33*(2), 135–147.

Fischer, Z. N. (1996–1997, Winter). On zen work. *Turning Wheel: The Journal of Socially Engaged Buddhism,* pp. 13–15.

Larson, E., & Witham, L. (1997, April 3). Scientists are still keeping the faith. *Nature, 386,* 435–436.

Lyons, L. (2005, January 11). *Religiosity measure shows stalled recovery.* Retrieved February 5, 2005, from http://www.galluppoll.com/content/?CI=14584

Muirhead, R. (2004). *Just work.* Cambridge, MA: Harvard University Press.

Roof, W. (1999). *Spiritual marketplace: Baby boomers and the remaking of American religion.* Princeton, NJ: Princeton University Press.

Weber, M. (1930). *The Protestant ethic and the spirit of capitalism.* New York: HarperCollins Academic.

Wrzesniewski, A., McCauley, C., Rozin, P., & Schwartz, B. (1997). Jobs, careers, and callings: people's relations to their work. *Journal of Research in Personality, 31,* 21–33.

Wuthnow, R. (1996). *Poor Richard's principle: Restoring the American dream by recovering the moral dimension of work, business, and money.* Princeton, NJ: Princeton University Press.

Wuthnow, R. (2001). *Creative spirituality.* Berkeley: University of California Press.

7

RESPONSIBILITY AND LEADERSHIP

Andreas Schröer

Modernity fragments, it also unites.
—Anthony Giddens

ALL WORKERS ARE, OR SHOULD FEEL, RESPONSIBLE. But leaders have a special burden. They have a larger set of responsibilities at work (employees, boards of trustees, voters, mission statements) and often—because of scheduling demands, for example—more complex situations at home as well. How do leaders, particularly those with an ethical conscience, parse out their responsibilities? Thanks to the range of leaders interviewed in the GoodWork Project, I had the opportunity to examine this question with respect to two contrasting populations: established leaders, defined as exemplary workers who have found themselves in or beyond the peak of their professional life and changed their domain significantly; and leaders-in-formation. In the latter case, I studied two groups of individuals under the age of forty: social entrepreneurs, who are tackling societal problems with business strategies; and young political activists, who have shown strong political engagement at an early age.

The effects of age on styles and approaches to leadership have been examined in broad terms by Bennis and Thomas (2002). They found that the difference between two generations of leaders is due to the impact of the era in which those leaders emerged. Whereas the older generation grew up in an era that included World War II and the Cold War, a period that Bennis and Thomas describe as an *Era of Limits* (1945–1954), the younger generation grew up in an *Era of Options* (1991–2000) that included a variety of powerful new media, globalization, and the end of the Cold War, as well as more troubling phenomena like AIDS and terrorism. The major difference between the two groups, Bennis and Thomas found, is their attitudes toward work-life balance. Whereas the older generation puts everything on the line to accomplish its mission, the younger generation is much more aware of the work-life balance issue.

Although Bennis and Thomas have proposed that the social and ethical frames of reference have changed, I focus more on cognitive aspects of leadership (Gardner, 1995). I contend, first, that leaders-in-formation tend to have a broader and more fluid concept of responsibility than preceding generations of leaders; they create individualized mixes of responsibility for different spheres of their lives. In contrast, established leaders have a more focused notion of responsibility. Second, leaders-in-formation struggle with conflicting responsibilities; established leaders talk much less about such conflicts, instead reflecting a sense of purpose and putting a high value on integrity. For leaders-in-formation, work-life balance is indeed an issue; they want to work in or lead an organization in a way that also allows them to respond to the needs of their families. Leaders-in-formation have a rather interwoven and pluralistic understanding of responsibility that calls on them to construct and reconstruct continually their personal concepts of responsibility. This form of hyperresponsibility (Lenk, 1998) might be needed, because leaders respond to different needs and use different abilities in different spheres—the public sphere, the private sphere, and the realm of normative ideas.

In principle, responsibility can denote different relations: somebody (a) is responsible for something (b) to somebody else (c), within the framework of certain (professional, ethical, universal) standards (d). According to the cognitive approach adopted here, I focus on what or whom leaders in good work feel responsible for or to. A person can feel responsible simultaneously to different causes, such as another person, a community (or country), an organization (or company), a value (such as truth or liberty), and an ideal (such as excellent work) (see Haydon, 1978).

Responsibility is more likely to become a motivation for leadership when (1) responsibility is based on a personal encounter, a (family) tradition, or another strong ethical framework; (2) the person has an entrepreneurial sense of transforming the responsibility into strategy and action; and (3) a supporting environment such as a team, peers, or mentors helps the subject to act according to his or her responsibility (compare Damon and Bronk on ultimate purpose in Chapter One of this volume). According to positions in moral philosophy, the first aspect explains why people act responsibly. In Kant's understanding of moral action, the moral standard itself is the mainspring (*Triebfeder*) for moral action. Other motivations can be the power of the existing tradition (Hegel) or a deep interpersonal encounter (Buber). The entrepreneurial sense stands for the person's willingness to accept the responsibility he feels and his ability to create something new or productive out of it, and the supporting environment helps us to understand that we are talking not about purely individual achievements but about leadership in a certain social and professional context.

Methods

I examined the interview transcripts of two sets of leaders: eight established leaders and seven leaders-in-formation. I sought to find indications of a personal sense of responsibility and of differences in terms of focus, continuity, and conflicting responsibilities between the two sets of leaders. The eight established leaders were selected by polling GoodWork Project researchers about which interview subjects they considered to be the best and most inspirational of the more than twelve hundred good workers interviewed for the project. People nominated multiple times were considered, and an attempt to represent multiple professions and both genders influenced my ultimate selection. Ultimately, the six men and two women chosen came from three professions: two from journalism, three from business, and three executives of philanthropic foundations. The leaders-in-formation were selected at random from among social entrepreneurs and young political activists. The five men and two women were, at the time of the interview, between twenty and thirty-nine years old.

In what follows I present several examples of how responsibility can play out as a positive force for leadership. I've selected examples that capture well the themes that emerged in the larger population. In the latter part of the chapter I cite other subjects who help to flesh out the patterns I have discerned.

Established Leaders

I begin with examples of how established leaders conceptualize their principal responsibilities.

Responsibility to the Community: Paul Brainerd

Paul Brainerd, born in 1947, is founder of Social Venture Partners (SVP) and the Brainerd Foundation. In his first career, he was founder and chairman of Aldus Corporation, a company that produced the first desktop publishing software, PageMaker. After an extraordinarily successful career in business, Brainerd set up a new foundation. The Brainerd Foundation focuses on environmental issues such as global warming. In the process he also created a new, engaged form of philanthropic action. A group of one hundred successful people, including Brainerd, operates SVP like a venture capital firm. They invest in organizations and help them grow in order to tackle specific social or environmental problems.

Brainerd was brought up in a small town in Southern Oregon. His mother, who was active in church and several charitable organizations, nourished in him the idea of giving back to the community: "When I formed my company, Aldus Corporation, in the 1980s, we had four pillars of values in that company . . . one of those was *service to the community.*" For Brainerd, community service was not only an ethical principle; it also attracted employees to his company and helped to retain them. Responsibility to the community has also been the driving force behind his philanthropic enterprise. Asked to whom he feels most responsible in the work he does with SVP and the Brainerd Foundation, he answered, "to the public that's ultimately served by the nonprofits. You play a very indirect role here in that you're supporting organizations that in turn serve others. And ultimately you're responsible to those people who are receiving these services . . . to ensure that whatever is being done is *in the public interest* as defined by you."

The ethical framework of a philanthropist shapes Brainerd's interpretation of the public interest and his definition of responsibility to the public. This interpretation is not arbitrary. On his account, philanthropy should always help to build trustful relationships, recognize and use resources and human capital effectively, and prevent harm. Therefore accountability is an important aspect of responsible leadership. "How do you get the accountability component into organizations in terms of outcome-based measurement? . . . That requires a whole new infrastructure in terms of systems to keep track of outcomes . . . in terms of *making a difference in people's lives.*" The accountability "measure" that Paul Brainerd proposes is closely related to his "broader theory of change. And that is based on that it's all about people and leadership. . . . That—fundamentally, in organizations as well as individuals that make a difference—it's all about their ability to engage people, provide a model or a perspective or an idea that leads and results in change."

Paul Brainerd has a clear and focused view of responsibility in his work, one based on an ethical framework that goes back to the charity work of his mother: "The whole context of giving back to one's community was established at a pretty early age for me." This sense was enriched by positive experiences in business and in philanthropy. He has a strong entrepreneurial sense and has had a supportive environment for his ventures.

As I found with respect to other established leaders, Brainerd did not mention conflicting responsibilities or the feeling of being torn between different responsibilities. He also could not remember any ethical conflicts related to his work: "Nothing comes to my mind that would be a major issue for me." To be sure, he is aware that philanthropy can do harm to a society. He tries to create as many accountability and learning mechanisms in his organizations as possible in order to be able to cope with these risks. Brainerd's responsibility to the community, his values, and his beliefs, are aligned with what he does in his work and with what he has achieved throughout his career. His responsible leadership is combined with personal integrity in the sense that he remains true to his values and has aligned his actions and his beliefs.

Corporate Social Responsibility: Anita Roddick

Dame Anita Roddick, born in 1942, is founder and former CEO of The Body Shop, an international company that sells natural skin and hair care products. The Body Shop operates in fifty countries, with more than nineteen hundred shops worldwide. Roddick was originally trained as a teacher. She founded The Body Shop in 1976 in her hometown, Littlehampton, in England, when her husband was traveling and she had to take care of their two children. She decided to open a shop where she sold homemade skin and hair care products with minimal packaging. The products were made from natural ingredients, and the ideas for her product lines were a direct result of her extensive journeys to various parts of the world. Probably the most famous example is her disclosure of the secret of why Tahitian woman have such soft, smooth, and elastic skin—cacao butter, which became an important element in The Body Shop's first skin care product line. Roddick is an optimist and a great storyteller, with an infectious sense of humor (Roddick, 2005).

Roddick's innovation in the business world is her way of understanding a business and shaping its conduct. In view of the circumstances surrounding its founding, the company became her way of living and doing what she wants to do. The financial bottom line was not at center stage for her but rather was an appropriate vehicle for her higher goal: "I think if I can look back and I look back at my tombstone, it would be, 'She tried to make business a kinder, gentler place.' And that's a real big goal." The Body Shop is appropriately seen as a values-driven company, one that engages in local economies, women's rights, and the protection of animals, and fights against animal testing and inhumane working conditions. So that she could concentrate on her other interests, Roddick sold The Body Shop in 2006 to L'Oreal.

In her role as a business leader, Roddick feels most responsible to her employees and to the local trading communities and cooperatives with which she does business. This responsibility is based on personal encounters—with her employees on a daily basis, and with women in the local communities during her travels and project work. These immediate relationships have helped her to develop a truly global perspective on business. Her project and campaign work as well as her business strategies are driven by the idea of service to humanity, an idea rooted in a sense of responsibility for people she knows personally. In her view, responsible business practices include ethical components: respect for countries and cultures "south of the equator"; humane working conditions, including education and child care for employees; and support for small-scale local ventures and initiatives. Roddick regards organizations such as Businesses for Social Responsibility, alternative trade associations, the World Business Academy, and *Inc.* magazine as good value-based business models. These stand in contrast to the usual business practices that she rates 'hugely irresponsible.'

One of the reasons for Roddick's responsible leadership, she believes, is her background as an Italian immigrant in the United Kingdom. She cites the values instilled in her by her parents: "There was a work ethic. . . . So service was everything. I knew how to serve customers; I knew how to be quick." Even so, she recognizes the role of self-interest, broadly construed: "*Everything I do is for myself,* and I think anybody who says it's for the world's part is a load of crap. . . . I'm always looking to please some imaginary people—my dead father, a couple of nuns that helped shape my identity. So they're my mental moral guardians of my gatepost."

From all indications Roddick has integrated her life and her work. Like Brainerd, she did not report conflicting responsibilities or ethical dilemmas in her work. She sees her office as an extension of her own kitchen. As a businessperson, she acts no differently than a citizen or family member. She lives an aligned life. In her business she acts according to her values and beliefs, using her company and the money it makes as a vehicle to serve a higher purpose. Her sense of responsibility is paired with personal integrity. Her view of life is holistic: "I just thought life was love and work, end of story."

Responsibility and Loyalty to Employees: John Sperling

Born in 1921, John Sperling founded the for-profit University of Phoenix for working adults in 1976. He is also president of Seaphire International, a salt water agricultural company; chairman of the Kronos Group, which practices age-management medicine; and an activist on the issue of drug law reform. Sperling received his undergraduate education at Reed College, Oregon; a master's degree from the University of California, Berkeley; and a doctorate in economic history from Cambridge University. Before becoming an entrepreneur at age fifty-two, he taught as a tenured professor at San Jose State University (Sperling, 2000).

In his work, Sperling feels most responsible to the employees of his companies. "I try to feel loyal to all of the ten thousand employees that I have, that the companies have. I think loyalty is very important, but you only get it by giving it. So I think that's a very important part of knitting a company together and making it successful."

Sperling also stresses the centrality of integrity: "You have to have absolute integrity within the company so that there's no doubt as to what the ethics are." On the other hand, Sperling does not think much of explicit statements of goals, because he perceives them as limiting. His motto is, "He goes furthest who knows not whence he goes."

Owing to his pioneering role in for-profit higher education programs Sperling is a controversial figure in education. But he does not see himself torn between conflicting responsibilities or different kinds of constituencies. "I see no conflict at all. . . . I have no conflict at all. For a person who runs a controversial company, it is important to have a strong value base."

Sperling deems his Calvinist upbringing as an important source for the values he still holds. "Calvinists believe they can determine the difference between sin and virtue that habit of mind has carried over. So once I decide to do something, I never have any doubts."

Sperling's notion of responsibility is clear, and focused on his employees. It is not only an ethical principle; it also reflects his convictions on how to run a business. In his view, a successful company needs to be knitted together by mutually loyal relationships. His beliefs and actions are very much aligned, and he insists on the centrality of integrity and focused responsibility.

o

MY SURVEY SUGGESTS THAT ESTABLISHED LEADERS do not report conflicting responsibilities or ethical dilemmas in their work. Their professional accomplishments are aligned with their values and beliefs; the latter may even be an important source for their success. Integrity, identity, and responsibility for the different aspects seem to belong together inseparably. Brainerd and Roddick also point to the integration of life and work as an important aspect of their personal concept of life and leadership.

Leaders-in-Formation

As a contrast, I turn now to leaders-in-formation, whose conceptions of responsibility differ in instructive ways from those of the established leaders already discussed. The senses of responsibility of these younger subjects are much less certain, both in terms of focus and in terms of balance among conflicting forces.

Responsibility to the Vision to Change Lives: Gerald Chertavian

Gerald Chertavian, thirty-six,[1] is president and CEO of Year Up. Prior to founding his training program for urban young adults, he graduated from Harvard Business School and cofounded and ran an Internet strategy consulting firm, Conduit Communications, based in London. In 1999 he sold his firm and started to "run a school . . . a program to enable urban adults to realize their potential." In 2001, *Boston Business Forward* magazine recognized Chertavian as one of "Boston's forty most-promising individuals under the age of forty." He currently serves as a trustee of Cambridge College and Bowdoin College, and is on the board of advisors for the New Sector Alliance.

Chertavian invested half a million dollars of his own money in his program, with the goal of reaching ten thousand students. He feels primarily responsible to his "students—yes, they are at the center of everything we do, so when we draw visual pictures of our program and we think about our program . . . you always have to keep your eye on the ten thousandth student."

The means of this empowerment are basically education and support. Young adults in Greater Boston can apply for a Year Up program that teaches them technical skills, professional skills, and soft skills "that

---

[1]All ages are from the time of the interview.

enable them to make a positive and successful transition." The program also provides support for other priorities, including help with immigration, tutoring in English as a second language, and housing.

Chertavian considers himself a "people-focused executive director." Whether in business or in running his nonprofits, he gets "a 'high' in seeing someone grow and develop, whether it is a baby, or a student, or staffpeople." This orientation toward personal development emanates from values he absorbed from his father, a "workaholic" dentist: "You earn what you get. Nothing comes for free. Dad would often say, 'Step up, you pay the price and you shall receive.'" Chertavian believes that "you can achieve what you want to provide if you want to work for it." And this belief has become a cornerstone of his philosophy in Year Up. The program is "very, very demanding. There is a seven-page work agreement you need to sign, and if you don't meet the expectations, you're fired. . . . I am into people earning their opportunities."

The broader context for his working philosophy is Chertavian's conception of what American society should be. "This country was founded on a belief that you work hard and get ahead. It was the foundation upon which we built America." He sees this dream endangered by soaring high school dropout rates among Hispanic and African American kids, which leaves them with a 6 percent chance of securing a college degree. "I get to live my dream. I get to do on a daily basis what most excites me both intellectually and emotionally, which is to enable people to realize their potential." It is to this dream that he feels most responsible; the dream has encouraged him to found and ultimately scale up a successful nonprofit program for urban young adults. But Chertavian's sense of responsibilities extends not only to his students; he also feels a direct responsibility to the business side of his job, and that includes his staff and his funders.

Chertavian is married and has two children. To cope with the different and sometimes conflicting responsibilities, he has developed his "multiple firsts" theory: As he expressed it, "on a given day, when one of my roles may be demanded because it is placed first, you have to allow that to happen." Although he believes that he has "learned to balance work better," Chertavian is still searching for a way to balance the different roles, to be as good and responsible as possible, "as a friend, as a businessperson, as a community member."

Reflections on his family background indicate to Chertavian that he is seeking to integrate two different role models: His father worked very hard to provide for his family; he was driven by the quality of his work and used to tell his son, "Good, better, best, never let it rest until the good is better and the better is best." On the other hand, Chertavian described his mother as a kind, good-hearted person "with a beautiful soul." Chertavian feels responsible to a double heritage. He first became a successful businessman by working extremely hard; now he is doing what he always wanted to do: serve urban young adults in their career development.[2]

Responsibility to a Humane Organization: Sara Horowitz

Sara Horowitz, thirty-nine, is founder and executive director of Working Today. She founded the organization in 1995 to represent the concerns of the growing independent workforce, including freelancers, consultants, independent contractors, temps, part-timers, and the self-employed. Working Today seeks to update the nation's social safety net in order to make it possible for independent workers to gain access to services (such as financial services) and benefits (such as health insurance and life insurance) previously available only to "traditional" full-time, long-term employees (see http://www.freelancersunion.org/about-our-founder-a). In her work Horowitz feels most responsible to the idea of a good and humane organization, a "new kind of organization . . . a real structure for people. . . . We want to provide services to get people to feel a direct connection to you—like a mutual aid society."

In recognition of her efforts to create a self-sustaining organization of flexible workers, Horowitz was awarded a MacArthur Foundation Fellowship in 1999. In 1996, the Stern Family Fund named her a Public Interest Pioneer, and she was also an Echoing Green Fellow for four years.

The area of work that Horowitz has chosen is in line with her family tradition. "My grandfather came here as an immigrant and he became a union organizer. . . . My father was a union-side labor lawyer, and my husband is a union-side labor lawyer. And so that's what my family does." Horowitz was interested in labor already as a freshman in college; she cited not only her family background but also the whole of the "environment that I grew up in. I just thought everybody was for unions." Another source of Horowitz's notion of responsibility was the Quaker school she attended: "There was something about mission and having a commitment to something higher that gives you a kind of resilience like nothing else." Honoring the family tradition, Horowitz became a labor attorney and a union organizer before founding Working Today.

[2]See Erikson (1969), who argued that successful adults do what their mothers wanted them to do in the way their fathers would have done it.

Horowitz combines a basic notion of professionalism with an entrepreneurial approach to realize her ideas. Wryly, she cited famed director Billy Wilder, who explained the secret of his movies: he shows up on time and gets his movies made on budget. That "funny kind of professionalism" Horowitz finds "inspiring." Resilience and steadiness are her way to show strength: "The secret is to just wake up in the morning and just put one foot in front of the other foot."

Even though Horowitz told us "I think I have a pretty balanced life," she has to deal with conflicting responsibilities, which she referred to as "conflicting ideologies." Horowitz calls herself a "realistic idealist." Like the Quakers in her old school and other personal heroes such as Franklin and Eleanor Roosevelt, she believes that "dreams really matter." But she also cultivates a distance from the people on the "do-gooder" left, with their "sloppy ideas" and unsophisticated analyses. On the one hand, there is her entrepreneurial approach; on the other, she embraces a tradition on the side of labor and a strongly felt social responsibility. She was once invited to the elitist World Economic Forum, which for her "was like the classical example of pitting two parts of yourself against the other." She felt that going there would be "crossing the picket line" and would identify her as an entrepreneur talking about globalization.

Horowitz's vision and responsibility tend to answer to different callings. One calling—reflecting her family tradition—leads her "to create a new labor organization that has staying power that acts in the democracy to make sure that there's a safety net for how people really work." To make it "a very real, on-the-ground organization," she needs to be an analytical entrepreneur, thinking in economic terms of growth, value, and turnout. For Horowitz, the tension between conflicting responsibilities is not as strong as for other leaders-in-formation; rather, tension for her revolves around conflicting identities. When she encountered people from the Central American Movement or anti-globalization protesters who criticized her for not "being labor," "that was above anything else the most painful thing I had to deal with." At least one thing is clear: "The thing that is probably closest to my heart is trying to think of new labor structures for people who aren't traditional workers anymore."

Responsibility to the Children and to Our Ancestors: Earl Martin Phalen

A graduate of Yale College and Harvard Law School, Earl Martin Phalen, 35, is CEO and cofounder of BELL (Building Educated Leaders for Life) Foundation, an organization that seeks to increase the educational and life achievements of inner-city children. Founded in 1992, this community-based, nonprofit organization currently serves elementary school children in first through sixth grade in Boston, Washington, D.C., and New York City. Adopted at the age of two, Phalen grew up in Massachusetts as an African American child in a white, middle-class family. Phalen describes the family as loving and supportive; his parents fostered in him a love of children. But throughout his school experience he was confronted with quotidian racism in American society.

After a year in the Lutheran Volunteer Corps in Washington, D.C., Phalen reached a decision: he would support other people who were struggling to survive. He saw Latin American and African American kids as the least served group in U.S. society; virtually nobody believes in them or wants to help them realize their full potential. Reflecting on his ancestry, he told us, "[I feel] responsible to our children and to our [African American] ancestors. So for everybody who laid down their lives to open up opportunities for me and for everybody else around, I feel a very, very big responsibility." In his stated responsibility to ancestors, Phalen echoes a sentiment that we found chiefly among African Americans in our larger study (Horn, 2004).

In the spirit of his ancestors, who gave their lives for the freedom of their people, Phalen founded the BELL Foundation to help these too-often-neglected children. He hopes to grow his organization so that it helps to educate one thousand children in ten years.

This is where Phalen's own struggle begins. It is not primarily a struggle with conflicting responsibilities or with conflicting identities; rather, it is a struggle in light of the odds against reaching his goal. It has been hard for him to realize and accept that not every employee in his organization brings the same commitment to the cause as he does. Even with engaged staff, he feels "that's not the spirit that our ancestors brought to this." He also has to force himself to do things he was not comfortable doing before, like "doing fundraising, running educational programs," which he describes as "stepping outside my comfort zone." Fulfilling entrepreneurial tasks, doing management, and fundraising bring him into conflict with his convictions about what matters in "the whole grand scheme of the world," because he is convinced that these procedural considerations do not "matter even a bit." Phalen also feels torn between a focus on productivity, on the one hand, and the burning desire to help, to be passionate for the good cause, to honor the heritage of his ancestors. Because of the organizational tasks he has to fulfill, and the size of the responsibility he feels to his ancestors, he doesn't always believe he can live up to it: "I think [my ancestors] were focused on freedom and understood the price of freedom. I don't live up to that standard, but that's the standard I have." So he concludes, "That's where I'm still—it's still a conflict. It's still in conflict."

When he started the BELL Foundation, Phalen "was obsessive about working to get to where he wanted to be." It was a period in his life when he did nothing but work, and he hired a staff that had the same work ethic. After focusing completely on his job for five years, he decided he wanted to marry, have a family, and take time for himself. For the first time he hired a senior management team for his organization. Although this move has freed up time for other activities and priorities, Phalen has had to give up some of the responsibility for the operation of the organization. Even as he has done so, he has still had some doubts about the legitimacy of his decision, because "when folks talk about life-work balance. . . . I just don't think our ancestors were focused on balance."

Phalen feels strongly responsible to his causes, to the children in his program and to his ancestors, in order to achieve "the broader goal [which] is to impact, is to change society." How best to fulfill his strong sense of responsibility is a permanent struggle for him. At present he feels that he is not working as hard as he used to and that he is not "as focused as having that burning desire light" in him. He feels a conflict between the values that are important to him and the tasks of an entrepreneur and manager. And if he is to have a meaningful relationship with his family, he must also temper his engagement with the organization that is integrally tied to his sense of identity and self-worth.

Generational Differences: Focus and Balance

Among established leaders I have found a focused sense of responsibility that clearly relates to their achievements. Paul Brainerd's responsibility to the community resulted in a community-oriented corporate culture at Aldus and the creation of new, socially oriented forms of philanthropic action with the Brainerd Foundation and Social Venture Partners. Anita Roddick's strongly felt responsibility to her employees and to local trading communities resulted in the widely known and highly touted corporate social responsibility of The Body Shop. Roddick created a company that has good working conditions for its employees, is active in fair trade, and has supported a whole slew of social and environmental campaigns. John Sperling felt most responsible and loyal to his employees; this loyalty constitutes an important aspect of the corporate culture within Phoenix University and the Apollo Group.

This pattern also appears in other leaders not discussed here. For Katharine Graham, long-time publisher of the *Washington Post,* responsibility to editorial quality and independence inspired a tradition of investigative journalism (see Damon and Bronk, Chapter One in this volume). Graham took over as publisher of the *Washington Post* after the death of her husband, Philip, and continued the family tradition that had started with her father, who bought the *Post* in 1933. Graham was influenced by the notion of public service to which her father devoted the last twenty years of his professional life. Not only was the paper itself at the center of her concerns, but she also felt most responsible to the editorial quality of the paper. This deeply rooted responsibility, based on a strong moral identity, allowed Graham as publisher to make hard decisions that were highly controversial and politically uncomfortable—namely, to publish the Pentagon Papers and to support Bob Woodward and Carl Bernstein's investigation of the Watergate scandal (Graham, 1997).

Striking in these select GoodWork interviews is the lack of discussion about issues of balance and conflicting responsibilities. Within the group of established leaders, the narratives are rarely marked by conflicts; the subjects all tell stories of alignment between their responsibilities and achievements. They give fascinating examples of identity and integrity developed over their entire lives.

For example, Paul Brainerd was not aware of any ethical dilemma or conflicting responsibilities. In his two careers he found a way to act according to a strongly felt responsibility to the community and the integrity of his personal values and professional action. Anita Roddick exemplifies the integration of business life and civic engagement. Her story is one of engaged balance and integrity. Katharine Graham noted one important conflict in her professional life, resolved long before our interview: the conflict between the profitability and the editorial quality of a national newspaper. She always knew that, as publisher, she was responsible for both, so she took a balanced stance on this conflict. But even if profit and editorial quality were important, for her, profit served primarily as a means to allow reporters and editors to excel at their jobs. So she resolved this tension successfully by leading a profitable media company and maintaining the *Washington Post* as a national newspaper of extraordinary editorial quality, even when facing political pressure or personal risk.

When we now take a look at the leaders-in-formation, things become more entangled. There is a strongly felt need to balance different responsibilities; responsibilities are often not clearly focused; and conflicting responsibilities were quickly cited.

As one example, Gerald Chertavian feels "primarily responsible" to many people simultaneously. His idea of responsibility is nourished by "the American dream". He does not focus on one particular task in his life but seeks to live up to his responsibility to his students, staff, and funders; he wants to fulfill all the roles in his life as well as possible—be a good friend, a good businessperson, a good community member. But obviously because he is an active entrepreneur, this ambitious agenda creates tensions in his schedule and priorities, tensions that he seeks to solve with his "theory of multiple firsts."

Earl Martin Phalen seeks to balance different conflicts of responsibility. First, he needs to cope with his responsibility for the good cause, that is, helping young urban adults, alongside his responsibility to run a successful organization. Phalen feels strongly about the conflicts between ethically valuable work and his daily fundraising and management tasks. Second, he needs to balance his wish for a strong family with his commitment to the BELL Foundation. His crushing mission haunts him: he cannot always live up to the responsibility he feels to his ancestors, who were focused not at all on issues of work-life balance but on freedom for their people.

Sara Horowitz noted the conflict between the entrepreneurial aspects of her work and her identity in union organizing, the tensions between her realism and idealism. She seeks to be identified as one who cares for a social and humane organization with entrepreneurial strategies, and who stands apart from people on the "do-gooder left." Yet she recoils from being considered a traditional businessperson.

We found this pattern of conflicting responsibilities in other leaders-in-formation in our sample. Aaron Lieberman, thirty-one, successful social entrepreneur and founder of Jumpstart, feels responsible primarily to his family, especially to his grandfather and his little daughter. He feels a strong obligation to help others; an important point of orientation for him is the Jewish principle of *tikkun olam* (repair the world). Lieberman told us about the conflict between the challenging process of creating a new and successful organization and living a fulfilling family life. He recounted conflicts between responsibility for the economic success of his organization and responsibility to its mission, which in his view do not always seem aligned. He also reported frustration because the responsibility he has assumed has not provided the economic security required for his family.

A twenty-two-year-old graduate student at Stanford University whom we interviewed is cofounder and technical director of a national student think tank devoted to political innovation. The youngest subject in our sample talked about the struggle of dealing with conflicting responsibilities to his own education, to his girlfriend, and to his political goals. He wondered whether it is even possible to balance the life of a political activist with a fulfilling personal relationship.

By and large these examples indicate that leaders-in-formation are willing and able to take on responsibility for a lot of different causes, but they are still struggling with accepting any limits to their responsibility; their notion of responsibility lacks the focus we found among established leaders.

To be sure, these conflicts do not result in fragmented personalities or irresponsible leadership; on the contrary, they are part of the leaders' narratives, showing who they are and how their sets of values are different from those of others. Leaders-in-formation are balancing different responsibilities. They seek to integrate them into a consistent narrative, a distinctive way to express who they are and what they are seeking to achieve. Striving for an integrated sense of identity and integrity, they are still in the process of developing a personal concept of responsibility. Chertavian summarized the plight of his cohort: "I admire people who are self-actualized, people who know what they are about and don't have to prove it. . . . It is such a gift in life that many of us, I think, struggle for many years and decades to get there."

Conclusions: Ongoing Individualization of Responsibility

In their twenties and thirties, leaders-in-formation need to balance their family needs, the needs of their partners, and their commitment to their jobs. A person seeks satisfaction through productivity in career, family, and civic interests. Erikson (1950, 1968) characterizes this period of life as a conflict between principles of *generativity* and *stagnation*. In his view, the main question of middle-age adulthood is, "Will I produce something of value with my life?" In addition to vocational and avocational activities, and managing the house, a person needs to take care of and nurture children and help to form the next generation.

It seems from our interviews that, in contrast to the leaders-in-formation, established leaders reflect the final stage in Erikson's model: the tension between integrity and despair. So far as we can determine, the leaders we interviewed have succeeded in developing a sense of integrity. Their reflections on responsibility reveal feelings of fulfillment with a deep sense that life has meaning and that they have made the contribution to life for which the leaders-in-formation are still striving.

To be sure, it is not surprising that the younger group is facing conflicting responsibilities in balancing family, job, and community involvement. What is revealing is that they are so outspoken about it. There seem to be two reasons for this kind of open reflection. First, in the context of a changed understanding of family roles (Barnett & Hyde, 2001), constantly evolving working conditions (Giddens, 1991; Sennett, 1998), and the challenge of building trusting relationships (Kramer & Cook, 2004), these tensions may be more salient for workers now than they were in earlier eras. Second, the outspoken reflection on conflicts of responsibility is an important aspect of creating a distinctive self-identity as a leader.

Our study cannot answer one important question. We do not know which of two situations prevails. Perhaps if they had been interviewed thirty-five years ago our established leaders would have sounded like our leaders-in-formation—in which case we are dealing with a *life-stage transition* that remains relatively stable over time. But perhaps our established leaders would have sounded much like they do today—in which case we are dealing with a so-called *cohort effect*. Only longitudinal studies can help to resolve this question. So perhaps some day in the future we or some other investigators could revisit our leaders-in-formation and determine whether in fact they resemble the established leaders of today.

In any case, we feel encouraged by the interviews of our younger subjects. Leaders-in-formation perceive their conflicts of responsibilities as part of a process of integration. Despite challenges to the concept of identity and integrity under postmodern conditions, despite doubts about the trustworthiness of leaders today, we have identified a group of nascent leaders who are developing a sense of leadership based on ethical frameworks and a notion of responsibility to others that they seek to balance with other responsibilities in their lives. These leaders illustrate that contextual diversity does not necessarily entail fragmentation of the self (Giddens, 1991). The leaders-in-formation are making use of their different contexts to create a self-identity and a sense of integrity that incorporates elements of different settings and reflections of different needs into a cohesive narrative. The established leaders have already succeeded in this integrative effort; we have reason to hope that our nascent leaders will as well.

What can we learn from this study for preparing new leaders to take on responsibility? Responsibility and commitment are aspects of personal growth for any leader. Therefore, conflicting responsibilities can also be understood as aspects of personal development of leaders, as psychologist Erikson suggested in his analysis of the great religious leader Martin Luther; they might also be a result of our era of multiple modernities, ethical plurality, and the new definition of family and gender roles; The tensions could rise from new organizational forms such as public-private partnerships, social entrepreneurships, or other entities that combine once rival models of operation. However, leadership education should help to reflect and analyze these existing tensions. Leaders-in-formation should not seek easy solutions but rather learn to understand their struggle as an opportunity to define their personal concept of leadership and their specific narrative. A person should stick to her personal sense of responsibility, even if that implies responding to conflicting needs, values, and moral ideas. The continuum of reflection, of struggle about the proper way to lead one's life and organization, and of honoring one's own sense of responsibility might constitute the privileged path to outstanding good work and ethical leadership; it also might lead to new creative solutions: As can be seen in our examples of leaders-in-formation, the social entrepreneurs have developed economically sound ways of tackling social problems.

REFERENCES

Barnett, R. C., & Hyde, J. S. (2001). Women, men, work, and family: A new theoretical view. *American Psychologist, 56,* 781–796.

Bennis, W., & Thomas, R. (2002). *Geeks and geezers: How era, values, and defining moments shape leaders.* Boston: Harvard Business School Press.

Erikson, E. H. (1950). *Childhood and society.* New York: Norton.

Erikson, E. H. (1968). *Identity: Youth and crisis.* New York: Norton.

Erikson, E. H. (1969). *Gandhi's truth: On the origin of militant nonviolence.* New York: Norton.

Gardner, H. (1995). *Leading minds: An anatomy of leadership.* New York: Basic Books.

Giddens, A. (1991). *Modernity and self-identity: Self and society in the late modern age.* Stanford, CA: Stanford University Press.

Graham, K. (1997). *Personal history.* New York: Vintage Books.

Haydon, G. (1978). On being responsible. *Philosophical Quarterly, 28,* 46–57.

Horn, L. (2004). Passing it down: The role of cultural history and ancestors in good work. GoodWork Project Report Series, no. 31. Available at http://pzweb.harvard.edu/eBookstore/PDFs/GoodWork31.pdf

Kramer, R. M., & Cook, K. S. (Eds.). (2004). *Trust and distrust in organizations.* New York: Russell Sage Foundation.

Lenk, H. (1998). *Konkrete Humanität: Vorlesungen über Verantwortung und Menschlichkeit.* [Concrete humanity: Lectures on responsibility and humanity]. Frankfurt am Main, Germany: Suhrkamp.

Roddick, A. (2005). *Business as unusual.* Littlehampton, UK: Anita Roddick Books.

Sennett, R. (1998). *The corrosion of character: The personal consequences of work in the new capitalism.* New York: Norton.

Sperling, J. (2000). *Rebel with a cause: The entrepreneur who created the University of Phoenix and the for-profit revolution in higher education.* New York: Wiley.

8

SERVICE AT WORK

Lynn Barendsen

*I've come to believe that each of us has a personal calling
that's as unique as a fingerprint—and that the best way
to succeed is to discover what you love and then find a
way to offer it to others in the form of service.*

—Oprah Winfrey

IN THIS CHAPTER I EXAMINE THE DIFFERENCES in the views of
responsibility expressed by two groups. One group I have labeled the
caring group. It includes those who work directly with others and whose
work directly benefits those others—or whose primary professional identity inheres in working with others. The second group I term the *individualized group.* It consists of people in professions where much of the
work occurs in offices and does not involve relating directly to other people. I compare three caring professions—teaching; medicine, including
doctors and nurses; and social entrepreneurs—to three individualized
professions—business, law, and journalism. It should be noted that there
is not a sharp line of distinction between these two groups, and some
points of crossover may be identified. For example, social entrepreneurs
have many businesslike qualities, while some journalists and lawyers see
themselves as working in direct service of others.

My analysis reveals that caring workers focus on the human core at
the center of their responsibilities. Like many of us, these workers feel

responsible to a multitude of parties, yet the individuals they directly serve become the focus when decisions and pressures become acute. Doctors and nurses focus on patients, teachers focus on students, and social entrepreneurs focus on serving particular communities in need. Although one might anticipate that such an immediate human connection could become a drain, in fact these workers derive strength and purpose from it.

My study reveals the following:

1. Workers in caring professions typically describe themselves as filling in or taking over a responsibility that others have abandoned.

2. The line between personal and professional is a source of conflict for all professionals, but the nature of this conflict is fundamentally different in the two groups. Caring professionals do more than bring work home; when the line between their professional and personal lives is blurred, they risk caring too much. For some caring workers, their personal and professional lives are guided by the same values, and this alignment can make personal sacrifices easier to bear.[1]

3. When faced with a choice between conflicting responsibilities, caring professionals typically base their decisions on the individuals or communities they serve.

Taken together, these findings demonstrate that caring workers are guided by one responsibility over all others: responsibility to the individuals they serve.

What Are the "Caring Professions"?

For the purposes of this chapter I am defining *caring professionals* as those who devote their work lives to serving others. These individuals include those who work in soup kitchens or homeless shelters, those who dedicate careers to social services, as well as teachers, medical professionals, and social entrepreneurs.[2] Mahatma Gandhi and Mother Teresa provide two

---

[1]The concept of alignment and its relationship to good work are introduced in Gardner, Csikszentmihalyi, and Damon (2001).

[2]In Chapter Two of this volume, Susan Verducci discusses Nel Noddings's concepts of caring and morality and then applies this framework to her own analysis of responsibility in work. There are points at which Verducci's analysis and my own overlap, and indeed many of the "caring" characteristics she looks for are present in the following pages.

"ideal type" examples of individuals whose lives are devoted fully to helping mankind.

Several factors help to explain why some individuals become deeply committed to service work. Studies of the health and social service professions indicate that the desire to help others is a major motivating factor for individuals entering these fields (Kutner & Brogan, 1980; Powell, Boakes, & Slater, 1987). Role models are particularly important in inspiring and sustaining commitment to service work (Damon, 1995; Youniss & Yates, 1997). Several studies mention a "triggering event" or "framework experience" that brings about newfound awareness of purpose in life or a change in life choice (Feldman, 1971; Seider, 2005; Walters and Gardner, 1986). Personal hardships, often experienced early in life, may also be responsible for motivating individuals to help others (Colby and Damon, 1992). In their study of moral exemplars, Colby and Damon are skeptical, however, of attributing too much weight to any single factor, either family background or early experience. Instead, they emphasize that "one of the characteristics of highly moral people is their ability to learn from their experience all throughout life" (p. 8).

Methodology and the GoodWork Project

The majority of analysis in this chapter is based on interviews conducted by the GoodWork Project. The single exception to this is the nursing sample, for which I am indebted to Joan Miller.[3] I began by conducting an analysis of subjects' responses to a single question: *To whom or to what do you feel responsible in your work?* Responses were then divided using a series of subcodes, and these responses were compared across professions. When possible I have supplemented my analysis with additional examples from the subjects' interviews.

Considerations of Responsibility: Findings

Workers in some caring professions describe themselves as filling in or taking over a responsibility that others have abandoned.

---

[3]In consultation with the GoodWork Project, Miller studied eight young nurses and sixteen veteran nurses who were mid-level managers or leaders in the profession. The results of her analysis are discussed in Miller, "Opportunities and Obstacles for Good Work in Nursing," in press. Miller was kind enough to share the transcripts of this study with me, and my understanding of the caring professions has deepened as a result.

As mentioned earlier, caring workers are distinct from the other professions examined in that they each identify one clear, primary responsibility: doctors and nurses to patients, teachers to students, social entrepreneurs to groups in need. In addition, teachers and social entrepreneurs believe that, in fulfilling this responsibility, they are taking on obligations that others have neglected. Lawyers, businesspeople, and journalists are not as focused in their responsibilities; in fact, when asked about their primary responsibilities, they typically name multiple parties.

Teachers

Above and beyond all other responsibilities, teachers list their responsibilities to students (or their "kids") first. On a very basic level, teachers point out that they spend significant amounts of time with their students, "in some cases, I see the child more than the parent does." Beyond the considerable time they devote to teaching, teachers also act as role models and mentors:

> I don't even like to say this but I'm afraid that there are parents who've abdicated the kind of responsibility that we all felt as parents a number of years ago. And it's probably not all their fault either. It might be the economy. It's the way of the world. It's the exposures that parents have as well as children. . . . I think the lack of modeling, respectable kind of modeling for kids, is lacking in some situations. I mean, who are their heroes?

Although most teachers realize they are not simply teaching history or mathematics, they are not always at ease with these additional responsibilities. One teacher described how he and his colleagues find themselves filling parental roles:

> We're not babysitters, we're not parents, we're not even camp counselors; we're teachers. We're trying to impart knowledge of a particular subject matter. I'm not here to be a surrogate parent for these children, even though that's basically what ends up happening a lot of times. So you don't get the parental support. A lot of times parents are overwhelmed. This is a city, and you've got a lot of single moms out there who are barely scraping by with three jobs, trying to put food on the table, and I respect that.

Frustrated by lack of parental support, this teacher nonetheless understands that many parents find it difficult to meet all their children's needs.

As families become more fragmented, consistency in teacher-student relationships gains importance. Teachers do more than meet the needs of their students; they care deeply about them. Like parents, they understand the desire to comfort and nurture: "I feel like a parent a lot of the time; I want to make it all better, I want to be able to solve the problems, make it all go away if they're in pain, and I want to be able to, I don't like to see them struggling and I wish I could magically take it away."

In addition to these examples in which subjects specifically refer to parenting, several teachers also talked about feeling a responsibility to the "whole" student—not only teaching subject matter but responding to personal needs, teaching life skills, or helping students with whatever they need. Sometimes this additional service involves explaining basic skills of preparation that were at one time covered at home: "You're coaching more than you're teaching out there. You're motivating, you're encouraging fundamentals, fundamental skills . . . that they lack because no one taught them. Nobody ever sat them down and went to Target and got them the folder, got them the dividers, got them their pencils before school started in September."

At times, responsibility to the student involves being aware of and open to helping with emotional crisis:

> When you say responsibility, what I'm thinking is more need, and . . . also a lot of emotional things. I see everything, I'm not sure why I see everything. . . . You don't know how many kids slip through the cracks, who are in serious crisis, but I feel responsible, I do. You've got to be like, "Are you okay? What's going on? You want a jelly-bean? I've got some jellybeans; I know it's not going to make your pain go away, but are you all right?" You have a responsibility to check in with them; unfortunately, the structure of the school all the time does not allow that type of commitment.

All of these responsibilities are the type that parents feel toward their children. The teachers in our sample sound parental at times; they care about their "kids," and they also care about the kinds of adults these young persons will become:

> The students and society; there are days when I get, or times when I get very tense at what I'm doing because I know that three years, four years from now, these kids are going to be adults. And my obligation to them is to help them integrate into a society; and for society, it's to deliver citizens who can think and not just be quote, unquote, good model citizens, but productive, valuable, critical

citizens and not just critical for the sake of being critical; critical in the meaning of analytical.

Social Entrepreneurs

Social entrepreneurs are individuals who apply business acumen to social causes. By definition, their work serves a need that others in society have neglected. Social entrepreneurs see a societal void (such as part-time workers who lack medical benefits or elementary-age students who lack safe schools) and fill it with a new organization or service. Some stated overtly that they believe it is their responsibility to do so. Like teachers, their interest is not in placing blame (for example, on parents), but rather on helping the individuals in need.

When asked to whom or what they feel responsible, social entrepreneurs talk about the communities or people they serve. One social entrepreneur whose organization works to encourage peace makes a distinction between responsibility and motivation:

> On an immediate level, I would say I feel most responsible to my staff . . . if I don't do something well, my staff won't get paid. . . . But if I slice this a different way, which is who I feel motivated for, and who do I think about when I need to be picked up, I think about kids that I know and I think about [girl's name] who I knew when she was ten who got shot and lived and is fine, covered her one-year-old cousin in the middle of a gunfight on her playground.

Although this subject clearly feels responsible for keeping his staff employed, he is motivated by a concern for the children in need of protection.

A number of social entrepreneurs point to particular populations that are neglected and express a sense of personal responsibility to help these groups. Consider the perspective of one social entrepreneur, an African American who was adopted by a white family at the age of two:

> So I think there is a part of me, as early as elementary school, [that] knew that I wanted to devote my life to helping out groups within society become accepted, become fully human, become full participants in the American dream . . . full participants in their humanity. In our humanity. So I knew that very, very early on. And later experiences really helped resurface that and bring me to the place I am today. But I think that's the deep—the belief set. And also just feeling very blessed because at the time that I was adopted there was some

statistic that some 70 percent of black boys in the foster care system
ended up in the penal system by the time they were twenty-one.

Another social entrepreneur, though not a member of a minority
group, addressed the same broad issue: the fact that many are denied
opportunity and that he imagines himself as part of an equalizing force:

> I mean having a vision of America that is a bunch of affluent, semi-
> affluent people doing the daily grind, and then huge pockets that are
> totally left out and blocked inadvertently or not inadvertently from
> participation in the dream, is a totally dispiriting vision of the world.
> Just incredibly unmotivating. Yes. I just wanted to see what I could do
> to align myself with people who wanted to make changes like that in
> that series of problems.

Social entrepreneurs may talk more than others about ideals because
they daily confront the fact that the ideals are often far from reality. Many
social entrepreneurs explain that they feel a responsibility to contribute to
society or to work toward change. At times these beliefs stem directly from
a spiritual or religious upbringing. As he described his own work, one subject referred to the Judaic ideal of *tikkun olam*, or the "repair of the
world." According to him, "we're here to repair the world." Another social
entrepreneur, who referred to himself as "spiritual" but not following any
religion formally, described his beliefs as follows, "I believe that . . . we all
come from a higher power and that while even though society is very
segmented, that there's a responsibility to reach out to those . . . pockets of
society that are less served."

Medical Practitioners

Teachers feel responsible to students. Social entrepreneurs feel responsible
to particular underserved groups (the poor, inner city youth). Nurses and
doctors feel responsible to their patients. Additionally, many doctors cite
responsibility to their patients' families. This difference between doctors
and nurses may well be explained by the immediacy of the care that
nurses typically give. The majority of their interaction is directly with the
patients whereas doctors spend more time talking over treatments, medi-
cations, and care with one another, with other staff, and with families of
the patients. Neither doctors nor nurses describe their work as comprising
responsibilities that others have neglected. This difference within the
sample of caring workers might be explained by the differences between
occupations. Social entrepreneurs are, by definition, taking on neglected

communities. Teachers' responsibilities have grown increasingly complex as families have become more fragmented and burdened with responsibilities. The medical professions, by contrast, are established and less subject to major cultural shifts. Nurses do, however, describe a particular sense of responsibility demonstrated by the most effective members of their profession. One subject described the difference between nursing students who have developed the "caring competencies" and those who have not:

> Nurses can go in and they can check the monitor and hang the IV or insert the line or the tubes or whatever. Hemodynamically they're excellent, but when it comes to being with and truly being present to patients and families and knowing what to say and how to say it and when to say it and to truly be able to learn the whole skill, which I believe it is . . . of true empathy . . . the mere coming into a room, their way of being with other people, what they said, how they said it, their whole character, comes through as far as being very transparent and very authentic. And it's interesting with patients, that they see it quickly. Most patients—it's like they'll say you're different.

The difference between technical skills and the ability to empathize is significant. Nurses claim that patients easily discern which nurses "care" and which nurses are simply going through the motions. As one subject described it, these differences directly affect the level of care received by the patient:

> In nursing and medicine it is such an intimate relationship . . . that your framework, your beliefs really impact the care and the outcome of that patient. And patients do know when you don't care. . . . You can teach someone the concept of person, environment, health care, caring, compassion, but I think that caring—you can also demonstrate caring, but you cannot make someone want to care.

According to some subjects, caring is the very basis of the nursing profession, and therefore one of the most basic responsibilities of nurses:

> I think we have a wonderful opportunity and possibility because of the very roots of, I think, nursing and what it truly, I believe, [what] Florence Nightingale and so many that have gone before us really envisioned it to be. And I think it's a trust, an obligation I see to continue to be a voice, to be change agents, to continue—because we're entrusted with people's lives at a time of great vulnerability. And I think it's a wonderful privilege, but it also can be so tragic with the absence of caring and competency.

Additionally, several nurses reported that they and their colleagues are increasingly expected to take on ever-expanding responsibilities without proper preparation. It is unclear if these are responsibilities that others once held or if the profession itself is changing. One subject believes that the increase in responsibility has to do with changes in our health care system:

> I think it's a combination of things, the way health care has changed and technology has increased. The role of the nurse has expanded far beyond what many people imagine, the expertise that they have to have, and there's always one more thing that they need to learn how to do. So, besides your basic physical care of the patient, you have new medicines that you're responsible for giving, you have new therapies that you need to direct, at least. So, it seems like the role of the nurse is ever expanding, but the supports aren't necessarily there to help that.

In part this situation seems to be a result of the shortage of qualified nurses in the United States. Nurses are being thrust into positions of responsibility before they are fully trained. Another subject, the chair of a nursing department at a prominent and well-respected school of nursing, talked about how necessary it is to prepare nurses for the expanding levels of responsibility they will have:

> I'm not sure that we always do, nursing as a whole, prepare them for the responsibility that they're suddenly granted their first day off of orientation. The complexity of today's health care delivery system and treatments far exceed what we can ever teach in school. We can't teach them everything they need to know, but many practice settings expect students to come out knowing everything.

It is important to emphasize that these nurses are not dissatisfied in their work. They worry about increasing responsibilities, and they worry about what this means for the care of their patients, but they are nonetheless deeply fulfilled by their caregiving. Like the other caring workers in this sample, the nurses are less interested in the *causes of these shifts* in responsibility and more interested in the *focus* of their responsibilities. Similarly, the teachers expressed some understanding of the plight of overcommitted parents and focused on the students' needs. Social entrepreneurs focused more on individuals in need than on the details of how they arrived there.

Individualized Professions

I have used the term *individualized* to describe three professions that are less oriented to an "other" than are the professions in the caring group.

The work of some of the individualized professions is mediated, the work of others is more compartmentalized.

Journalists' work is mediated in that journalists relate to others through the written word. They reported a variety of responsibilities. Among these, responsibility to the "truth" is primary; however, some journalists also reported responsibility to an imagined reader or viewer. For some journalists, loyalty to either of these somewhat abstract concepts makes little sense. Instead, these individuals expressed primary responsibility to their own personal standards. Journalists also talked about responsibility to sources, to their employer, and to their colleagues.

Lawyers' work is more compartmentalized than mediated, in two senses: first, they work with people on specific matters, not with their entire well-being in mind; and second, they deal with a variety of cases bearing no particular relation to one another and are unlikely in most instances to feel a personal attachment to any one of them. Lawyers described even more varied types of responsibility than journalists—to the firm, to the client, to the law, to justice, to themselves. This variance depends in part on the type of law practiced (and in our sample several different fields are represented).

Like lawyers, businesspeople do work that is more compartmentalized than mediated, although depending on the particular goods and services provided there may be elements of both types of work. Additionally, businesspeople have rare or infrequent contact with their consumers. And like lawyers, businesspeople described a number of responsibilities, with no clear entity emerging as primary. A few business people talked about how the nature of their responsibilities has changed over time—either as the business itself has grown or as their own positions have shifted:

> In the latter part of my career I was responsible to the shareholders. They are the ones that put up the capital and they are the ones that fundamentally own the company. Early in my career I didn't have a line of sight to the shareholder. I didn't know how my decisions affected the shareholder. That was one of the big issues I found when I became CEO. I think it changed who I am responsible to. I think more in my earlier career I was more responsible to see that the job got done well for the customer—which is still important. Don't get me wrong. We don't ignore the customer. But it definitely migrated to the owner of the company.

In our study, we interviewed individuals at all levels or career stages—those who were just starting out, those who were in the middle of their work lives, and those who were near retirement. The study of nurses, for example, includes both established faculty at top nursing schools and nurses who are just beginning their careers. In both cases, the nurses were clear about their primary responsibility: it is to the patient. Teachers who have been working for more than thirty years still consider students their first responsibility. This emphasis has not shifted over time. Social entrepreneurs are very entrepreneurial in mind-set, and in this way perhaps are the closest of the caring professionals to businesspeople. Like their counterparts in the business world, they begin and grow their organizations; and like business-people, they experience shifts in responsibilities as their organizations grow. They have to balance funding pressures, employee needs, and the needs of the communities they are trying to help. But because their organizations are mission driven, most social entrepreneurs point to one constant responsibil-ity: serving the needs of their particular group or cause. In business, as I have argued, experience and growth change both the company (its reach) and the responsibilities of the primary stakeholders.

In summary, caring workers each identify a single primary responsibil-ity: to the individual or groups they serve. Some caring workers believe they are taking over responsibilities that others have abdicated. Journal-ists, lawyers, and businesspeople are more diverse in their responses. Most workers, however, share a common dilemma: the pull between familial and work-related responsibilities.

The line between personal and professional is a source of conflict for all professionals, but the nature of this conflict is fundamentally different between the two groups.

The discussion of personal and professional boundaries involves two separate issues. The first of these is a common theme heard throughout the working world: the problem of imbalance between work and familial life. This problem is more acute for the caring workers in this sample. Simply put, caring workers risk caring too much. The second issue involves an overt and positive connection between personal and professional life: car-ing workers often describe the same values guiding their personal and pro-fessional lives. If caring workers feel they are at risk (of burnout, of becoming too involved in the life of a patient), they find sustenance when their personal and professional values are in alignment with one another.[4]

---

[4]Jeffrey Solomon also discusses the issue of balance in teachers' lives in Chapter Five of this volume, on time management. Solomon's emphasis is on those teach-ers who are able to establish a boundary between work and personal life in order to keep themselves from burning out. My emphasis falls on those teachers who give all to their students and risk becoming too involved. For these teachers, establishing boundaries is quite difficult.

Work and Family Balance

In the caring professions, individuals risk becoming too involved with the party served (patient, student, community in need). Some of these individuals attempt to set boundaries between their professional and personal lives. They do so with varying degrees of success. As related by a teacher, establishing boundaries is part of a deliberate attempt to preserve time as well as energy: "I think I'm really committed to doing a good job, but I've also really made a conscious effort to try to put limits to the amount of time that I spend doing school stuff, partly for my own energy level so that I don't burn out."

Some teachers acknowledge that there are simply not enough hours in the day to complete every task. Like teachers, nurses run the risk of burnout. Maintaining balance is one way to combat this risk:

> And I think that every one of us in health care, we have to pay attention to our own balance. I have to pay attention that, okay, I've gone three months without a day off—I really need to try to take a day off. That's not a bad thing. Or I need to make sure that once a week or twice a week I get to one of my children's basketball games, or something like that. It may not seem like much, but it keeps me balanced as an individual and then I feel as if I'm not giving up one thing for another.

Nurses face heavy loads of responsibility and emotionally demanding relationships. Social entrepreneurs also face these demands, but additionally they experience the demand that accompanies running an organization. One social entrepreneur described how he puts additional pressure on himself during his time at work, to try to squeeze as much work as possible out of these hours:

> Every hour that I am spending at the office is an hour that I am not with the family, and every hour that I am with the family is an hour I am off task, and it's really a zero sum game. . . . It is brutal. It is probably one of the most painful things I have to deal with. . . . I push myself hard. . . . if I am at work I make every hour count because if an hour at work expands to two hours unnecessarily, that's an hour that I lost with my family.

For many caring professionals there is no balance: many openly admit they have difficulty drawing a line between professional and personal time. One doctor, for example, explained that vacations are not always an escape. He also was not clear that he really wants to leave his work responsibilities behind: "I'm going away tomorrow. I'm not going to be around tomorrow. I have a couple of pretty sick patients, and I'm worried about what's going to happen to them. And so the conflict I have is, do I keep checking in with my nurse to see what's going on? Or do I leave it up to the nurse to deal with and speak to the on-call physician, which is normally what happens?"

Teachers frequently described problems with setting boundaries between work and family life. One teacher described how heavily her work concerns weigh on her: "The responsibility that I feel is sometimes the kind that keeps you up at night, not sleeping." Another teacher realized that the kind of time and energy he is investing now is possible only because he does not have a wife and children at home:

> Sometimes I'm putting too much of myself into my job. And so relationships are strained, and my time, I feel like I spend a lot of time worrying about my job. . . . I think I won't be able to teach the way I'm teaching right now for the rest of my life. There's just no way. And I'm not married, I don't have children right now, so I have some time and some energy to invest in my job, but I don't know if I'll do that for the rest of my life.

For these teachers, the inability to establish and maintain boundaries is a casualty of the deep bond they feel with their students. Many subjects were aware of how connected they are to the individuals they serve. One teacher tied her success or failure directly to that of her students: "I feel when a kid fails, I've failed too." Lawyers, journalists, and businesspeople also struggle with issues of balance between work and family life, but the struggle is less pronounced in these professions. Some did not mention any issues of balance between work and family, and a few reported that they have no problems in this regard. For one businessman, leaving the worries of work behind was not an issue at all: "I've always had one very good personal trait and that is that I've always been able to open and close the hot water faucet and the cold water faucet. So, when I walk away from business I forget about it. If I go to sleep tonight and I don't set the alarm clock, and my wife doesn't wake me, I will sleep for twelve hours."

There are of course journalists, lawyers, and businesspeople for whom issues of balance between work and family life are difficult. However, these problems are almost always an issue of time constraints. Unlike the caring workers in this sample, they do not risk becoming too involved with particular individuals. One lawyer's response to questions about work and family balance is representative:

> I am not sure I manage it well. The best way I can do it, unfortunately, is to give up other things that I personally would like to do. I mean it's

not a sacrifice—I don't want to sound noble, like it's a sacrifice, but if you divide your life into the three parts of work and all the related commitments, and there are a lot of them; family; and then sort of things I am interested in personally but don't necessarily involve the family, it's that third which has to give.

As noted, the caring group faces similar issues, but the quality of the conflict is fundamentally different. Bringing home paperwork is not the same as caring too much—losing sleep over a sick patient or becoming too involved in the life of a troubled student. Further distinctions between these two groups of workers go beyond issues of work and family balance.

Personal and Professional Values

Some caring professionals make a direct connection between their professional and personal lives through their values, explaining that they are guided by the same principles in work and in life. The teachers in our study described this as *modeling*, or setting an example for their students with their own behavior. For example:

> I've got a friend who's a CPA. . . . Let's say he got arrested for drunk driving. He'd go to work the next day, no big deal. If it's a teacher that does it, it's a big deal. So to say that you aren't a role model or that you don't have that responsibility to the kids is a lie and you're just kidding yourself. So I try to, I live in town here, and I try to keep myself out of the news, if you will. . . . I'm not a very religious person. I don't really believe in a higher authority. I just live my life the way mom and dad taught me. . . . It's the way you conduct yourself in the class, the way that I am at home, and I don't have to turn it on and off.

This teacher realizes that he is a role model and that his behavior is carefully observed by his students. If professional and personal values are in alignment with one another (if he practices what he preaches), acting as a role model is less difficult.

Medical professionals also talk about agreement between personal and professional values. In fact, one nurse explained that she was particularly drawn to her workplace because of its philosophy, one she describes as "values-based health care education":

> It's something that I know can be operationalized because I practice nursing that way and I live my life that way. And so the common

phrase that the Jesuits use is that they want students who graduate from here who are men and women for others, which really encompasses the core values in the values-based health care education. Because if you're for others, you're always going to look at social justices. If you're for others, you're going to want to find common ground. If you're for others, you're going to want to be as excellent in the knowledge you learn so that you can impart the best that you can in serving others, whether it be a nurse or doctor or teacher or whatever.

This subject lives her life and practices nursing guided by the same principles. When these values are in agreement, there is less conflict. Similarly, a doctor described her understanding of "what's meaningful" as consistent across personal and professional lines:

I guess I feel—probably this sounds funny to you; I don't usually hear doctors talk like this as much—but I think it's important to be loving in the world. . . . Because of that I structure my whole approach to people in my life in a very particular way. . . . I think that generally what's personally meaningful to me and what's meaningful in my clinical work with patients and with learners and with employees, I think those things pretty much line up. If I stick to what I just said a minute ago, it lines up just fine.

A single philosophy, to be "loving," guides both professional and personal lives.

Interestingly, the aforementioned social entrepreneur who described the pull between work and family as "brutal" expressed consistency with respect to his personal and professional values:

I never attempted to separate my career from my values, and I believe that those who are given much in life have a greater responsibility to give back. And I am not necessarily talking about giving financially. . . . But if you look at my opportunities for education, my opportunities to spread my wings and explore the world as a young man, whether it is through travel, the blessing of having grown up in a very strong, supportive family, those are all the things that I look at when I feel fortunate for what I have been given in life. So I play out a career that's very much about doing my part and giving back and attempting to make change, in however a small way to change the world for the best, for the better. And so those values are a huge part of the career choices that I have made.

Although this subject, like workers in many professions, struggles to find time for his many responsibilities, he is resolute in his commitment to "give back." The values that are important to him personally are the same values that guide his work.

Another social entrepreneur also talked about consistency between personal and professional values. He placed his own work within the context of history:

> I feel most responsible to our children and to our ancestors. So for everybody who laid down their lives to open up opportunities for me and for everybody else around I feel a very, very big responsibility. So I often ask myself, "What would Harriet Tubman do in this situation?" And it's an easy guide; it makes the question so simple, especially when folks talk about life-work balance and keeping a balance and maintaining. And I just don't think some of our ancestors were focused on balance. I think they were focused on freedom and understood the price of freedom. I don't at all live up to that standard, but that's the standard that I have.

Although the particular context this subject laid out—African American history—is not typical in our subject population, his argument is characteristic of caring workers. Striking a balance between work and family is never easy, but when personal and professional values are in alignment, sacrifices seem less bitter. Caring workers are guided and, in fact, supported by a deep sense of responsibility to the individuals they serve.

When faced with a choice between conflicting responsibilities, caring professionals typically base their decisions on the communities they serve. Indeed, the three caring groups are distinguished by the fact that each constituency identifies a particular group to which it is primarily responsible. This primary responsibility is further solidified and articulated in the face of conflict. In the caring professions, one favors the needs of the patient over the interest of the practice, the needs of the student over the interests of school administrators, and the needs of an underserved population or a cause, usually over the interests of a funder. As mentioned earlier, there is a contrast between nurses and doctors in how they list their primary responsibilities. Nurses assert their primary responsibility to patients, even when they are balancing other duties:

> I have a dual role. One is as the nurse leader for the organization, and then the other is [as] the administrator for the hospital, with a team of individuals. So, it's a little bit different in both. First of all, I think the way I look at things is everything I do, what it entails, needs to focus around patient care. So everything, whether it relates to our

financial situation—I'm responsible for our budgets, I'm responsible for employee relations, I'm responsible for assuring standards of practice are where they need to be, nurse vacancy rates, a lot of data, patient satisfaction—all the things that we do center around the patients.

Or as another nurse explained it, "no, I don't experience a tug. It's very clear to me. . . . The core business of this industry is patient care, and that's my focus."

Doctors also asserted their primary responsibility to patients, especially when faced with other pressures. Additionally, some doctors asserted a responsibility to their patients' families. For example, describing a conflict he faced with respect to a living will, one doctor explained that he was perceived as being involved in a "mercy killing." In the end, he was at peace with his actions because he felt he was true to his primary responsibilities to the patient and the patient's family: "You have to do some things that you don't like in the profession. And in this case I believe my responsibility to the patient and his family was properly and professionally carried out"

In the example just presented, when faced with a life and death decision a physician based his decision on his primary set of responsibilities. But even more mundane workplace dilemmas are guided by the singularity of purpose embraced by caring workers:

> My priorities are always foremost what's in the best interests of the patient. An example is, if I have a meeting scheduled at two o'clock in the afternoon and I have a patient that's not doing well, I won't show up at the meeting. I'll be at the bedside taking care of a sick patient. That's just the way it's going to be. I may get criticized and so forth, and people may frown and not like that, but that's just tough. It's easy to set your priorities in this business. Patients come first.

Social entrepreneurs face conflicting responsibilities as well. They have invested much of themselves, both emotionally and financially, in establishing organizations. If that organization struggles, they feel the negative consequences quite personally, much in the way that a business entrepreneur might. Their livelihoods are intimately connected to the success of the organization. Additionally, social entrepreneurs feel particularly responsible to the people they support. One social entrepreneur founded a program geared toward educating low-income urban adults. The program offers a combination of hands-on skill development and real work apprenticeships in information technology. This subject talked about making a difficult short-term decision (to fire an employee) in order to maximize long-term results (and reach more students):

> You always have to keep your eye on the ten thousandth student. We want to touch at least ten thousand people, so everything you do, you have got to be thinking about the ten thousandth student. So decisions you make today may not be right for your current situation, but it brings you closer to that goal. You may fire a staff member who is good but not great, and if you are going to get to ten thousand, you better have great staff people.

Ultimately he makes his decision based on how best to serve the students.

Another social entrepreneur has established an organization designed to improve urban high schools. When faced with conflicting responsibilities, he is guided by his mission:

> I am accountable to our mission of fostering high levels of academic achievement by attracting and preparing all—what I told you before. So when something comes up and I'm torn between what I'd like to do personally, or even a friend that I'm interacting with, someone that's in the professional community, or something I'd like to do—a variety of things come up all the time that tempt you to do different things, but I feel very, very accountable to this mission. The mission's bottom line is about helping every child really reach high levels of learning through the strategies we've set out.

Again, when push comes to shove, the focus returns to the level of the individual, and "helping every child."

Similarly, when teachers are faced with conflicting responsibilities, they almost always make their choices in favor of their students. For example, an art history teacher in an urban public school told us,

> And there are conflicts sometimes with people, placement of people; you see teachers in positions that sometimes you don't think it's best for them or best for students, but it's a bean-counting deal where things get, positions have to be filled. And I don't think students are always best served that way; in fact, I know they're not, and so I'm conflicted in how far do I take my complaints and how far do I stay in my little world and make my difference in my classroom. And that's why I'm slowly moving into administration, is to be able to do what I think is best for everybody. I'm always students first, and it will always be teachers second, and I think there are some people here

who are teachers first and students second or third. And I think as long as we keep our eye on the prize, which is the students, then the decisions will all fall into place, in my opinion, in the right way; as soon as we go for teacher comfort, then we've made a mistake.

As this teacher explained, focusing on his primary responsibility, his students, helps him in his decision making. The students themselves are a source of support in that they provide focus and a sense of purpose.

In another example, a teacher explained that keeping the needs of students first *is* good teaching. When asked if she ever feels torn between conflicting responsibilities, for example, between students and colleagues, she responded:

> No, I never have because I think [that] . . . doing the right thing by a student does the right thing by the colleague. And I feel like my kids' needs, like say a kid has an emotional need, their academics don't work if the kid's crying in class. So if a girl's in here crying, I'm not going to say, "Sorry, honey, you've got your MCAS [Massachusetts state test] right now," because the kid's not going to take their MCAS that day, so you get them to counseling. Maybe there's a hierarchy of needs, that sounds kind of phony, but I really don't see a conflict. . . . There tends to be a right thing to do, and if you tend to think it out and do the right thing for the student, you're going to be doing a good job as a teacher.

Caring workers, like all of us, face conflict in their responsibilities. They are guided in the choices they make by a clear sense of what's most important. Patient, student, inner city youth—these take precedence when a difficult choice must be made.

People in the other professions considered in this study face conflicting responsibilities in varied ways. Journalists are most parallel to caring professionals in that many assert a primary loyalty to the group they serve—their audience (reader or viewer). Although the largest percentage of journalists focus on responsibility to audience, or to truth, this abstract relationship is not enough for some of them. Some journalists reported that, when faced with conflicting responsibilities or difficult choices, they rely instead on their own personal standards or instincts. Journalists quite often asserted other responsibilities as well: to their sources, to their place of employment (newspaper or television station), to colleagues. When faced with conflict (for example, to print or not to print), most journalists asserted, they try to respond with their audience in mind. It is important to realize, however, that a journalist's relationship to his audience is not a personal one. Journalists rarely know their readers, and if they do, this relationship is quite different from that of teacher and student, for example. Most readers are imagined. As a result, when journalists are pressed to make a difficult ethical choice, keeping the audience in mind does not always help. As one journalist explained: "I don't think about the reader so much. I am not going to pay any of that stupid lip service. . . ." "Well, we always think of the reader." If you think of the reader, you are suddenly thinking about that little old lady in Peoria, and you are writing about some cliché-riddled flagpole, and you're lost. You have to please yourself."

In times of conflict, some journalists are guided not by an imagined audience but instead by a principle: to report the truth. Of course "truth" too is an abstraction:

> I think trying, integrity is important, try to say things that I think are true and offer some kind of verifiable evidence for it even if it's not strictly scholarly or scientific. Which is a long way of saying what they used to call The Truth, which I'm somewhat sort of suspicious that there is such a thing as The Truth, but I think it's important to try to provide evidence for what you're saying. . . . When is the defining moment for you in terms of truth? When you say, "Yeah, OK, I'm going to go ahead and publish this or back it up." It has a lot to do with knowing that I'm going to have to stand by those words.

Because many stories are not black and white but grey, many journalists acknowledged that responsibility to "truth" is not always the best guide.

Lawyers described conflict between what is "right," or legal, and what the client wants or described conflict between serving the needs of the client versus serving the needs of the firm. Although on the surface the lawyer-client relationship is parallel to the relationships in caring professions (doctor-patient, teacher-student, social entrepreneur–community in need), choices made by lawyers are rarely in favor of their clients in any simple and straightforward manner. Rather, primary responsibility is typically to the firm, to a partner, or in favor of personal principles. For example,

> [there is] the conflict between what I want to do, what I think is right, what level of research I think would be appropriate to dig into a particular issue and come out with the right answer versus the client's willingness to pay for it. And when your billing rate is $400 an hour, you can't spend much time digging into things, researching things, and expect the client to keep you as a lawyer. You have to move pretty

quickly and sometimes more quickly than you would like. I guess there
is also a tension between what the law is and what the client wants to
do. Clients may want to do things that the law just doesn't permit.

The relationship between lawyer and client described here is vastly different from the relationships described in the caring professions. In the
caring group, workers are guided in times of conflict by one responsibility
over all others—to the individuals they serve. The legal professional is
much more torn, and clearly this lawyer will not base his decision merely
on what best serves the individual client. As mentioned previously, the
work lawyers do is compartmentalized: they work with people on specific
matters only and are unlikely to become as personally involved as caring
workers do. The relationship between lawyer and client may be complicated; in fact, one criminal defense lawyer went so far as to refer to clients
as "the enemy":

> Not only criminal defense, in every lawyering field . . . the client is your
> worst enemy because the client can be ungrateful, they can . . . manipu-
> late you, the situation, everything, not only criminal defense clients, but
> all clients. And so a lot of lawyers spend a good deal of their time pro-
> tecting themselves against that, the client turning against them. . . .
> How do you communicate an affinity and an enthusiasm and an empa-
> thy for the client while at the same time protecting your ability to
> remain an effective professional for the next case down the line?

Perhaps most distinct from the caring group, businesspeople worry
about the treatment of their employees, pleasing stockholders, and optimiz-
ing resources. They try to determine whether it is preferable to fire employees and keep the company healthy, or retain them and invite financial
difficulties. In our business sample, two very different stories emerged when
subjects spoke about facing difficult decisions. Some experience little or no
conflict in their decision making: "I see no conflict at all. If the employees
know that they should be devoted to the welfare of the customers and then
through that devotion the company continues to grow and prosper and the
shareholders are happy as can be . . . so I have no conflict at all."

But other subjects acknowledge that they sometimes have to make
tough choices. In making these tough choices, no single responsibility
guides most businesspeople. Rather, this group describes a process of
weighing variables and making the best choice at a particular moment:

> So it's an optimization philosophy rather then maximization philoso-
> phy, so we just try . . . at any given time . . . to optimize the value we

add to all the different groups, and that's the trick of management in terms of doing our best—sometimes the objectives are conflicting. We traditionally paid a significant year-end bonus to our employees, but over the past four years our performance hasn't enabled us to do that. So there's some upset on that part because we're not able to pay our annual bonus, but at the same time we can't pay the bonus without jeopardizing the financial strength of the enterprise and reinvestment for the good of all the other stakeholders, so. . . . It's easier to be a good company in good times than it is in bad times, so our challenge is to be a good company in bad times.

In the group of professionals who do not work in direct service of others, then, there is little consensus about how difficult decisions are made. By contrast, the caring group is, without exception, guided and supported by an overriding sense of responsibility to the individual served.

Conclusion

Although the nature of the work carried out by caring professionals varies quite a bit, they uniformly expressed a passion for their work and for the individuals they serve. Journalists, lawyers, and businesspeople may also be passionate about their work, but their passion is for the ideals of the profession (uncovering the truth, upholding the public trust, capitalism, and opportunity), not for a community of individuals (students, patients, people in need). This human difference is crucial in the way these professionals understand responsibility. It is the human dimension that seems to take its toll———the reason teachers lose sleep over their students—yet it reenergizes the caring worker. As one nurse explained it, the deep sadness of working with a terminally ill patient is eased by knowing her work is having a direct, human impact:

> I think what brings me back is that a lot of days—sometimes I have frustration and sadness, but a lot of days I will make a difference. People will say, "I don't want you to leave. Please stay. Are you coming back tomorrow?" and "Thank you so much for brushing my hair. Thank you so much for talking to us," and will be so grateful. . . . And that's everything. And that's one of the reasons I love nursing is, I think very few people have that level of reward for what they do.

Caring workers are not necessarily "called" to their professions in a way that other professionals are not. However, our findings do reveal that caring workers have a very particular, human focus to their responsibilities.

Doctors and nurses focus on patients, teachers focus on students, and social entrepreneurs focus on serving particular communities in need. Caring workers are supported in their work by this overarching sense of responsibility.

In the more individualized professions there is much less consistency around the issue of responsibility. Nonetheless, there are some professionals in each domain examined for whom a particular responsibility is clearly dominant. This may be a responsibility to one's own principles, to God, or to the ideals of a profession. Individual lawyers, journalists, and businesspeople report each of these factors as their primary responsibility. Perhaps for those professionals who are able to cite one primary responsibility, difficult decisions are more easily and confidently reached. For example, a lawyer torn between listening to a client or listening to his colleagues draws on his personal principles, or a journalist unsure about whether or not to report a particular story remembers her journalistic responsibilities to report the truth objectively. Presumably this rule of thumb would also be true for other workers—in the military, in the sciences, in the arts; when guided by a single sense of responsibility, a worker faces less conflict than when motivated by more than one.

Individual workers within these professions may be at peace with their responsibilities, but what about the professions as a whole? When lawyers do not agree on a single primary responsibility, the profession itself may suffer from a kind of misalignment. Individual lawyers may work with a clearly defined set of responsibilities, yet one definition may vary quite a bit from another.

Changes in technology and increased market pressures mean that individuals are working longer hours, often on weekends. Those in the individualized professions often do so in an office (sometimes in both a home and a workplace office). Although caring professionals experience a unique set of pressures and are certainly at risk should these pressures overwhelm them, they are supported by a community of like-minded colleagues. What does it mean for a profession if its individual workers operate with quite diverse understandings of their responsibilities? Bad or compromised work is likely to result when a professional lacks a primary audience (caring for people), a primary responsibility (to a principle such as truth), or support from colleagues (compare Gardner, Chapter Twelve, this volume). In the absence of these conditions—ones that catalyze work worthy of the descriptor *good*—pathological forms of work can result.

REFERENCES

Colby, A., & Damon, W. (1992). *Some do care: Contemporary lives of moral commitment*. New York: Free Press.

Damon, W. (1995). *Greater Expectations*. New York: Free Press.

Feldman, D. H. (1971). Map understanding as a possible crystallizer of cognitive structures. *American Educational Research Journal, 8*, 485–501.

Gardner, H., Csikszentmihalyi, M., & Damon, W. (2001). *Good work: When excellence and ethics meet*. New York: Basic Books.

Kutner, N., & Brogan, D. (1980). The decision to enter medicine: Motivations, social support, and discouragements for women. *Psychology of Women Quarterly, 5*, 341–357.

Miller, J. F. (in press). Opportunities and obstacles for good work in nursing. *Nursing Ethics*.

Powell, A., Boakes, J., & Slater, P. (1987). What motivates medical students: How they see themselves and their profession. *Medical Education, 21*, 176–182.

Seider, S. (2005). "Framework experiences": A key to the development of social responsibility in young adults. GoodWork Paper 36. Available at http://pzweb.harvard.edu/eBookstore/detail.cfm?pub_id=172

Walters, J., & Gardner, H. (1986). The crystallizing experience: Discovery of an intellectual gift. In R. J. Sternberg & J. E. Davidson (Eds.), *Conceptions of Giftedness*. New York: Cambridge University Press.

Youniss, J., & Yates, M. (1997). *Community service and social responsibility in youth*. Chicago: University of Chicago Press.

9

BEYOND THE GENDER STEREOTYPE

RESPONSIBILITIES TO SELF AND OTHERS

Carrie James

I definitely feel most responsible to my children and my husband in terms of they are my first priority in life and everything that involves them is more important than everything else. And I feel responsible to myself in all contexts. And in order to be responsible for myself, I have to professionally be doing what I feel is good work. And it just all comes out of there. If I am responsible for myself, I'm doing a good job, I'm loyal to my clients, and I'm ethical.

—Criminal lawyer

ACCORDING TO POPULAR WISDOM AND SOCIAL SCIENTIFIC CONSENSUS, gender matters in nearly every aspect of our lives. Sociologists commonly refer to gender as a prototypical "master status." Some scholars contend that not only are core societal institutions "gendered," but gender itself should be considered an institution (Lorber, 1994). That is, masculinity and femininity, social constructs though they are, carry powerful expectations that actually guide social relations. In this chapter I discuss the ways in which gender affects—and perhaps more importantly and more surprisingly, does *not* affect—how professionals define their key responsibilities at work and beyond. I also provide an account of how specific responsibilities—to self and to others—are conceptualized; this account considers both gender and profession influences.

For decades social scientists have documented the ways in which our interests, values, politics, and career choices—indeed, our very identities—are fundamentally shaped by gender. In the realm of work, gender is understood as a key factor mediating opportunity structures and commitment to work and family (Gerson, 2002; Hochschild, 1989; Padavic & Reskin, 2002). Research in numerous professions has shown that occupational choice, focus, and work style are affected by gender. For example, studies of medicine have shown that women physicians have distinct practice styles; they spend more time with and ask broader, "whole person" questions of their patients (Bertakis, Helms, Callahan, Azari, & Robbins, 1995; Franks & Bertakis, 2003). By way of explaining such patterns, social psychologists have argued that as a result of early childhood psychoanalytic dynamics, women's and men's self-concepts are deeply gendered (Chodorow, 1978; Gilligan, 1982; Miller, 1976). Still stronger claims have come from social cognitive neuroscience, which traces gender differences to genetics or brain wiring.

Regardless of whether gender differences are explained by biology, psychoanalytic dynamics, or socialization, the "differences lens" holds a strong appeal. As an example, Gilligan's well-known argument that women speak "in a different voice" (1982) continues to be noted a quarter of a century after the publication of her book. More specifically, Gilligan argued that women often feel encumbered by their responsibilities to others or "caught in a web of relationships," especially when making difficult choices. Men, on the other hand, generally assert a more independent sense of self and make decisions by reference to abstract principles. In short, women feel greater responsibility to others and men feel greater responsibility to themselves and to their deeply held ideals and values. Some researchers link the appeal of such arguments to larger concerns about social order, suggesting that this gender split has, at least historically, helped to reconcile a fundamental conflict between self and other.

Caring for self and caring for others have traditionally been cast as dichotomous and competing responsibilities in popular discourse and social scientific thought. Conceptualized on the broadest level, the tension between the individual and society, or "the problem of order," has been a—if not *the*—fundamental concern of sociology since its inception (see Bellah, Madsen, & Sullivan, 1985; Wrong, 1995). Traditional gender roles, it has been argued, have helped resolve this tension by prescribing a neat division of labor: men focus on independent achievement while women specialize in care for others (Gerson, 2002). Historically this division of expertise corresponded to the public-private split in which men toiled in the public sphere while women tended to the home. The opening of the public sphere to women weakened the rationale underlying these gender roles. Therefore there is good reason to believe that gender differences in responsibilities to self and other—if indeed they were as deep as some have suggested—may be waning.

Accordingly, evidence is accumulating that women are placing greater emphasis on an independent self and, at the same time, care for others (specifically family) is becoming a greater draw for men (Gerson, 1994, 2002). Despite this research, the appeal of the lens of differences continues to be strong. Take as examples the enduring popularity of *Men Are From Mars, Women Are From Venus* (Gray, 1993) as well as the recent media hype about young ivy-league-educated women planning to forge careers as stay-at-home moms (Story, 2005). And as noted earlier, Gilligan's theory of "different voices" continues to be widely cited.

In interviews conducted as part of the GoodWork Project, my colleagues and I asked leading professionals, *To whom or what do you feel most responsible?"* In examining responses to this question, I sought to understand whether professional women and men do in fact emphasize different kinds of responsibilities. I also explored how women and men manage potentially competing obligations, such as those to self and those to others. If Gilligan (1982) is correct, one would expect men to assert an independent self as a core responsibility and, in turn, to conceive of connections to others as potential threats. Women, on the other hand, would cite a myriad of other-oriented responsibilities as priorities, and the self would be discussed more rarely or as an extension of caring for others. In undertaking this analysis, I wished to test such claims using our large data set of interviews with professionals.

Our data suggest that women and men are more similar to than different from each other in the kinds of responsibilities they feel. More pointedly, men are just as likely as women to emphasize responsibilities to others; in turn, women emphasize self-responsibility as often as men do. Moreover, and also contrary to expectations, our sample of professional women and men conceptualized their responsibilities to self and others in comparable ways. Looking at the domains of journalism, law, and theater, I discovered three distinct ways in which subjects understand responsibilities to self and others—as conflicting, coexisting, or congruent. I found that gender does not independently affect how individuals understand self and other, while professional domain emerges as a significant influence. Overall, this analysis shows that the domain of work mediates how responsibilities to self and other are perceived and reconciled, and how (if at all) gender matters.

The Many Shades of Responsibility: Patterns in the Data

I analyzed narratives about responsibility from professionals in the fields of business, genetics, higher education, journalism, law, medicine, philanthropy, precollegiate education, and theater. I searched interview transcripts for the protocol question, *To whom or what do you feel most responsible?* If this question was not present, I looked for related questions, such as *Have you felt torn between conflicting responsibilities?* Transcripts in which responsibility questions were not asked were disregarded; I did not read entire transcripts, nor did I make interpretive judgments (read between the lines) about subjects' responsibilities. In total, I coded transcripts of 599 subjects who were explicitly asked about responsibilities; the gender distribution of this sample was 259 women (43 percent) and 340 men (57 percent). Responses were coded in categories developed inductively as the analysis proceeded; these categories included responsibility to God, to self, to colleagues, to superiors and mentors, to clients (students, patients, audience, and so on), to institution, to society, to abstract values, to professional domain, and so on. As I discuss later, I first compared the types of responsibilities that women and men cited. I then undertook a closer analysis of a subsample of responses in three domains (journalism, law, and theater) in which a responsibility to the self was often cited. Relationships among gender, domain, and responsibilities were examined through cross-tabulations. Statistical significance was determined through the use of chi square tests.[1]

Overall, a handful of significant gender differences in types of responsibilities were found. Women were slightly more likely to discuss responsibilities to superiors, including mentors and teachers (28 percent of women versus 19 percent of men; p = .02); to their colleagues (20 percent of women versus 14 percent of men; p = .04); and to their institutions (24 percent of women versus 16 percent of men; p = .02). Men were slightly more likely to cite God as a responsibility (7 percent of men versus 1 percent of women; p = .001). In addition, women were slightly more likely to name multiple responsibilities (85 percent of women versus 80 percent of men), but this difference is not statistically significant.

---

[1]A total of 166 chi square tests were conducted from cross-tabulations of responsibility type by gender, and self-other stances by gender and professional domain. Of these, only eleven cross-tabulations were statistically significant (p ≤ .05).

More gender patterns were found within professional domains, yet again only a select few turned out to be statistically significant. Among these, in higher education women were more likely than men to cite multiple responsibilities (77 percent of women versus 63 percent of men; p = .05) and responsibility to superiors (62 percent of women versus 28 percent of men; p = .03). In genetics women were more likely to cite responsibility to funders (24 percent of women versus 5 percent of men; p = .02) and to family (54 percent of women versus 31 percent of men; p = .04). In pre-collegiate education, men spoke about values more often than women did (27 of men versus 0 percent of women; p = .01). Finally, in law men were more likely to cite responsibility to society or the public interest (48 percent of men versus 18 percent of women; p = .01).

Beyond this handful of differences, and contrary to expectations, women and men were strikingly similar in most of their reported responsibilities. Notable among these similarities is the finding that women and men were almost equally likely to cite responsibility to family, with men mentioning family slightly more often; 28 percent of women and 32 percent of men cited their families or personal relationships. And with regard to responsibility to the self, women and men were again very similar; 28 percent of women and 27 percent of men cited the self as a key responsibility. Overall, what stands out is how alike these women and men were in the types and numbers of obligations they felt to others.

On their face, these findings about responsibility to others and self call into question the popular wisdom that men and women lean toward opposite poles of the autonomy-connection continuum. However, women and men can mean very different things when they assert a responsibility to themselves. Moreover, regardless of how self-responsibility is defined, it is important to know how the self is conceptualized vis-à-vis responsibility to others. To answer these questions, I undertook a deeper analysis of subjects' narratives in three domains (journalism, law, and theater) in which responsibilities to self and others both were frequently discussed. As noted, my analysis uncovered three distinct ways of conceptualizing the self vis-à-vis others—conflicting, coexisting, and congruent; professional domain turns out to exert a significant effect on the stances that individuals hold.

Responsibility to Self and Others

What do professionals mean when they name the self as a key responsibility? Our interviewees specified such things as their personal values and ethics, their standards for quality work, their interest in and passion for their work, their happiness and well-being (self-care, leisure time), and their professional reputations and success. The following examples are illustrative:

> I have the greatest obligation to myself—not to mislead myself, to be honest, to be brave, not to compromise.—Theater director
>
> Myself. . . . It is my standards that I live up to and it is my sense of how things should be done which motivates me. . . . There are lots of broad things in our society that we feel responsible for, but I think that, ultimately, I think it comes down to your own sense of your vision of the world and who you are accountable to. And you want to feel within yourself that you are living up to those standards that you set up for yourself.—Corporate lawyer
>
> [Being responsible to myself] means that I have to wake up in the morning and like myself.—Corporate lawyer

Among subjects in journalism, law, and theater who cited the self, 45 percent pointed to personal standards for quality work and 40 percent spoke about their core values and ethics as composing the self to whom they felt responsible. A comparison by gender across these domains revealed no significant differences in how responsibility to self is defined. Looking within domains, no gender patterns were found in law, although there were some notable differences among journalists and theater artists. Female journalists are more likely than males to define responsibility to self in terms of their quality standards or personal values (80 percent of women versus 42 percent of men). A greater percentage of male journalists assert a responsibility to their personal satisfaction, interest, or passion for their work (25 percent of men versus 0 percent of women). In theater, males are more likely to stress ethics and values (44 percent of men versus 18 percent of women). Again, our data suggest that professional domain seems to mediate how, if at all, gender matters.

Interesting in their own right, these findings may warrant further investigation. Yet it seems even more important to examine how the self is understood in relation to others, especially given the ways in which self and others are often understood as competing constituencies. Our subjects' narratives speak not only to discrete responsibilities, but also and often to the relationships between those responsibilities. These data can thus show how responsibility to self meshes, or is reconciled with, responsibilities to others, including colleagues, superiors, clients (audience, students, patients, and so on), and family, among others.

Self-Other Approaches in Journalism, Law, and Theater

I conducted a close analysis of the narratives of journalists, lawyers, and theater subjects and discovered three distinct ways in which responsibility to self is framed vis-à-vis responsibility to others:[2]

1. *Conflicting.* Self and others are dichotomous and competing constituencies; misalignment exists. As an example, several lawyers spoke about having to make trade-offs between serving their clients' wishes (to have their cases resolved quickly or to test the limits of the law) and satisfying their personal standards in their work (for example, doing adequate background research and following their ethical principles).

2. *Coexisting.* Self-responsibility neither explicitly conflicts with nor is congruent with responsibilities to others. For example, several journalists portrayed their responsibilities—to their readers, to their editors, to their own sense of satisfaction in their work—as separate obligations, relatively independent of one another.

3. *Congruent.* Self and others are experienced as congruent or aligned; responsibilities to self are fulfilled through responsibilities to others, and vice versa. In theater, for example, many actors described their responsibilities as intimately tied to one another; their personal enjoyment of their work was bound up with supporting their fellow actors or with providing the audience with a truly engaging experience.

CONFLICTING SELVES AND OTHERS. The conflict approach is consistent with the familiar idea that self and others are dichotomous and competing constituencies. In narratives representing this stance, tensions or explicit conflict between meeting obligations to self and tending to others are highly salient. In the terminology favored by the GoodWork team, a misalignment exists between the needs of self and others. Some subjects' narratives suggest a zero-sum equation in which compromise is likely if not inevitable; in order to be responsible to others, the self must be sacrificed in some way, or vice versa. As subjects most often frame it, self-responsibility is vulnerable

---

[2]These approaches are ideal types. Although most responsibility narratives fit into one category or another, some responses contained reference to more than one approach to self and others. In those cases, the dominant self-other theme of the narrative was coded. If entire transcripts had been reviewed, I may have found more evidence of multiple approaches.

to infringement by the needs or ideas of others. One young actress articulated this feeling:

> The only person you can really make happy is yourself. You really can't think about what other people think and what other people want. . . . I try not to worry about pleasing other people, because you can really hurt yourself when it comes to that. And you really are your own best critic I think. And like I said before when, you know when, if something—no matter how many people tell you it was good or it was bad, if you have an opinion about it you really can't shake that, because you're the only one that really knows what you think. And you're always going to be with yourself.

As is suggested by this narrative, personal quality standards are a kind of self-responsibility that often arises with the conflict stance. Loyalty to one's ethics and values, happiness and satisfaction with work, and wellness are also mentioned, although less frequently. The "others" to whom conflicted individuals feel responsible are most often clients, colleagues, or superiors. A corporate lawyer first spoke about her numerous responsibilities to others, and then about how her own physical well-being is compromised by striving to meet them:

> Oh, it's hard to say who I feel responsible to. It's really kind of a—it's almost something I don't have any control over. I just have a sense of responsibility; I've had a sense of responsibility since I was a little girl. I was a firstborn, and it was my responsibility to take care of my brothers . . . responsibility is just built into my hardware, it seems like. And so I feel responsible to my students; I feel responsible to my institution; I feel responsible to people in my field; I feel responsible to the nation at large. Is that big enough for you? . . . It's a conflict within me. I actually don't like working all the time, but actually. . . . I work all the time. I work all the time, and my main conflict is that I actually am out of shape. I work too hard, I know I invest way too much in my work, and I have a responsibility to myself, actually, not to be in bad physical shape. And I have a responsibility to myself to enjoy some things in the world other than eating, and I don't hike anymore. I really like hiking, and so that's where my conflict is.

Not surprisingly, family is also mentioned as a responsibility that renders feelings of conflict, as one lawyer discussed:

> I definitely feel most responsible to my children and my husband in terms of they are my first priority in life and everything that involves

them is more important than everything else. And I feel responsible to myself in all contexts. And in order to be responsible for myself, I have to professionally be doing what I feel is good work. And it just all comes out of there. If I am responsible for myself, I'm doing a good job, I'm loyal to my clients, and I'm ethical.

After describing these responsibilities, this interviewee went on to talk about her struggle to fulfill them:

I think often the result is that I feel—and I know other people in this position feel—that I'm not really doing anything as well as I could be. I'm not doing my job as well as I could. I don't have as much time as I really need to have with my children, with my husband, for myself. And all I can say to myself is that this is just the way it is right now. There is no—for me at least, in my specific circumstances, there is no clear answer. There is no solution. It's just living with that conflict.

For this attorney, conflict between self and other results in sacrifices on both fronts. The high standards she sets for herself—her definition of good work—ultimately conflict with her responsibility to her family, the result being that she feels compromised on both ends.

PATTERNS IN THE CONFLICT APPROACH: A "RULING" DYNAMIC IN THE LAW? Despite longstanding concerns by social theorists about the "problem of order"—the idea that if individuals are left to pursue their own self-interests, society will devolve into anarchy—the conflict approach to self and other appears less often than other stances. In the sample of lawyers, journalists, and actors who cited responsibility to self, 22 percent noted tension or conflict with obligations to others. Women and men in these domains are nearly equally likely to be conflicted; thus gender does not appear to be a key factor related to feelings of conflict. However, professional domain does appear to affect the way in which responsibilities to self and others are understood. Lawyers were more likely than actors or journalists to mention conflict: 38 percent of the lawyers in the sample exhibited this stance compared with 22 percent of actors, and no journalists discussed self-other responsibilities as central conflicts for them (p = .01). Within the conflict group, 63 percent were lawyers and 47 percent were theater artists.

The fact that a majority of subjects who demonstrated the conflict approach were lawyers suggests that the nature of the domain may encourage this mind-set, or at the very least convey an understanding of certain responsibilities—to client, for example—as probable sources of conflict. As one criminal lawyer pointed out,

One piece of advice that I have gotten, and I haven't really given it
out, is that the client is always an enemy. And that's fairly common in
criminal defense—not only criminal defense, in every lawyering field,
that the client is your worst enemy because the clients can be ungrate-
ful . . . they can manipulate you, the situation, everything—not only
criminal defense clients, but all clients. And so a lot of lawyers spend
a good deal of their time protecting themselves against that, the client
turning against them. And that happens. It happens a lot. . . . So I
think lawyers are always dealing with that. How do you communicate
an affinity and an enthusiasm and an empathy for the client, while at
the same time protecting your ability to remain an effective professional for the next case down the line? *How do you?* . . . I think
always by not overidentifying . . . keeping the relationship a professional relationship, not taking the client out to lunch a whole bunch
of times, not going shopping with the client. Just keeping, maintaining
the professional boundaries, I think, are very important. And trying to
protect your—to keep the client in role and to keep yourself in role.
And there's a reason for that. It's not just—you're not just being
snooty or anything. It's really about understanding that your interests
are not, this isn't a lifetime partnership or anything of that sort.

According to this lawyer, maintaining strict roles or boundaries between
self and other is necessary in order to do good work in the law and to protect his integrity as a professional. Furthermore, he explicitly suggested
that the mind-set of the "client as enemy" is normative in the law.

Similarly, a general-practice attorney traced her sense of conflict to the
nature of the lawyer-client relationship:

I do find that there is frequently a conflict with myself between responsibility to my client and to myself. And by that I mean not so much a
simple time conflict. . . . It's more—it is sometimes my duty to my client
to do and say things that are really contrary to my own temperament
usually, not so much ethics, but—and it isn't even always just temperament. . . . If I have the lawyer on the other side who is just being a complete jerk to me, and it is in my client's best interests for me to maintain
that relationship with the lawyer on the other side, I am not free to do
the human thing, which is tell him where to get off. . . . I'm not free to
be angry and to act on that. My job is to do whatever is best for the client, and my self is subjugated to that. That also manifests itself in my
direct relationship to the client. I recently had an incident where the client was unhappy with me because of something that she thought I
hadn't done that I had. And so the client was way off base, and that

happens with a lot of frequency. And my role, once again, is not to say, "You know what, you're way off base." I apologize. My job is to apologize even when it isn't my fault, to take responsibility for things that are not my responsibility. That's another piece of the essence of this relationship with the client. It's the deepest manifestation of "the customer is always right," in some sense.

This attorney perceives service to her client to be her primary responsibility, with the result that her self is "subjugated" to the client's needs.

Finally, a corporate lawyer spoke about a number of responsibility conflicts that were common among lawyers in our sample: family versus firm and clients, firm versus clients, and most pertinent to this analysis, self versus client:

> There is always a conflict between family and firm and clients because there are a limited number of hours in the day and the practice of law can be all consuming. It can really crowd out everything else. And so as between family and firm, there is constant conflict. If I put more time in here, I take time away from seeing my nine-year-old. And there is a conflict between the firm and the clients. In a sense, the firm wants me to bill everything I do for clients. Clients don't want me to bill for everything I do for clients. I have to tread the line between those two desires and bill what is fair and not bill what is not appropriate, and that is difficult. And there is also the conflict between what I want to do, what I think is right, what level of research I think would be appropriate to dig into a particular issue and come out with the right answer versus the clients' willingness to pay for it. And when your billing rate is $400 an hour, you can't spend much time digging into things, researching things, and expect the client to keep you as a lawyer. You have to move pretty quickly and sometimes more quickly than you would like. I guess there is also a tension between what the law is and what the client wants to do. Clients may want to do things that the law just doesn't permit, and some of the lines that get drawn in the law, in mergers and acquisitions, in the investment area, the regulated industries area, are not bright, crisp lines that it's obvious that you are stepping over. It takes a lot of experience and judgment to know where the line is, what you can advise the client he can legally do in good faith without adverse consequences, and what minute variations in the facts would cause him to stray across the line. And because it is so nuanced and it's based on such a totality of circumstances, and it's such a subjective judgment, clients will press you on it.

This lawyer's self-other conflict is less about personal boundaries with clients than about his feeling pressured to compromise his quality standards—what he thinks is the "right" level of research—in order to meet his clients' expectations. Moreover, although he does not appear to compromise his ethics, he suggests that clients "press" him to "stray across" the lines of the law.

Interestingly, male and female lawyers are almost equally likely to hold a conflict approach to self and other. This finding may be surprising given how much attention is given to the difficult plight of women in the law (O'Brien, 2006). In our sample, profession appears to exert the strongest influence over how responsibilities are construed. Overall, our data suggest that certain characteristics of the legal profession may contribute to perceiving conflicts between self and other. The long hours that legal work requires frequently pose dilemmas for lawyers, who at once feel responsible to their families and to their personal quality standards for their work. The lawyer-client relationship is frequently characterized as a service relationship in which the clients' needs push up against the lawyers' self-responsibilities; this tension results in either disappointed clients or frustrated attorneys. Finally, lawyers may emphasize conflict because it is a key metaphor for their work; after all, law is the domain in which conflicts between individuals or institutions are adjudicated. For trial lawyers in particular, a key marker of success in the law is beating the other side by convincing the jury that their client's claims are more credible than those of the other party.

Despite this evidence about conflict in the domain of law, it is important to note significant variation in self-other approaches within our sample of lawyers. In fact, a slightly greater percentage of lawyers described self-other responsibilities as congruent. Therefore, while features of law that are absent in other domains may contribute to greater sensitivity to conflict, conflict is not the only self-other dynamic felt by lawyers. At the same time, law's discourse of conflict is sometimes mentioned by subjects even when they personally embrace a more congruent approach.

Although law is the domain in which the conflict stance is most likely to appear, some theater subjects also spoke about self-other conflicts. Theater is a domain in which one might expect frequent conflicts over the definition of quality work and of artistic visions. As this veteran actor suggests, such tensions may contribute to a feeling that one's very self is at risk:

> You feel responsible to yourself, for one thing; I mean almost primitively . . . it's related to what I'm now just talking about. I mean, the

opportunity you give yourself to degrade yourself is so enormous
that some huge self-protective thing helps you, which is a good thing
on the one hand and a bad thing on the other because you can't
really do the work you need to do if you're worried about protecting
yourself, so that's a two-edged sword. . . . But you do feel, on a very
primitive level, responsible to yourself, you know? That you're just
going to permanently cause some permanent injury yourself by what
you're doing. But also to a standard, to a criteria, and usually you go
into the theaters. Or to film, or anything, because you've seen things,
you've experienced things when you were younger that really meant
something to you, and you see the power of this form of expression.
And to feel that that's being violated, or worse, that you are violating
that, it's like you're violating something that's important to you
and that has given you a lot of sustenance, so you feel responsible to
a criteria and the standard.

Taking a self-protective approach is an understandable strategy in a
field such as acting in which significant pressures exist to meet the expectations of the audience, producers, and directors. One might expect that
journalists experience similar tensions, especially given our other findings regarding misalignment of goals and values in the domain of journalism (Gardner, Csikszentmihalyi, & Damon, 2001). Yet although
some journalists referred to the potential for conflict, none of them discussed outright conflicts between self and other—at least not in their
narratives about responsibilities. Rather, journalists who spoke about
self-responsibility were most likely to construe self and other as coexisting obligations.

As in the case of law, among theater subjects gender does not seem to
be related to perceptions of conflict between self and others. Rather,
regardless of gender, it seems that particular tensions in the domain of
theater contribute to a conflict stance. Nevertheless, the domain of theater more often "sets the stage" for individuals to perceive deep connections, a congruence, between obligations to self and others.

COEXISTING SELVES AND OTHERS. Some individuals interviewed for the
study describe the self as neither explicitly conflicting nor congruent with
responsibilities to others. Rather, the self is described as if it were one
among many peacefully coexisting, even disconnected, obligations.
Responsibilities to self, to colleagues, to clients, to one's audience, and so
on are presented as if they are distinct pieces of the same pie; each is

apportioned a certain amount of attention, without apparent conflict.[3] Indeed, responsibilities are often listed in a compartmentalized fashion: to myself, to my family, to my colleagues, to my clients. Ideally, all responsibilities are balanced—each is given a comfortable share of one's energy and attention. A young journalist described three distinct responsibilities:

> [To whom] do I feel most responsible? A combination of the audience, myself, and . . . whatever higher power guides me. And you can substitute that for conscience or something like that, but those three. . . . Is the product that I'm putting out on the air; is that of quality to the viewer? Am I misleading them? Am I offending them? So that's in terms of my responsibility to the viewer. My responsibility to myself; again, that mirror test: can I look at myself in the mirror and be proud of who I am? Do I feel good about the decision that I made morally, ethically? And then the third, in the scheme of things, am I doing good work for humanity? Am I contributing something good to this planet? Am I fulfilling whatever purpose I am supposed to, whatever this earth plane is? And I don't necessarily pretend to be able to answer that. But I think I have a pretty good feel for whether or not I'm on the right track personally, professionally, and spiritually.

While the responsibilities cited here can certainly be intertwined (conflicting or congruent) in some way, this subject described them as separate elements. His responsibility to the audience did not seem to pose any conflicts for his ethical self, nor did he describe these responsibilities as mutually reinforcing. Similarly, a young actor talked about his self-responsibility as distinct from his obligation to his audience:

> *To whom or to what do you feel most responsible?* I think, myself. I don't think I've ever gotten on stage and tried to perform for anybody. So, I'd just say, myself. *Are there any secondary responsibilities you feel?* Well, responsibility to the audience, like I would always ideally want to—I'm performing for an audience, so, I guess the responsibility equal to me would be the audience. And I try to do my best in terms of communicating with them.

---

[3]*Note:* This characterization does not mean that neither conflict nor congruity between responsibilities exists for these subjects. Rather, their narratives on responsibility did not contain references to conflict or alignment, although they may have been discussed in other sections of the interview.

This actor suggested that his responsibility to his audience may be as important as or equal to his own sense of fulfillment in playing a role, but the two obligations are otherwise unrelated.

The meanings of self that most often arise with the coexisting stance are personal quality standards, ethics and values, and satisfaction or interest in one's work. A lawyer spoke about his personal definition of good (high quality and ethical) work: "I think it's just my personal sense of how I define a good job. I mean, I want to do a good job. So, it's my personal, ethical standard. [A good job is that which] in my internal space . . . makes sense to me, and covers what I have researched and felt to be is the entire—or a good portion of the issue. I come out with a logical and fair work product." This subject asserted that his conception of good work emerged from an "internal space," and so implies that it is relatively disconnected from the expectations of others.

PATTERNS IN THE COEXISTING APPROACH: THE MIND-SET IN JOURNALISM. Approximately 37 percent of the narratives suggested a stance of coexisting self and others. Once more, no significant gender differences were found: 36 percent of women and 38 percent of men in this group described self and others in these ways. Domain again seems to be the key influence: the coexisting stance is most likely among journalists. Indeed, 73 percent of journalists held this stance compared to only 22 percent of lawyers and 27 percent of theater subjects ($p = .001$). Features of journalism that may explain this pattern include the nature of the relationship between journalist and audience, and the need to strive for objectivity in reporting despite the fact that objective truths rarely, if ever, exist.

Journalists' narratives about self-responsibility suggest the centrality of personal satisfaction and contentment with their work. While journalists also cite obligations to various other constituencies (and sometimes struggles among them), these obligations are described as separate from their core interest in and passion for what they are doing. As one documentary filmmaker put it, "I really think you have to do what interests yourself. I mean, within certain limits. I can't go off and make a movie about this chair, so I think there are certain commonsense things. But in terms of what do people want, I've kind of given up on that. I think I just have to go with whatever instincts I have." This subject spoke about past unsuccessful attempts to cater to an audience's interests above his own; he has now resolved to satisfy his own interests. If luck has it, he will at the same time create something relevant and important for his audience, but a responsibility to them does not drive his artistic choices.

Similarly, a national newspaper correspondent talked about herself as her "number one" responsibility:

Well, I feel responsible [pause] to myself, in the sense that I have to be proud of and live with the consequences of what I write and what I say. Television has a slightly more ephemeral quality to it . . . you get used to being a little more loosey-goosey on TV; you say, "Achh, that's just television." It's not quite true, but you say it. You don't worry about it so much. But in print especially, and especially because it stays there, the old joke being about that doctors bury their mistakes, but the journalists have them out there all day, or in our case all week. And just because I need to feel satisfied with what I do, I mean, that's number one. Number two, I guess would be . . . doing your best to tell the story whole and tell it clearly. I don't think there is any such thing as objective truth in public affairs. There are quantifiable truths in science; this is not a science, this is a human endeavor . . . that relies on perspective and perspectives, and can get to be [unclear] sometimes. But you have to give it your best effort to see it whole and see it clearly. . . . I feel loyal, I guess, to the craft of journalism.

This narrative points to a feature of journalism that may explain why self and others are often perceived as separate responsibilities. Journalists are responsible for telling stories as accurately as possible; however, journalism "is a human endeavor" that "relies on perspective and perspectives." Therefore, reporters must gather different points of view and "do their best to tell the story whole." Achieving this end may require journalists to segment their responsibilities, to keep their own interests and perspectives separate from their obligations to others. Lawyers spoke about this separation as well; however, the need for boundaries in the immediate service relationship between lawyer and client is quite distinct from a journalist's more distant relationship to her audience.

In addition to being committed to objectivity, the journalists we interviewed sometimes attempted to segment their responsibilities to themselves and others as a strategy for coping with misalignments in their domain. That is, reporters sometimes responded to conflicting pressures from editors, audiences, and market forces by, sadly, abandoning the ideal that self and other can be fulfilled simultaneously. These journalists were sometimes resigned to the current state of affairs in journalism, and therefore past the point of struggling over compromises or fighting for a win-win scenario.

One notable gender finding here is that male journalists are somewhat more likely to exhibit this stance than women, who tend to emphasize congruence between self and other. This result suggests that women in journalism may be more optimistic than men or more sensitive to positive connections between self and other. This pattern may be related to the previously mentioned finding that male journalists are more likely to define responsibility to self in terms of personal satisfaction, interest, or passion for their work. Female journalists more often define self in terms of their quality standards or personal values, particularly those that are consistent with giving to others.

CONGRUENT SELVES AND OTHERS. A number of theater artists, lawyers, and journalists construe their responsibilities to self and others as congruent or symbiotic. That is, responsibility to oneself not only dovetails with but is fulfilled through obligations to others, and vice versa; self-other obligations are mutually reinforcing, and benefits to each are greater when alignment occurs. A journalist discussed her efforts to align her core values with her numerous responsibilities to others:

> I guess I feel . . . the fundamental responsibility is to my own sense of integrity, and that links to this notion of aligning myself with the best . . . that is life serving, life enhancing. And so that's what I feel fundamentally responsible to, is this integrity that keeps pushing me out of the comfort zone. And now of course you know life is so complicated and there are so many things you have to weigh in terms of being responsible. You know, there are funders, there are employees, you know, there's a jillion things that are constantly competing for your loyalty at any one moment. . . . [My] loyalty is—fundamentally has to be—to my own sense of integrity, and that is defined as loyalty to my devotion, I guess, to that which is life enhancing, that which is life serving.

Quality standards and core values are self-responsibilities that are typically discussed in congruent narratives. A young actor articulated how a good performance fulfills both types of obligations:

> *To whom do you feel most responsible?* I think, that's tough. I think, honestly, probably myself. But I think ideally that then feeds into a sense of responsibility to both the text, the play, and what it's trying to do and say, and the audience, and the other people on stage. So there are sort of a lot of different things operating. Now I think when I say "myself" that means that if I feel that I'm serving those things, then I feel like I'm doing myself a service through serving those other things. . . . So it's both a responsibility to the audience, to give them something that has clarity and vision and meaning and a reason to be watched. . . . I think ultimately there needs to be a reason to speak. That's what I look for. Why do I have to speak this? Or not even speak, but why am I here? Why should they watch and why am I here and do I have anything valuable to offer?

Aligning responsibilities requires constant reflection and the ability to take the perspective of the other into consideration when considering one's own needs. When alignment is achieved, this actor finds his own needs are fulfilled *through* attention to others.

Not surprisingly, the personal values discussed in congruent narratives are typically other-oriented: being socially responsible and sensitive to others' needs and ideas. Some subjects describe the self in largely social terms, as inseparable from interactions and relationships with others. One actor remarked,

> I feel most obligated to being the best person that I can be as a human being, first and foremost, and being complete. . . . Being a good listener. Being somebody who doesn't jump to conclusions; a person who gets the big picture and understands every aspect of whatever situation is coming up, so that judgments aren't made hastily, so that you can make decisions that are based on truths for everybody that has given you input. . . . But it's also—getting to where I am now was an inner search for who I really was, and that was probably part of why I left the acting business for X amount of time and then getting in touch with myself, being comfortable with who I am and what I do. Being a good person; I think we all strive to do that, and at times it's really hard. I think being connected, being balanced, being open, and being honest and truthful. Never trying to hurt or tear down someone's ideals or ideas about something but listening and just really embracing what people have to say. I'm very open in that way, and I think that really gets me much further than the way some people I've seen in the way that they operate.

This actor's conception of self as "connected" and "open" is strikingly different from the language of boundaries and the implied separation between self and others suggested by the conflict and coexisting approaches. As he sees it, attention to others' needs actually brings greater rewards to himself.

PATTERNS IN THE CONGRUENT APPROACH: THE MIND-SET IN THEATER. The belief that responsibilities to self and others are, or should be, congruent and aligned appears more frequently than the other approaches discussed here. More than 40 percent of narratives of journalists, lawyers, and theater subjects contain this perspective. Interestingly, slightly more men than women spoke about alignment between self and others, although the difference is not statistically significant. With regard to domain, theater artists are slightly more likely than lawyers and somewhat more likely than journalists to talk about congruence of self-other responsibilities. Over half of actors, producers, and directors who cited self conceive of self-other obligations as positively intertwined, compared with 41 percent of lawyers and 27 percent of journalists.

The domain of theater has distinct features that support the belief that self and others should be congruent, including the nature of performer-audience relationships and characteristics of theater's "product." As one actor discussed, the immediate presence of the audience in theater creates a relationship that may be more intimate than that between writer and reader:

> In the theater there is a sense of they know where you are and where you're sitting. It's really painful, actually; even if the play is very successful, if the audience is having an emotional response, you feel responsible for that in a way that you might not with the novel, because the novel is such a personal experience. And you can take it out and put it in your bag or put it in your drawer or whatever, and the social, political act of going to the theater and witnessing something, it's a much more visceral responsibility in some way, I think. And that's something I'm learning how to deal with more; [it] is like disconnecting from that so I don't feel so terrible if the audience is crying, or if they're angry, or if they're pissed off; I have to let them have their own experience.

The dynamic between performer and audience member is quite distinct from "client" relationships in the other domains. It is more immediate and intimate than that between journalist and distant reader or viewer. At the same time, the link is less "contractual" than the attorney-client relationship; actors, playwrights, and directors produce for audiences but *ideally* not in service of specific audience members' interests or demands. Rather, as subjects describe it, theater is an expression of human truths and, at its best, fulfills a responsibility to the broader public by helping them see things in a new and different light.

Among actors, the interplay between self-responsibility and obligation to the audience is often complicated and certainly holds the potential for conflict. However, many subjects respond to this dynamic by establishing a clear sense that being truly responsible to one's audience means *not* catering to them.

> I would say [I feel most responsible] to myself, really, because if I'm not being honest about what I'm doing, then I'm not doing the best work that I can do, and therefore I'm not being responsible to the

audience and anyone who comes to see it or pays to see it, or to the world of theater—or contributing as an artist to—I mean if I'm going to consider myself as artist, then I have to be truthful in my creation of whatever it is I do. I think if I'm selling out and not constantly reevaluating what I'm doing, it's really easy to lose your creative edge and your vision, hence purpose. . . . We generally try not to cater toward an audience, although I think it's good to know who your audience is gonna be in a specific community or place. That's based a lot on how much you can charge for tickets—you know your community or whatever. I feel a responsibility toward the audience in terms of doing the best work that we can do, and doing something we believe in, and not catering toward them is probably one of the best things you can do because by doing so, you are maybe opening up new experience for them, which is the ideal result.

As this subject conceives it, doing her best work and not "selling out" fulfills her responsibilities to her self and to her audience. Although some journalists spoke about not catering to the audience as well, theater subjects more often articulated a belief that refusing to cater was equivalent to being responsible to self and others.

The collaborative nature of theater's "product," the play, may also contribute to congruent self-other stances. A good show is the result of actors being personally invested in what they are doing and committed to their fellow cast members, the playwright's conception of plot and character, and the message being conveyed to the audience.

After theater subjects, lawyers are the next most likely group to discuss congruence between obligations to self and others. Interestingly, lawyers are nearly equally likely to exhibit congruence and conflict stances, the two distinct poles of the self-other continuum. This finding suggests that a discourse of conflict exists in law but may be counterbalanced by other discourses or actively rejected by our (admittedly unrepresentative) sample of lawyers. For example, one corporate lawyer emphasized connections between self and others but also implied that doing so requires rejecting the conflict discourse prevalent in law:

I do know that winning at all costs is not part of my makeup . . . it turns out that the best comes not from simply acting in your own interests but [from] acting in your interests and the interests of the group. And that what I do in terms of—and I have to be careful [of] the jobs I take in that regard because this would not necessarily be the appropriate job for some circumstances—is that I try and find the best result for all of us, which is best for my client. That is a simple . . . and that means there may be a rank order amongst good results for all of us, but this one is better for my client than the others. They could all be equally good for the group, but this one is better for mine, and this could be a little bit less good for someone here. But my effort is not to beat the other guy but to achieve the best result for my client. And that is why I am in the negotiated transaction business, not the hostile takeover business, not the litigation business, not any of those things.

While this lawyer recognizes the need to focus on what is best for his clients, he also favors and looks for opportunities to create a "win-win" outcome. His standards for good work and his values, implied by his remark that "winning at all costs is not part of my makeup," are consistent with a congruent self-other approach.

Similarly, a criminal lawyer talked about her deep sense of social responsibility and her belief in the interconnection among all things:

Responsible? I guess [to] my children and responsible to myself and my own self expression; and I think the one thing I feel responsible for [is] everything with whom I am connected in some way. Part of what I have been learning and sharing I've been sharing with everybody that comes into my world. So in that sense I feel responsible, and it's actually a part of my tradition to, whenever you do anything for anyone, like to dedicate it, to pray for all the beings in the universe. Like if I am feeding my children, then to kind of wish at the same time that you would be feeding, that all the children throughout space would be fed. So it's extending out, increasingly extending out your sense of responsibility. So while today I am most responsible to getting thank-you presents for the people who took care of my children last weekend while I was meditating, fundamentally I do actually take seriously my responsibility to everything, including the earth and my teacher and what he has given me. So I guess it's not a single answer. Everything.

Given her values, this lawyer cannot but conceive of self- and other-responsibilities as congruent: she positively equates self-expression with caring for others. The strength and salience of her sense of responsibility to "everything" may buffer the influence of discourses such as "the client as enemy" noted by other lawyers.

Compared with actors and lawyers, journalists were least likely to describe self and others as congruent. The nature of journalistic work—the effort to portray stories as objectively as possible—likely contributes to journalists' predilection for separating rather than connecting self- and other-responsibilities. A rare gender finding in this analysis is that those journalists who do mention congruence are women who define self-responsibility in terms of their work standards and deeply held values, which are about caring for others.

Conclusion

Gender is widely understood to influence most aspects of individuals' lives, including the kinds of responsibilities people feel. Gender differences are often routinely accepted as social facts. However, our data suggest that women and men in fact rarely speak in different voices; at least with regard to responsibilities, their narratives are more similar than different. Or rather, gender alone does not dictate how the professionals we interviewed conceive of responsibility at work and beyond. When gender does matter, professional domain seems to mediate the difference. While it would be hasty to suggest that the professionals we interviewed escape the effects of living in a world in which gender is a powerful social construct, the interplay between gender and responsibility may be weaker for these individuals than conventional wisdom might predict.

Beyond general findings about types of responsibility cited, my analysis uncovered three approaches to conceptualizing self-responsibility and loyalty to others: conflicting, coexisting, and congruent. In the narratives I examined there was little evidence for the argument that women tend primarily to others at the expense of themselves, nor for the belief that men inevitably perceive other-obligations as conflicting with their cherished autonomy. Findings from this research are consistent with a growing body of research in sociology of gender that explores how such gendered self-concepts may be changing in response to larger cultural and economic shifts. Gerson's work (1994, 2002) has documented hints of change as economic opportunities have increased for women and the "involved father" ideal has emerged for men. Perhaps our data lend support to this argument, but it is important to note that our sample of professionals is not representative of the population at large, nor necessarily of all women and men in the professions we studied. What we can say is that among a select group of accomplished women and men, gender has little bearing on how self-responsibility and obligations to others are conceptualized.

More generally, the prevalence of the stance that self- and other-responsibilities are congruent suggests that, at least in our sample of professionals, self and others need not be competing nor dichotomous in the ways that many scholars have proposed. Importantly as well, domain of work appears to influence how self-other responsibilities are understood. Conflict stances are most often found among lawyers, coexisting approaches are common among journalists, and the mind-set of self-other congruence is articulated by theater subjects more often than by the others. I have traced these domain differences to characteristic features of these domains, including the nature of the relationship between subjects and their clients, readers, or audience members. A discourse of the "client as enemy" in law contributes to sensitivity to tensions between self- and other-responsibilities and the subsequent drawing of boundaries between attorney and client. The more distant relationship with the reader and, perhaps more important, a responsibility to present stories as objectively as possible contributes to a desire to separate self and other in journalism. Finally, in the theater, subjects point to the intimate interaction between actors and audience, the need to be personally invested in the work, and the collaboration with one's fellow performers as core responsibilities and essential features of good work.

Although this analysis focused on journalism, law, and theater, these findings may allow us to speculate about other fields of work. For instance, medicine shares some characteristics with law, including the immediate service relationship between doctor and patient. Doctors may feel the need to subjugate themselves (particularly their physical wellness) by working long hours in service of patients' needs. At the same time, medicine is beyond doubt a "caring profession"; its core mission, as defined by the Hippocratic oath, dictates that physicians be responsible for others above all. One would expect that individuals who embark on a career in medicine have a strong personal drive to care for people. Especially today, individuals entering medicine can expect to work long hours for less competitive financial rewards and less autonomy than in the past. Therefore, I speculate that physicians are likely to perceive congruence in responsibilities: fulfillment for oneself lies in caring for others.

Despite some observed differences across domains of work, a key takeaway from this analysis is that achieving congruence between self- and other-responsibilities was an overriding concern among our interviewees. Along with the absence of significant gender findings, this analysis calls into question the assumption that self and others are typically conflicting responsibilities that women and men manage differently by specializing either in caring for self *or* in tending to others. Again, characteristics of our sample should be noted. Our studies of "good work" have sought in large part to identify points of intersection between caring for the self and tending to others. The project thus set out to identify individuals who manage to do high-quality work that is both personally fulfilling and

socially responsible. Therefore, our interviewees are more apt to understand their responsibilities to themselves and to others as interconnected,
and to seek strategies in their work for aligning them.

Ideally, in our view, responsibilities to self and others *should be* congruent, or aligned, and we have much to learn from individuals who succeed in aligning them. So while our sample of professionals may not
represent larger trends in the general population, our interviewees present
a positive way of conceiving responsibilities that may provide inspiration
to others. Nevertheless, an important finding from our studies is that an
understanding and *desire* to do good work—that which is both beneficial
to others and fulfilling to oneself—can only take one so far. Forces
beyond the individual, in the profession and in the organizations in which
people work, can facilitate or derail workers' efforts to meet their responsibilities to others and to themselves. As noted earlier, aligning self- and
other-responsibilities requires constant reflection and the ability to take
the perspective of the other into consideration when considering one's
own needs. Institutional supports are needed for this kind of reflection to
occur. Above all, professions need a lively discourse about responsibility
at work—one that embraces the ideal of aligning obligations to self and
obligations to others, one that acknowledges conflicts and offers support
for reconciling them, and one that applauds exemplars of good work.

REFERENCES

Bellah, R. N., Madsen, R., & Sullivan, W. M. (1985). *Habits of the heart:
Individualism and commitment in American life*. Berkeley: University of
California Press.

Bertakis, K. D., Helms, L. J., Callahan, E. J., Azari, R., & Robbins, J. A. (1995).
The influence of gender on physician practice style. *Medical Care, 33*(4),
407–416.

Chodorow, N. (1978). *The reproduction of mothering: Psychoanalysis and the
sociology of gender*. Berkeley: University of California Press.

Franks, P., & Bertakis, K. D. (2003). Physician gender, patient gender, and
primary care. *Journal of Women's Health, 12*(1), 73–80.

Gardner, H., Csikszentmihalyi, M., & Damon, W. (2001). *Good work: When
excellence and ethics meet*. New York: Basic Books.

Gerson, K. (1994). *No man's land: Men's changing commitments to family and
work*. New York: Basic Books.

Gerson, K. (2002). Moral dilemmas, moral strategies, and the transformation of
gender: Lessons from two generations of work and family change. *Gender
and Society, 16*(1), 8–28.

Gilligan, C. (1982). *In a different voice: Psychological theory and women's development.* Cambridge, MA: Harvard University Press.

Gray, J. (1993). *Men are from Mars, women are from Venus.* New York: HarperCollins.

Hochschild, A. (1989). *The second shift: Working parents and the revolution at home.* New York: Avon/HarperCollins.

Lorber, J. (1994). *Paradoxes of gender.* New Haven, CT: Yale University Press.

Miller, J. B. (1976). *Toward a new psychology of women.* Boston: Beacon Press.

O'Brien, T. L. (2006, March 19). Up the down staircase. *New York Times,* section 3, column 5, p. 1.

Padavic, I., & Reskin, B. (2002). *Women and men at work.* Thousand Oaks, CA: Pine Forge Press.

Story, L. (2005, September 20). Many women at elite colleges set career path to motherhood. *New York Times,* section A, column 5, p. 1.

Wrong, D. (1995). *The problem of order: What unites and divides society.* Cambridge, MA: Harvard University Press.

10

CONTROL AND RESPONSIBILITY

A DANISH PERSPECTIVE ON LEADERSHIP

Hans Henrik Knoop

In the name of all the competitors I promise that we shall take
part in these Olympic Games, respecting and abiding by the rules
which govern them, committing ourselves to a sport without
doping and without drugs, in the true spirit of sportsmanship,
for the glory of sport and the honour of our teams.

—The Olympic Oath taken by nineteen-year-old Greek
swimmer Zoï Dimoschaki at the opening ceremony of the
2004 Olympic Games in Athens

AT EVERY LEVEL IN THE LIVING WORLD, if a system is to grow and be
sustained, a balance must be struck between opposing forces, such as the
interests of the parts and of the whole, the tendency to be independent
and the tendency to belong, the necessity for local self-organization and
the necessity for unifying governing principles (Camazine, Deneubourg,
Franks, Sneyd, Theraulaz, & Bonabeau, 2001; Csikszentmihalyi, 1993,
1996; Knoop, 2005). Therefore, at its core human leadership can be
assumed to depend directly on the ability of leaders to attain and maintain such balances (Knoop, 2001). At the organizational level, this perspective suggests a necessary combination of three basic ideals: (1)
guiding ideas of the organization are understood, justified technically

and morally, and shared by leaders and workers; (2) the aims of the organizations are adequately challenging to leaders and workers; and (3) the organizational infrastructure matches both aims and external pressures (Knoop, 2000; Senge, 1990; Senge, Kleiner, Roberts, Ross, & Smith, 1994). Relating to this, at the individual level both leaders and nonleaders seem to depend on generative combinations of intrinsic and extrinsic motivation; combinations of positive emotions, engagement, and higher purpose; and combinations of compliance and creativity in regard to professional mastery and improvement (Csikszentmihalyi, 2003; Damon, 2003; Gardner, 2004; Knoop, 2006; Seligman, 2002). Even at the societal level it is evident how these basic ideals need to play out if a society is to thrive.

Thus at least in the ideal, every society has to provide sufficient predictability for the well-being of its citizens by using some kind of control mechanisms while at the same time allowing for openness, adventure, emergence, and freedom for individuals to choose and take control of their own lives. Serving as examples, democracy and capitalism can, at least ideally and in part, be regarded as systems that comply with this combinational ideal. Thus democracy's finest tenet may be the vision of bringing the diversity of human interests together in common form, as "rule by equal citizens," in contrast to alternatives in which power is highly concentrated in one or a few individuals. Although many dictatorships have claimed to be democratic, such rhetoric is clearly deceptive. Parallel to ideal democracy, capitalism (Smith, 1776/1904) was originally thought to provide the best guarantee for social reciprocity and responsibility: those holding goods or services could sell only if they served the purpose of *others* well enough for the others to want to buy.

However, it is now clear that the social qualities of democracy and capitalism are quite easily corrupted in that both structures may degenerate into social polarization. Such polarization has become particularly evident in the wake of the globalization of information, trade, and transport, massively boosted by digital technology. For example, the world now has only one militarized political superpower, the United States, and the United States is under tremendous moral attack for failing to accept and act out the social responsibility that so many are convinced must go hand in hand with such power. Similarly, the financial world is increasingly controlled by relatively few exceedingly wealthy people and institutions, rendering the idea of free markets more and more exotic, and thus inviting protests around the world.

In short, the necessary balance of individual control (stimulating individual responsibility) and sociocultural control (preventing individual irresponsibility) has proven very difficult to strike in both the political and the economic spheres. This unstable situation may well explain why politicians and leaders of private companies, along with other key institutions all over the world, are facing severe deficits of trust (Gallup Organization, 2002; GlobeScan, 2005). In any case, the irony of global leaders (such as those at the World Economic Forum) acquiring still more extreme measures of wealth while asking for trust from billions who are in despair is difficult to ignore. It seems relevant to recall moral philosopher John Rawls's (1971) advice: if one wishes to be trusted as leaders in a united society, permit economic inequalities only insofar as they *clearly* benefit also the least fortunate members of society.

To be fair, compared to the alternatives, *the combination* of democracy and capitalism as the basic structure of a healthy society is disputed by few. Democracy and capitalism have been driving both wealth and welfare in many countries. And intriguingly, both structures have been extremely resistant to change: they do not have to change themselves as their "contents" (political parties, institutions, private companies, and so on) come and go, win and lose—for these competitive processes of change are defining ideals of both democracy and capitalism. Still, it seems highly unwise to disregard the severe problems now shown to be latent in these structures, as indicated by the low levels of trust referred to earlier (Gallup Organization, 2002; GlobeScan 2005). Sinking trust predicts sinking responsibility, because it is obviously very difficult to take genuine responsibility for something one does not trust, and therefore we cannot do without trustworthy leaders demonstrating clear social responsibility. Considering the present pace of sociocultural change, it is difficult to imagine a time in history when good leadership was more important than it is today, and when the lack of it was more dangerous.

Against this background, leadership in a Nordic country such as Denmark may be of broad interest. The Nordic region is consistently found to be among the most successful in balancing freedom and equality so as to maintain true democracy, and in moderating the economy through taxation and welfare so as to maintain genuine free markets. As direct evidence for this, Denmark currently has the world's highest level of social equality, as indicated by the Gini Index (Förster & Mira d'Ercole, 2005). Likewise, the very limited corruption among leaders found in the Nordic region indirectly supports the claim (in Transparency International's Corruption Perceptions Index, 2005), as do the high levels of broad social trust registered by the GFK Center for Market Research (2003). Furthermore, the Global Competitiveness Report (World Economic Forum, 2005a), the World Competitiveness Index (International Institute for Management Development, 2004), and the Networked Readiness Index (World Economic Forum, 2005b) rank the Nordic region as very well prepared for global interaction, according to measures ranging from targeting creativity and technology to gender equity and social welfare. It also goes without saying that such findings go a long way toward explaining why broader measures of happiness and well-being also often place these countries among the most fortunate in the world (Veenhoven, 2006). Thus, given the overwhelming global challenges facing humanity today, it seems likely that important lessons can be learned from studying Nordic leadership firsthand.

Studying Danish Leaders: Methodology

At the Royal Danish School of Education (1998–2001) and the Danish University of Education (2001–2004), my colleagues and I investigated three domains within the frame of the GoodWork Project: education (Denmark) (Knoop, 2001), journalism (Finland, Denmark, Norway, and Sweden) (Knoop & Vestergaard, 2002), and business (Denmark) (Knoop, Znaider, & Ravn, 2004). The aim of all three studies was to gain better understanding of the preconditions and circumstances for doing work that was at the same time personally engaging, of high professional quality, and good for the broader society. Within each domain, professional, political, and academic leaders were included in the sample. In each case, leaders were nominated by expert informants. To be included in the samples, the leaders had to be recognized by peers for having achieved significant results regarding both processes and outcomes, and preferably but not necessarily involving notable creativity; and they had to have a record of being involved in ethical issues at their own workplaces and (preferably) in public debate. The leaders were all interviewed using a tailored version of the GoodWork protocol developed by Gardner, Csikszentmihalyi, and Damon (2001, pp. 259–268). Questions sampled the purposes, values, assumptions, strategies, pressures, formative influences, and communities of the leaders.

For the present study the responses of forty-six Danish leaders from these three studies were aggregated with the purpose of mapping the most important patterns (Kvale, 1996; Miles & Huberman, 1994; Thomas, 2003). The sample encompassed education (ten professional leaders, five political leaders, and seven academic leaders), journalism (four professional leaders, one political leader, and four academic leaders), and business (eleven professional leaders, three political leaders, and one academic leader). The categories used in the analysis for the present study are

Figure 10.1. Driving and Controlling Forces Affecting the Production of GoodWork.

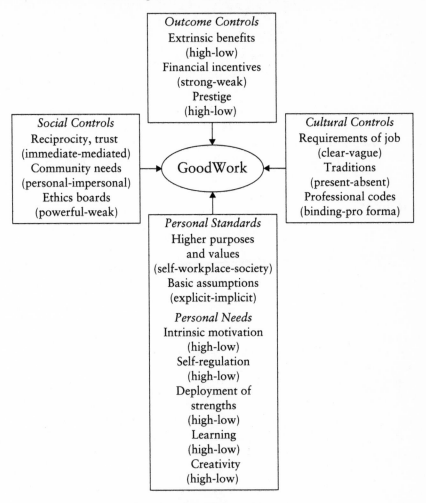

Outcome Controls
Extrinsic benefits
(high-low)
Financial incentives
(strong-weak)
Prestige
(high-low)

Social Controls
Reciprocity, trust
(immediate-mediated)
Community needs
(personal-impersonal)
Ethics boards
(powerful-weak)

GoodWork

Cultural Controls
Requirements of job
(clear-vague)
Traditions
(present-absent)
Professional codes
(binding-pro forma)

Personal Standards
Higher purposes
and values
(self-workplace-society)
Basic assumptions
(explicit-implicit)

Personal Needs
Intrinsic motivation
(high-low)
Self-regulation
(high-low)
Deployment of
strengths
(high-low)
Learning
(high-low)
Creativity
(high-low)

Source: *Adapted from Overview,*
www.goodworkproject.org.

shown in Figure 10.1, an elaboration of a model used by Gardner, Csikszentmihalyi, and Damon (see Introduction); note that I have placed slightly more emphasis on the personal standards and added personal needs in accordance with the focus of the Danish studies.

The key assumption underlying Figure 10.1 is that good work depends on all four systems being aligned both internally and as a whole in order for cultural, social, outcome-related, and personal incentives to function synergistically. In addition, a third alignment for good work in the Danish context exists between intrinsic and extrinsic motivators within individuals and groups. Indeed, most problems in education or work seem to involve misalignment of these drivers. For instance, when focus on tests trumps the well-being of students in school (to no one's benefit except perhaps that of the test makers), such misalignment results; the same characterization applies when excessive hours at work trump healthy lifestyles. Thus, to balance our focus on internal motivation with more external controls, we included the category *intrinsic motivation* along with the categories *deployment of strengths, learning,* and *creativity,* which tend to correlate with the experience of intrinsic motivation (Csikszentmihalyi, Abuhamdeh, & Nakamura, 2005; Peterson & Seligman, 2004).

Findings

Findings Regarding Satisfaction of Personal Needs

In what follows, I examine the findings with respect to each of the principal foci of the study. Beginning with personal needs, my colleagues and I looked at *intrinsic motivation,* possibilities of *self-regulation,* and *deployment of strengths, learning,* and *creativity.* Apart from being strongly interrelated in human life, these features are often positive predictors of spontaneous social responsibility. For instance, if a person does not experience any influence over a given event, he or she may also not be inclined to feel responsible for it, following the logic, "If I didn't do it, I am not to blame." Furthermore, because human beings are designed to pursue maximal control over their own situation through learning and creative endeavors, loss of intrinsic motivation and possibilities of self-regulation will often have depressive and anxiety-provoking effects—such as more or less covertly undermining responsibility toward the authorities. Therefore, the success of professional controls, as in the cases of democracy and capitalism already discussed, very much depends on how much control over their own situations professionals thereby *gain.* In other words, the effect of top-down control in a profession seems to depend directly on how much bottom-up control it provides for the individual worker.

Regarding the *responsibility* for satisfying personal needs in the workplace, a uniting sentiment was found among the leaders. "By default" workers should have large degrees of freedom, consistent with responsibility to the overall aims and principles of the workplace; individuals were expected to work hard, though not too hard (mirroring the measured version of the Protestant work ethic shared by most Danes); and they were expected to provide for others—directly by simply being helpful, considerate, and kind in the company of others, and indirectly as highly taxed citizens enjoying welfare throughout the Danish society. Of course there was political disagreement regarding exactly how much economic equality there should be; that Denmark consistently registers as an economically egalitarian country (Förster & Mira d'Ercole, 2005) also seemed reflected in the priorities of our sample.

We found that almost all leaders were highly *intrinsically motivated* and driven by what first inspired them to apply for the position. Yet many leaders also reported stress, and more than a few had experienced early warning signals in the form of disease and nascent depression. These warning signs appeared to correlate inversely with the degree to which *self-regulation* was possible. For instance, if misalignments between organizational aims and personnel resources were detected, it would obviously be necessary for the leaders to be able to regulate aims, personnel, or other variables in order to ensure realignment. However, though all leaders were clearly sensitive to this elementary fact, many reported being unable to escape these "failing states" quickly enough to remain entirely unharmed. Such a continuing state of affairs may ultimately have consequences for their sense of commitment and responsibility as well.

The majority of the leaders were clearly able to employ their *strengths* in their work. Yet many also reported that administrative burdens often interfered with their ability to play from strength: they described themselves as not strong in administration and often not particularly interested in becoming so. Without exception, the leaders came across as individuals focused intensely on *learning*—including dedication to the creation of learning communities of colleagues. However, many also described frustration about contradictory and confusing conditions making learning, and thus indirectly work, difficult and ineffective. Work overload—leaving too little time for deeper reflective learning—and the rate of change—leaving too little time for deeper implementation—were reported as negative constraints in this area.

Nonetheless, most leaders found that they were able to remain reasonably *creative* as leaders, and many were indeed promoted to their respective positions on the basis of earlier creative accomplishments. This fact may partly explain the leaders' widely shared respect for creative employees, often even for those who surpassed the leaders themselves. Indeed, one business leader told us that he was actively trying to hire people who were smarter than he was, while another reported regularly going "mentor shopping" for the same purpose. Thus, assuming that the benefit of learning and creativity predicts at least some spontaneous responsibility in return (Peterson & Seligman, 2004), these findings encourage an optimistic perspective.

When looking at differences across domains, educational leaders, much more than leaders in journalism and business, reported declining satisfaction of their personal needs. The main reason was the new forms of public government and management introduced to reform education; these innovations often clashed violently with traditional ways of doing pedagogy and of realizing educational leadership. Indeed, there was a special irony for the educational leaders trying to uphold pedagogical traditions for doing good work: many of these very traditions were regarded by others as signs of bad work. Also, although each educational leader understood that the increasing rate of change somehow spelled "stronger traditions for breaking traditions," as one person said, and although all leaders appeared sympathetic to some measure of continuous change, many were ambivalent on the issue. Some were squarely hostile to both the quality and the quantity of this change, often seen as "pseudo-change" or "the emperor's new clothes"; several of the interviewees even seriously considered resigning from their leadership positions. And the majority simply found that the way the educational world was administered was inadequate, judging by the plummeting well-being of many students, professionals, and leaders—all telltale signs of a misaligned domain. It bears repeating how personal responsibility to a large extent seems to go hand in hand with satisfaction of the personal needs in focus here. Therefore, if not dealt with expeditiously, the frustrations just mentioned forewarn cheating and distrust.

Within journalism, the paramount worry regarding personal needs pertained to the future of professional autonomy. Large-scale mergers were creating ever more concentrated power structures to *run* journalism, rather than *being watched* by it, as was quipped more than once during the interviews. Similarly, the old joke about the free press being reserved for those who own one was ominously emerging as more than a joke for several of the journalist leaders. I shall return to this point. At this juncture it may be important to note that these changing conditions also seemed to touch the individual journalist leaders (and professionals) at the very basic level of personal needs and responsibilities.

Findings Regarding Personal Standards

We looked at the leaders' *higher purposes* in their work, their expressed *values,* and the more *basic assumptions* underlying these purposes and values. These categories are interrelated: it is important for any person to experience substantial alignment among basic philosophical assumptions about human life, explicit and broadly guiding values, and work on meaningful projects. Furthermore, the deeper anchoring the personal standards have, the more broadly they can be used; accordingly, any issue of professional responsibility seems to be quite strongly related to the strength of conscious justification. For instance, if a leader proclaims a vision for the future that has no specific rationale and that does not carry any expressed values or worldview, chances are it will blow across as "hot air." This does not mean that every professional ideal should be up for debate at all times, for no profession can operate without simple guiding principles *above* debate. What it means is that both simple and more complex guiding principles need to be well understood and effectively argued if workers are to comply responsibly with them.

In general, the leaders across the domains appeared genuinely committed to their work and to the well-being of those who were served by that work. And although not many planned to remain in their respective positions for more than a few additional years, and with too many not enjoying their work fully, the immediate commitment across the sample was unmistakable. As such, the leaders were generally aiming not only at their own career interests but also at those of their employees and respective organizations, as well as at higher professional and societal ideals. For the majority, a primary motivation for having chosen a leadership position was that they expected their professional ideals thereby to be realized more extensively, leadership simply being the logical next step in their professional career. Indeed, for the majority of the leaders, the idea of applying for a leadership position came only after gaining self-confidence through years of professional success. Thus, with a few exceptions we found strong personal motivation and responsibility underlying the professional commitment.

However, these overall positive impressions were modified in several ways. For instance, we found practically no statements indicating *pure altruism*—that is, no stories or examples in which a leader had decided or done something that was not *also* in her or his own interest. Thus, rather than the leaders being directed only at the well-being of others, they came across as *reciprocal altruists*, for whom social responsibility was based on mutual benefit. A sharp example of the sentiment was provided by the chief editor of a leading newspaper talking about how he responded to criticism: "Being a pragmatic person, I don't mind handing people excuses, if that makes them happy—as long as it does not harm me or my paper." In this vein, we found very few, indeed almost no, references to universal projects regarding society, let alone humanity, as a whole, although on the other hand neither did anyone speak negatively about responsibilities toward the larger whole. Yet at the personal level the entire sample did come across as actively pursuing possibilities to contribute and make a difference to the larger whole, to leave a lasting mark, and to make the world a better place. Thus, the best estimate to be drawn from this part of the study may be that Danish leaders appear truly driven to do good work for the benefit of self, profession, and society alike—but also that, as pressures increase, they tend to prioritize in that order.

We sought to probe the *basic scientific, philosophical, and religious assumptions* underlying the higher purposes and values expressed by the leaders. We did this because of our belief that it is important for leaders to be able to voice rational and moral justifications for their chosen course of action. In our modern world it does not appear possible to dismiss deeper rational justifications for key political and professional priorities without thereby generating indifference and meaninglessness. Of course it may be argued that the quality of leadership and morality ultimately rests on what a person *does* rather than on what a person *says*, but in our knowledge-based world, doing something without some kind of articulation appears increasingly unlikely to be effective, if not ignored altogether.

We had expected substantial justifications of higher purposes and values at the level of basic assumptions. Yet we found little evidence across the domains. Rather, apart from responses from the relatively few academic leaders, we found only very limited reference to deeper scientific, philosophical, or even religious grounds. Instead, the vast majority of the leaders appeared to base their work of leadership on relatively few guiding principles and appeared to be unmotivated by more abstract considerations. Here we may recall Albert Einstein's statement that "everything should be made as simple as possible, but not simpler." Einstein acknowledges both the potential effectiveness of simplicity and the danger of oversimplifying rational and moral justifications of complex issues, thereby deleting their deeper meaning from human discourse. Indeed, we argue that unjustified decisions are *by definition* devoid of meaning, and thus at odds with the criteria for good work proposed in the present study.

A few statements from political leaders at the highest level may illustrate the troubling state of affairs. For instance, when probing justifications, a typical answer from a minister was, "This [the basic personal priority discussed] is what I have chosen because I think it is the right thing" (a quasi tautology). Other politicians answered the same question in an equally unsubstantiated manner with statements such as "This is what I have chosen because I have always felt this was the way it had to be" (habits, not rationality, are given as reason) or "I am in favor of a high level of welfare because I do not think we can decently do otherwise" (reference to other, hidden or unarticulated, priorities that determine what "we can decently do") or "I am doing this because we have to do this in order to keep up" (external forces have set the priority for the person). In essence, many of the most important, foundational "decisions" are simply made "by heart," emotively, and apparently such decisions are often better described as some kind of *internalized, unconscious coercion* (disguised as free will, as the devil's advocate may quip).

Again, to be fair, modern philosophy contends that we shall never acquire an *absolute* basis for our decisions and that there is this thing called *endless regress,* which simply means that you can go on asking for deeper reasons forever, without ever reaching "the bottom." Still, this is a common circumstance that all humans enjoy (or suffer) and it does not in any way remedy the need for *substantial* justifications for decisions, least of all by responsible leaders in professional work.

An example: In Danish education all professionals are taught the discipline of didactic justification based on a personally chosen view of humanity. This stance has created a culture among educational practitioners that is akin to William von Humboldt's ideal of wide degrees of freedom in the academic world, trusting that this will ultimately lead to both high technical performance and high morality: "Coercion may prevent many transgressions; but it robs even actions which are legal of a part of their beauty. Freedom may lead to many transgressions, but it lends even to vices a less ignoble form" (Humboldt, 1791/1993). Thus when a leader is not readily able to defend decisions—especially the constraints brought about thereby—on both rational and moral grounds, civil and professional disobedience, if not frank cheating, is more likely to take effect.

Among the business leaders, the demand for deeper philosophy was not as patent as in education and journalism, but there was nevertheless an intense focus on "values" that were in effect serving as basic assumptions and justifications for action. One curious finding deserves special mention here. When stating their basic values, for obvious reasons many of the leaders mirrored the values of the workplaces to which they had committed as leaders. Furthermore, these values were often thought to provide a "profile" or to "brand" the workplace as "standing out" for employees to identify with. Yet ironically the values stated were to a large degree completely identical across the sample. Thus, almost without exception the leaders wanted to provide a variant of "the best product, at the best price, through the best work processes, to the satisfaction of everyone." To be sure, these ideals are completely aligned with market forces, but to most workers, "identifying with the market" probably does not provide much identity, if any at all. Thus, such use of "values" may actually do damage, turning higher meaning into meaningless words. A material impression of this sentiment was given during an interview in a large, modern business building: the tension between "the best" glass and steel and "the worst" lack of corporate soul could almost be felt physically.

Finally, when asked about *religious beliefs,* only a few leaders had any to report. Indeed, only two of the forty-six leaders expressed religious affinities of any importance in their life, and even those two gave no indication of religion affecting their work. Thus, the secular culture of Danish society seems clearly mirrored in the culture of leadership. To be sure, existential issues were of broad interest, often expressed in ways akin to spirituality, but again, religion as such was not in any way brought to bear as justification or responsibility in the work life of the leaders.

Findings Regarding Outcome Controls

We looked at the influence of *extrinsic benefits such as money and prestige* on the performance of good work. Ideally, extrinsic and intrinsic motivators are aligned. Extrinsic aims are meaningful and supportive drivers for intrinsically motivated, joyful processes, which can be assumed to make good work more likely to occur. However, in general, both at the level of a profession and at the more personal level, extrinsic motivators often appear to trump the intrinsic. The result indirectly erodes professional standards through loss of personal commitment and sense of responsibility.

In line with the findings regarding personal needs and personal standards, the essential output controls appeared to be well aligned with the professional codes within each domain. In other words, broadly speaking we found very little evidence that extrinsic motivators were corrupting the intrinsic motivators in our sample. Thus, even though extrinsic goods such as financial compensation and prestige *did* count in the careers of the leaders across the three domains, these rewards did not seem to interfere much with the wishes to do good work; rather, most leaders simply regarded the prestige and money as "going with the job," as extra incentives for working harder and proceeding further in the *right* direction.

The leaders in education came across as highly committed to the success of their employees and students, with this commitment often nobly linked to broader pedagogical ideals regarding society. However, the outcome controls in education did not appear to be particularly strong. For instance, the performance of teachers or students did not seem to have much immediate effect on anything. The general spirit was that "everyone did the best he or she could, and that was the way it was going to be." (It may be noted that the interviews took place before any public ranking of schools and higher education worth mentioning was undertaken, and before national testing in school became a serious issue in Denmark.) This is not to say that the present study found no outcome controls in education. For instance, parents did have the option of transferring their children to other schools if they disagreed with the professionals, just as citizens more broadly could obviously give their vote to other educational policies if dissatisfied with the given. What we found was, rather, signs of changing educational control systems. Many educational leaders were increasingly challenged by political, professional, and civil "stakeholders" placing them under rather intense cross fire of conflicting interests, with the political system demanding more output control, in forms quite alien to traditional Danish educational leadership.

In business, the leaders' financial success was obviously of paramount importance, in both the short and the long run. It was also generally acknowledged by the interviewees that results were best created through the well-being and happiness of employees. The financial output control, which often had some measure of associated prestige, thus appeared to be aligned with the ideals defining good leadership. Also, this finding seems to mirror the broader impression of Danish leadership presented earlier that despite "the business of business still being business," very strong critiques emerge when businesses fail to live up to the ethical responsibilities linked to their freedom to act. Clearly, in Danish culture few incidents are judged as more despicable than those in which powerful companies fail to assume the responsibilities implied by this freedom; all the leaders in our sample seemed critically aware of this imperative. Yet business was clearly changing in the light of globalization. As several leaders told us, the complexity and confusion inherent in these trends may often lead individuals to focus more narrowly on the immediate pecuniary outcomes, which are more certain, rather than on long-term effects that are increasingly difficult to estimate. However, we found no concrete evidence that this state of affairs was leading to moral decline.

With regard to journalism, testimony was dominated by concern about media mergers and the concentration of power over the free press in the hands of more or less anonymous investors. Though not everyone saw the ownership issues as immediately threatening in Denmark, two worries stood out: that the owners could become too remote from journalism (mainly in it for the money, thereby rendering professional standards second), and that the owners could become too embroiled in journalism (mainly in it for the policy, thereby overriding the editorial independence of a free press). However, apart from these premonitory worries, we found it difficult to judge the kind and strength of output controls in journalism. Clearly journalism judged inadequate or inferior would have consequences, for it would presumably lead the audience to withdraw from it, with certain financial consequences. But because it is often not clear when journalism passes the quality test, and because Danish journalism enjoys rather limited public trust, the audience may not be that sensitive to poor journalism. Moreover, because most people cannot do without some minimum of news information, they may simply take what they can get and thus not really function as a significant output control.

Bearing these problems in mind, we still found overall reason to be optimistic. Across the three domains there appeared to be very little evidence of output controls, whether cultural or social, corrupting personal standards. Rather, when professional codes *were* in conflict with other forces, such as political or financial pressures, the leaders appeared to take an active role in protecting the core values of their organization and finding ways to prevent further professional damage. In short, output controls did not seem to have had negative effects on the commitment and responsibility of Danish leaders, although increasing pressures to account for economic performance were unmistakable and the source of considerable concern.

Findings Regarding Cultural Controls

We looked at *requirements of the job, traditions,* and *professional codes.* As bases for effective work, these features are critical: the acceleration of cultural evolution implies complexities still difficult, indeed often impossible, for individuals to grasp. Furthermore, deep ambivalences are likely to follow the confusion harbored within those complexities. For instance, often a person will experience simultaneous demands for both pressing the accelerator and pumping the brakes, psychologically speaking, as overwhelming challenges prompt simultaneous fight or flight responses. When such a pervasive problem hits a profession, as it now has almost everywhere, some workers will be prompted to cheat because they can suddenly get away with it or because they are afraid of being left behind in the competition. Others may choose the opposite approach and take on more responsibility, while still others may opt for cheating for what they believe is a (good) cause. Few issues seem more important to understand than how social responsibility unfolds under these conditions (Fischman, Solomon, Greenspan, & Gardner, 2004).

Although strong and binding codes of conduct were formally installed in almost all the respective organizations, the overall impression of the cultural controls among the leaders was not entirely positive. Thus in all three domains the professional demands of the jobs were rising and under intense flux, while the traditions needed to counterbalance the flux were faltering. To reiterate, these are the signs of our time, but they add up to immense pressure on the leaders to be dynamic, adaptive, and willing to readjust, often without the support from a well-aligned profession that is necessary for being able to enjoy, or at least contend successfully with, turbulence.

In certain ways the domain of business stood out as least problematic in regard to cultural controls. The challenges of business leaders are primarily quantitative, so to speak, because economic and informational flows increased while the basic rules of the game remained the same. Thus, despite the rapid pace of change, the leaders in business appeared to remain strongly embedded in social reciprocities and continued to trust their partners and colleagues. (To be sure, they relied mostly on a legal basis, such as written contracts and commitments regarding their position, to "trust from.") All worked in places with written codes of what may appropriately be called *business excellence*—some even used this copyrighted term (Center for Leadership, 2003) as an overall professional and ethical framework—with deep commitment to good work in the full meaning of the phrase.

This being said, however, the leaders did not hesitate to vex or wax cynically about the increasingly competitive landscape. Still, none of the interviewees came across as morally broken or even pessimistic on behalf of their respective professions and work. The main worries were directed toward the larger economic and political dynamics at the national and international level, toward which many felt rather powerless, even some who were working at the level of CEO or as director of a governmental agency. Like so many others, the business leaders were observing the global situation with considerable alertness while being able to act out their responsibilities chiefly at the local level. Overall (maybe in light of the alternatives), very few regrets were recorded about being business leaders in the Danish context.

In contrast, the leaders from journalism gave numerous accounts of misalignments, though their individual estimates of the profession varied considerably. One quite critical professor of practical journalism provided a good summary of public perceptions of journalism, foregrounding new types of relations misaligned with traditional ideals of the profession. To paraphrase him, these perceptions were as follows:

> Journalism is increasingly enmeshed with the entertainment and advertisement industry, leading to more fictionalized journalistic forms and means of expression, as well as to more superficiality and conformity.
>
> Journalism itself is still deeply commercialized.
>
> Journalism is rather intimately engaged with the administrators of power, along with being a power itself rather than a watchdog of power, thereby becoming an increasingly closed elite brotherhood.

Maybe worst of all, this professor, a former CEO of a branch of a national television station, thought that the public deemed many journalists to be untrustworthy and irresponsible; according to him the public believed that journalists used unethical methods as well as news criteria that distorted reality and ultimately threatened democracy. Without claiming to have exact numbers, he elaborated that "my basic viewpoint is not that all journalists are morally corrupted but simply that dilemmas that were always part of journalism have been accentuated . . . and that one of the problems for journalists is in fact that they have come to live in a closed social sphere, which sharpens other problems as they get out of touch with large segments of the population."

Several respondents were significantly more positive in their estimates. For instance, the chief editor of a leading newspaper said,

> My experience is that economical interests and commercial considerations in general have no direct influence on content in [Danish] journalism. This sounds unbelievably naive . . . nevertheless, it is my well-considered opinion . . . of course there are owners and money to be made . . . but that lies very far from the question about which news should be brought. . . . However, this does not mean that we do not have problems with upholding "intended objectivity" [regarded by him as a core ideal in Danish journalism]. We most certainly do . . . the main causes being journalists not being sufficiently skilled, making mistakes, working too quickly, sloppy . . . and sometimes much too biased by personal engagements as when a journalist falls in love with the story and ends up blinded by it.

In education we discerned severe problems of misalignment in the form of unclear requirements of the job, partly outdated traditions of teaching and leading, and widespread confusion among practitioners regarding which professional codes to adopt, because ideas about teaching and learning were so many and so different, and much too often escaped intelligent debate (see Fischman, DiBara, & Gardner, 2006). Thus, although the educational leaders all signaled strong integrity and commitment to provide for good work, the findings in this category illustrate how difficult their task is and provide unmistakable signs of warning.

Findings Regarding Social Controls

We looked at *trust and reciprocity, professional power structures and ethical boards,* and the relation of leaders to *community needs on the larger scale.* These variables target social relationships within each domain as well as the perception of social relations with the larger world as experienced from within the domain. Social controls are strong predictors of responsibility in several ways. For instance, if peers engage in reciprocal win-win relationships, they will be spontaneously motivated to assume responsibility so that these relationships may continue to thrive. Likewise, if one works in a strong but legitimate public or private power structure, the structure will often provide welcome degrees of freedom; much need not be debated, there are clear goals and rules on which to act with adequate degrees of professional autonomy, and the benefit of being part of a well-led system is likely to prompt responsibility from workers in return.

However, the reverse is also true: if workers find themselves embedded in no-win games, or even "just" win-lose games that idealize the destruction of the competitors or enemies, a more cynical and less socially responsible culture is a plausible consequence. Therefore, when living in societies with competitive politics and economics, it is of utmost importance for competing citizens to trust these systems as being fair and beneficial overall, no matter who wins a particular competition. If they are to remain trustful citizens with genuine rights and heartfelt responsibilities, they should adopt a stance akin to the Olympic spirit in sports: it is great to win but even more important to take part. And as regards leadership: the more political, economic, or professional power a person acquires, the more social responsibility *must* be demonstrated in order for the power structure to remain intact and effective. As alluded to earlier, this is what gatherings such as the World Economic Forum appear to *aim* for; but as many of the growing economic inequalities in the world are brought about by decisions made by exactly the kind of influential individuals represented at these kinds of summits, popular trust may not rise until the golden ideals materialize substantially.

The overall impression across the three domains was that most social controls were formally in place: nearly all interviewees agreed on the importance of trustful and reciprocal win-win relationships because the formal power structures and ethical boards were well established. However, the speed of change appeared to make it difficult to maintain sufficient social continuity for people to invest themselves completely or even sufficiently in their work. One business leader speculated how, on average, a leader in an organization would be performing at optimum for only a year. He arrived at this conviction through a perhaps whimsical but still thought-provoking calculation: he assumed that the average length of employment at a given organization was five years, of which the first two were in part tutorial and the last two were in part colored by the leader increasingly looking for new job opportunities (and in some cases for a successor), thus leaving just one year in the middle—the third.

Also, in all three domains the overriding forces were skewing the traditional relations within the fields. Thus, within education, the relation to the larger community had become ambivalent, to say the least. The external political and economical controls were increasing in combinations of top-down approaches and market pressure. In part this situation can be explained by domain-external causes. For example, on the one hand, there is increased global competition. On the other hand, increasing political forces aim to keep educational conditions in control by more restrictive, and often more detailed, top-down regulation and accounting. The educational leaders were all highly aware of these new conditions; they implied that the roles of leaders were changing to being more tightly bound to top-down policies, to being governmental agents rather than professionals amongst equals. This trend stood in sharp contrast to the tradition of primary schools being more autonomous in both theory and practice. Indeed, the difficulties of leading under these conditions prompted several of the hitherto highly successful leaders sampled for our study to consider early retirement or change of position.

To be sure, as has already been alluded to, every educational leader we interviewed came across as *wishing to be* highly responsible to the societal ideals stated in acts of education, to professional standards, and to the people depending on their work. What often made their work perplexing, and thus made it difficult for us to determine how their responsibility played out, was that political, economic, and to some extent professional frames and standards were often contradictory, sometimes even incompatible, and changing faster than the institutions could be reasonably expected to accommodate.

Within journalism, the already mentioned megamergers in the media world were the most mentioned indicator of changing relationships. As in education, this huge external transformation did not occur without affecting many social relationships within the field. Indeed, in darker moments during the interviews, several leaders worried about the future of the free press, seeing on the horizon early warning signs that the concentration of power in the media world may become so socially distorting as to vitiate the core values of the domain (see Gardner, Chapter Twelve, this volume).

Within business, the key issue regarding social control proved to be quite different from the issues found in education and journalism: namely, the challenge of being open to what was called *self-leadership,* in which skilled professionals were increasingly able to "lead" themselves, as long as the guiding ideas of the organization were understood and accepted. Yet in business as well we found no lack of concern on the larger scale. For example, respondents worried about what would happen if good Danish companies were bought away by foreign investors, and how it was possible to have trust in an increasingly uncertain and unstable future. We did not find this sentiment to be antiglobal as such. It was simply a shared state of heightened awareness of rapid transformation that often stretched individuals and social structures beyond their capacities. For instance, one leader discerned a race between tendencies of centralized mass production on the one hand and tendencies of decentralization into smaller units on the other: the dilemma was that the size of companies often did matter in obtaining "market control" (Anderson, 2006). For his part, a director of a governmental agency saw three main "wars" (that is, conflicts) taking form in society, all contributing to social instability: (1) a political war in which politicians insult each other to a degree that renders politics unworthy of respect and trust, and leads to a weakening of overall social control in society; (2) an economic war in which the competition in the private sector becomes so fierce as to lead to corruption in the form of cheating and loss of trust in private companies; and (3) a scientific war in which experts play against one another to a degree that the public may lose trust in science.

To sum up, the leaders across the three domains agreed that most basic social structures were in place and that there was much that leaders could do on a daily basis to ensure good work. Yet we found consensus across the entire sample, including among the business leaders, that effective controls against the excessive concentration of economic and political power were necessary for society to function broadly, and to maintain professional standards in the face of possible corruption by financial or political powers.

Likewise, it was heartwarming to learn that so many leaders, responsible for upholding and controlling standards of work on a daily basis, stood united in demanding that whatever standards or controls were to be installed, these would have to comply with the standards of humane life.

Conclusion

Our research indicates that Denmark has a strong leadership base in the domains of education, journalism, and business, giving support to personal, professional, and societal excellence alike. These results confirm other favorable studies of Danish and Nordic leadership; they indirectly support international praise for Nordic countries successfully balancing freedom and equality, creativity and responsibility, antiauthoritarian culture and high welfare—all widely regarded as crucial components for a civilized and effective society.

A strong sense of genuine responsibility was found throughout the sample, this convergence representing a broad variety of leadership positions. Yet rapidly changing circumstances were seen as potential threats to crucial professional norms and traditions, placing leaders in both technical and moral cross fire. Of particular importance here were the larger forces of globalization. As political and economic decisions were increasingly determined by international considerations, issues of responsibility became perplexing, and perhaps beyond the scope of the individual leader. It was strongly indicated that the competitive, and hence often blind, forces that characterize both political democracies and economic markets should be limited to a level that allows professional standards to remain intact and honors broad humanitarian considerations.

Looking forward, I make the following proposal: we need to acknowledge how societies with competitive politics and economics depend on their citizens actually trusting these systems as being fair and beneficial overall, *no matter who wins* a particular competition. This stance is akin to the Olympic spirit in sports, where it is clearly great to win, but even more important to take part. Indeed, what obviously makes a sport function is that participants can keep losing games without losing the will to go on playing. Who would care to play at all if they knew beforehand that they would win? And even more ironic: those who learn to lose games without losing their spirit are *ultimately* most likely to win, because their ability to lose in Olympic manner makes them more tolerant to optimal levels of challenge, where by definition there is a high risk of losing but also where learning proceeds most effectively and joyfully (Csikszentmihalyi, 1993; Knoop, 2005). Losing is thus a necessary and clearly positive part of the game if framed rightly in the background of the grand game of life on earth. This fact appears to be of crucial importance if we are to succeed in governing societies by democratic and competitive means: we have to organize for momentary losers to stay spirited and in the game, from the most basic to the highest levels. For example, in order to trust democracy, citizens need to see losing politicians clearly acknowledging that winning political opponents (*not* enemies) are OK— that indeed by democratic definition they are the *best* choice—without thereby being damaged as politicians themselves. Because if such a perspective is not achieved, it is likely that one is confronting either ignorant citizens, flawed democratic procedures, corrupt individuals in political office, or combinations hereof, all of which effectively undermine trust in democracy. Likewise, in order to trust market mechanisms, citizens need to see very clearly that the mechanisms are fair, even for those who lose. Because if citizens do not see this, they may rationally conclude that for some people it is more or less legitimate to cheat in order simply to escape the no-win game they're in—ultimately contributing more to a cheating culture in society at large than to a culture of good work.

I believe that the Olympic code, which unites the world of sports, can provide a beacon of hope as well in the professions, in politics, and in economics. However, today in many places the world looks increasingly like a Social Darwinian nightmare rather than an Olympic event. In light of this situation, it seems wise simply to insist that the more political, economic, and even professional power a person acquires, the more social responsibility he or she *must* demonstrate in order for the power structure to remain intact, effective, and humane. And the success of this process may be measured simply by the degree to which demonstrations in the streets voluntarily disappear.

REFERENCES

Anderson, C. (2006). *The long tail*. New York: Hyperion.

Camazine, S., Deneubourg, J.-L., Franks, N. R., Sneyd, J., Theraulaz, G., & Bonabeau, E. (2001). *Self-organization in biological systems*. Princeton, NJ: Princeton University Press.

Center for Leadership. (2003). *EFQM excellence model*. Copenhagen: Author.

Csikszentmihalyi, M. (1993). *The evolving self*. New York: HarperCollins.

Csikszentmihalyi, M. (1996). *Creativity: Flow and the psychology of discovery and invention*. HarperCollins.

Csikszentmihalyi, M. (2003). *Good business: Leadership, flow, and the making of meaning*. New York: Viking.

Csikszentmihalyi, M., Abuhamdeh, S., & Nakamura, J. (2005). Flow. In A. J. Elliot & C. S. Dweck, *Handbook of competence and motivation*. New York: Guilford Press.

Damon, W. (2003). *The moral advantage: How to succeed in business by doing the right thing*. San Francisco: Berrett-Koehler.

Fischman, W., DiBara, J., & Gardner, H. (2006). Creating good education against the odds. *Cambridge Journal of Education, 36*(3), 383–398.

Fischman, W., Solomon, B., Greenspan, D., & Gardner, H. (2004). *Making good: How young people cope with moral dilemmas at work*. Cambridge, MA: Harvard University Press.

Förster, M., & Mira d'Ercole, M. (2005). Income distribution and poverty in OECD countries in the second half of the 1990s. OECD Social, employment and migration working paper no. 22. Paris: Organisation for Economic Co-operation and Development.

Gallup Organization. (2002, November 7). Survey on trust. Report on trust for the World Economic Forum.

Gardner, H. (2004). *Changing minds*. Boston: Harvard Business School Press.

Gardner, H., Csikszentmihalyi, M., & Damon, D. (2001). *Good work: Where excellence and ethics meet*. New York: Basic Books.

GFK Center for Market Research. (2003). *Trust levels: Much room for improvement*. Retrieved July 16, 2006, from http://www.gfk.hr/press_en/trust.htm

GlobeScan. (2005, December 15). *GlobeScan report on issues and reputation*. Report on trust for the World Economic Forum. Retrieved July 16, 2006, from http://www.globescan.com/gsr_overview.htm

Humboldt, W. V. (1993). *The limits of state action*. Indianapolis, IN: Liberty Fund. (Original work published 1791)

International Institute for Management Development. (2004). *World competitiveness index*. Geneva, Switzerland: Author.

Knoop, H. H. (2000). *En harmonisk kommune er kompleks—Om balancen mellem individ og fællesskab*. [A harmonious municipality is complex—On the balance between individual and community]. Copenhagen: Royal Danish School of Educational Studies.

Knoop, H. H. (2001). *Humane creativity in Danish education*. Copenhagen: Danish University of Education.

Knoop, H. H. (2005). Kompleksitet: Voksende orden ingen helt forståaar. [Complexity: Growing order that nobody quite understands]. *Kognition & Pædagogik, 57*(15), 6–24.

Knoop, H. H. (2006). Kreativitet [Creativity]. Copenhagen: *Dansk Pædagogisk Tidsskrift, 1*, 24–32.

Knoop, H. H., & Vestergaard, E. (2002). *God journalistik—Arbejdspapirer*. [Good journalism—Working papers]. Copenhagen: Danish University of Education.

Knoop, H. H., Znaider, R., & Ravn, I. (2004). *Godt lederskab—Et eksplorativt interviewstudium om harmoni og disharmoni i dansk ledelse.* [Good leadership—An exploratory interview-study on harmony and disharmony in Danish leadership.] Copenhagen: Danish University of Education and Center for Leadership.

Kvale, S. (1996). *InterViews: An introduction to qualitative research interviewing.* Thousand Oaks, CA: Sage.

Miles, M. B., & Huberman, A. M. (1994). *Qualitative data analysis* (2nd ed.). London: Sage.

Peterson, C., & Seligman, M.E.P. (2004). *Character strengths and virtues—A handbook and classification.* New York: Oxford University Press.

Rawls, J. (1971). *A theory of justice.* Cambridge, MA: Belknap Press of Harvard University Press

Seligman, M.E.P. (2002). *Authentic happiness.* New York: Free Press.

Senge, P. M. (1990). *The fifth discipline: The art and practice of the learning organization.* London: Century Business.

Senge, P., Kleiner, A., Roberts, C., Ross, R., & Smith, B. (1994). *The fifth discipline fieldbook: Strategies and tools for building a learning organization.* London: Nicholas Brealey.

Smith, A. (1904). *An inquiry into the nature and causes of the wealth of nations* (5th ed., E. Cannan, Ed.). London: Methuen. (Original work published 1776)

Thomas, D. R. (2003). *A general inductive approach for qualitative data analysis.* Auckland, NZ: University of Auckland.

Transparency International. (2005). Corruption perceptions index. Retrieved July 15, 2006, from www.infoplease.com/ipa/A0781359.html

Veenhoven, R. (2006). What we know about happiness. Updated version of paper presented at the Dialogue on Gross National Happiness, Woudschouten, Zeist, The Netherlands, January 2001. *Kognition & Pædagogik, 60,* 14–49.

World Economic Forum. (2005a, September 28). *Global Competitiveness Report 2005–2006.* Originally retrieved July 15, 2006, from http://www2.weforum.org/site/homepublic.nsf/Content/Global+Competitiveness+Programme.html. This report no longer appears on the Web site of WEF but is sold commercially as Augusto Lopez-Claros (Au.), Michael E. Porter (Ed.), Klaus Schwab (Ed.), A. *The global competitiveness report 2005–2006: Policies underpinning rising prosperity* (new ed.). Houndsmills, Basingstoke, Hampshire, U.K.: Palgrave Macmillan, 2005.

World Economic Forum. (2005b). *Global information technology report.* Retrieved July 16, 2006, from www.weforum.org/en/initiatives/gcp/Global%20Information%20Technology%20Report/index.htm

PART THREE

THE LIMITS OF RESPONSIBILITY

11

CONSTRAINING RESPONSIBILITY

CHOICES AND COMPROMISES

Laura Horn
Howard Gardner

*One thing I'm really good at is compartmentalizing in my head,
to say that's not my problem. Here are my boundaries. This is
my challenge and that's just a condition that I have to live with.*

CHOOSING TO FOCUS RESPONSIBILITY IN CERTAIN AREAS means letting
go of other responsibilities. Across the professions, one obvious area in
which people make trade-offs is in the balance between work and other
spheres of life. Such choices and compromises must also be made within
each professional realm, as competing pressures pull from inside and
outside of the profession. In this chapter we address three primary
stances by which people limit their professional responsibilities. Each
stance can happen with an individual in any domain. But each stance
turned out to be particularly common for one of the domains we studied
(at least at a certain historical moment in the life of the domain).

We are grateful to our colleagues Bill Damon, for his conceptual contributions
to this chapter, and Carrie James, for her helpful comments on early drafts.

One way in which individuals limit their responsibility is by conforming to the consensus of the domain. In other words, they follow established professional norms without giving much thought to competing responsibilities. This stance was particularly common among the genetic scientists we interviewed in the middle and late 1990s. Other professionals carefully weigh competing professional responsibilities and make difficult choices among these responsibilities. This process proved especially prevalent among the primary care physicians we interviewed in 2005 and 2006. In both of these approaches, individuals uphold the core purpose of the profession, but in the second approach, people are more aware of the ways in which they limit their responsibilities.

In a third stance, individuals limit their responsibilities in a way that strays from the core purpose and tradition of their profession. Because the professionals we interviewed were nominated for their exemplary work, examples of this third stance emerged primarily in people's criticisms of others' work, a dynamic that presented itself in our interviews with print journalists in the middle and late 1990s.

The analysis in this chapter is based on an extensive review of interview transcripts in genetics, primary care medicine, journalism, philanthropy, and corporate law. Building on previous analysis of genetics, journalism, philanthropy, and education transcripts, we examined transcripts in each domain for instances where participants imputed responsibility to others or acknowledged the need to choose between important responsibilities and looked for patterns in how they made these assessments. For this analysis, we analyzed fifty-four transcripts in genetics, twenty-five transcripts in primary care medicine, twenty transcripts in journalism, twenty-three transcripts in philanthropy, and seventeen transcripts in corporate law.

Conforming to Consensus: The Example of Genetics

To become a researcher in the science of genetics requires years of rigorous training and highly structured practice. Even after completing a doctorate, young scientists typically conduct postdoctoral research under supervision, and then continue on as a junior researcher or faculty member, climbing the highly structured hierarchy of the profession. Throughout the long process of professionalization, which arguably extends throughout an entire career (even the most senior researchers must submit their work for peer review), professional researchers are trained to execute specific tasks in society—to create new knowledge.

When asked about their responsibilities, 70 percent of the fifty-four geneticists we interviewed spoke about a commitment to the core purpose of the domain: research and discovery. The strong consensus about the purpose of science and the intensive training procedures for carrying it out provide scientists with a clear message about their responsibility to pursue knowledge. Their focus allows them to set clear boundaries about their primary responsibility when presented with competing responsibilities, such as thinking through the potential social implications of their research and perhaps acting on the basis of their conclusions.

Many of the scientists we interviewed located ethical questions about the application of knowledge squarely outside of the responsibility of science. When asked directly about ethical issues regarding the application of scientific knowledge, such as cloning and gene therapy, 59 percent of geneticists imputed the responsibility for such questions to others, such as the government or society at large. The attitude of the genetic scientists toward the ethical application of knowledge represents one stance professionals can take toward limiting their responsibilities. They stay narrowly focused on what is widely agreed to be the purpose of their professional work.

When discussing responsibility for determining the line between eugenics and "deliberate and targeted improvement of some traits," one subject said, "I don't know whose responsibility it would be to identify those traits. That's a societal issue. It's not a scientific issue." This refrain separating social responsibility from scientific responsibility was one we heard many times from our subjects, who often used similar words: "Society has to decide, not a scientist." When presented with questions about the ethical application of genetic science in the late 1990s, scientists had a clear, collective narrative that allowed them to impute that responsibility to others and remain determinedly focused on the core purpose of their work.

Some of our interview participants expounded on the common refrain; they elaborated on the sharp distinction between social responsibility and scientific responsibility. They described it as an essential part of science that investigators limit their responsibility in such a way; as one researcher told us,

> I just have an abiding faith that it's society that has to make the decisions about how new technologies are implemented or applied. It is not the scientist's job to think about all the potential applications that their science will generate, or else you just emasculate the kind of science you do. At every stage you would be making a decision: could this be misused? Scientists' job is to really develop the knowledge. You can have faith and I have it that in the end, more knowledge is better than less.

Another common response was that scientists have no special qualifications to make ethical decisions, and therefore no special responsibility.
As one subject said about his responsibility to talk about such ethical
issues, "I am not in the possession of any knowledge that would make it
more important for me to talk on this than you. Because whatever I
know, within five seconds you'll know it. And so your views are as good
as or better than mine on it." Another subject responded in a similar
fashion: "Society has to decide, not a scientist. I don't think scientists
have any special wisdom. If anything, they probably have special igno-
rance in the areas . . . that are going to affect society."

Not everyone in the field has to recreate this logic. Workers can readily
fall back on the professionally sanctioned idea that scientists have a
responsibility to create knowledge and others have a responsibility to figure out how to use it in prosocial ways. Such boundaries are so embedded in the domain that only the rare scientist grapples daily with the
question of where to set the limits of his or her responsibility with regard
to the issue of the ethical application of knowledge.

Weighing Conflicting Responsibilities: The Example of Primary Care Medicine

Professions do not always provide clear instructions on how to think
about competing responsibilities. In the current medical environment,
physicians are faced with many conflicting responsibilities but have no
master narrative that allows them to focus comfortably on just one of
those responsibilities. The primary care physicians we interviewed
presented many conflicting narratives regarding the best way to care for
their patients. Some focus on providing the highest quality care for a few
patients while others choose to focus on providing adequate care for
many patients. Some believe that their patients receive the best care from
specialists while others focus more on developing a continuous relationship with each patient over the life span.

As with the geneticists we interviewed, a strong consensus emerged
among physicians regarding their core responsibility. They consistently
reported that they were responsible primarily to their patients. However,
with the recent explosion of medical knowledge, technology, and special-
ization, the nostalgic ideal of a single family physician knowledgeable
enough to care for all of the medical needs of each patient is no longer
realistic. Physicians face difficult choices among competing responsibilities; without one dominant narrative on which to rely, many manifest an
awareness that no matter which responsibility they focus on, they are

sacrificing other important professional responsibilities. The attitudes of the physicians we interviewed toward competing responsibilities in medicine represent a second stance that professionals can take toward limiting responsibility. They weigh competing responsibilities and make difficult choices among them, knowing that in the process they must inevitably sacrifice or minimize other important responsibilities.

One set of conflicting responsibilities that physicians must negotiate is whether to provide high-quality care for individual patients or to provide care for a wide range of patients, including those less able or wholly unable to pay for care. Some physicians choose to preserve the old ideal of taking responsibility for all aspects of care for each individual patient by limiting their responsibility to a small number of patients (two to three hundred patients instead of the typical caseload of three to five thousand patients). These physicians focus their responsibility on providing optimal care for relatively few patients.

One such "concierge" doctor described how his choice to limit his responsibility to a manageable number of patients enabled him to take more responsibility for each patient than he would in a normal practice. He told a story about discovering a blood clot in a patient's leg that would have been overlooked by the emergency room physicians. By remaining in close phone contact with the emergency room physicians and insisting that he be involved in the medical decisions, the concierge physician arrived at the proper diagnosis. Before starting his concierge practice, he would have had too many patients to be able to provide this kind of personalized care for all of them. "I would have basically said 'All right, I'm sending you to an emergency room. It's someone else's responsibility. That doctor's there. I'm not there'."

In order to take responsibility for providing this level of personalized care for all enrolled patients whenever they need it, concierge doctors limit their responsibility. They opt out of the current medical care structure, instead providing care for a relatively small number of patients, most of whom can afford to pay a lot of money for their care. They realize that if all doctors followed their lead, the medical system would collapse. "There was a fear that if we do this, everybody is going to do this. If this is successful, then there will be a wholesale stampede of physicians out of regular practices into this kind of a practice. And that has not happened. . . . It is not a particularly deep market in terms of the number of people who are willing to pay for these kinds of services."

Other physicians deal with the conflicting responsibilities by choosing to practice in an imperfect system that serves a greater number and a wider range of patients. However, this group concedes that this choice has a detrimental effect on the quality of care they can provide to each patient:

> People's care falls through the cracks when no one person is taking responsibility. I mean people do get lost. There are a lot of specialists. You've got people with multiple problems that get out and end up seeing five doctors, and you have to work hard to find out what's going on with those patients. And the patients presume that you know, but you don't always know. . . . There's not enough time. You can't do much about it. You can leave the practice. I mean there are things you can do. I got an e-mail right now from . . . one of these concierge groups. You can do concierge medicine, but then you don't take care of all your people. You don't take care of the people you [would ordinarily] take care of because everybody can't afford $2,000, $3,000, $5,000 to get concierge.

Another physician aptly articulated the conflicting responsibilities with which many doctors grapple. "[I feel] totally responsible to the individual patient. But I think there is a responsibility that we all have and [that] is more difficult to fulfill because it's more difficult to define, and that's to the community at large. . . . Medicine is an ongoing daily, hourly ethical issue, and that's between the macro-environment [and] the micro-environment. . . . It is, I think, at some level an important issue that comes up every day."

A second tension in medicine involves the use of hospitalists—doctors dedicated exclusively to the care of patients in the hospital. By passing the care of their inpatients on to doctors who specialize in hospital care, primary care physicians compromise continuity of care and the patient-physician relationship. On the other hand, these physicians prevent burnout for themselves. Moreover, some think that hospitalists may provide better quality care because they have more specialized knowledge about hospital care.

A well-respected primary care physician we interviewed worked in a group practice that set up a rotation system for handling its hospitalized patients. Each week one doctor in the group was responsible for visiting the hospital patients for the whole practice. Originally the doctor we interviewed chose to opt out of this system because he felt an overarching responsibility to care for his own patients, even when they were hospitalized. As he told us, "Until this year, I didn't actually participate in that. I would go in and see my own patients because I felt the need for that connection and I felt there was an expectation on me as a physician that I would be there when patients were sick in the hospital." Recently, when the group practice shifted to the use of hospitalists, this physician changed his policy. After careful reflection, he decided to embrace the use of hospitalists, letting go of the responsibility he felt to care for his own patients in the hospital. He cited three reasons: (1) he thought his patients may get better care that way, (2) he felt pressured into it, and (3) it would take too much energy to keep up with all of the information necessary to provide good hospital care.

The core responsibility in medicine—to provide quality patient care—has not changed. However, with the field of medicine changing so rapidly, individual physicians must figure out for themselves how best to uphold the core professional responsibility. Whether they choose to provide exceptional care to a few or adequate care to many, to pursue the continuity of the patient-physician relationship or to yield such continuity to the specialized knowledge of other practitioners, many medical practitioners carefully weigh the trade-offs with no clear consensus from the profession guiding them in how to make these choices. Unlike the primary hegemonic stance in genetics, many physicians face tensions in their daily work that force them individually to negotiate where to focus their attention and where to limit their responsibilities.

Straying from Tradition: The Case of Journalism

A third way of limiting responsibility in the face of competing professional considerations is to focus on a responsibility that lies outside of the traditional purpose of the domain. As with genetics and medicine, we identified a consensus among the journalists we interviewed on the core purpose of their work: to inform the public and support democracy. None of the participants mentioned entertainment or profit as a central purpose of journalistic work (Gardner, Csikszentmihalyi, & Damon, 2001); however, most print journalists we interviewed criticized the increasingly large number of people in the profession who pursue fame and money. Those whom they criticized reflect a third stance toward responsibility in the professions. They focus their responsibility on something external to the core values of the profession, in this case fame, monetary success, and self-aggrandizement.

Consider Haynes Johnson's criticism of television broadcaster George Stephanopoulos:

> Starting with Watergate, there was an enormous change in the lure of success and fame. . . . George Stephanopoulos is a good example. He's going to teach a course at Columbia University. He's marketing the book for two million dollars, his memoirs. And he will be on the

lecture circuit for probably twenty thousand a pop. And he will also be on maybe ABC Brinkley and maybe CBS too, as a commentator. This is a man—I mean I like George very much. And it's a guy who started politics when he was twenty-nine and he's been an aid to a president for four years, has never held elected office, hasn't crafted a law or whatever. But it's kind of an interesting commentary about where journalism is, in particular the celebrity field. So I think the values have changed, the standards have changed.

Without pointing to specific individuals, veteran editor Bill Kovach expressed a similar concern: "Most people I've worked with have really believed in the work they do as kind of an obligation and a service, rather than, you know, just a way to fill your time or to make a lot of money or to make yourself important. I do see a change in that. I do see a lot of people who are attracted by the celebrity possibilities in journalism now, which is one of the things that troubles me a lot."

Those whom Johnson, Kovach, and many other participants criticize have limited or redirected their sense of responsibility in a way that compromises the core mission of the domain. Some observers believe that the actions of these self-serving individuals do not even count as journalism. As famed editor Bill Bradlee said, "There were people who were great journalists, or allegedly great journalists, who really are no longer journalists. They are performers. Whether it is George Will or Al Hunt or Bob Novak. That is a trap."

Unfortunately, because we interviewed people nominated as exemplars in the field, we did not have an opportunity to explore firsthand the perspective of the individuals they criticized. We do not know which responsibilities would have been cited by journalists who pursue celebrity. The critiques of those who pursue fame and money in journalism were so prevalent in our interviews, however, that they merit analysis as individuals who represent a third stance toward limiting responsibility: making choices based on a responsibility to something that is widely considered not to be a central or defining facet of the profession.

If the largest and best-known journalistic institutions continue to move away from the traditional responsibilities of the domain and more toward entertainment or "news lite," those who pursue the limelight at the expense of presenting information that people need to hear could be conforming to a newly emerging consensus in the profession. Some observers worry that this could be the direction in which journalism is headed. As Haynes Johnson observed, institutional structures in journalism are beginning to encourage the pursuit of fame and money in the face of increasing commercial competition. "It used to be that the *New York Times* would not permit people to go on these talk shows, and other newspapers wouldn't permit their people. Now they hire PR people to get them on them. . . . So the younger reporters, they're in there trying to be like McLaughlin Group, shouting. Not giving any kind of intelligent—I'm appalled by that."

Stances Across the Professional Landscape: Philanthropy, Education, and Law

Conforming to consensus, weighing conflicting responsibilities, and straying from the core purpose of the profession are common ways in which professionals set boundaries on their responsibilities. At the time of our interviews, the professions outlined in this chapter presented particularly strong prototypical examples of each stance. However, the conditions in other professions we have studied also lead professionals to exhibit more of one stance than the others when faced with competing pressures. In philanthropy, for example, professional grantmakers and executives in private or community foundations do not agree on the core purpose of the work. Entering the field requires no formal training, and grantmakers tend not to identify strongly with the profession (Horn & Gardner, 2006).

Such conditions leave grantmakers with little guidance when faced with competing responsibilities. Accordingly, much like the doctors we interviewed, these grantmakers must spend considerable energy weighing competing responsibilities and defining for themselves the limits of their responsibilities. Consider the reflection of one philanthropy executive we interviewed, who has spent considerable energy figuring out how to set limits on her responsibilities:

> Great philanthropy is created on the heels of great capitalism . . . and on the heels of great capitalism are people who are not getting paid a lot of money, who are sort of the have-nots. And so there's irony in this whole work . . . but I decide not to define my work in that political context because I would go crazy. . . . So I just have to live with our economic structure, our political structure. There are people who acquire great amounts of capital or inherit it, and my job, the way it's defined, is to find ways to take parts of that and make it social capital and give it back into the world. And I can live with that. If it were my job to change the political economic structure, I'd have a really hard time knowing what to do. But one thing I'm really good at is compartmentalizing in my head, to say that's not my problem. Here are my boundaries. This is my challenge and that's just a condition that I have to live with.

Like those in medicine and philanthropy, the primary school educators we interviewed also tend to exhibit the individually reflective stance. Teachers feel primarily responsible to their students; however, there is no clear message about how to carry out this responsibility in their profession. In addition to meeting students' diverse social, emotional, and academic needs, teachers must answer to different stakeholders, including government, school administrators, and teachers' unions, all of whom have different ways of defining teachers' responsibilities and evaluating their performance (Fischman, DiBara, & Gardner, 2006). Some stakeholders focus on teacher qualifications, others on student attendance and retention or on test scores. In the absence of clear and consistent guidelines on how to uphold their responsibilities to their students and to the other stakeholders, teachers must make difficult individual choices about where to focus their energy and how to limit their responsibilities. As one teacher pointed out, "We are expected to be parent, psychologist, and then teacher, and that's very difficult" (also cited in Fischman, DiBara, & Gardner, 2006). Much like physicians who individually weigh competing responsibilities, teachers are keenly aware that upholding any of their important responsibilities means cutting corners in other areas.

In many ways corporate law has a structure similar to that of genetic science. It is a highly structured hierarchical profession with formal training that begins in law school and continues as individuals climb up the ranks through law firms. Not surprisingly, the corporate lawyers we interviewed limited their responsibilities in a way similar to those in genetics—chiefly by falling back on a narrowly defined role. When asked about their responsibilities in relationship to unethical business and accounting practices of their clients, several lawyers imputed that responsibility to others outside of the legal profession. They responded with similar phrases, such as, "These were accounting issues; they are not legal issues," or "I don't get involved with things like that; that's not my area." When faced with ethical dilemmas, they were able to limit their responsibilities easily by following the consensus of the domain about their sharply delineated role.

Influential Conditions

Which stance characterizes a domain depends largely on the structure of the profession. For instance, the amount of formal training in a domain is likely to influence the stance that practitioners take toward responsibility. Without formal training, individuals can more easily evade the core responsibilities of the domain. Journalism provides a good example of such a dynamic. Compared to medicine and genetic science, which both require extensive formal training, journalism requires very little training. When faced with competing pressures or lures, such as fame and money, there is more opportunity for people to focus on responsibilities outside of the core responsibility of the domain without internal conflict or professional repercussions. Indeed, as the example from the *New York Times* suggests, journalists may even feel internal or external pressures to deviate from the core mission.

On the flip side, intensive training requirements, such as exist in genetic science and medicine, can help preserve a focus on the core responsibilities of a profession, for good or for bad, even in the midst of rapid change and competing pressures. A disciplined focus instilled by rigorous training can prevent individuals from considering broader responsibilities that lie external to a profession. In the case of genetics in the latter years of the twentieth century, most scientists were able to impute the ethical responsibilities to others without much deliberation, in part because their training defined their responsibility as pursuing knowledge. In the case of medicine, rigorous training helps doctors stay focused on patient care, even as increasing medical knowledge and the financial structure of medicine force them to weigh competing responsibilities such as quality care for a few versus adequate care for many. Without such training, individuals in either profession might be more likely to stray from the core responsibility of the profession.

Flexible Stances

While the different stances characterize different professional domains at a given time, a range of stances can be detected across professions. Some of the geneticists we interviewed, for example, were more reflective than others about the ways in which they limited their responsibility. They did not simply repeat the mantra that ethical application of knowledge lies beyond the mission of science. They considered how they could take on part of this responsibility.

When asked about the uses and misuses of research, one researcher had clearly thought about what individual responsibility he wanted to take for these issues:

> I talk about this when I present discussions to laymen, meet with classes, talk to alumni. It's issues that I want to raise the visibility of, I want people to think about, because I believe those are the issues that society will need to make decisions about and I want to participate in

educating people to be prepared for making those decisions. . . . I am
comfortable in the belief that most knowledge has been used to the
good of mankind, and that if good-willed people engage themselves in
debating that knowledge, pushing that knowledge, educating another
generation in how it could be used and misused, you're preparing as
well as you can for culture and society to control that knowledge and
to use it to the betterment of people.

Some geneticists even considered how the domain as a whole might shift
its role to assume more responsibility for the ethical application of
knowledge. Such reflection could be characterized as refocusing responsibility in a way that has so far been deemed external to the core purpose
of the profession. We speculate that just as physicists lost their innocence
after the detonation of the first nuclear weapons, in the ensuing decades
of the twenty-first century more geneticists will devote time to ethical
issues.

The characteristic stances of each domain have their exceptions.
Some doctors limit their responsibilities by just doing their job,
and some journalists weigh conflicting responsibilities within the
domain and carefully choose between them. Consider the following
two examples.

One obstetrician-gynecologist we interviewed complained about the
pressure to see more patients and work longer hours. "I think we're
working harder, longer hours now than we used to. The problem is much
more intense. Especially in OB, you have to be in the hospital basically
when the patient's in the hospital as well. Before you could wait until
they were getting close to delivery and then come in. Now you have to
be here. But it's been a gradual change, so you just count it as a way of
life." When asked how he deals with these challenges, he responded,
"Just accept them, bitch about them, go on. There's not much one individual can do." Rather than outlining competing responsibilities and
contemplating various ways in which he could approach the problem—
the most common stance among physicians we interviewed—his professional stance is better characterized as following the consensus of the
domain. He just rolls with the punches and frames the challenges and
changes in medicine as something to weather.

One journalist we interviewed faces competing responsibilities as an
editor of two prominent Miami newspapers. She must balance her
responsibility to preserve the independence of the papers' reporting with
a responsibility to cooperate with the business side of the paper. She
clearly prioritizes journalistic integrity over business interests; however,

she carefully weighs her competing responsibilities each time she is presented with a story from the promotions department. She described her thought process to us:

> Before, news and advertising were worlds apart and never the twain met. Now you meet all the time so that relationship must be established that, yes, I can work with you to a degree, but you can't ask me to publish a story just to please an advertiser. . . . It's become more complicated to deal with ethics because you're dealing with [rival] sides. I would never, ten years ago, have had to deal with promotions as an editor. And now, community relations sends me something or promotions sends me something. Like tomorrow, they have a spelling bee that both papers are promoting. The spelling bee would be covered anyway. So in my mind I am covering it because it's a national spelling bee. It's seven thousand little kids. They go to Washington. That's a news story, okay. . . . You cover it because it's a news story. You don't cover it because it landed on your desk as a promotion.

This editor's reflective stance toward competing responsibilities aligns more closely with the characteristic stance of the medical doctors in our research sample. Individual characteristics such as age, personality, beliefs, and values likely contribute to the stance an individual embraces toward limiting his or her professional responsibility.

As conditions change, different stances are likely to characterize different domains at different times. External factors, such as an explosion of knowledge in genetic science or medicine, can present professionals with new conflicts in responsibilities, causing individuals in the profession to reconsider how they limit their responsibilities. In the twenty-first century, with the increasing presence of important ethical concerns such as cloning, stem cell research, and genetically modified food, the field of genetic science might present itself as much more conflicted about competing responsibilities. The increasing prevalence of ethical issues in science may make it more difficult for scientists to pursue pure science without a more self-conscious and conflicted choice on how to position themselves with respect to the ethical application of knowledge. In retrospect, genetics at the time of our interviews may come to be seen as akin to medicine in the innocent days of Martin Arrowsmith or Marcus Welby. When a single physician could more easily keep up with all of the important medical knowledge, practitioners might not have had to make as difficult choices as they do now about how to provide quality care for patients.

What Are Appropriate Limits?

The stance an individual takes toward limiting her or his professional responsibilities does not in itself constitute a value judgment. Regardless of how individuals set limits on their responsibilities, there is always room for debate about what constitutes good work and what counts as irresponsible work. Following the consensus of a well-defined profession serves society well in most cases, yet it is not always the right course of action. In the case of genetics, even when the professional consensus is strong and people agree on the boundaries of their responsibilities as scientists, some might argue that such limits are not appropriate given present misuse or potential misuse of genetic knowledge in a Huxleian future. When people weigh conflicting responsibilities, they are often aware that there is no one right choice to make, and any choice can be applauded or criticized. When concierge doctors first started practicing, many people inside and outside of the profession criticized the new type of practice as irresponsible. On the other hand, some viewed their alternative choice— to practice in an environment that does not provide the best possible quality of care for each patient—as equally irresponsible.

In the case of journalism, well-respected leaders in the field consistently criticize those who prioritize fame over journalistic integrity. While such consistent criticism might constitute a good criterion for judgment, the evasive stance that those they criticize represent does not necessarily depend on a normative claim. Prioritizing a responsibility that is not core to the profession can also be good or bad depending on the situation. Returning to the example of genetics, one could argue that someone who prioritizes the ethical application of knowledge over the creation of new knowledge might be making a responsible decision that could benefit society in the long run, even though it strays from the core purpose of science as currently construed. People resist change, and those who in retrospect are seen as creative leaders are often judged negatively at first.

The stance that professionals use to constrain their responsibilities is largely influenced by the current state of the profession—the conflicts facing the profession, the amount of tradition and training a profession provides. Nonetheless, each professional must decide when to follow tradition and when to rely on individual interpretation of professional responsibilities. Whether they end up following or diverging from professional mores, individuals can choose to reflect on or ignore conflicting responsibilities. Society is best served by those who weigh trade-offs in responsibilities and consider the consequences of their choices, not only to their personal reputation and status, but also to the profession and the broader society. Whether their decisions are appropriate is an important question that is examined in the next chapter in this volume.

REFERENCES

Fischman, W., DiBara, J., & Gardner, H. (2006). Creating good education against the odds. *Cambridge Journal of Education, 36*(3), 383–398.

Gardner, H., Csikszentmihalyi, M., & Damon, W. (2001). *Good work: When excellence and ethics meet.* New York. Basic Books.

Horn, L., & Gardner, H. (2006). The lonely profession. In W. Damon & S. Verducci (Eds.), *Taking philanthropy seriously: Beyond noble intentions to responsible giving.* Bloomington: Indiana University Press.

12

IRRESPONSIBLE WORK

Howard Gardner

*I would never go wrong so long as I could look anyone
I wrote about in the eye both before and after the story
ran in the paper. You can only do that if you are honest
and fair in what you write.*

—Bill Kovach

STARTING ON JULY 6, 2005, JUDITH MILLER, a well-known investigative reporter for the *New York Times,* spent eighty-five days in jail. She chose prison rather than naming the sources who had revealed to her the identity of a clandestine CIA operative named Valerie Plame. Interestingly, Miller had never published the information she had obtained, but it became known that she harbored that information. Miller was sentenced to up to eighteen months because she refused to pass this privileged information on to Patrick Fitzgerald, the special prosecutor, and to the grand jury charged with investigating the leaks of this sensitive, privileged information. To many observers, including me, Judith Miller appeared to be a hero. She was remaining true to the central mission of journalism: finding

I gratefully acknowledge several persons who gave me useful feedback on earlier drafts of this chapter: Katie Davis, Carrie James, Lindsay Pettingill, Scott Seider, Susan Verducci, and Ellen Winner. Special thanks to Ben Heineman, Alex Jones, Bill Kovach, Sara Rimer, and Allan Siegal, who have gently and generously educated me about journalism and the *New York Times.*

out the facts, speaking truth to power, protecting sources who might otherwise be unwilling in the future to share information that was sensitive but vital for the public to know.

The status of hero did not last long. Within days of her release Miller was being attacked from all sides, not least by some of her own colleagues on the *New York Times*. She was seen as disingenuous, dishonest, self-aggrandizing, even a traitor to her profession. Within a month of her release, Miller resigned from the newspaper. No longer a prize-winning journalist, she was now a celebrity ex-journalist.

Even those who had embraced Miller's original stance became confused. Hardly simple, the published reports and several background interviews on which I have relied reveal separate facets. On the one hand, there is the renowned reporter, Judith Miller, widely considered by colleagues to be a "piece of work" who had committed two sins. First, in the past she had consistently behaved in a high-handed manner, pursuing stories at all costs, being rude to subordinates and peers, and ignoring the directives of her immediate supervisors to avoid certain beats. Second, she had been the leading reportorial source—perhaps in the nation—of the claim that Iraq possessed weapons of mass destruction and that this violation of United Nations resolutions justified the U.S. invasion of Iraq in March 2003. According to many observers, Judith Miller had been too close to her sources and had helped them spread a narrative for which there was little, if any, solid evidence. Although she might have been seen as using her sources to inform the public, perhaps they were using her for their own misinforming or disinforming ends. Long before the particular incident that led to her time in jail, Miller had burned a lot of bridges.

Another facet concerned the leak itself. Joseph Wilson, a former ambassador, had traveled to Africa to investigate rumors that the African nation Niger was making nuclear-grade uranium available to rogue states, such as Iraq under Saddam Hussein. Having determined that the rumors were without foundation, Wilson published his conclusion in an Op-Ed piece in the *New York Times* in July 2003. By all reports, this publication infuriated officials high in the Bush administration and they determined to retaliate against Wilson. This they did by revealing to reporters—including Judith Miller—that Wilson was married to Plame, that Plame worked in the CIA, and that Wilson was, accordingly, an interested party in this affair. The clear purposes of this intentional leaking were to embarrass and discredit Wilson, on the one hand, and to render Plame's vocation untenable, on the other.

This much of the story became clear quite early in the saga. What confused many were the ensuing events. Conservative columnist Robert

Novak actually published the story about Wilson and Plame on July 14, 2003, but was never penalized in any way. Another reporter, Matt Cooper of *Time Magazine,* did not publish the material but was hauled in front of the grand jury. It looked like Cooper too would go to jail to protect his sources; but then his superior, Norman Pearlstein—a lawyer and head of Time Inc.—intervened and instructed Cooper to cooperate with the grand jury. On Pearlstein's account, and that of other legal experts, Cooper's legal obligation to the grand jury trumped his journalistic obligation to protect a source. Moreover Cooper's sources had apparently released him from the obligation to maintain confidentiality, so there was no compelling reason for him to remain silent. Cooper cooperated with the investigation and went free.

Which left Miller. She and her attorney, well-known First Amendment expert Floyd Abrams, saw the matter differently. Miller took a position on principle: one should not reveal a source in the absence of a full, explicit, and wholly voluntary release; and she was willing to pay the price for adhering to this principle. Only when explicitly released by her principal source—who turned out to be Lewis "Scooter" Libby, a high aide to Vice President Dick Cheney—did she agree to talk to the grand jury, and only on very narrow grounds. So Miller was free, Cooper and Novak had avoided any censure, Libby was indicted (and ultimately convicted), and the *Times* moved rapidly away from its support of Miller—in part because after her release she apparently did not cooperate fully with the *Times's* own investigations of the affair. There were lots of major and bit players, but clearly no shining heroes and, perhaps, no unredeemed villains.

Great cases may not make great law, but they certainly raise profound questions, including ones about the nature, locus, and extent of individual and corporate responsibility. There is the responsibility of the individual: the reporter, Judith Miller; the prosecutor, Patrick Fitzgerald (who in his zealous pursuit of the leaker may have gone beyond his investigative brief); the named and unnamed sources (Libby, Bush aide Karl Rove, perhaps others).[1] There is the responsibility of institutions: the *New York Times, Time Magazine,* the CIA, the grand jury, and the offices of the president and the vice president. There is the responsibility of the professionals from various domains—journalists, publishers, defense lawyers, public prosecutors, and other current and former public servants.

---

[1] In August 2006 it was reported that Richard Armitage, a high-level State Department appointee, may have been the first administration official to leak the identity of Valerie Plame Wilson (N. Lewis, 2006).

Irresponsible Work: Toward a Definition

In what follows I analyze the gray area of responsibility. I focus on those occasions when individuals lose track of the core responsibilities of their profession and engage in actions (or inactions) that I deem irresponsible or compromised (Gardner, 2005a). Irresponsible work spans the area between work that, on the one hand, clearly embodies the core values of the profession, and work that, on the other, is frankly illegal.

In so doing, I adopt a stance that differs significantly from that assumed by other authors in this collection. That is, while seeking to understand the emic perspectives of various players, I reserve the etic right to label certain activities *irresponsible* or *compromised*—even if, from the point of view of the players, what they did was excusable, proper, even laudable. I do so because ultimately we cannot leave such judgments exclusively to those who have an interest in self-preservation, if not in self-promotion. At a certain point, informed outside observers have the right—indeed, I would argue, the obligation—to say, "This is good work, that is OK work, the third example is illegal work. And this right extends to the recognition of a fourth variety: work that, while not strictly illegal, ought to be labeled *irresponsible."* Although by no means my exclusive focus, the Judith Miller case allows me to test the notions being developed here, with particular respect to individuals, institutions, and the overall profession of journalism.

How do we recognize irresponsible work? As argued by Horn and Gardner in the preceding chapter in this volume, every individual must limit his or her responsibilities in some ways. Responsibilities are properly limited when one or more of the following conditions are met: (1) the worker embraces a core value of the profession and places a high priority on its realization; (2) the worker assumes certain responsibilities, with reasonable confidence that other, equally compelling responsibilities will be assumed by peers; and (3) the worker elects to pursue an idiosyncratic responsibility, seeks to make this responsibility central to the "domain" and the "field," and is willing to accept the consequences should knowledgeable peers find his work lacking over the long haul.

Following Horn and Gardner, we can apply this metric to the profession of medicine. A physician is properly limiting her responsibility if she elects to devote all of her attention to her patients. The physician may elect to pursue concierge medicine but should have reasonable confidence that other physicians will serve the large majority of patients who cannot afford the fees of a concierge practice. Finally, a physician such as Jack Kevorkian may elect to devote his energy to the noncore value of physician-assisted suicide and to alert his colleagues to the importance of his stance, but he has to be willing to accept censure or even imprisonment if his behavior is judged to be irresponsible, unethical, or illegal.

By implication, then, we can make judgments of irresponsible work in medicine. A physician's work is irresponsible if the core responsibilities are shirked, if he pursues a course that serves only certain constituencies and fails to consider or to care whether other equally deserving constituencies will also receive treatment, or if he refuses to accept the consequences should his work be judged inadequate by informed associates. Put differently, the profession could no longer function if all (or even a majority of) workers proceeded in an irresponsible fashion.

Three Lenses on Journalism

I use the Judith Miller case as a point of entry for considering three realms within the profession of journalism: the level of the individual reporter (such as Judith Miller or Matt Cooper), the level of the news organization (such as the *New York Times,* CNN, or Fox News), and the profession of journalism as a whole. In each case I suggest the factors that can lead to a judgment of irresponsible work, as well as those that might mitigate that harsh judgment. In passing I consider examples of irresponsible work in other domains, such as higher education. In conclusion I suggest the forces that lead to irresponsible work and those that might prevent or minimize such irresponsibility.

Before embarking on this analysis, a word about the domain of journalism. My focus here falls on what one might term *serious investigative reporting.* This professional practice—barely a century old in the United States—features careful and thorough interviewing of sources, study of relevant documents, and consideration of broader contextual factors. The reporter (or, as has often been the case, the team of reporters) is expected to get the story right and complete, and insofar as possible, to avoid bias, prejudice, distortions, or special pleading. While not always living up to these high standards, publications such as the *New York Times* and the *Wall Street Journal* in the United States, the *Financial Times* in the United Kingdom, and flagship papers in Europe (such as *Neue Zuericher Zeitung* and *Frankfuerter Allgemeine*) aspire to this form and level of reporting. On this high standard many American newspapers and most so-called broadcast news outlets (though not National Public Radio) fall lamentably short—indeed, many would merit a judgment of irresponsible or compromised reporting.

The Individual Reporter

From her perspective, Judith Miller was being true to the core values of journalism: she was pursuing stories vigorously and defending the anonymity of her sources (http://www.judithmiller.org). Moreover, she was willing to accept the consequences of her perhaps idiosyncratic construal, going to jail for an unspecified period rather than compromising the principle of confidentiality by revealing her sources.

Yet Miller ended up being judged harshly by informed colleagues and observers. While she did indeed pursue stories vigorously, in their view she crossed at least two lines. She blatantly disregarded her editors' instructions to stop covering stories having to do with national security—instructions given after she had committed several abuses of her reportorial role. By this sin of commission she placed herself above the judgments of her superiors. A news organization cannot operate if reporters do not honor the lines and limits of responsibility laid out by editors.

The second line entailed her excessive personal contacts with powerful sources. To be sure, these close ties helped her to get prized stories, but they were purchased at a high cost: clouding of judgment and, perhaps, an inability to separate personal from professional relations. The public will not get accurate news if reporters stop being reporters and become friends or mouthpieces of their sources. One should always ask, who is using whom?

As suggested, there appears to have been an additional reason that Miller was judged so strongly. Once she had been released from jail, she was asked to cooperate completely with the management of the *Times* as they sought to unravel the full history of her case. Her failure to honor this request may have been the final straw, causing her to lose support and to embolden the many associates who had disapproved of her earlier personal and professional peccadillos.

Note that these issues of special treatment are not restricted to Judith Miller. Indeed, they may be prevalent among superstar reporters. Bob Woodward was justifiably honored for his path-breaking uncovering (with Carl Bernstein) of the Watergate scandal. But in the ensuing thirty years, Woodward has carved out a unique place in Washington journalistic circles. He has access to powerful figures that no other reporter has, and he writes best sellers that no one else could write. Woodward has been rightly criticized for excessive intimacy with his sources, a status that threatens his independence and sometimes gives the impression that he is endorsing the status quo. Woodward was also chastised for his role in the Wilson-Plame affair. Apparently, on the basis of his source in the

State Department, he knew about the Plame-Wilson link even before Miller and Cooper did. Yet in his reports he never revealed his knowledge of the case and dismissed the case as unimportant. Lack of candor with one's editors is a cardinal sin for a reporter. Although there is no smoking gun in the Woodward case, he may fairly be charged with a regrettable compromise (Carr, 2006).

One may reasonably raise questions about other individuals involved in the case. It seems that the other reporter, Cooper, and the publishers in the case, Pearlstein and Arthur Sulzberger Jr., took justifiable stands; according to a 1972 Supreme Court decision, a summons from the grand jury takes legal precedence over the protection of sources. It may appear to outsiders that Robert Novak benefited from special treatment, because he actually outed Plame and yet suffered no public exposure or censure. As far as I can determine, Novak spoke to the grand jury and did not compromise his role as a columnist. Lawyer Floyd Abrams may well be faulted for his poor judgment in construing this as a First Amendment case; but because this has been his stated cause for decades, he was acting according to his long-standing principles. Identified leakers Libby, Richard Armitage, and Karl Rove were to be judged by public opinion, if not (as in the case of Libby) in a court of law. Prosecutor Fitzgerald was caught on the horns of a dilemma: Should he drop a case that was important but incredibly murky? Or should he risk the charge of pursuing the case too zealously (Johnston, 2006)?

While Miller (and possibly Woodward) may be seen as having compromised their positions as reporters, it is important to stress that their sins were not venal. In this respect, they can be contrasted with the notorious case of Jayson Blair. This young reporter for the New York Times was steadily advanced through the ranks during the first years of the twenty-first century. This increase in responsibility and status occurred despite serious misgivings on the part of various supervisors and peers. In the spring of 2003 it was discovered that Blair had totally shirked his responsibilities as a reporter: he had plagiarized some stories, made up others, and lied consistently to his supervisors about where he had been and what he had spent on his corporate expense account. Blair was promptly forced to resign, and his misdeeds were laid out in excruciating detail in a lengthy Times cover story on May 11, 2003 (see also Blair, 2004).

Blair epitomizes the irresponsible journalist. The profession could not survive if many reporters behaved in the way he did. And indeed, both friends and foes of rigorous, disinterested reportage had a field day, attacking the Times for its mishandling of Blair's reportorial niche prior to his forced resignation.

Even in cases of plagiarism or fabrication, journalists do not go to jail. These misdeeds are crimes against professional standards, not violations of statutes. And in most cases the punishment is the appropriate one: plagiarists such as Blair and fabricators such as Janet Cooke of the *Washington Post* and Stephen Glass of the *New Republic* are driven out of the profession. Even those who manage to find another position—such as one-time *Boston Globe* columnist Mike Barnicle—operate under a cloud, one visible at least to those who care about the standards of reportorial journalism.

The News Organization

Just as Judith Miller underwent intense scrutiny for her actions in the early 2000s, the *New York Times* itself has been widely critiqued for its actions and inactions during the same period. In part, of course, this criticism comes with the territory. When you are widely considered the premier organization in your sector, it is expected that you will consistently perform at the highest levels, that you will be subjected to considerable scrutiny, and that you will censured whenever you fall short. Such is the lot of universities like Harvard or Stanford, or museums like New York's Metropolitan Museum or the Museum of Modern Art.

Still, a series of events during this period justified a close look at the operation of the *Times*. Neither the Miller case nor the Blair case involved just the protagonists. In the Miller case, the question was raised about whether her supervisors scrutinized her actions carefully enough, whether her reporting received adequate in-house criticism, and whether her involvements with the rich and the powerful—including publisher Sulzberger—insulated her from the scrutiny she should have undergone and the censure she might earlier have merited. In the Blair case there was little question that this talented but testy young reporter was given a "pass" on many occasions when he should have been reprimanded or even fired. In all probability this special treatment reflected both a desire to help a minority reporter on a staff that was short on minorities and to advance a young reporter who had the makings of a star—at least as *star* was being defined at the time.

Inevitably, once one speaks of the organizational level, one has to consider the individuals who composed the institution in the past and who constitute it today. The buck stops with those at the head of the organization: in this case, publisher Sulzberger, the board of directors of the New York Times Company, and editors Howell Raines (2001–2003) and Bill Keller (2003–present). Of these people, Howell Raines has by far been the subject of the most discussion. Raines was a gifted reporter for many years and a talented if controversial head of the editorial page during the 1990s. In an open competition during the spring of 2001 he beat out Keller for the coveted role of executive editor.

Upon assuming the post, Raines immediately announced that the *Times* had been resting on its laurels and that it was his mission to increase "its competitive metabolism" and make it all that it could be. As he declared, "the world's greatest newspaper is not nearly as good as it could be and ought to be" (2004, p. 49). He critiqued "the calcified front page we had inherited ... the neglected underfinanced 'soft' sections" (2004, p. 49); he pointedly added, "the first thing you noticed upon being hired by the *Times* was that on many stories it was a churning urn of underachievement" (2006, p. 137). He described the newsroom as full of "lifers, careerists, nerds, time-servers, and drones" (Hagan, 2006, p. 3) And indeed Raines appeared to be making good on his aspirations to improve the quality of the coverage. The paper's reporting in the wake of the 9/ll attacks was superlative, and the following year the *Times* snagged a record seven Pulitzer Prizes.

Yet by the spring of 2003 Raines was out of a job, his editorship having lasted a mere eighteen months. The proximal cause of his resignation was unquestionably the Blair affair—an event that many considered the low point in the paper's recent history. Yet Raines would undoubtedly have weathered this storm, and perhaps even the Judith Miller brouhaha (which began during his tenure), had he not lost the support of most of his newsroom. From his own vantage point, Raines had been arousing a sleeping giant, but from the point of view of most other observers, he had played fast and loose with his prestigious position. He had promoted favorites (including, it was charged, young Blair and middle-aged Miller); he had disrespected well-regarded, long-faithful journalists and staff on the paper; he had pushed certain issues far beyond their merits (notoriously, thirty-three stories about restricted admissions at an Augusta, Georgia, golf club and the unprecedented canceling of two columns critical of this excessive coverage); and not least his constant self-promotion. When a crisis occurs on your watch, you had better have a reservoir of goodwill on which to draw. In less than two years, Raines had squandered nearly all of that reservoir.

After the fact, if not during his reign, *Times* staffers were graphic in their criticisms of Raines. Speaking of Raines's self-glorification, Stephen Engelberg said, "I was staggered. The sheer ego of it. It wasn't about getting the story right, it was about his obituary" (Mnookin, 2004, p. 63). Long-time reporter Clyde Haberman added, "Howell seemed to think that if the September 11 attacks had occurred one week earlier [that is, before Raines took over as executive editor], we'd all have been sitting at our desks with our thumbs up our asses" (Mnookin, 2004, p. xvii) With reference to Raines's misuse of his journalistic pulpit, Jon Landman, the editor who first blew the whistle on Blair, made this comment: "When the making of a statement [by an editor] doesn't coincide with good journalism, you have a real problem" (Mnookin, 2004, p. 75). And *Times* public editor Daniel Okrent wrote critically about the Raines era and particularly about the Miller-led coverage of the Iraqi war: "An old *Times* hand recently told me there was a period in the not-too-distant past when editors stressed the maxim, 'Don't get it first, get it right.' That soon mutated into 'Get it first and get it right.' The next devolution was an obvious one. War requires an extra standard of care, not a lesser one" (Okrent, 2006, p. 110).

However, it would be a mistake to leave the *Times* issues at the doorstep of individuals—whether reporters like Miller and Blair, or editors like Raines and his successor, Bill Keller. According to my analysis, the *Times* was dealing with two separate issues, both far larger than the influence of particular individuals. One could even make the argument that the aforementioned individuals were at least in part victims of rather than contributors to these larger issues. In addition, entities other than reporters and editors also bear responsibility for the health of an institution.

To begin with, there were the rapid and unpredictable changes that were occurring in the media. Fifty years ago, print news was supreme and the *Times* stood at the head of the pack. In the intervening period, broadcast and Internet sources took an ever larger share of audience interest and profits, and most news organizations were purchased by multinational corporations that were interested primarily in high quarterly profits and not in quality journalism. (Most had nothing against quality journalism as long as it was also highly profitable.) The *Times* was one of the very few outlets that remained under family control. Yet in an effort to remain competitive and profitable, it had to diversify its holdings (buying and selling various newspapers, owning and divesting television channels, trying desperately to crack the mysteries of the Internet and derive financial rewards from it). Needless to say, not all of these purchases and experiments worked. The *Times* also continually expanded the range of its coverage to areas that were widely considered to be soft (witness its regular sections called "Escape" and "Dining" and "House and Home") and peripheral to the central mission of "all the news that's fit to print."

In addition, there are problems associated with being widely considered the leading institution in your sector. (To be sure, there are worse problems to have.) There is the temptation to rest on your laurels, to dismiss criticism, to ignore competitors to whom you had better be paying attention. This stance was well captured in a remark made by reporter Elizabeth Kolbert with reference to the Blair scandal: "the paper of record" cannot afford to "check up" on its employees; it has to assume they are trustworthy (2003). Of course that is precisely the assumption that the *Times* should *not* have made with reference to Blair and, it turned out, to several other "free pass" reporters as well.

In courting the leadership of the *Times* for the job of executive editor, Raines had directly addressed these issues. He had argued strongly that the *Times* was most likely to retain and strengthen its supremacy by delivering the highest-quality coverage to its most sophisticated readers. In that sense, he had endorsed the core values of the domain. At the same time, however, he had strongly criticized the current staff as being lazy, self-satisfied, and immune to self-correction and improvement. Of course, short of dismissing his whole staff, Raines had to work with the very individuals he had critiqued. So, while addressing real needs and proposing a genuine solution, he had poisoned the atmosphere at the very institution he was trying to reform. As journalist Seth Mnookin put it, "Under Howell Raines, the frustration that simmered just below the surface seemed to explode. Desk editors weren't speaking to one another. Reporters were almost at the point of open revolt. There was such fear of Raines's temper and dismissive attitude that some editors said they kept to themselves concerns about shoddy stories or reporters. A newsroom where editors are scared to voice their concerns is a disaster waiting to happen" (Mnookin, 2004, p. 157; see also Auletta, 2002; Hagan, 2006).

I had the opportunity to observe an eerily parallel situation at Harvard University. Lawrence Summers assumed the presidency of Harvard at the same time as Howell Raines took on the leadership of the *Times*. Like Raines, Summers was an articulate, brilliant, and in some ways larger-than-life figure who promised to affirm the core values of the domain—in this case, quality liberal arts education at the tertiary level—while arousing its stagnant staff and reforming its anachronistic processes. If anything, Summers initially had more support from both staff and management than Raines had. His broad goals of emphasizing undergraduate education, interdisciplinary scientific initiatives, and international experiences for students were not particularly controversial; bringing about these changes would indeed require rethinking some current institutional processes and priorities.

Yet Summers could not resist critiquing the very individuals, departments, schools, and research centers with whom he had to work; and like Raines, he gave the impression that he saw the institution as an extension of himself rather than as the collective efforts of thousands of others who were working in quiet good faith. He described Harvard as essentially unchanged in a century, and implied that he was the anointed successor to Charles William Eliot, who had created the modern Harvard during his long presidency. Summers made a number of publicly embarrassing gaffes, and by the time he realized that he had to fight to keep his position, his supporters were too few and insufficiently powerful. In the end, Summers lost the support of Harvard's governing corporation, just as Raines had lost the support of the board of the *Times*.

The fates of Raines and Summers underscore that institutions are more than single individuals, and despite Ralph Waldo Emerson's phrase, more than the "lengthened shadow of an individual." Legally and properly, a chief executive officer is appointed by a board of directors; it is up to the board to monitor the executive, to offer counsel when there are problems, and in the extreme, to dismiss the executive. Ultimately both executives were in fact forced to resign, though with little alacrity or enthusiasm on the part of the New York Times Company and the Harvard Corporation.

More crucial in both cases were the attitudes of those who were close to the executives on a daily basis. As documented here, Raines succeeded in earning the fear, if not the enmity, of many of the staff of the newspaper. Their collective uproar after the Blair affair made Raines's tenure untenable. By the same token, while Summers enjoyed support among many students, alumni, and some faculties, he lost the support of the central faculty of arts and sciences and was not defended publicly by any of his deans. The threat of a second vote of no confidence by the Arts and Sciences faculty sufficed to bring about his removal. I would argue that those closest to the executive—peers, direct reports, and workaday employees—have a responsibility to stand up for the deepest values of the institution.

What can compromise a highly regarded institution such as the *Times* or Harvard? As with individuals, the identification and preservation of key values is definitional. Once a newspaper stops pursuing the most important stories in the fairest and most complete manner, it is in trouble. Once a college or university places other values on the same level as providing a superior education, it rapidly loses its reason for existence. I have watched with mounting despair as major educational institutions have moved in perceptible steps from *.edu* to *.com* (Gardner, 2005b; H. Lewis, 2006)

In times of extremely potent market forces and few counterforces of equivalent power, the tendency to focus on the bottom line—on everything from favoring wealthy applicants to requiring the university press (that publishes scholarly monographs) to show a profit—is patent; pity those institutions that lack the fortitude to withstand these pressures.

But institutions can be undermined from within as well as by external forces. To the outside world, the *Times* and Harvard did not look very different in 2006 than they did in 2000 or even 1990. But to those within the organizations they had become increasingly roiled under management that was ill-fitted to its task—at least within the institution as currently constituted. Leaders must be prepared to fight for needed changes, but they need troops who support them, not troops who are waiting for an excuse—in some cases, any excuse—to topple them.

These examples underscore the difficulty of a clean separation of the institutional from the individual level. Institutions exist before and, in most cases, after the individuals occupying their helm at a specific moment. They have distinctive cultures and they respond to field pressures that extend well beyond particular persons or moments. Yet practices and policies are at any time announced, implemented, and nuanced by particular individuals who must assume responsibility—both credit and blame—for what occurs on their watch. The *Times* was not the same institution under Haines as it was under his predecessor, Joseph Lelyveld, or as it is under his successor, Bill Keller; and the Harvard of Summers is easily distinguished from the Harvard under the leadership of predecessor Neil Rudenstine or interim successor Derek Bok.

It is possible for an institution to recover from a characterization of "irresponsible work." The *Times* took many steps in this direction. In addition to publishing detailed accounts of and apologies for the Blair and Miller affairs, it appointed a series of internal committees under the supervision of a highly respected editor, Allan M. Siegal. The committees recommended several changes, most of which have since been put into effect by the paper (Seelye, 2005a). The corrective measures included a diminished use of anonymous sources, regular reporting of corrections of errors and changes "for the record," clear delineation of the line between reporting and commentary, and appointment of a public editor who serves as an ombudsperson for readers and whose work is not subjected to routine editing. (The position has so far been filled by Daniel Okrent and Byron Calame, two highly respected journalists of very different backgrounds.) Of course such moves can be seen as mere public relations. But on the basis of my own observations I would say that the *Times* has taken its responsibility as the paper of record very seriously.

And provided there are no scandals of the sort that roiled the paper in the early part of the decade, the middle part of the decade will be seen as a time when the newspaper regained stature.

The Profession

For most of the nineteenth century, newspapers were quite different entities than they are now. They were openly partisan, they promoted the values and friends of their owners, and their reporters were more known for their drinking habits than for their reportorial zeal.

William Randolph Hearst, the most powerful publisher of the time, was notorious for his inappropriately large role in fomenting the Spanish-American War and was immortalized in Orson Welles's movie *Citizen Kane* as the egomaniacal Charles Foster Kane.

The *New York Times* reflected, and in many ways led the way to, a professionalization of journalism (Tifft & Jones, 1999). Although journalists do not acquire official credentials, reporters have come to be seen as belonging to a skilled craft. They are expected to identify stories worth reporting; to carry out due diligence, such as verification of facts and checking of sources; and to report stories in as fair, objective, and complete a way as possible. Bill Kovach, a well-known and much-admired editor, reflects on the lessons he learned from his mentor: "[Tim Pridgen] told me I would never go wrong so long as I could look anyone I wrote about in the eye both before and after the story ran in the paper. You can only do that if you are honest and fair in what you write" (B. Kovach, personal communication, September 12, 2006).

The trend in journalism mirrored trends in most other major domains. From law to medicine, from architecture to engineering, the Progressive Era of the early twentieth century saw a sharp trend toward the professionalization of the sphere. Trainees were expected to get a formal education and a license; they participated in supervised mentorships, apprenticeships, or internships; and they were informed of the relevant codes of practice and expected to adhere to them. Positive exemplars were recognized and rewarded while those who defied or ignored the codes were subject to excoriation and, on occasion, banishment from the profession. Almost no rookie reporters went straight to work for a major paper like the *Times;* they were expected to put in their time at small local newspapers (often in the South), then to move to second-tier cities. They started with the least prestigious beats (education, the police) and moved gradually to more prestigious beats (Washington, key international capitals). The pinnacle, such as a position at the *Times,* was reached by only the most talented, and often only after a considerable period of surveillance over a considerable period of time. The process was reasonably meritocratic.

Quite possibly the high point of the professions in America was achieved in the early 1960s. This was a time when a few newspapers and the three networks dominated news coverage; when doctors, lawyers, engineers, and even politicians were the object of high levels of admiration and trust; when disinterested trustees or "wise men" were recognized and honored. In the fall 1963 issue of *Daedalus,* the journal of the American Academy of Arts and Science, editor Kenneth Lynn declared, "Everywhere in American life, the professions are triumphant" (quoted in Gardner & Shulman, 2005, p. 13). Today, when gifted young college graduates often head directly to Hollywood or to a Wall Street hedge fund, it is doubtful that any observer would utter that phrase.

What can compromise a profession? Part of the answer, paradoxically, may be its democratization. By the late 1960s, many professions were under attack for being exclusive, exclusionary, and the redoubt of white males, typically of Protestant Anglo-Saxon background. There began an inexorable broadening of the professions to admit those of different backgrounds, including those who had hitherto been marginalized in the American workplace. Although few today would question the benevolent aspects of these trends, they may have occurred at a cost. In some cases, standards for entry were lowered—for example, for members of certain previously underserved groups. In many cases, the ideal of disinterestedness was attacked as unrealistic or even wrongheaded. Relativists (both those in the academy and those on the streets) argued that all issues are fundamentally issues of power, that the attainment of power is the aim of every interest group, and that those who hold power determine what is right or wrong. There is no room in this dispensation for the lonely reporter or designer or physician who seeks to remain loyal to a code even when it goes against his perceived self-interest—let alone when it diminishes or undermines his own power.

Of course one can open up a profession without undermining its ethical core. Indeed, I believe this has been the case in certain regions—for example, in Northern Europe—and in certain professions, such as medicine. But when demotic trends are coupled with a frontal attack on once-respected institutions and individuals, fundamental domain beliefs are often toppled in the process. As legal authority Russell Pearce (2001) has argued, the professions of mid-century America had lots wrong with them, but at least they foregrounded a sense of the public good.

In this regard, journalism has had relatively few protective coats. For one thing, it has never been a *bona fide* profession. Anyone can declare herself a journalist; and although that declaration may not be taken seriously at the *New York Times* (or the *Wall Street Journal* or the *Financial Times*), the distinction is lost on most of the public. Neither Judith Miller nor Jayson Blair served the kind of apprenticeship that was routine earlier in the twentieth century. The newscaster who reads the story without fully understanding it (let alone researching and writing it) is seen as no different from the chain-smoking reporter who beat the pavement in order to uncover the facts surrounding a scandal. Indeed, it is sometimes difficult to distinguish news outlets from entertainment or advertising outlets. (If you doubt this, surf the local TV channels in any American city at ten or eleven o'clock on any weekday night.)

Nor can journalists count on institutional forms to protect them. Unlike physicians and lawyers, journalists do not set up partnerships that can pledge to uphold core values and decide on an acceptable profit. If the newspaper is owned by a family, the journalists are at the mercy of the values—both financial and political—of that particular family. And when the newspaper is part of a publicly traded company, quarterly profits are likely to trump considerations of quality reporting or long-term viability. Once-admired papers such as the *Louisville Courier Journal*, the *Los Angeles Times*, and the *San Jose Mercury News* have all been battered by an excessive bottom-line mentality—and the family-controlled *New York Times* is not immune from such pressures (Gavin, 2006).

Finally, there is the threat of government control—patent as I write early in 2007. Cases like that of Judith Miller have emboldened federal officials and courts to place tighter controls on journalists and to subject them to severe penalties if those controls are ignored. Thomas Jefferson said, in a 1787 letter to Colonel Edward Carrington, "Were it left to me to decide whether we should have a government without newspapers, or newspapers without a government, I should not hesitate a moment to prefer the latter." One certainly does not hear such proclamations in governmental circles today.

For these and other reasons, many doubt that the journalistic profession as it was practiced in the middle twentieth century in the United States will survive (Carroll, 2006). Print newspapers are likely either to become promoters of local news and local products or to go out of existence altogether. Journalists are likely to divide into the few who become celebrities and the many who are looking for another job (which paradoxically could involve teaching at a journalism school). Reliable and thorough broadcast news hardly exists anymore, except perhaps on CNN during a time of crisis and National Public Radio in those communities that can afford to subsidize it. Rupert Murdoch's News Corporation may well survive—along with Silvio Berlusconi's virtual monopoly in Italy. But donning my etic hat, I do not consider these to be journalistic outposts. (They are better described as partisan entertainment outlets.) Currently, blogging is a fad, but most blogs are of interest only to intimates of the blogger. Those blogs that have widespread appeal will survive, but they will face a choice: either remain parasitic on existing journalistic media, or develop staffs that can feed the needs of the consumers and secure sources of revenue to pay those staffs—in other words, attempt to reinvent journalism in a nonprogressive era.

Professions rise and fall for various reasons, and if journalism goes the way of barbering-as-surgery, nothing can be done about it. But professions rise for reasons, and those reasons do not evaporate just because a particular role or institution has become dysfunctional and ultimately disappears. Surgery is well carried out by physicians, and if lawyers become too costly for ordinary citizens, licensed or unlicensed mediators will take their place in the noncorporate world. Individuals will continue to need reliable and objective reporting about what is happening in the world, and if they do not get this information from print journalists at little cost, other institutions and professions will eventually arise—and people will pay what they need to pay to get these services.

Preventing or Countering Irresponsibility

Through an examination of journalism at three levels, I have sought to illustrate examples of irresponsible or compromised work. One can find comparable examples across various domains—for example, the instances of irresponsible work in medicine cited earlier. Close ties often exist across these levels. Thus, turbulent conditions in the wider profession often cause boards to embrace risky strategies and to appoint leadership that promises to pursue these strategies vigorously and uncritically. This newly installed leadership is in turn likely to reward individuals who test the limits of responsibility and—either directly or by omission—to penalize those individuals who appear resistant to change—for legitimate, even idealistic reasons, or because of stubbornness or sloth.

Yet irresponsibility can occur even when systemic pressures do not exist. When the Harvard Corporation appointed Lawrence Summers as president, Harvard University—with its endowment of more than twenty billion dollars—was certainly not under the same profitability or survival pressures as was the *New York Times*. (I fall short here of attaching the label *irresponsible* to Summers or to the Harvard Corporation.) The profession of accounting was comfortable and well established on the American scene in the 1960s and 1970s; greed rather than external pressures motivated many individuals and many firms to blur the lines irresponsibly between accurate reporting, collusive winking, and frank massaging of the numbers. And even when a domain is almost free of external constraints—as is the case with philanthropy—it is still possible for boards and leaders to behave irresponsibly. According to many published reports, this is what happened to the enormously wealthy and powerful Getty Trust, with its endowment of more than eight billion dollars, at the beginning of the twenty-first century.

So, with the possibility of irresponsibility ever present, what steps should be taken to reduce the incidence of irresponsible behavior and, when it appears, to identify it, isolate it, and make sure that as little damage as possible results?

From one perspective, the answer to this question is simple—indeed, elementary. The core values of the domain need to be made widely known, to be loudly and regularly articulated and to be powerfully embodied in individuals and practices. During training, individuals need constant exposure to these values; they need regularly and vividly to observe the differences between full realization, competent practice, mere lip service, and frank flouting of these values. When individuals, institutions, or professions behave in an exemplary fashion, this fact should be celebrated. Conversely, when cases of frankly irresponsible behavior occur, they should serve as a wakeup call. The behavior of the offending party should be carefully examined, corrective measures should be installed, and regular, tough surveillance should be instituted in order to determine whether a sense of responsibility has in fact been regained and maintained.

Indeed, when and where a profession is well established and conditions are stable, instances of irresponsible behavior ought to be relatively scarce, readily recognized, and easily repaired. Perhaps this was the case during the early 1960s when professions in American life occupied a hallowed status. Yet while clarity and stability may be desirable, they do not guarantee universal responsibility. Indeed, sometimes the most treasured institutions fall prey to irresponsible behavior just because of the widespread assumption that "it can't happen here."

While the road to good work—or the prevention of irresponsible work—is not difficult to describe, its realization proves to be anything but straightforward. Our GoodWork project amply documents threats to good work at this time—even as this chapter documents or alludes to cases that would widely be deemed irresponsible. Now, to be sure, there will always be some people, some institutions, and even some professions that look for opportunities to behave irresponsibly; these compulsive cheaters are not our concern here. Rather, the difficult question to resolve is how individuals, institutions, and on occasion entire professions that start out or have been on the right track end up behaving in ways that are irresponsible, lamentable, and injurious to society. To put it perhaps too bluntly: Could steps have been taken that would have made Judith Miller and Howell Raines exemplars of good work, not only in their own eyes, but also in the eyes of their peers and of informed observers? Or to ratchet up the question several levels, what in the early years of the twenty-first century might have pushed the *Times* or the profession of journalism decisively toward the responsible side of the ledger?

My own position on these questions is cautiously affirmative. While no one should minimize the potency of external pressures, in the end it is individuals who compose our institutions and professions. If they cannot or will not hold themselves accountable, then it is up to their peers to do so. Had Miller and Raines been strongly sanctioned by their peers and supervisors, they might have followed a much more benign course (compare Seelye, 2005b). By the same token, the examples and behaviors of other new outlets could have pushed the *Times* either toward more sensationalistic coverage (as occurred in the middle of the nineteenth century) or toward more high-level reporting (as has happened intermittently in the ensuing eras) (see Fallows, 1997). As a professional cohort, journalists could promulgate standards of performance and pointedly ostracize those who do not meet them—as happens, at least in theory, in the traditional professions. In the absence of such checks, the prognosis for journalism in the United States is bleak.

Speaking more generally, professions need to respect their current instantiation but not be paralyzed by it. Change for change's sake is rarely indicated, but reflexive adherence to the status quo is equally problematic. Those professionals and professions that keep their principal values and goals centrally in mind are the ones most likely to thrive; they can peer through accidental changes in methods of delivery while making certain that the most important needs and desires are being appropriately fulfilled. As argued throughout this volume, this task is most difficult at times of flux and when the ambient society is sending mixed or destructive signals. At such times, a strong sense of individual responsibility is crucial—and may prove to be the only reliable bulwark against irresponsible behavior.

REFERENCES

Auletta, K. (2002). The Howell doctrine. *The New Yorker,* June 10, 2002. http://www.kenauletta.com/howelldoctrine.html

Blair, J. (2004). *Burning down my master's house: My life at the* New York Times. Beverly Hills, CA: New Millennium Press.

Carr, D. (2006, October 2). A reporter who scoops his own newspaper. *The New York Times,* p. C1.

Carroll, J. (2006, April 26). Last call at the ASNE saloon. Speech delivered at the 2006 American Society of Newspaper Editors' convention.

Fallows, J. (1997). *Breaking the news. How the media undermine American democracy.* New York: Vintage Books.

Gardner, H. (2005a, Summer). Compromised work. *Daedalus,* pp. 42–51.

Gardner, H. (2005b). Beyond markets and individuals: A focus on educational goals. In R. Hersh & J. Merrow (Eds.), *Declining by degrees.* New York: Palgrave/Macmillan.

Gardner, H., & Shulman, L. (2005). The professions in America today: Crucial but fragile. *Daedalus,* pp. 13–18.

Gavin, R. (2006, November 5). Major shareholder challenges *Times* corporate structure. *The Boston Globe,* p. A16.

Hagan, J. (2006, September 11). The United States of America vs. Bill Keller. *New York Magazine.* Retrieved http://nymag.com/news/media/20334/

Johnston, D. (2006, September 2). Leak revelations leave questions. *New York Times,* p. A1.

Kolbert, E. (2003). Tumult in the newsroom. *The New Yorker.* June 30, 2003. Available http://www.newyorker.com/archive/2003/06/30/030630fa_fact

Lewis, H. (2006). *Excellence without soul.* New York: Public Affairs Books.

Lewis, N. (2006). Source of C.I.A. leak said to admit role. *The New York Times,* August 30, 2006. Available http://www.nytimes.com/2006/08/30/washington/30armitage. html?ex=1314590400&en=371ecd094bbd6ae6&ei=5090 &partner=rssuserland&emc=rss

Mnookin, S. (2004). *Hard news: The scandals at the* New York Times *and their meaning for the American media.* New York: Random House.

Okrent, D. (2006). *Public editor #1: The collected columns (with reflections, reconsiderations, and even a few retractions) of the first ombudsman of the* New York Times. New York: Public Affairs Books.

Pearce, R. (2001). Lawyers as America's governing class: The formation and dissolution of the original understanding of the American lawyer's role. *University of Chicago Law School Roundtable, 8*(2), 381.

Raines, H. (2004, May). My times. *Atlantic Monthly,* pp. 49–81.

Raines, H. (2006). *The one that got away: A memoir.* New York: Scribner's.

Seelye, K. (2005a, May 9). Panel at the *Times* proposes steps to increase credibility. *The New York Times,* p. C6.

Seelye, K. (2005b). Times editor expresses regret over handling of leak case. *New York Times,* October 22, 2005. Available http://select.nytimes.com/gst/abstract.html?res=F10B13F8385B0C718EDDA90994DD404482

Tifft, S., & Jones, A. (1999). *The trust: The private and powerful family behind the* New York Times. Boston: Little, Brown.

Who killed the newspaper? (2006). *The Economist,* August 24, 2006. Available http://www.economist.com/opinion/displaystory.cfm?story_id=7830218

PART FOUR

TOWARD GREATER RESPONSIBILITY

13

PRACTICING RESPONSIBILITY

Jeanne Nakamura

*Where learning is the accompaniment of continuous activities
or occupations which have a social aim . . . , the school
becomes itself a form of social life, a miniature community
and one in close interaction with other modes of associated
experience beyond school walls.*

—John Dewey

IN THE GOODWORK PROJECT, we have examined questions about working
life through the lens of current conditions in the professions. This perspective has sensitized us to internal forces, such as self-interest, as well
as to external ones, such as competition, that erode professionals'
responsibility for others. These "others" include both the community
represented by the organization in which the professionals work (hospital, school, newsroom) and the wider community their work is meant to
serve (patients, students, the general public). In this chapter I address
responsibility for others in the two different senses implied by this distinction, calling the first *civic responsibility* (responsibility for those with
whom one works and lives) and the second *social responsibility* (responsibility for those served by one's work).

Work organizations often discourage habits of responsibility for others
through the very way the work life is structured within their walls.
Indeed, sometimes the architecture itself drives home the message. In our
study of good work in the business world, one Fortune 500 CEO

described arriving for the first time at the headquarters of a company he had been hired to run. The looming building plainly communicated, "We are very big and you are very small. . . . Just go along and no one will get hurt." How, he wondered, could workers be expected to do anything other than check their sense of responsibility at the door and succumb to the silently shouted demand that they perform as dutiful cogs in the corporate wheel?

The impact of living in organizations is not limited to the adult workplace. Jackson's *Life in Classrooms* (1968), Willis's *Learning to Labour* (1982), and other studies have shown how the explicit curriculum of schools is shadowed by a second one that is built into the very organization—social, spatial, temporal—of the small worlds in which students spend their days. For example, Jackson argues that, while learning arithmetic and spelling, school children wait their turn, do what they are told, and thus are also learning to be patient and obedient. Dutiful obedience might look like responsibility superficially, but the underlying impulse is fundamentally different. John Dewey (1916) cautioned that to act only on the basis of a sense of duty or obligation, in classroom or workplace, is to stop at merely performing the required offices of a job. It is a thin basis for responsive participation in, and responsibility for, a community.

In this chapter I am concerned with the kind of learning that takes place through participating in work environments, especially those of an educational nature. In particular, given the theme of the book, I ask, In what ways can educational settings foster rather than discourage habits of responsibility? I explore a kind of pedagogy that may hold lessons for structuring workplaces as well as schools: *practicing, rehearsing, experiencing responsibility for others day by day, within the microcosm or small world of an institution.* The premises are essentially ones articulated decades ago by Dewey (1916, 1921, 1938). We learn through experience: "You cannot teach people a virtue by requiring them to read books about it. You can only teach a virtue by calling upon people to exercise it" (Menand, 1997, p. 17). We learn civic and social responsibility through civic, social experience: "Education could prepare people for life in a democracy only if the educational experience were also democratic, only if learning mimicked the processes of living socially in a democracy" (p. 12).

Our studies of graduate training in leading science labs provide insight into what this process is like. Graduate students in the sciences learn by apprenticeship, virtually living in the training lab. Labs become small communities—some full of rivalries and tension, others stimulating or harmonious. There is little doubt that in this initiation into professional life, students may absorb forms of civic and social responsibility along with technical expertise, standards of excellence, and specialized knowledge.

For example, a distinguished scientist and mentor organized his large space-science lab so that learning occurred via high-stakes doing (Hooker, Nakamura, & Csikszentmihalyi, 2003). Novice students were assigned small tasks that needed to be completed with perfect accuracy. Should errors be made, the novice might place at risk years of data gathering on which much knowledge and many careers depended. In addition to acquiring the specific technical skills required by the tasks and a general commitment to precision, students rapidly acquired a keen sense of responsibility to the collective enterprise, by being given what they experienced as almost overwhelming responsibility for a part of it. Consider how fundamentally this pedagogy and its outcome differ from one in which apprentices are given tasks with only their own standing at stake. It makes sense that this pedagogy has evolved in space science, where students routinely go on to plan and conduct projects as members of large teams.

To take another example, a leading geneticist was admired by former graduate students as a scientist's scientist (Nakamura, Shernoff, & Hooker, 2004). He modeled for them the practice of willingly sharing information and materials with colleagues outside his own lab, as one aspect of being a responsible member of the scientific community; he expected his students to do the same. Inside the lab where they spent their days (and many nights), he made it easy for them to cooperate with one another, organizing the lab so that students' projects did not overlap and there was thus no incentive to compete or to withhold information. The lab was remembered by his students as harmonious and happy. Consider how dramatically this pedagogy differs from one that is not unheard of in elite labs, in which two students are given the same research problem to solve and made to compete head to head.

These examples suggest one fruitful approach to the present topic: study the educational experience closest to the start of a practitioner's career in a given profession. As the preceding cases illustrate, *specific* expressions of responsible practice as a scientist (or physician, lawyer, or engineer) begin to form during these years of specialized training (Sullivan, 2006).

However, it is undergraduate education that today represents the nearly universal pathway into professional life in the United States. If students learn responsibility for others in college—or if they do not—this emerging stance may affect both what kind of work they choose and how they approach whatever occupation they enter. Further, educating citizens—in our terms, cultivating responsible participation in communities to which one belongs—has traditionally been the charge of liberal arts colleges (Colby, Ehrlich, Beaumont, & Stephens, 2003). In contrast to vocational schools, which resemble professional schools in their emphasis on technical preparation, cultivating responsibility is arguably part of the liberal arts college's raison d'être. (For one counterargument, see Fish, 2004.) Finally, small residential colleges that foster civic and social responsibility should reveal this process with clarity. Even more than graduate science labs, they are microcosms, small worlds unto themselves, in which students live for an extended time.

The need to investigate and to intervene as appropriate is urgent. The decline of civic engagement and the rise of forces undermining social responsibility (Gardner, Csikszentmihalyi, & Damon, 2001) have not spared college campuses—despite a strong response from educators, such as the widespread introduction of service learning into curricula. We studied a select group of liberal arts colleges—schools admired within higher education for doing good work. To our surprise, educators on these campuses talked remarkably little about the development of students' sense of responsibility for others. It was an even less salient goal among the colleges' students themselves, who as a group were far more concerned with their own personal and academic growth.

In the rest of this chapter I explore how three schools we studied—Swarthmore, Morehouse, and Mount St. Mary's Colleges—are designed in key respects as *microcosms* of life in the wider community. I suggest they are designed so that what is "practiced" within them (such as civic and social responsibility, of particular interest in this chapter) will also be practiced later, in the larger world. I aim to illuminate how our experiences of responsibility for others can be structured by our daily lives within institutions.[1]

Choosing the Schools to Study

In our study of good work in higher education, my colleagues and I investigated what ten highly regarded colleges and universities seek to accomplish for their students (GoodWork Project, 2006). We interviewed

---

[1]The chapter focuses on the cultivation of responsibility for others. It does not explore, despite their prominence as aims of undergraduate education, the cultivation of responsibility for self or the nurturing of responsibility for a particular domain or discipline.

key stakeholders (primarily faculty and administrators) about their personal and institutional purposes and practices. To understand how well the schools' aims are communicated and how well those aims align with the students' own priorities, we also surveyed juniors and seniors at each school.

Of the schools studied, seven provide a liberal arts education. I identified the three liberal arts institutions with the strongest commitment to cultivating students' responsibility for others. Rather than relying on official mission statements (which universally mentioned responsibility for others) or on the assertions of the educators (on which the case studies would be based), I selected the schools where students themselves reported a commitment to social responsibility.

In the eyes of the students surveyed, Swarthmore, Morehouse, and Mount St. Mary's are the three schools with the highest *institutional commitment* to service and social change. On a seventeen-item question (1 = highest ranked, 17 = lowest ranked), the mean rank orders were 6.5 for service and 7.8 for social change.[2] In contrast, for the other four liberal arts institutions, the mean rank orders for these items were 11.0 and 13.0, respectively.

According to the surveyed students, these three colleges are also the ones making the greatest *institutional contribution* to student development in the areas of service and social change. The mean rank orders were 8.5 for service and 10.0 for social change, compared to mean rank orders of 13.3 and 13.8, respectively, for the other four liberal arts institutions.

Applying this set of criteria, these three liberal arts institutions emerged as the ones that place greatest emphasis on service and social responsibility. It did not escape our notice that cultivation of responsibility for others was ascribed intermediate importance even at these schools. Thus they may yield different insights than the schools studied by Colby, Ehrlich, Beaumont, and Stephens (2003), where cultivating responsibility for others is a primary and defining institutional mission.

All three schools are small, private, significantly residential, and religious in origins. Ideally, however, they differ enough in their approaches to cultivating responsibility for comparison to be fruitful. Mount St. Mary's is an ethnically diverse Catholic women's college. Swarthmore, which has Quaker roots, is one of the country's most selective coeducational liberal

---

[2]The question items were "Contributing to your community, becoming a good citizen" (service) and "Preparing to actively transform society for the better" (social change).

arts colleges. Founded in a Baptist church, Morehouse is a leading historically black college for men. One is on the West Coast, one is on the East Coast, one is in the South. No three schools will generate a comprehensive taxonomy of pathways to civic and social responsibility, but this set puts multiple dimensions into play.

The primary data are twenty interviews with faculty, administrators, and trustees (Swarthmore, $n = 6$; Morehouse, $n = 6$; Mount St. Mary's, $n = 8$). The interviewees were conceived as expert informants, jointly illuminating the way the colleges cultivate responsibility. Student survey data are also drawn on as relevant (Swarthmore, $n = 101$; Morehouse, $n = 103$; Mount St. Mary's, $n = 162$).

Practicing Civic and Social Responsibility at Three Liberal Arts Colleges

Analysis of each school's data was guided by the questions *Responsible for whom?* (For whom does the college hope students are learning to be responsible by living in this community?) and *Practicing how?* (What ways of practicing responsibility do most students at this college share?). I looked for themes and practices that recurred across multiple interviews and that were echoed in the student surveys.

Taking responsibility for others is practiced through the kinds of activities pursued and through the social, temporal, and spatial contexts in which these activities occur. These are basic dimensions that structure all experience. Here I focus on the activities and social relations that cultivate habits of responsibility.

In the pages that follow I introduce each school and discuss its approach to civic and social responsibility. First, I provide a thumbnail sketch of each small world and the forms of responsibility it seeks to create. Second, I describe how the milieu (in particular the faculty) supports students' development of responsibility. The third and fourth sections of each discussion describe how the school's students practice responsibility for others. In the third section, I describe the social relations, especially with peers, through which students practice *civic* engagement, or responsibility for colleagues. In the fourth section, I describe the activities through which they practice *social* responsibility, applying their skills and knowledge in order to improve the welfare of others. Fifth, as Dewey (1916) cautioned, it is not enough to learn how to function in a microcosm that lacks connection to the wider world. Accordingly, I point out the connections to the wider community that help students take what is learned and utilize it out in the world. Sixth, even if daily practices shape people most strongly, ceremony and ritual can also be influential if they embody a living culture and connect with a tradition that is still a going concern. For each school I identify a campus event that crystallizes its approach to cultivating responsibility for others. Finally, although the chapter addresses colleges' aims and practices, the measure of a school's good work is its actual impact on students; I conclude with a word about what students do when they leave each school, in terms of responsibility for others.

The Engaged Mind: Collegiality and Social Action

Swarthmore College, situated on a handsome, 350-acre campus outside Philadelphia, is among the nation's most highly regarded and selective liberal arts colleges. It is deliberately small, boasting an eight-to-one student-teacher ratio. It was founded as a coed college in 1864 by Quaker farmers. President Frank Aydelotte, who championed the liberal arts nationally, introduced the honors program at Swarthmore in 1922: "The effect on the whole institution was to uplift and intellectualize it" (Schall, 2003, p. 49).

MICROCOSM. A key thesis of this chapter is that responsibility for others can be learned through practicing it in a small world designed with that purpose in mind. Swarthmore is a true microcosm: self-contained, set apart, a deliberately structured community with a residential student body and many of the faculty living nearby. In key respects, students are consistently exposed to a single ethos; in this way, habits—including habits of responsibility—are redundantly cultivated and reinforced across settings and relationships. The community is characterized in precisely the terms of this chapter, in a statement on the college's Web site (Swarthmore College, 2002):

> These students will live the life of the mind as participants in A
> COMMUNITY OF LEARNERS dedicated to the highest standards of
> intellectual achievement. They will learn from faculty members who,
> as gifted educators, actively seek to extend the boundaries of knowl-
> edge and at every turn encourage their students to join them in that
> pursuit. . . . Their pursuit of truth will involve something more as
> well. This community of learners is an INTENTIONALLY ETHICAL
> COMMUNITY. It seeks to be a microcosm of a just, generous, and
> inclusive world and to place intellectual acuity at the service of
> developing such a world.

This is the life of the mind as an intrinsically social rather than solitary enterprise. This is community with civic life organized around common dedication to intellectual inquiry rather than other possible pursuits. Of particular interest for this chapter, the community possesses a distinctive notion of *how* to live the life of the mind together, and a characteristic or "signature" pedagogy (Shulman, 2005) for cultivating that capacity. In addition, while practicing civic responsibility takes the particular form of collegial participation in an intellectual community, practicing social responsibility takes the form of using the intellect to better society.

INSTITUTIONAL MATRIX: COLLEGIALITY AND DIALOGUE. Learning responsibility for others is supported at each school by the institutional matrix in which it takes place. At Swarthmore, this is particularly true of *civic* responsibility. Students enter a strong community: among the faculty there is "good esprit-de-corps"—a general sense that pervades this college of respect of each faculty by the other faculty who reach out across disciplines and find "accessibility and dialogue that is not available in some other institutions"; there is a "level of decency." What binds the faculty together is love for the life of the mind (which by itself could inspire disciplinary isolation) and commitment to the community. A weekly faculty lunch enables colleagues "to see what other people are doing, to ask questions about it, to see connections with it." Responsible participation in the life of this community lies in engaging others receptively but critically in dialogue, an approach with connections to the school's Quaker roots—the "endless good argument" (Schall, 2003). That is, the form of civic engagement that students practice is modeled by faculty not only in academic contexts but also in the general life of the college: the school immerses students in a coherent culture of civic responsibility. An administrator described the approach to governance: "If it's a close vote and it's an important issue, we feel that we better stand back and not accept that vote, but come back and vote again after much discussion. . . . There is a sense that we need this because we want to make sure that everybody is heard and that the ideas that they bring are factored into the decision . . . so that the decision is not imposed but is a community resolution."

Although interviewees freely say that it can be time-consuming, tiring, and contentious, they believe in this decision-making process. A professor stated, "I have struggled in situations with colleagues and students when it would have been easier to say, 'Done! Vote!' No . . . I've been here long enough now to see the worth of that struggle to reach consensus." Another professor called Swarthmore "a much more democratic institution than many" and attributed the tumult following a recent institutional change to the failure to "follow through the full spectrum of Quakerly consensus before the decision was made."

Students enter this community on equal footing; like the faculty, they are intellectuals. There is a sense that faculty and students are engaged in a common enterprise, and that their roles are less complementary (parent-child, expert-novice) than parallel (learner-learner). Faculty members engage students in their scholarship and research, and find their students interesting; their attitude is collegial. Their impact is testified to by the student survey: the item "[having] role models for an intellectually engaged life" received higher ratings at Swarthmore than at other schools.

PRACTICING CIVIC RESPONSIBILITY: COLLEGIALITY AND DIALOGUE. Civic responsibility is most distinctively practiced by Swarthmore students through collegial dialogue in the small seminars that characterize upper-level courses, including the honors program. All interviewees agreed that this is a signature pedagogy, just as all stressed a single set of themes when describing the school's civic habits more broadly. One interviewee contrasted this dialogical pedagogy and the opportunity it creates for learning civic responsibility with the familiar model of "each individual person digesting material" alone: "The most distinctive aspect of a Swarthmore education is the Swarthmore seminar. And the seminar is exactly an opportunity for the faculty to become more colleagues with a set of students who are all pursuing a topic together. And who are accepting the imperative of listening to each other, learning from each other's contributions, and becoming a team in the creation of knowledge." The emphasis falls on working together: "talking and listening and the weaving of these threads of connection and contradiction in the discussion as it goes along."

Equally committed peers are a crucial factor in learning to be responsive to others through these exchanges. An administrator asserted, "We have a student culture which really has a transformative impact on the students." The survey confirms that students feel that "stimulating peers" are critical contributors to their educational experience. Also contributing to the formative impact of coursework, intellectual exchange is integrated more organically into the rhythm of Swarthmore students' days than is typically true of college life. One professor observed, "Office hours are essentially every hour except those in lecture." To accommodate students' cocurricular activities, seminars may take place late in the evening.

In part, the school is a microcosm of the academic world at its best, and indeed many students go on to pursue careers in the academy. Students learn through daily practice how to participate as responsible and responsive, engaged and collegial members of an intellectual community—with the expectation that they will do the same in whatever communities they subsequently join.

PRACTICING SOCIAL RESPONSIBILITY: USING THE MIND TO BETTER SOCIETY. Currently, consistent with Quaker tradition there is great institutional self-consciousness about preparing students to use the educated mind in the service of making the world a better place. Just as a responsible and responsive form of intellectual engagement is modeled by faculty and practiced by students, a responsible and responsive way of connecting intellectual engagement to the wider world's challenges is increasingly modeled and practiced. A professor commented: "There seems to be this theme of . . . trying to do decent things for humanity." Field study, community-based learning experiences and projects (locally and abroad), internships in nonprofits, and major social change projects are increasingly supported. Another associated pedagogy is project-based, open-ended learning; an engineering professor described a semester spent building an energy-efficient house from straw bales. Students learn to use the dialogical skills they have acquired to contribute to the wider world. An arts professor explained: "They have to go to the community in which they expect to site their [art]work and see what would be useful there. What would be appropriate? What do people need? What do they want? What can I do, then, that makes an avenue for discussion?"

Like-minded peers are again critical. An interviewee saw a "tremendous amount of mutual reinforcement among students" for being concerned about society. Students do not shrug off peers' social concerns by saying, "I really don't care. I just want to prepare for my profession." Rather, they reinforce each other "for being not only academically exciting, and pursuing ideas, and creating knowledge, but for thinking about how to use [knowledge]" to "do something important" for society. One professor challenged the easy criticisms of Swarthmore privilege:

> A colleague of mine, who teaches at an inner-city institution, says, "Well, you teach at Swarthmore. That's not the real world." And my response to that has been, "Actually it is a real world, and I wish that more of the world could be very real in the ways that this world tries to be real." I think that sending our students out with hope and resolve is very, very valuable. They say, "What do you mean I can't do that? Oh, no. I will." "I will," as a young man from Ghana who came to Swarthmore as a scholarship student . . . said, "I will dream that I can open a liberal arts college in Ghana to help people." And ten years later, this January, it is happening.

CONNECTING TO THE WIDER COMMUNITY. Swarthmore students live in a well-defined microcosm, but they interact with the wider world in the course of practicing both civic and social responsibility. First, external academic examiners come to the campus and evaluate the honors students, who show they are practiced at responsible participation in an intellectual community by entering into dialogue with these examiners about their areas of study. Second, students move beyond the campus to tackle social problems through courses, study-abroad programs, internships, and civic ventures of their own design.

DEFINING RITUAL. If responsibility for others is a salient goal, it will enter into institutional ceremony and ritual. An emblematic Swarthmore event, First Collection, takes place in the grassy, tree-shaded outdoor amphitheater during freshman orientation. The ritual's symbolism conveys the communitarian aspect of the life of the mind as students will learn to live it at Swarthmore, and the school's joining of intellectual and civic formation. As described on the college's Web site (Swarthmore College, 2002):

> Each student holds a candle. After the speakers have finished, one candle is lit, then another from the first, and so on until, as dusk turns to dark, some 370 separate dots of light form a collective glow, illuminating the night. . . . It acknowledges the INNER LIGHT in everyone gathered there as it unites them around the common purposes at the heart of Swarthmore's mission. And it brings each student face to face with a personal and a shared commitment to the search for truth.

ENTERING THE WIDER COMMUNITY. Can civic and social responsibility be perceived in students' lives after college? In terms of civic responsibility, many graduates continue as engaged citizens of the academic community that Swarthmore exemplifies. Large numbers leave Swarthmore with degrees in traditional liberal arts concentrations; the most popular majors continue to include English literature and history alongside economics, biology, and political science. The intensity of intellectual engagement is reflected in the 30 percent who enter the honors program, the many graduating with double majors, and the high numbers who go on to graduate education and lives of research and scholarship. Swarthmore is among the top colleges nationally in producing PhDs; its alumni include four Nobel Prize winners. In terms of using the intellect to solve social problems, alumni pursuing socially responsible work include Harvard professor Robert Putnam, author of *Bowling Alone*; Eben Moglen, a Columbia professor who advocates free software as one requirement of a democratic society; Neil Gershenfeld, an

MIT professor whose Fab Labs foster entrepreneurship in underserved communities; and Patrick Awuah, the aforementioned graduate who founded a liberal arts college in Ghana in 2002.

Through Fraternity to Leadership

Morehouse College, in downtown Atlanta, is the nation's only all-male, historically black college. It was founded by a Baptist minister in 1867 to serve former slaves. Its first black president, John Hope, refashioned it as a liberal arts college and strengthened an already solid academic reputation. Its president in the mid-1900s, Benjamin Mays, coined the term *Morehouse Man* for the ideal graduate.

MICROCOSM. Historically, Morehouse has provided a clear example of how the microcosm of a school stands in relation to the wider society. Founded in a time of institutionalized racism, its mission was to raise up the African American community in an unequal world. The school was traditionally seen as preparing the "talented tenth" to lead responsibly and well (Eaves, 1999) by creating a microcosm where they could temporarily "lay down the burden of race," as one interviewee put it. Believing that leadership must be earned by possessing strength of character, the latter has been demanded by the institution's high expectations; modeled by faculty, successful alumni, and African American community leaders; and practiced along with responsibility for one's brothers by participating day by day in the close, competitive, proud fraternity of Morehouse students.

INSTITUTIONAL MATRIX: "TOUGH" LOVE. Interviewees focused less on curriculum, classroom pedagogy, and infrastructure than on personal relationships in describing the institutional matrix within which the capacity for responsibility is forged. Many faculty and administrators take a parental interest in students; one administrator labeled the attitude "tough" love. Faculty and administrators described challenging, preaching, and mentoring, and the alumni among them recalled an even more potent milieu during their own years as Morehouse students. The college has sought to instill high aspirations, and it has pushed for cultivation of the qualities that make an individual deserve to lead.

PRACTICING CIVIC RESPONSIBILITY: THE BROTHERHOOD. At the center of the "Morehouse family" has always been genuine fraternity among students. Immersion in this fraternity has traditionally been key to the school's cultivation of responsibility for those with whom one works and lives. Responses to the student survey were filled with references to the "brotherhood" experienced at Morehouse—the nurturing, the camaraderie, the unity; the bonds formed; the importance of "being surrounded by brothers with like minds"—which is seen as making the college special.

Faculty and administrators also described how Morehouse has exemplified the community in which peer ties are strong, salient, and influential, thus binding the student body together. They articulated how this aspect of daily experience fosters fraternal responsibility for others:

> The bonding that takes place between Morehouse Men is something that's just not experienced anywhere [else]. It is not. It's like one big fraternity with the good qualities . . . you're joining a proud community. . . . There's a sense of tradition that's so deep and embedded. And the older students having gone through that; when the freshmen come, they become big brothers to them as mentors and guides, academically, but also as part of this whole experience of what it means to be a Morehouse Man. It means respect for your brother. It means support for your brother. Morehouse Man. Helping, and not just helping in the classroom but helping in a way to make sure they follow these unofficial codes of conduct . . . how you behave, how you behave with others, what is the image you project as a Morehouse Man? We spend a great deal of time just talking about these things.

In their conversations with students, the faculty and staff underscore the centrality and broad significance of fraternity. As one faculty member observed, "We talk about the fraternity and real brotherhood that needs to pervade the world."

PRACTICING SOCIAL RESPONSIBILITY: LEADERSHIP. Morehouse holds a view of social responsibility as bettering the world through effective leadership. Traditionally this emphasis has meant leadership within the African American community. Today the range of application has grown wider and at the same time less focused. At a time when "leadership development" has acquired great cachet, it is worth underlining that Morehouse historically produced leaders, and acquired a reputation for doing so, without making the cultivation of leadership per se a part of the college's official mission statement or formal curriculum. Morehouse alumni include history-making lawyers (such as James Nabrit of *Brown v. Board of Education*), government leaders (such as Maynard Jackson, the first black mayor of Atlanta), and activists (most famously, the Reverend Martin Luther King, Jr.). Instead of teaching leadership, the college has historically focused on cultivating a sense of responsibility for the welfare of a community and a set of habits and qualities that merit others' respect: learning "how to make waves so things can move, not making waves so that ships sink." The qualities that recurred in the interviews include "integrity, honesty, civility, accountability," a "well-developed sense of [self]," and "the sense you can do anything you set your mind to do." Only in recent years has Morehouse formally institutionalized leadership development.

Although the interviewees focused on the cultivation of character, they also pointed to multiple ways that students may practice leadership in the course of their campus lives. According to one faculty member, "It's a process . . . of small exposures to, and small practices in, leadership. Small opportunities to lead." The occasions include practice leading in the classroom, beginning in freshman year; in student clubs and organizations, including a student court; on dormitory councils; and in campus governance, including positions on the Morehouse board of trustees.

CONNECTING TO THE WIDER COMMUNITY. In striving to nurture social responsibility, understood as leadership, Morehouse draws on connections with the world beyond the campus. The school makes efforts to expose all of its students on a regular basis to leaders in the wider African American community. This is institutionalized in the required all-college "Crown" assemblies, named to evoke the words of alumnus Howard Thurman, a noted theologian and civil rights leader: "Morehouse holds a crown over the heads of her students and then challenges them to grow tall enough to wear it." Morehouse stands out among the schools we studied in the extent to which community leaders were perceived as influential by students, who rated their impact as significantly greater than did students at the six other liberal arts colleges we studied.

DEFINING RITUAL. Ritual and ceremony play a significant role at Morehouse. An event during the lengthy freshman orientation marks initiation into the Morehouse family, especially the brotherhood of Morehouse students, with and for whom the freshmen will learn responsibility. The forging of character, the prerequisite for leadership, is also foreshadowed. An administrator explained:

> The students are in silence from four o'clock until seven o'clock, when the ceremony begins. They eat in silence and they walk in silence because they are now at a point of reflection, examining their goals, who they are. . . . The dean of the chapel uses the metaphor of ferrymen and we

are now about to take them across the waters to another shore. . . . The parents are asked to write on a slip of paper their wishes, hopes, and dreams for their sons over the next four years. The students write on a piece of paper the bad habits that they have that they need to get rid of. . . . The oldest Morehouse alumnus is ninety-some years old and he was the man who got the first Ph.D. way back when. . . . He comes down from the stage and when the students have filled [an] urn with all their bad habits, [he ceremonially burns them], the flames representing their getting rid of their bad habits. Then we have a beautiful box . . . that brought the ashes [of Howard Thurman] here before their interment [in an obelisk on the plaza]. . . . Two parents, a father and a mother, stand at the foot of the stage and the parents walk around and music is playing softly, "On Jordan's stormy banks I stand, and cast a wistful eye." . . . They drop into the box their wishes for their sons. Then the young men file out and they form a corridor all the way down to the street and the parents walk through the corridor. They can't speak to their sons or anything, and the man and the lady who have the box, they enter the obelisk and place these wishes there. Then the young men gather in the street where they lock arms and sing the college hymn, "Dear Old Morehouse."

This ritualized transition, the parents' parting ceremony, is deeply affecting: "Parents leave here crying. The students are all revved up, ready to change the world."

ENTERING THE WIDER COMMUNITY. Is the Morehouse variant of responsibility for others evident in students' lives after college? Business administration is currently the most popular major. The college has a long reputation, however, for producing African American leaders across many sectors of society, beyond business. In addition to the professions that Morehouse originally supplied—education and the ministry—alumni now include leaders in the law, in government, and in activism.

Transmuting the Experience of Care into Service to Others

Mount St. Mary's College was founded in 1925 by Catholic nuns, who "hiked up their skirts and hiked up the hill" to establish the school on a then-remote Los Angeles hilltop (Andion, 1998). It was created to prepare women to be contributing members of their community by providing them with a liberal arts education. The school has traditionally served daughters of immigrants; many students are first-generation college-goers pressed by concerns about educational costs, grades, and securing a job after graduation. A sizeable number transfer from the school's two-year campus in downtown Los Angeles.

MICROCOSM. The microcosm of Mount St. Mary's lies at the intersection of a religious world of compassionate action and a society with many unmet needs. It is set apart from the rest of the city physically, an oasis of beauty and order, although many current students are unable to immerse themselves fully in the small world of the college because of the pull of their neighborhoods and families (95 percent are from the region, one-third commute) and of jobs required to pay for college (98 percent qualify for financial aid). The student body is more than two-thirds Hispanic, Asian-Pacific, and African American—a microcosm of the ethnically diverse surrounding area.

The forms of civic and social responsibility cultivated by practicing them in this close-knit, caring community are appreciating diversity and putting knowledge and skills in the service of beneficial action in the world. Learning these forms of responsiveness to and responsibility for others is fostered by the faculty, staff, administrators, and sisters of the religious order, through example and explicit encouragement as well as practice.

INSTITUTIONAL MATRIX: CARE. In terms of the matrix in which responsibility is learned, every interviewee emphasized the intimate, welcoming community that the students enter and the unstinting dedication to students' welfare. The language of care is pervasive: faculty, administrators, staff, and trustees all spoke of "caring," "nurturing," "supporting," "enabling," and "encouraging." The school's atmosphere is "generous," "hospitable," "warm," and "safe." A trustee called it a place with "heart and compassion"; another lauded its "tell me what you need" stance. When the amount of interview material referring to support is compared to the amount referring to challenge, it runs 4 to 1 in the corpus of Mount St. Mary's interviews; at Morehouse, it runs 1 to 3. In this regard the two are at opposite ends of the spectrum, among the seven liberal arts institutions we studied. Swarthmore falls between them.

Care registers in students' daily lives in a host of ways. Teachers are highly accessible; doors are open. Small classes allow personal attention and the dedication of time, which faculty use both to facilitate student learning and to learn about the students as individuals. For every student, a faculty member serves as an advisor. The school's limited resources are invested in programs, such as one-on-one tutoring, that demonstrably respond to student needs. Running throughout the interactions is the *quality* of care. Students recognize it and respond strongly. In identifying what makes the school special, participants in the student survey stressed the experience of care: professors are "available," "very helpful," "invested in you as a student," "know you personally," and "actually care for you and what you plan to be in the future." The supportive environment fosters a variety of student outcomes; this milieu has a particular impact in fostering responsibility because it models the school's variant of social responsibility: service to others.

PRACTICING CIVIC RESPONSIBILITY: RESPECT AND APPRECIATION. Responsibility for those with whom one works and lives is practiced in daily interactions with peers at Swarthmore and Morehouse. At Mount St. Mary's, where many students commute or work or both, it is perhaps not surprising that peers are experienced as less influential than at the other schools. Compared to the transformative relationships with Mount St. Mary's faculty, staff, and administrators, peer relations are less salient. This said, students reported that they receive considerable help learning to work with individuals from different backgrounds—much more than at the other liberal arts schools we studied. Given the college's remarkable diversity, it is noteworthy that some survey respondents singled out the friendly relationships among students as a distinctive feature of the school.

The school actively cultivates habits of responsibility for the universal other: as a senior administrator put it, "respect each other without distinction," pointing out that "it's the 'without distinction' that's the challenge." The phrase formulates in secular terms a core element of the founding order's mission: "love your neighbor without distinction." The practice is fostered throughout the college community—among students but also between faculty and students and among campus offices.

Respect for the ethnic diversity of the community is only the starting point, however. The more ambitious response that the school cultivates is an active appreciation of difference. As the president observed, enrollment numbers alone are not a measure of success; they give students the opportunity to live amid diversity, but not habits for responding well across difference. Mount St. Mary's incorporated a curriculum-wide multiculturalism requirement years ago, supports numerous campuswide celebrations of ethnic heritage, and designs its major events as opportunities for students to broaden their horizons. And they talk: "I had a class last semester with ten students. Every single student there was born in a different country. The wealth of human experiences is really alive and well here. I was just talking to a student about that. . . . She didn't [previously] recognize the benefit of that for her."

PRACTICING SOCIAL RESPONSIBILITY: SERVICE. Students at Mount St. Mary's live immersed in a culture of service, the value of which they know because they themselves are its primary recipients. Like the related ethos of care, a theme running through every interview is the cultivation of social responsibility in the form of service to the community. Students continually confront expectations that they too will (in the interviewees' words) "view their professional life in a service context," "succeed so you can serve," "contribute to improve the world," "make a difference," "give back to society," and find "a fulfilling life of service."

Service learning is an established part of coursework in most departments. Volunteering and community service are important parts of the cocurriculum. Students in applied majors (such as education) experience extensive supervised practice. In these ways, students practice responsibility for others in daily life. Engaged practice is supplemented by explicit discussion. In addition, members of the community actively model the life of service and invite students to join them. A nursing faculty member said:

> If I'm doing a volunteer clinic at my church to check blood pressure, I might say that day in class, "Does anybody want to come help me do that?" Not for extra points . . . just for the act of doing. . . . Students are really savvy in terms of knowing faculty are just giving them a line. You can push and tell them they need to try to make a difference in their community, but if you can't provide any examples for them, what value is that? Not much.

CONNECTING TO THE WIDER COMMUNITY. As I've reported, the school makes a concerted effort to create opportunities for students to engage the community beyond the campus: social responsibility is practiced in cocurricular and impromptu volunteer work, in community service, and in internships. Although the school values its remote location, it seeks ways for students to use the things they learn through meeting needs in the wider world.

DEFINING RITUAL. Like Morehouse, Mount St. Mary's is rich in ritual, and works to keep the stories and heroes of the institution alive. Although some interviewees singled out events that celebrate diversity, several cited Mary's Day, the symbolism of which both links success to service and honors diversity, all within the framework of Catholic tradition. An interviewee's account conveyed how the ceremony affirms the college's variants of civic and social responsibility:

> Mary's Day happens every spring, and it's our honors and awards convocation, but it isn't just about honors and awards. It's about receiving an honor or an award so that you can go forward and do good. We start the program with students dressed in all their different ethnic costumes, processing in with fruit and candles and incense, and placing them by the picture of Our Lady of Guadalupe, including a crown of flowers. Then we read the *Magnificat,* which is the part of the New Testament where Mary is asked if she is willing to do this thing, to be the mother of God. And she is very afraid, but she says, "Yes." And then they sing it. They sing, "My Soul Magnifies the Lord," and they dance, and then they get their awards. And the whole notion of the awards is that "I say yes. I have this ability, but now it's my turn to say yes."

ENTERING THE WIDER COMMUNITY. Can responsibility for others be perceived in students' lives after graduation? Social responsibility is instantiated in the form of service at Mount St. Mary's, and large numbers of its students graduate in nursing, education, and psychology. Each of these three leading majors provides preparation for a traditional caring profession. The school's most prominent alumni include teachers and administrators at all educational levels, nurses and physicians, and in growing numbers, medical researchers. Of course many students who choose to attend these three schools are to varying degrees already oriented toward responsibility for others. As one Mount St. Mary's professor put it, we "make it possible for them to become more fully who they already are"; to some extent at least, students often "already have this notion of doing good for others, and achieving for their families and themselves."

Ways of Practicing Responsibility

I have illustrated how three schools create microcosms that teach forms of responsibility for others as an integral part of social life writ small. Across campuses, the clear intention is that habits of responsibility acquired by living within these small worlds will be carried out beyond them, into students' subsequent lives in workplaces and other communities.

Two factors help all three schools cultivate civic responsibility: small size and residential character. These factors make possible the cultivation of community, including immersion in a way of life, creation of strong social ties, and extended exposure to role models. Some of their lessons may generalize not only to other residential colleges but also to workplaces.[3]

I examined the schools' signature ways of structuring what students do and with whom, and the forms of community participation and social responsibility that the schools hope their students will pursue in the future. Living in each microcosm entails participating in at least three kinds of relationship: (1) with faculty, (2) with other students, and (3) with segments of the larger community beyond the campus. Through these relationships, students practice responsibility in two respects: by learning what it is to participate responsibly within a community, living civic engagement day by day; and by learning what it is to do work motivated by a sense of responsibility for others. Each set of experiences has the potential to affect an individual's approach to his or her subsequent professional life—to colleagueship in the first case, and to commitment to work that helps others in the second.

First, daily life cultivates a distinctive form of *civic responsibility* at each college, as manifested in students' relationships with one another: collegiality at Swarthmore, fraternity at Morehouse, and respect "without distinction" at Mount St. Mary's. Contacts with professors provide a critical matrix for student development of responsibility: *collegiality, tough love,* and *care.* To differing degrees, interactions with faculty model the kind of responsibility for others that students are meant to be practicing and preparing for. It is tempting to see these as traditionally gendered practices and forms of responsibility, characterizing as they do a coed, a men's, and a women's college.

Second, each college provides somewhat different opportunities to practice *social responsibility,* doing work that serves others: project- and community-based learning focused on social problems, campus leadership opportunities

---

[3]In any given school or workplace, space and time may also be crafted in distinctive ways that contribute to the cultivation of responsibility for others. One school we studied instituted a period called *Common Time,* an hour during the week when no classes were held. Interactions among any and all became possible. Several colleges designed new buildings with common spaces to encourage the kind of spontaneous exchange on which community thrives.

and continual occasions to show the qualities of a leader in daily life, and service learning and service opportunities, both planned and impromptu. The schools emphasize three different ways of enacting responsibility for others; these might be labeled *solving, leading,* and *serving.*

As instantiated at each of these schools, the two sets of practices create a constructive balance. The practices in the first set foster cohesive ties that provide a basis for ongoing engagement in the shared life of a community, and in this sense are conservative and integrative. The practices in the second set foster efforts on behalf of social betterment, and thus are inherently oriented toward change.

Contact with members of the wider community supports one or both aspects of student learning. For example, at Swarthmore, the honors students' responsibility to external examiners rehearses responsibility to the wider intellectual community, of which the honors course is a microcosm. And students' engagement with community partners in tackling environmental, economic, and other problems rehearses social action in the community beyond college.

Less frequent experiences reinforce the daily practices. Especially at Morehouse and Mount St. Mary's, traditional institutional commitments to social responsibility are vitalized through ritual and ceremony, recollection of defining events in the school's history, and contact with the school's religious roots.

These colleges, which place substantial but not primary importance on cultivating responsibility for others, provide an instructive comparison to schools studied by Colby, Ehrlich, Beaumont, and Stephens (2003). At many of those schools, cultivating moral and civic development is the essential mission; it lies at the heart of institutional identity, curricular requirements, and assessment efforts. At the three colleges portrayed here, in contrast, responsibility practices appear to be most effective when integrally bound up with pursuit of the school's primary aims. At Swarthmore, for instance, practicing social action occurs less universally than practicing constructive dialogue. This may be because the latter pedagogy fosters both civic engagement and the school's defining goal for students: rigorous intellectual engagement. There may be a lesson here for schools (or workplaces) that want to encourage civic engagement and social responsibility when another mission is already in place.

The cases presented here illustrate the importance of modulating an institution's dominant messages. Inherent in each approach to cultivating responsibility is a distinctive way that campus life can *fail* to result in civic and social responsibility through too much of a good thing. At Mount St. Mary's, the emphasis on support can lead to dependence or passivity, undermining the ideal of proactive service to others. At Swarthmore, the ethos of intellectual intensity and social action can lead to burnout. One student wryly bemoaned the "unrealistic expectation that students will be able to both completely devote themselves to their academic work and change the world in their spare time." A favorite T-shirt proclaims, "Guilt without sex." At Morehouse, an interviewee noted that "we're trying to instill self-confidence without arrogance. There is a phrase, 'You can always tell a Morehouse Man—but not much.' And that's what we want to avoid, is casting that image that you're a person who is really arrogant."

Changing conditions also pose challenges to schools' cultivation of responsibility for others. Some of these conditions are widespread and mirror the challenges to good work in professional life. In particular, growing numbers of college students today come to campus "not to learn but to finish," as one professor put it. To employ Bellah and colleagues' (1985) useful distinction, they may be too concerned with securing a job or launching a career to hear a call to serve. Other challenges are institution specific. Until the 1990s, the judgment of external examiners substituted for grades in Swarthmore's honors program, letting faculty function like coaches rather than evaluators. Grading was instituted at the insistence of students looking ahead to requests for GPAs and transcripts; this shift weakened the dynamic, although interviewees felt that the original spirit of the relationship lingers. At Morehouse, the struggle for racial equality rendered the brotherhood a moral force and tied leadership to the betterment of the black community. With the passing of the civil rights movement, it is no longer self-evident that (in one student's words) "working together is so much more effective than working alone, albeit side by side"; nor is it evident that the brotherhood is so much more than an old boy's network. At Mount St. Mary's, the sisters, who have always been the visible embodiments of the school's ethic of service and care, are a shrinking presence. Led by the first lay president in its history, the college is challenged with sustaining the values of the aging religious order.

At the same time, these schools draw on well-defined, strongly held traditions, including religious traditions, to respond positively to changes that other institutions might see as problems. One example is the increased diversity of American society. All three schools work to integrate diversity into their discussions of what it means to be responsible, and for whom. At Morehouse, where students' daily experience of brotherhood is grounded in gender and racial similarity, students are challenged to embrace diversity and think of unity in terms of the "world church" and "universal brotherhood" as well as the cohesion of the African American community. At Swarthmore, appreciation of diversity is assimilated into the notion of dialogue and bringing all voices to the table. And at Mount St. Mary's, the celebration of diversity has been deliberately woven through the rituals, curriculum, and daily life of the college (Andion, 1998).

Responsibility, Educational Workplaces, and Beyond

At the outset of this chapter I remarked on the limitations of *duty* as a basis for engaging in the work of a community: the cog in a wheel might be dutiful but not responsible. The *self-interest* expressed in the careerism of many current college students (Astin, 1998) provides even less basis for willingly choosing responsibility for others. The daily practices encouraged at these three colleges may be variations on the third relationship between individual and community that Dewey (1916) identified in *Democracy and Education: interest*. It is a relation not ordinarily associated with responsibility. At first blush it might seem odd to think of responsibility for others in this way. Yet what these schools aim to cultivate, what they invite students to practice during their college years, is a genuine interest in the communities to which they belong—most broadly, the global community. Only such interest will inspire responsive engagement with others in the project of a community's betterment.

Analogously, underlying these educators' own collegial dialogue, "tough" love, and enabling care is a deep interest in their students' welfare and development as human beings and citizens, as well as an abiding interest in the welfare of the society the students will inherit. That is, these colleges are not just learning environments. For their faculty, staff, and administrators, they are also places of work. The example of these schools suggests that if a *work organization* wants to cultivate civic and social responsibility, it must begin by recruiting individuals with a genuine interest in those served (here, faculty, staff, and administrators who care about students and their education), making clear how the organization's efforts express this interest; and it must foster the workers' genuine interest in the workplace community they have joined. In the best of cases, it would also——as at these three colleges—cultivate a broader responsibility for other members of the global community.

The faculty, staff, and administrators interviewed at these schools understood and enthusiastically embraced the student-centered aims of their institutions. More than a few invoked the language of family when referring to the campus community. One might object that the case of colleges and their workers does not generalize to other sectors. But one former CEO interviewed for the GoodWork Project observed that in his decades of experience, "there seems to be a pretty widespread longing to have work that counts, that matters for people; and to be in a place where you care about the folks around you and believe they care about you. That's really a *longing*." Likewise, surveys show that when people contemplate retirement, they anticipate missing what amounts to social and civic responsibility: *the opportunity to make a difference* and *the experience of being part of a community*. The puzzle, this former CEO mused, is "If most of us really want that kind of place, what's preventing us from having it? Why doesn't that exist?" "How," he asked, "can you make that just a part of the way things are?"

These schools would suggest that work organizations must attempt to do exactly that: to shape daily practices, encourage social relations, organize physical space, and structure time so that each of these factors supports responsible work. The specific practices are myriad. They need not be large or costly. To take one small example, Swarthmore maintains a weekly lunch at which faculty from across the disciplines gather for an hour to eat together, learn about each other's work, and discuss pedagogy. Such regular occasions for meaningful exchange strengthen ties. One Swarthmore interviewee avowed, "As many of those things as you can do, the better it will be." It is probably only against this sort of backdrop that workers are lastingly affected by the occasional ceremonies and rituals, the reminders of defining events and heroic actors from the past, that an organization may sponsor to spotlight responsibility. That is, it seems most important that acts of responsibility at work are (as the same ex-CEO put it) "*uniformly* acknowledged, applauded, recognized, and imitated."

Of course, for a host of reasons many work environments unfortunately impede rather than support and celebrate practicing responsibility for one's coworkers and for those served by one's work. Under these conditions, one sometimes sees individuals take it upon themselves to respond by remaking or "crafting" their jobs, developing ways to make a difference to others and create community even if this is not characteristic of the organization as a whole. On one hospital's cleaning staff, for example, some workers adhered to their formal role; others redefined both the task boundaries and interpersonal boundaries of their jobs so that they routinely contributed to patients' morale and the efficiency and cohesiveness of their unit (Wrzesniewski & Dutton, 2001). In many organizations, practicing responsibility for others depends on such individual improvisations.

After all, in key respects, the three colleges construct one possible relation between the microcosm lived in and the larger social system: a small community is crafted that possesses qualities not consistently realized in the larger system, with the intent that those who pass through will go on to live by and foster the qualities in question in the wider world. At Swarthmore, for example, we saw that the college "seeks to be a microcosm of a just, generous, and inclusive world and to place intellectual acuity at the service of developing such a world." One can imagine other relations between microcosm and macrocosm, notably colleges designed to replicate the qualities of the larger system and aiming to prepare their students to thrive within the status quo. Indeed, because they are "of" the larger social system, the small worlds of schools—and workplaces—often, if inadvertently, tend to instantiate its prevailing values. It requires work to sustain a microcosm committed to social action, social change, or service to others; and it takes courage and hope to do so if other commitments of attention and energy guide the wider society.

REFERENCES

Andion, M. (1998). *Keeping promises: Multicultural education in Mount St. Mary's College.* Unpublished doctoral dissertation, University of California, Los Angeles.

Astin, A. W. (1998). The changing American college student: Thirty-year trends, 1966–1996. *Review of Higher Education, 21,* 115–135.

Bellah, R. N., Madsen, R., Sullivan, W. M., Swidler, A., & Tipton, S. M. (1985). *Habits of the heart.* Berkeley: University of California Press.

Colby, A., Ehrlich, T., Beaumont, E., & Stephens, J. (2003). *Educating citizens: Preparing undergraduates for lives of moral and civic responsibility.* San Francisco: Jossey-Bass.

Dewey, J. (1916). *Democracy and education.* New York: Free Press.

Dewey, J. (1921). *Human nature and conduct.* New York: Modern Library.

Dewey, J. (1938). *Experience and education.* New York: Collier Macmillan.

Eaves, J. H. (1999). *Determining which factors lead to the academic success of African-American college students at the nation's only all-male, predominantly black post-secondary institution.* Unpublished doctoral dissertation, University of South Carolina.

Fish, S. (2004, May 21). Why we built the ivory tower. *New York Times,* p. 23.

Gardner, H., Csikszentmihalyi, M., & Damon, W. (2001). *Good work.* New York: Basic Books.

GoodWork Project. (2006). Research profile: GoodWork in higher education. Retrieved September 15, 2006, from http://www.goodworkproject.org/research/highered.htm

Hooker, C., Nakamura, J., & Csikszentmihalyi, M. (2003). The group as mentor: Social capital and the systems model of creativity—A case study in space science. In P. Paulus & B. Nijstad (Eds.), *Group creativity* (pp. 225–244). New York: Oxford University Press.

Jackson, P. W. (1968). *Life in classrooms*. New York: Holt, Rinehart, & Winston.

Menand, L. (1997). Re-imagining liberal education. In R. Orrill (Ed.), *Education and democracy* (pp. 1–19). New York: College Entrance Examination Board.

Nakamura, J., Shernoff, D., & Hooker, C. (2004). *The cultivation of good work in science: Mentoring and optimal development.* Paper presented at the second European Conference on Positive Psychology, Verbania Pallanza, Italy.

Schall, L. M. (2003). *Swarthmore College: The evolution of an institutional mission.* Unpublished doctoral dissertation, University of Pennsylvania.

Shulman, L. S. (2005). Signature pedagogies in the professions. *Daedalus, 134*(3), 52–59.

Sullivan, W. (2006, April 10). *Professional apprenticeships: The challenge of integration.* Paper presented at the annual meeting of the American Educational Research Association, San Francisco.

Swarthmore College. (2002). *The meaning of Swarthmore.* Retrieved April 4, 2007, from http://web.archive.org/web/20040812212033/www.swarthmore.edu/support/meaning_of_swarthmore.html

Willis, P. (1982). *Learning to labor: How working class kids get working class jobs.* New York: Columbia University Press. (Original work published 1977)

Wrzesniewski, A., & Dutton, J. E. (2001). Crafting a job. *Academy of Management Review, 26,* 179–201.

14

THE GOODWORK TOOLKIT

FROM THEORY TO PRACTICE

Lynn Barendsen
Wendy Fischman

You can't escape the responsibility of tomorrow
by evading it today.

—Abraham Lincoln

THE ISSUE OF WHO IS RESPONSIBLE FOR "GOOD WORK" is obviously an important one, but its exploration begs an equally important consideration: how to encourage individuals to assume responsibility for work. As highlighted in several previous chapters, carrying out good work is not a matter of chance—its achievement is based on individual traits, influential role models, and the ambience of working environments and the broader society. We know, for example, that exposure to positive models and mentors, deeply rooted religious beliefs, and alignment of individual and professional values are strong predictors of good work.

Even when the stars of good work are well aligned early in life, things can go wrong. Young people are under tremendous pressure, and even

---

The creation of the Toolkit and the research on which it is based was made possible through the generous support of the Christian Johnson Endeavor Foundation. We thank President Julie Kidd and her colleagues Susan Kassouf and Elaine Schapker for their keen interest and unstinting support.

those with the best of support systems (involved parents, committed teachers) may be tempted to cut corners when tasks feel too burdensome. We have heard high school students talk about the debt they feel to their parents, who have sacrificed so that they might attend prestigious private schools. Accordingly, some students are willing to use dishonest tactics to achieve the highest grades possible. Other students, working long hours that mirror those of professionals, tell us they deserve to win recognition. If judges or mentors disagree, they are willing to cheat to achieve the result they feel they have earned.

As documented in Chapter Twelve, by Gardner, and in much current writing (see Callahan, 2004; Fischman, Solomon, Greenspan, & Gardner, 2004), lack of responsibility for work is regularly detected among many novice and veteran professionals. Disappointed and unsettled by the stories and justifications offered by professionals, especially the young professionals in our study, we set out to tackle a new question: *How can we encourage individuals to develop professional responsibility?* We believe that early intervention can make a difference. In other words, we need to move beyond a reliance on serendipity to facilitate the development of professional responsibility.

In this chapter we explore the rationale and strategies for nurturing professional responsibility in the young. We have gathered significant data that warn us of pitfalls in the way of, and optimal aids to, the development of responsibility. We seek to encourage conversation across the various stakeholders within a community to develop a common language and come to agreement, or alignment, about what constitutes good work in their setting. We advocate a multipronged approach that targets responsibility in students, responsibility in teachers, and responsibility in school communities.

But why speak of work when one is dealing with young people who are still in school?

In many ways, work is central to students' lives. While in school, students spend hours concentrating on school work (we use the term *work* broadly to include school work as well as traditional modes of employment). For these students, work entails learning and mastering disciplines, preparing college applications, and participating in extracurricular activities and clubs (such as student government, the school newspaper, and athletic teams). Beyond school walls, many students also "intern"—that is, work in fields they might pursue in the future. Most of the young participants in our research study, especially those driven toward a particular career, identified these early work experiences as important in helping them to form decisions about what to focus on in college, and in some cases, graduate school. Their early experiences (for example, as a scientist in a university lab setting or as an editor of a school newspaper) were pivotal in shaping their views about work and their responses to ethical quandaries. These budding professionals took note of such factors as heavy workload, diminution of personal life, pressure to produce, and difficult interpersonal dynamics among peers. On the basis of their early work experiences, many students were struck by the disjunction between what has been preached to them about work values and ethical approaches and what they have observed on their own, overheard at home, and read in the newspaper headlines. Though many observers claim that adolescence is too early to be tackling ethical issues in work, we have found that young students grapple with the same tensions that seasoned professionals face. By starting to work with them at a young age, we seek to help students consider the meaning of work in their lives and the impact of their work on others.

With this in mind, we have over the last several years developed *The GoodWork Toolkit*. Through conversations, discussions, and debate, this set of tools aims to encourage high-quality, socially responsible, and meaningful work. It engages individuals in reflection and conversation about their own work—how to negotiate demands, expectations, and standards in responsible ways. We also seek to challenge certain commonly held assumptions about work. For example, in the Toolkit we ask, *"What is a "good" professional?"* Is a "good" journalist one who frequently gets her stories on the front page, even if her tactics are questionable? Or is a "good" journalist one who will not compromise professional standards (such as fairness, honesty, and accuracy) but whose stories garner less attention? We aim to facilitate discussions with students, teachers, and parents about their disparate responsibilities. But even more centrally, we seek conversation among the various stakeholders within a community to develop a common language and come to agreement, or achieve alignment, about what constitutes good work in their setting.

Background and Methodology

The need for the Toolkit became clear after we had talked with many young people about whether they have a sense of responsibility in their work. We gleaned three related lessons: (1) Students have a hard time thinking about the broad concepts of good work without first discussing the individual constituents (excellence, ethics, values, and so on). (2) Students are interested in other people's stories; in talking about others, they move readily thereafter to reflections about themselves and their own struggles in work. And (3) students are interested in the difficult situations faced by different kinds of professionals at various ages, not only those confronting other high school students. Students seem relieved to hear that a veteran lawyer faces professional tensions similar to those they face in class, in the hallways, and on the playing fields. Though students are in a different position than working professionals, the challenges faced by the protagonists resonate with their own work. They too face situations in which one value is pitted against another—such as the decision to take the honest route even at the expense of a high grade, or the choice to spend personal time with family and friends or get ahead on schoolwork or into an attractive internship.

Theory Underlying The GoodWork Toolkit

Based on these lessons, we devoted particular attention to the organization of the material. Specifically, the Toolkit was designed using three guiding principles:

1. Participants first think about others and then turn inward to reflect on their own responsibilities and how they relate to work.
2. Participants approach the topic of good work by breaking down preconceived notions and considering all of its essential elements.
3. Participants understand the breadth and depth of the importance of good work in society by exploring how it relates to many different kinds of professions and to their own forays into work—at school, in summer jobs, in internships, and in dreams about their future.

The Toolkit represents a sustained attempt to move from research to practice—to adapt what we have learned from our own research, as well as from relevant theories and literature, in order to develop practical tools and interventions that can be used in schools. We also draw on other practical interventions developed by the GoodWork Project in journalism and in higher education. In journalism, for example, William Damon and colleagues at Stanford, in collaboration with the Committee of Concerned Journalists, developed the "Traveling Curriculum," which has been used in one third of the nation's print newsrooms. The curriculum consists of twelve modules from which newsrooms select three for a day-and-a-half-long workshop (see http://www.goodworkproject.org and http://www.concernedjournalists.org). Relatedly, in higher education, under the direction of Mihaly Csikszentmihalyi and Jeanne Nakamura, our colleagues at Claremont Graduate University have developed an approach using data collected from students, faculty, and administrators in college and university settings to reflect on good work at the institutional level—to engage disparate audiences in conversation about the overarching mission of the school (Nakamura, Yoneshige, & Csikszentmihalyi, 2007).

Existing Theories and Programs

Along with considering these good work models of how to encourage responsibility in the workplace, we also examined relevant perspectives on ethical training and existing programs in schools (Colby, Ehrlich, Beaumont, & Stephens, 2003; Damon, 1988; Damon, 1997; Damon, 2002; Damon, Menon, & Bronk, 2003; Lapsley & Narvaez, 2006; Lickona, 1991; Lickona, Schaps, & Lewis, 1996; Noddings, 1992; Turiel, 2006). Here we briefly note the work that has most influenced our thinking.

COGNITIVE DEVELOPMENTALISM. The cognitive developmental approach has its roots in the work of Jean Piaget (1932) and Lawrence Kohlberg (1964). Famously, Kohlberg posed hypothetical dilemmas—for example, is a husband justified in stealing expensive drugs that a pharmacist is hoarding so the medication can be used to treat his dying wife? This approach engages students in making use of hypothetical dilemmas that challenge them to think about complex moral issues. The hope is that the discussion of these dilemmas among students will elicit a "moral atmosphere" in the school (Simon, 2001, p. 84).

VALUES CLARIFICATION. In this approach, students are encouraged to discover their own value systems by working through ethical problems. There is no common, agreed-upon set of values, and teachers do not favor one response over another. Though students think for themselves through a range of possibilities, there is little to no structure to "help students distinguish better from worse moral decisions" (Simon, 2001, p. 187). In other words, individuals who favor this approach do not believe in consensus about moral values—various constituencies (that is, parents, teachers, and peers) prioritize and emphasize different values.

UNIVERSAL VALUES. Unlike values clarification, the universal values approach argues that there *are* some values that we can all agree on, such as honesty, responsibility, fairness, fidelity, and equality. Before students engage in moral complexity, they should be familiar with these "fundamental" values with which most individuals concur (Bennett, 1993, pp. 58–60).

Supporters of this approach believe that values education should focus on noncontroversial issues. Furthermore, proponents of this approach believe that these fundamental values can be taught in noncontroversial ways—through cooperative learning and modeling rather by grappling with moral dilemmas (Bennett, 1993; Lickona, 1991; Ryan, 1989).

PEDAGOGICAL NEUTRALITY. In direct contrast to the universal values approach, the purpose of pedagogical neutrality is to present all "significant sides of an issue" and to "help students see why an issue is controversial" (Noddings, 1993, pp. 122–123, 139). Pedagogical neutrality has its roots in Nel Noddings's "ethics of care" (compare Verducci, Chapter Two in this volume). According to this view, teachers should devote time to multiple perspectives, teach an issue from each perspective, and maintain neutrality. Proponents of this approach believe that pedagogical neutrality is a helpful model for addressing controversial issues, especially when teachers are faced with the problem of "whose values" to teach (Simon, 2001, p. 189).

Though our conception of the Toolkit drew on some of these premises, our goals and approaches for working with school communities to encourage responsibility in work were sufficiently distinctive to warrant our own good work program. To be specific, the Toolkit does not employ hypothetical dilemmas—all of the stories are based on real individuals. We also endorse direct thematic connections with the school curriculum. For example, the theme of *responsibility* might easily be linked to a history course that is tackling the issues of responsibility during the Holocaust. Furthermore, our approach privileges some professional values over others: high-quality, socially responsible, and meaningful work constitute the gold standard for good work. Rather than shy away from controversy, we discuss the stories of individuals who are conflicted, who feel drawn in various directions, but who strive to adhere to certain core values. As young people begin to observe and experience these same complexities in their work as students, teammates, and interns, they will be able to identify and reflect on these real tensions. When working with school communities, we do not want to tell teachers or students that one value is more important than another (for example, honesty versus responsibility); instead, we describe how those who carry out good work negotiate the tricky moments when they may have to sacrifice one value for another.

To convey the types of cases of which the Toolkit is composed, we offer a few examples:

Debbie is the editor of her high school newspaper at a prestigious, competitive boarding school. She works hard to balance the paper's content for a broad audience of students, faculty, parents, and alumni. Coming from a family of journalists and writers, she also works hard to meet the standards set by her predecessors. During the production of her first issue as editor, she faces a decision about whether to print a story about her school that could be potentially damaging to its reputation. In her work Debbie struggles to balance responsibility to her own standards, to the standards of journalism, to her audience (as mentioned, itself varied), and to her advisors, colleagues, and fellow students.

Allison is a dedicated high school scientist, already working in a neurobiology lab at a major university. In the high school science world of today, exceptional students compete in the prestigious Intel Science Talent Search. In spite of a warning that Intel judges do not typically award prizes to projects based on live animals, Allison chooses to conduct an experiment involving mice. She works long hours on her project. While preparing the research report for the competition, she represents her work in a way that is more appealing to the judging system but is dishonest. Claiming that she watches films of mice rather than handling them herself, Allison is named a semifinalist and wins a college scholarship. Accepted by an Ivy League university, she chooses to continue a career trajectory in scientific research. As described, she will continue to struggle with issues of responsibility (to scientific standards, to her colleagues, to herself) and competition.

Steven is an engineering professor at a top liberal arts college who is deeply committed to the teaching of undergraduate students. He prides himself on using techniques that require students to try new things that will facilitate their intellectual and personal growth. However, Steven faces a major dilemma in his work with respect to grading. He must decide whether to give his students grades that accurately reflect their work or to inflate their grades (as do many colleagues) in order to keep his students competitive with other undergraduate students applying to top graduate engineering programs.

After reading these kinds of stories, participants engage in open-ended discussion that brings out different perspectives on the protagonist and the situation that he or she is confronting. This discussion in turn prepares participants to consider how some of the highlighted complexities also arise in their own work. For example, we ask the direct (but evocative) question, *To whom or what do you feel responsible in your work?* Students write down a list that might include individuals (teachers, coaches, parents, friends, siblings), communities (church, team, ethnic group), or ideals (to do my best, to tell the truth, to show kindness). Very quickly participants come to realize that these many responsibilities can be the source of much stress and anxiety. Although they have not always considered responsibility before we begin to work with them, it does not take long to translate our terms into realities with which they are familiar—perhaps all too familiar!

Structure of the Toolkit

The Toolkit is made up of a series of cases and accompanying activities organized by themes central to good work. Each major theme constitutes a chapter featuring several cases about individuals who struggle in some way to carry out good work. These chapters include the following:

What Is Good Work? introduces the concept of good work and asks participants to begin to consider what constitutes good work in various professions and work environments.

Beliefs and Values explores how beliefs and values can help an individual overcome difficult situations and yet may also create tension in work.

Goals highlights the ways in which goals influence the kind of work individuals pursue, the strategies they use, and the decisions they make.

Responsibilities considers the various responsibilities an individual has and acts on in work, and how conflicting responsibilities might influence work.

Mentors and Role Models provides an opportunity to think about how veteran professionals can be supportive in work and how individuals can develop useful connections and relationships with others close by (supervisor, teacher) or at a distance (paragons), to draw on when needed.

Excellence explores what excellence means, how its definition varies across different areas of work, and which factors are key to maintaining it.

Perspectives creates awareness of the tension caused by differences in perspectives emanating from the varying roles and personal and professional responsibilities of working individuals. Issues of alignment are addressed—specifically, the extent to which various constituents agree or disagree on what constitutes good work, the mission of the school, and criteria for a successful school experience.

Good Work Revisited revisits the guiding questions of the Toolkit and explores how participants' understanding of the major concepts of good work have evolved and how to draw on these lessons in one's future working life.

How the Toolkit Can Be Used in School Settings

The Toolkit is not a prescribed curriculum. It is called a toolkit because it contains a variety of tools that may be used in a number of combinations. The materials are meant to be adaptable to a variety of contexts; for instance, the Toolkit can be used as part of a retreat, as a year-long theme in a particular class, or as the basis of a two- or three-day seminar. Furthermore, the chapters do not need to be followed in any particular order: the stories and activities are designed so that facilitators can pick and choose and adapt them as best suits their goals and needs.

To date the Toolkit has been used in a variety of educational contexts: it has been integrated into various types of course curricula, and used as a professional development tool and as part of an effort to align a school community around important topics. Across these diverse forms and forums, teachers, administrators, students, and parents have been exposed to the materials in both urban and suburban school settings, in public and private institutions, serving students from elementary school to the university level. For example, one of our collaborators, June Weissman, integrated and adapted some of the Toolkit materials in her fifth grade class of gifted and talented students. She used the concepts of good work to help students choose research topics that would be personally meaningful. She hoped that these topics might develop into lifelong passions, possibly resulting in work that would have a positive effect on their lives. One of our colleagues, Susan Verducci, has been using Toolkit materials in her humanities course Integration of Liberal Studies at San Jose State University. Verducci and her students explore the aims and purposes of liberal education, the nature of good work, and the connection between the two. Finally, we offer modules at the collegiate level. In collaboration with colleagues at the Institute for Global Ethics we have offered a course at Colby College entitled Meaningful Work in a Meaningful Life. Our goal is to encourage students to think about their work as college students and beyond, when they will enter the workplace. As we express it, "We are not interested in what work you choose to pursue—that's your decision. We are very interested in what kind of a worker you will be, wherever you decide to hang your hat."

In our experience to date we have identified three effective uses of the Toolkit: (1) to encourage individual students to think about responsibility, (2) as a form of professional development for teachers, and (3) as part of a schoolwide community effort for students, teachers, administrators, and parents.

Students and Responsibility

A choral director and music instructor at a Boston area high school (whom we will call Cynthia) piloted early versions of Toolkit materials. The Performing Arts Department is one of the most visible departments in the school, and the community shows support by attending concerts. Historically the arts have always been valued by the school and its surrounding community.

Cynthia originally wanted to use Toolkit materials because she thought it would provide a good opportunity for her students to engage in conversation about topics that are important to society—something she has not often been able to do. She was particularly interested to see how her students, who represent a wide range of individuals in grades 9 through 12, would respond to the notion of good work.

At the beginning of the year Cynthia asked her students to write about characteristics of a good worker and what it takes to carry out good work. Before introducing any of the cases she was curious to learn how they thought about good work. This pretest proved to be an instructive exercise; responses varied quite a bit, from comments like "following directions" and "time management" to "effort," "legality," and "teamwork." Some students defined good work in terms of the final product or outcome of work rather than the process itself. For example, students would equate good work with diverse measures of success. One student explained, "Good work is knowing how high your standards are and striving to break them." Of the forty students who completed this exercise, only one student mentioned "good grades."

Interestingly, the notion of engagement—passion for and a sense of commitment to work—emerged as a common theme among students. This surprising consensus was manifested through words like *dedication*, *pride*, and *excitement*. One student wrote that good work is "when you believe [in] your job no matter how important it is." Another student wrote that in order to carry out good work you need to "make sure you do a thorough job with what you're doing, be it cleaning someone's car or editing a business report. . . . I think if you're a good worker, you should love your job no matter if your job is the lowliest on earth or the highest paying there is." In our study of good work we have found that in order to carry out work that is both high in quality and socially responsible, enjoyment of and engagement in the work is a necessity.

Every few weeks Cynthia would take a break from rehearsing in class and draw on the Toolkit. The students seemed excited to read another case, and as she describes it, when she read aloud, "there was not a peep in the room." Specifically, Cynthia selected cases that focused on the arts in some way. Topics that the cases addressed included standards for work, conceptions of identity based on beliefs and values, relationship of personal and professional goals, influence of mentor-mentee relationships, and collegiality and teamwork. After she read a case, students would spend the rest of the time talking as a group about the details of the situation—specifically in terms of the protagonist's decisions and actions. Following these discussions, students were given homework—the discussion questions provided at the end of each case.

According to Cynthia, the cases and activities that focused on competition elicited the most discussion from her students. Though her course is an elective, students and their parents tend to be competitive about the roles and assignments they get in the choral group. Cynthia holds auditions for some of these roles. Sometimes after these auditions, disappointed students and their parents complain to her about the decisions she has made. For these reasons, a case entitled "How Far Are You Willing to Go?" about a young actress contemplating plastic surgery was a helpful tool to start conversation with students about competition and the risks involved with wanting to "win at all costs." In response to this particular case, a student reflected about the pressure he faced to succeed and the ethical consequences involved: "My boundaries may be threatened by many things. There is constant pressure to conform to social norms, which can mean compromising ethics in order to get ahead in life. This pressure can come from my peers, our society, or even my own drive for success." He added, "It is important to recognize these threats and not allow them to falter [sic] my personal beliefs for what success means to me."

This particular group of students approached the issue of responsibility from multiple perspectives. Whereas most high school students (*when* they think about responsibility) focus on academic work and responsibility to peers, teachers, parents, and themselves, this sophisticated group of students also considered their responsibilities as performers (rather than just as young persons or students). As part of a choral group, they each carried responsibilities to the group as a whole; and as aspiring performers, many of them were in direct competition with one another when it came to auditioning for solo opportunities or landing roles in musical theater. This additional layer of responsibility further complicated already vexed dilemmas as students struggled with issues of balance (how to divide time and energy among schoolwork-social life, schoolwork-musical performances) and stress (parental and peer pressure, high personal standards, college applications). At the end of the year Cynthia reflected on the Toolkit and its role in her class. She commented that what excited her most was that it "allows me to see another piece of who [my students] are," and lets students "get to know *me* in a different way." She explained, "As we discussed the cases, they heard my opinions and thoughts. I also began to recall situations I had experienced over the years. Students love to hear about their teachers in a 'real way.'" Ultimately Cynthia found that students began to understand that good work encompasses *both* the process and the product of work. Though "grade grubbing" is an issue at the school, this teacher commented that the topics discussed in her class as a result of the Toolkit "gave the students a window into the issues teachers face when assessing work, and that good work is not just the 'A' paper with all the correct answers. . . . They began to think about good work and all that impacts it. They began to think about goals, and I suspect that many had not thought beyond the idea of just making it through college."

Teachers and Responsibility

We have used Toolkit materials for professional development in a few different formats: with a single school department, with the full faculty from a single school, and in a conference setting with teachers from many different schools.

WORKING WITH A DEPARTMENT. At a regional high school outside of Boston, we were invited to work with the world languages department. There were no critical problems in this department (we were not helping out a "troubled" community); rather, a teacher at the school mentioned our work to the individual in charge of coordinating staff development days, and we received an invitation to lead a session. As it turned out, the world languages group was intriguing and we learned quite a bit about the challenges associated with teaching language in a high school setting.

We met first with a core group of faculty, to get a sense of what might be most useful for this particular community. On the basis of the feedback we received, we decided to begin a conversation about the mission of the department and see whether the group could draft a mission statement.

We structured the session itself on three ideas: model, mission, and mirror. We believe that these three ideas, or "levers," can increase the likelihood of good work (Fischman, Solomon, Greenspan, & Gardner, 2004). First, in thinking about models, we asked participants to consider how others handle their responsibilities, and to think in particular of an individual who exemplifies good work in the way he manages his responsibilities. We asked participants to describe these exemplary workers, and together we generated a list that included words like *creative, honest, full of integrity, attentive, giving, hardworking*, and *brilliant*. We moved the conversation from a consideration of qualities to one of standards, asking teachers to consider the standards they use to measure their own work and to think about whether these standards are similar to or distinct from the criteria they apply to others. Some key issues for this department emerged, including mixed standards for excellent work, varied understandings about the "client" (such as is the client the student, parent, or department head?), and issues specific to the most ethnically diverse faculty department in the school—in particular, alienation from the other major faculty departments—which they surmised was due to having a native language other than English.

Teachers in this department expressed frustration that other faculty in the school did not understand their goals. In addition to feeling a responsibility to teach the language of their native countries, these foreign language teachers also felt a responsibility to teach their students about other cultures. As one teacher explained, students will learn about Spain (in addition to every other country they must cover) for only a few days out of any given year in a history class. In his Spanish language class, he would not only teach Spanish, but also teach students about Spain and its culture. This strategy enabled him to turn his students' eyes outward— away from the self-oriented lives that so many high school students experience—to another culture and another way of life. These language teachers told us they felt a responsibility to teach their students that the world is bigger than one small town in Massachusetts.

Second, members of the group took a step away from their own work and read three case studies from the Toolkit. Each story offered them an opportunity to look at the work of others (a scientist, a social entrepreneur, and an actor) and to define, as a group, each worker's mission. After some discussion, the group began to draft a mission statement for the World Languages Department. A division emerged as some focused on teaching students about culture and ethnic diversity while others focused on mastery of the language. We encouraged participants to continue the conversation in department meetings. We hoped that leaving them with an "incomplete" task would ensure that this recommendation would be followed.

Finally, all participants were asked to sort thirty values (including creativity, honesty, hard work and commitment, relationships, and spirituality) in terms of importance in their work. This last activity asked each participant to look inward (or into a metaphorical mirror) and think about his or her own priorities and how these might or might not fit into those of the department and those of the entire school. This portion of the program was designed to begin to get at the issue of alignment, specifically in terms of whether the ways in which the values were sorted proved consistent across the department. Analyzing the data, we learned that most participants agreed that honesty and integrity, creativity and pioneering, and enjoyment were most important elements in their work.

We left materials with the world languages department that would help them continue the conversation on their own. Additionally, members of the faculty suggested that they would like to consider some of the challenges we had identified in thinking about a collective mission statement. If a mission is agreed on, is that mission in service of personal and professional standards? Additionally, we suggested that they think together about the goals and responsibilities of each of the following groups: parents, teachers, and students. Are they in alignment with one another? If not, what is the impact of their differences? If misaligned, is it possible to think of ways they might be able to bring their disparate goals closer together?

WORKING WITH EDUCATORS FROM DIFFERENT COMMUNITIES. The GoodWork Project is housed within Project Zero, a research group at Harvard's Graduate School of Education (see http://pzweb.harvard.edu). Every summer, approximately three hundred educators from around the world attend the Project Zero Classroom, a weeklong institute during which participants are exposed to various ideas developed at Project Zero and have the opportunity to reflect on their classroom practices. At this institute we offer a mini course entitled "Teaching 'Good Work' in the Classroom: The *GoodWork Toolkit*." During this short session, we meet educators who occupy many different roles: teachers, principals, and school administrators from a variety of school systems in many states and nations. We have a dual purpose for these sessions: to introduce the Toolkit materials as ways in which educators can start conversation about good work in their classrooms, and to give educators the opportunity to reflect on and think about their own work. We work with a few case studies (such as those of Allison and Steven mentioned earlier) and help the participants to wrestle with the issues raised by the cases.

Every summer we ask participants to tell us a story about an instance when they felt torn between conflicting responsibilities or a situation when they were unsure of the best course of action. One elementary teacher (whom we will call Alice) told us about taking over a classroom for a colleague who was on maternity leave. As Alice familiarized herself with the files on the various students, it became clear that the teacher on leave had kept sloppy records, and that her evaluations of students were very general and in most cases far too generous. Alice began her own evaluations and quickly faced quite a bit of resistance from parents. Whereas previously they had been told their children were doing quite well, now they were hearing something very different. Parents complained, and Alice soon faced an extremely upset principal. Although she did not want to blame her colleague (who planned on returning to the classroom after her leave), Alice believed that her own evaluations provided far more accurate assessments of her students' work. Alice also believed that her students were paying the price for her colleague's unprofessional actions.

When faced with these tough dilemmas, educators typically make their decisions on the basis of the needs of their students. "I have to think of my kids" is a phrase we have heard repeatedly, and with this in mind, difficult choices are made a bit more clear. For educators, their primary responsibility is certain, and this consensual view is often what sustains them in less than optimal working conditions (Fischman, DiBara, & Gardner, 2006).

These brief workshops can only scratch the surface of responsibility in teaching. In a few hours educators have the opportunity to reflect on their work and to learn about tools they might use in their own classrooms. Testimony documents the utility of the exercise: "Self-reflection is often lost in the fast-pace lifestyle of teachers. This course reminded me of the importance of ethics in education," or "It made me reflect on my own choices and made me wonder when I should be more aware of my actions and how they affect others." We hope that the teachers who take this course will return to their classrooms with a renewed sense of why they do what they do. We also hope they will work with their students and perhaps their colleagues to encourage discussion on issues of responsibility in work. In an attempt to bring about maximum impact of these ideas, we developed the option of working with entire school communities.

School Communities and Responsibility

Teachers (like the choral instructor) who piloted our materials told us they loved what they were able to accomplish in their classrooms, but they wished others were carrying out similar work. We set out the ambitious goal of "creating a culture of good work" in a school community and then began the process of finding a school interested in our ideas. In the fall of 2005 we began working with an independent K-12 school in Massachusetts. At this school we have approached good work with particular reference to the various constituencies that make up any school (such as students, faculty, and parents), and to what might be involved in bringing these constituencies into alignment with one another.

In our work we have led a workshop with academic department heads, convened a faculty retreat, and facilitated a full-day retreat for ninth grade students, who were joined in the evening by their parents. These meetings and retreats for faculty, students, and parents alike generally follow the same structure, outlined earlier, that we use in our work with faculty and students. Specifically, we begin by opening up a conversation about good work, such as thinking about attributes of someone admired or words that come to mind when the term *good work* is mentioned; we read and analyze stories of individuals; and then we relate these stories to participants' own lives. To collect data about what students, parents, and teachers think about their work at school, we have also developed an online survey about good work for students, faculty, and parents. In combination with the values-sorting activity completed by all of these community members, we are able to help the different stakeholders in the community launch a conversation about areas of alignment and misalignment. On the basis of much of this work, individual teachers have begun to use Toolkit materials in various classrooms, and GoodWork Project leader Howard Gardner has come to speak at the school on separate occasions to address students, parents, faculty, and staff. In sum, in collaboration with senior school administrators, we aim to approach issues of responsibility and good work via multiple paths, hoping to increase the likelihood that these ideas will be integrated into the DNA of the school community.

While formal evaluation remains to be done, we have received a great deal of positive feedback. For example, here is part of a letter sent by a faculty member following the ninth grade day. (According to our contacts at this school, this is a "typical" response—one of fifty-two parent and student e-mails received that evening.)

I know how important it is to try to engage around the many intense social issues that the kids deal with; I think you are heading in a very positive direction to go in through a different door, and center the focus on values, choices, and decision making. If kids (and all of us for that matter) think about building our lives around meaningful engagement and look at the pressures to succeed in the broadest terms, it is not a very long leap to apply those concepts to all the decisions in our lives.

The GoodWork team's message and issue seemed to resonate so strongly with everyone, and were the basis for important discussions about values and choices that were meaningful and approachable for all. The kids seemed to have had a great day themselves—it was wonderful to see them so engaged and charged up.

One of the key elements in our success thus far has been the key group of individuals who have championed these efforts. Throughout the process we have been in regular contact with the heads of the upper and middle schools, the provost, and the deans of the faculty and students. Each of these individuals brings a particular perspective to the table and thinks specifically about the constituencies to which he or she is primarily responsible. As a result, good work ideas are being incorporated into the school community and becoming a part of the culture.

Of course, other possibilities and approaches exist for working with entire school communities on issues of responsibility for good work. As an example, we worked with another independent school in Massachusetts to consider an issue they felt was particularly pressing: honesty. Upper and middle school students spent time in advisory sessions and in classes discussing the various pressures that tempt them away from honesty. Students and faculty filled out an anonymous questionnaire that asked them, "Have you ever intentionally . . . lied to a peer? . . . lied to an adult? . . . lied to avoid conflict? . . . cheated on a quiz or a test? . . . plagiarized a paper? . . . used Cliff Notes or Sparknotes?" The survey went on to ask if they had been lied to, and finally asked them whether or not they considered themselves honest individuals. Students and faculty also filled out the values sorting inventory, and the results showed that honesty was the value the entire community found most important.

All of this initial groundwork laid a foundation for a powerful town meeting in which students and faculty came together to try and answer the question *Why be honest?* Early on in the session, one student stood up and spoke about the sense of responsibility he feels he owes to his parents. Saying that his family has sacrificed quite a bit to give him an expensive secondary education, he feels he has to do "whatever it takes" to be successful and get into a good college. This single example demonstrates that responsibility may be experienced as a burden, and at times such a burden can feel overwhelming. Another student countered that honesty is "like a muscle; if you don't work it out, it will atrophy." For this student, waiting until college to "become" honest is not an option. These valuable discussions were only the beginning of a process that has continued at this school. The Honesty Committee, formed to "encourage open and honest dialogue about honesty as it applies to society and to [the school] community," continues to exist. This committee hopes to prepare these students "for the unavoidable moral conflicts they will face in life."

Summary

The goal of our Toolkit initiative is to develop, inspire, and sustain work-related responsibilities in young people. We believe we have assembled a valuable set of materials, even as we are still discovering the many and varied ways these materials may be adapted. As we expand our existing work—with teachers, in workshops, at secondary schools, and at the college and university level—we look forward to next steps. In particular, we hope to expand our university work to help those about to enter the workforce think deeply about meaningful work, taking into account their many responsibilities and attempts to mediate among them. Internships are an important precursor to work; we hope to work with students prior to and following their internship experiences, perhaps through the auspices of offices of career services. We envision workshops or seminars that question participants about what gives value to their work, what success means to them, and which institutions and individuals embody good work. We plan as well to establish a Web site that will help us reach a greater range of schools. We have had encouraging international interest (portions of the GoodWork Toolkit are being used in Taiwan, South Africa, Mexico, and Australia); a more extensive Web site should enable these various users to communicate with one another. Eventually we hope to encourage schools to carry out schoolwide efforts (like those outlined above) without our direct involvement. This goal is important because schools know themselves best (it takes time for us to understand particulars that they take for granted), but also because the school has to be fully committed if the materials are to be effective. For genuine progress to be made, each community has to be invested and ultimately take ownership of the efforts. We would like our own efforts to be catalytic rather than indispensable.

Our discussion of the Toolkit has focused on one part of the GoodWork Project, responsibility, in one domain, education. Ultimately, we can see our ideas and approaches expanded in three ways: (1) toward other aspects of the GoodWork Project (such as mentoring and trust), (2) toward other domains or professions (such as law, medicine), and (3) toward individuals experiencing professional transitions (such as individuals who are retiring or starting second careers). As happened with the interview questionnaire we have administered to well over a thousand individuals, the Toolkit proves a stimulus for individuals to reflect on the meaning of work in their own lives and on the importance of their work to others. With the Toolkit and adapted materials, we hope to inspire individuals of all ages and in a variety of areas to think deeply about the purpose of work and about the effects of their own work on the larger society.

Conclusion

Research about good work is clearly valuable in and of itself, but at the end of the day we need to be able to indicate how or whether good work can be inculcated. This is part of *our* responsibility, as researchers. Of many possible interventions we have developed one, but already we see many applications. They differ from one another, even at the high school and college levels, and it would be easy to see similar differentiation in other professions.

More specifically, there are clear leverage points at which to achieve positive impact on a young person's moral development. We have learned, for example, that several factors determine whether an individual is likely to do good work. These include long-standing belief and value systems, role models and mentors, and pivotal experiences. Optimally, we try to target as many of these points as possible, asking young people to think about what they value in work, encouraging exposure to role models and mentors early on, and increasing the opportunities for pivotal experiences (such as camp, work internships, travel, and service work).

Professionals of all types feel multiple and often conflicting responsibilities, with the pressures associated with these responsibilities beginning early and scarcely abating over time. A high school scientist may feel as much pressure as a veteran scientist; the difference lies in the impact of their decision making. If a young scientist decides to falsify her data, it is unlikely that anyone beyond her immediate community will feel the effects. However, if she achieves positive results (a prestigious award, entrance to a high-ranking university), it is likely that she will repeat this kind of behavior. Later in life, her behavior could impact millions. Cutting corners in scientific research might mean that a new drug hits the market without the scrutiny and fully informed examination that is so crucial to successful applications. We have witnessed this type of behavior across professions. Young people must come to realize that their decisions—how they choose to act on stated or implied responsibilities—have both immediate and long-term impacts on others.

REFERENCES

Bennett, W. (1993). *The book of virtues*. New York: Simon and Schuster.

Callahan, D. (2004). *The cheating culture*. New York: Harcourt.

Colby, A., Ehrlich, T., Beaumont, E., and Stephens, J. (2003). *Educating citizens: Preparing America's undergraduates for lives of moral and civic responsibility*. San Francisco: Jossey-Bass.

Damon, W. (1988). *The moral child: Nurturing children's natural moral growth*. New York: Free Press.

Damon, W. (1997). *The youth charter: How communities can work together to raise standards for all our children*. New York: Free Press.

Damon, W., (Ed.). (2002). *Bringing in a new era in character education*. Stanford, CA: Stanford University Press.

Damon, W., Menon, J., & Bronk, K. (2003). The development of purpose during adolescence. *Applied Developmental Science, 7*(3), 119–128.

Fischman, W., DiBara, J., & Gardner, H. (2006). Good education against the odds. *Cambridge Journal of Education, 36*(3), 383–398.

Fischman, W., Solomon, B., Greenspan, D., & Gardner, H. (2004). *Making good: How young people cope with moral dilemmas at work*. Cambridge: Harvard University Press.

Kohlberg, L. (1964). Development of moral character and moral ideology. In M. L. Hoffman & L. W. Hoffman (Eds.), *Review of child development research*, Vol. 1 (pp. 283–432). New York: Russell Sage Foundation.

Lapsley, D., & Narvaez, D. (2006). Character education. In W. Damon & R. Lerner (Eds.), *Handbook of child psychology*, Vol. 4 (6th ed., pp. 248–296). Hoboken, NJ: Wiley.

Lickona, T. (1991). *Educating for character: How our schools can teach respect and responsibility*. New York: Bantam.

Lickona, T., Schaps, E., & Lewis, C. (1996). *Eleven principles of effective character education*. Washington, DC: Character Education Partnership.

Nakamura, J., Yoneshige, K., & Csikszentmihalyi, M. (2007). On the development of college students: What they want, what they get, and its impact on their satisfaction. Unpublished paper.

Noddings, N. (1992). *The challenge to care in schools: An alternative approach to education.* New York: Teachers College Press.

Noddings, N. (1993). *Educating for intelligent belief or unbelief.* New York: Teachers College Press.

Piaget, J. (1932). *The moral judgment of the child.* London: Routledge & Kegan Paul.

Ryan, K. (1989). In defense of character education. In L. Nucci (Ed.), *Moral development and character education: A dialogue.* Berkeley, CA: McCutchan.

Simon, K. (2001). *Moral questions in the classroom: How to get kids to think deeply about real life and their schoolwork.* New Haven: Yale University Press.

Turiel, E. (2006). The development of morality. In W. Damon (Ed.), *Handbook of child psychology,* Vol. 3 (pp. 789–857). Hoboken, NJ: Wiley.

CONCLUSION

Howard Gardner

ALMOST EVERYONE AGREES THAT THE TRAIT OF RESPONSIBILITY is desirable; few argue, even facetiously, in favor of irresponsibility. Yet in matters both large and small, in world affairs and in the events of our daily lives, we regularly encounter examples of irresponsibility. (Sometimes I despair of clipping articles that document irresponsibility because the supply—medical malpractice, journalistic plagiarism, hedge fund irregularities, engineering shortcuts—seems endless.)

Clearly we human beings find it all too easy to shirk responsibility and behave in ways that may be good for us, and perhaps for those to whom we feel closest, but that are not healthy for the broader society. To invoke a higher standard, we may have recourse to the words of Winston Churchill: "Sometimes it is not enough to do your best. You just have to get the job done."

Matters conspire to undermine a sense of responsibility. Human beings are not born moral or ethical. These virtues need to be acquired and nurtured, often against the odds. Even those who start on the right track can deviate. Pressures and seductions are powerful. Moreover, historical and contemporary contexts exert powerful influence. We live at a time—and those of us who are U.S. citizens live in a society—where the material rewards for irresponsibility sometimes dwarf the plaudits for responsibility. Intrinsic motivation becomes essential in a milieu where the ambient signals combine to diminish an ethical sense.

Modulating Responsibility

In this book our emphasis has fallen on the positive. We have directed our attention to individuals who do an exemplary job—those whose concern extends to other individuals, to the core values of the domain in

332

which they work, to the benefit of the broader society, and even at times to the welfare of the planet. Our exploration has yielded surprising findings. For example, contrary to our expectations, the sense of responsibility works in similar ways in men and women; whether male or female, our subjects describe much the same obligations, pressures, and opportunities. Also, although various forms of spiritual involvement emerged, religious factors *per se* do not play a large role, at least in our sample of American professionals; rarely did our subjects invoke religious rationales for their professional beliefs and behaviors. On the other hand, the decision to enter a caring profession, the willingness to go against the odds, the capacity to persevere, and the skill to navigate uncharted domains are all symptomatic of individuals who do not refrain from assuming responsibility—indeed, who embrace it themselves, sometimes to the point of exhaustion, and model it for others.

As we expected, professions play an important role in shepherding a sense of responsibility, but that role turns out to be complex. In some ways it is easier to be part of a strong profession—such as medicine or science—that has a long and honorable tradition of embracing certain responsibilities (such as the obligation to come to the aid of anyone in distress or to report one's data completely and accurately). But the strength of the profession *per se* does not suffice. Both law and the media are very powerful today, but a sense of responsibility remains elusive, because each of these professions is constantly buffeted by powerful market forces. Paradoxically, one also detects a powerful sense of responsibility in domains that are only weakly professional—such as precollegiate teaching—and even in spheres where a sense of professionalism has not developed, such as social entrepreneurship. Yet responsibility seems strangely elusive in philanthropy, perhaps because it is so difficult to secure candid feedback on how effectively one is carrying out one's work. It turns out that the crucial variable is not the profession per se. What matters is the extent to which an individual in that vocation chooses to take on the responsibilities she deems important, whether or not support is available from others or from the long-standing values of the domain.

The Road Ahead

The work described in this book emanates almost entirely from the first phase of the GoodWork Project. During that initial phase, lasting more than a decade, my colleagues and I have interviewed more than twelve hundred individuals from nine separate vocational spheres. We have pored over our data and reported our findings in numerous publications and forums, including the present one, which focuses on a single one of the numerous issues that we probed. No doubt it will be possible in future years to conduct parallel investigations of other themes that permeate the initial clutch of interviews—ranging from a sense of purpose to the role of mentoring in the past and its status today and in the future.

The questions examined here are classic, going back to the time of Plato, Confucius, and other paragons of ancient times. Like other strategies for circumventing obstacles or addressing long-standing questions, such questions need to be revisited, especially in a rapidly changing era. As members of the GoodWork research team move beyond the first phase of the project, we expect to direct our attention principally to the following issues.

First, our focus has fallen largely on elite professions, ones open to those with ample education and viable career options. In future work it will be important to determine how those in ordinary industrial, commercial, service, or craft careers conceptualize issues of work and, in particular, how they parse the territory of responsibility under conditions in which their own degrees of freedom are relatively modest.

Second, until now our study has been conducted in the United States. The chief exception is the important work conducted in Scandinavia by Hans Henrik Knoop, a portion of which is reported in these pages. Knoop's study has delineated aspects of work in Scandinavia that appear healthy, as well as clear warning signs, particularly in the sphere of journalism. We hope to encourage comparable research and applications in many other societies. As an initial effort, my colleague Marcelo Suarez-Orozco and I have developed a course called Good Work in the Global Context. In the course offered at New York University, we and our students visit issues of GoodWork in cultures and societies from around the globe. Our Web site provides a venue for following such work and for contributing to it.

The new digital media hold promise, as well as considerable risk, for a sense of responsibility. Individuals can connect in order to lobby for a land mine treaty, but they can also network to plan terrorist attacks. Individuals can cultivate meaningful friendships, but also traffic under false identities. A particularly lurid example is a Web site called *alibinetwork.com,* which helps irresponsible individuals create alibis—for example, if they are having an illicit affair. How responsibilities are navigated, or absolved, in a digital age is a third focus for future work.

Final Thoughts

Finally, and most important, although this work began as scholarly research, we would not have undertaken it just to satisfy our own curiosity. To put it in the vernacular, we want to "give away" the results of our

GoodWork project; we seek to "make a difference." Two of our initial efforts are described in the final chapters of the book: the surveys of alignment on selected college campuses described in Chapter Thirteen and the adaptations of the Toolkit in secondary and college settings, as described in Chapter Fourteen. The materials and ideas behind these efforts are readily grasped; to implement the basic concepts, educators need neither fancy equipment nor elaborate statistics. Moreover, while as educators we have naturally begun with students in schools, the principles of responsibility elucidated here can be carried out by workers and leaders across the full range of professions and careers. In particular, the chapters in this volume yield a number of ready takeaways:

1. Understand the basic mission or missions of your occupation and your role(s) within it.

2. Explore the relation of your personal beliefs and goals to your chosen occupation and role(s).

3. Identify individuals and institutions that take responsibility seriously; seek to work in such a milieu; take positive lessons from these positive instances.

4. Note examples of irresponsible work, derive lessons from them, be prepared to change course or even institutions and to advise others to pursue the responsible course.

5. Realize that you cannot undertake complete responsibility to all possible persons and tasks; have a sense of priorities, an alertness to limits and boundaries, and a balance among responsibilities.

6. As you grow older, broaden your sphere of responsibility; be prepared to go beyond your own circle, to assume responsibility for the wider profession to which you belong.

7. As you grow older, direct increasing attention to the support of young persons, the good workers of the future.

Nearly all young people understand the notion of responsibility, and few seek to shirk it completely. But too many of them have not internalized the need to act responsibly, and too many of them regard responsibility as a task for the future, not as an imperative of today. Accordingly, the interventions we plan to undertake will be chiefly with young persons, who will one day determine how responsibility plays out in the workplace, and indeed whether it is operating at all. As aspiring trustees, we see our responsibility clearly: to portray what it means to be responsible, to model responsibility to the best of our ability, and to pass on a sense of responsibility to the future stewards of the workplace and the wider world.

NAME INDEX

A

Abbot, A., 10
Abrams, F., 264, 268
Abuhamdeh, S., 226
Anderson, C., 239
Andion, M., 299, 306
Appiah, A., 110
Applebaum, H., 3
Armitage, R., 264n1, 268
Astin, A. W., 307
Auletta, K., 272
Awuah, P., 296
Aydelotte, F., 291
Azari, R., 197

B

Barendsen, L., 15, 17, 91, 122, 172, 311
Barnett, R. C., 169
Barnicle, M., 269
Beaumont, E., 288, 289, 305, 315
Bellah, R. N., 197, 306
Bennett, W., 315, 316
Bennis, W., 154–155
Bentham, J., 44
Bernstein, C., 167, 267
Bertakis, K. D., 197
Bin Laden, O., 82–83
Bird, B., 90
Birkeland, S., 111
Black, S., 111
Blair, J., 82, 268, 269, 270, 271, 272, 277
Blumenthal, D., 110

Boakes, J., 174
Bogle, J., 12
Bohr, N., 82
Bok, D., 274
Bonabeau, E., 221
Bourdieu, P., 71
Bradlee, B., 34, 254
Brainerd, P., 95–96, 97–98, 157–158, 161, 166, 167
Brogan, D., 174
Bronk, K., 13, 21, 24, 26, 27, 82, 156, 167, 315
Bruner, J., 127
Brunstein, J., 23
Buber, M., 156

C

Caddell, D., 140
Calame, B., 274
Callahan, D., 312
Callahan, E. J., 197
Calvin, J., 136, 140
Camazine, S., 221
Cantor, N., 23
Carrington, E., 277
Carroll, J., 277
Casanova, J., 133
Cezanne, P., 72
Chertavian, G., 161–163, 167–168, 169
Chodorow, N., 197
Choe, I., 66
Churchill, W., 1, 21, 332
Colby, A., 25, 27, 33, 39, 82, 174, 288, 289, 305, 315

SUBJECT INDEX

A

Accountability, as responsibility, 29–30

Age, effect on leadership, 154–155

Age span, responsibility across, 11–12

Alignment: of elements of good work, 8–10; of forces affecting production of good work, 225–226; importance of, for caring professionals, 173; of responsibility to self and others, 202, 213–217, 218–219

American Medical Association (AMA), 130

B

Balance: needed for governing systems, 221–223; in Nordic countries, 223–224, 240. *See also* Work-life balance

BELL (Building Educated Leaders for Life) Foundation, 164–166

Bible History Online, 22

Bribery, 13, 30, 40

Business: Danish, influences on production of good work in, 231–232, 233, 235, 238, 239; example of ultimate responsibility in, 28–31, 40; facing conflicting responsibilities in, 192–193; humane creators in, 89–94, 93n3; responsibility as conceived in, 181; Work-family balance in, 184

C

Call to responsibility, as spiritual orientation, 135, 136, 140–144

Calling, 4–5, 79

Calvinism, 4–5, 160

Capitalism, democracy combined with, 222–223

Caring: concern for relationships with, 46, 52–55; for environment, 24, 93–96; expanded view of, 76–77; features of, and good vs. exemplary workers, 45–55, 46n4; journalism and, 56–60, 56n8; moral nature of, 44, 45; motivational displacement with, 46, 50–52; receptive attention with, 46, 47–50; teaching, to children, 77–78, 79; work/life integration and, 60–62. *See also* Ethics of care

Caring professionals: characteristics of, 173; defined, 172, 173; examples of, 173–174; facing conflicting responsibilities, 187–190; individualized professionals vs., 172, 193–194; methodology for studying, 174, 174n3; motivation for, 174; responsibility as conceived by, 174–180, 182, 193–194; values of, 185–187; Work-family balance for, 183–184. *See also* Nurses; Physicians; Social entrepreneurs; Teachers

Center for Leadership, 235

Children: difficult experiences of, as motivation, 52n6; teachers' responsibility to, 175–177, 189–190; teaching passion and caring to, 77–78, 79. *See also* Students